Emerging Issues in International Business Research

NEW HORIZONS IN INTERNATIONAL BUSINESS

Series Editor: Peter J. Buckley
Centre for International Business,
University of Leeds (CIBUL), UK

The New Horizons in International Business series has established itself as the world's leading forum for the presentation of new ideas in international business research. It offers pre-eminent contributions in the areas of multinational enterprise – including foreign direct investment, business strategy and corporate alliances, global competitive strategies, and entrepreneurship. In short, this series constitutes essential reading for academics, business strategists and policy makers alike.

Titles in the series include:

Globalizing America
The USA in World Integration
Edited by Thomas L. Brewer and Gavin Boyd

Information Technology in Multinational Enterprises
Edited by Edward Mozley Roche and Michael James Blaine

A Yen for Real Estate
Japanese Real Estate Investment Abroad – From Boom to Bust
Roger Simon Farrell

Corporate Governance and Globalization
Long Range Planning Issues
Edited by Stephen S. Cohen and Gavin Boyd

The European Union and Globalisation
Towards Global Democratic Governance
Edited by Brigid Gavin

Globalization and the Small Open Economy
Edited by Daniel Van Den Bulcke and Alain Verbeke

Entrepreneurship and the Internationalisation of Asian Firms
An Institutional Perspective
Henry Wai-chung Yeung

The World Trade Organization in the New Global Economy
Trade and Investment Issues in the Millennium Round
Edited by Alain M. Rugman and Gavin Boyd

Japanese Subsidiaries in the New Global Economy
Edited by Paul W. Beamish, Andrew Delios and Shige Makino

Globalizing Europe
Deepening Integration, Alliance Capitalism and Structural Statecraft
Edited by Thomas L. Brewer, Paul A. Brenton and Gavin Boyd

China and its Regions
Economic Growth and Reform in Chinese Provinces
Edited by Mary-Françoise Renard

Emerging Issues in International Business Research
Edited by Masaaki Kotabe and Preet S. Aulakh

Emerging Issues in International Business Research

Edited by

Masaaki Kotabe
Preet S. Aulakh

Temple University, USA

NEW HORIZONS IN INTERNATIONAL BUSINESS

Edward Elgar
Cheltenham, UK • Northampton, MA, USA

© Masaaki Kotabe and Preet S. Aulakh 2002

Published by
Edward Elgar Publishing Limited
Glensanda House
Montpellier Parade
Cheltenham
Glos GL50 1UA
UK

Edward Elgar Publishing, Inc.
136 West Street
Suite 202
Northampton
Massachusetts 01060
USA

A catalog record for this book
is available from the British Library

Library of Congress Cataloging in Publication Data
Emerging issues in international business research / edited by Masaaki Kotabe and
Preet S. Aulakh.
    p. cm. — (New horizons in international business series)
"The Institute of Global Management Studies (IGMS) at the Fox School of
Business and Management, Temple University sponsored the inaugural
International Business Research Forum on 'Emerging Issues in International
Business Research' during April 7-8, 2000 … at the Fox School"—Frwd.
Includes index.
1. International trade—Research—Congresses. 2. Business—Research—
Congresses. 3. Foreign trade promotion—Research—Congresses. 4. International
business enterprises—Research—Congresses. I. Kotabe, Masaaki. II. Aulakh,
Preet S., 1962– III. International Business Research Forum on 'Emerging Issues
in International Business Research' (2000 : Fox School) IV. New horizons in
international business.

HF1372 .E44 2002
382—dc21
                                                                    2001051075
ISBN 1 84064 836 8

Typeset by Manton Typesetters, Louth, Lincolnshire, UK.
Printed and bound in Great Britain by MPG Books Ltd, Bodmin, Cornwall.

Contents

List of figures	vii
List of tables	viii
List of boxes	ix
List of contributors	x
Foreword M. Moshe Porat	xvii
Foreword Arvind Phatak	xviii
Preface	xx

1. International business research: from functional to issue-based focus   1
   Masaaki Kotabe and Preet S. Aulakh

PART I   THE MACRO-ENVIRONMENT

2. Regional integration and foreign direct investment: theory and lessons from NAFTA   15
   Lorraine Eden
3. Intellectual property rights and international business   37
   Subhash C. Jain
4. Global financial markets and global firms: implications for international business research   65
   Jongmoo Jay Choi
5. Cultural Balkanization and hybridization in an era of globalization: implications for international business research   81
   Bryan W. Husted

PART II   INTERFACES BETWEEN BUSINESS AND INSTITUTIONS

6. Emerging issues in MNC–host government relations in developing countries   99
   Ravi Ramamurti
7. National export promotion: A statement of issues, changes, and opportunities   123
   Michael R. Czinkota

8. Industrial endowments in international business: an analytical
    framework   140
    Yadong Luo
9. Business groups and economic development: a resource-based
    view   163
    Mauro F. Guillén

PART III   STRATEGY AND COMPETITION

10. Globalization of firms: strategies and outcomes   201
    Saeed Samiee
11. Entering foreign markets through strategic alliances and
    acquisitions   223
    Michael A. Hitt and Klaus Uhlenbruck
12. Towards a research agenda on hybrid organizations: R&D,
    production and marketing interfaces   241
    Xavier Martin
13. The Internet and international business: a cross-regional study   260
    Indrajit Sinha and Yaniv Gvili

Index   273

Figures

3.1	Differing views on intellectual property protection	50
6.1	Bargaining model of MNC–host government relations	104
6.2	Liberalization of FDI policies of developing countries: subjective characterization of trends	107
6.3	Two-tier bargaining model	108
8.1	An integrated framework of industry selection	157
12.1	Functional interfaces within a firm	243
12.2	Functional interfaces between firms	246
12.3	Functional scope of 389 alliances among international airlines, 1982–94	248
13.1	Online shopping: relative importance of low price	264
13.2	Online shopping: relative importance of reputation	265
13.3	Online shopping: relative importance of convenience	265
13.4	Online shopping: relative importance of service	267
13.5	Online shopping: relative importance of branding	267
13.6	Percentage agreeing that prices are lower on the Internet	268
13.7	Percentage expected discount on the Internet	268
13.8	Difficulty in buying from another country's sites	269
13.9	Need fulfillment by domestic e-tailers relative to US sites	269
13.10	Product selection of domestic e-tailers relative to US sites	270
13.11	Quality of 'deals' offered by domestic e-tailers relative to US	270
13.12	Likelihood of shopping online	271

Tables

3.1   Losses suffered by US industries resulting from intellectual
      property inadequacies, 1986   44
3.2   International intellectual property rights protection: regime
      deficiencies   46
3.3   Major enforcement deficiencies   47
3.4   Effect of patent protection on inventions, 1981–83   52
3.5   Social and private rates of return from investment in innovation 53
4.1   A valuation framework   68
9.1   The effect of foreign trade and investment flows on business
      groups in emerging economies   171
9.2   Cross-sectional sample descriptive statistics and correlation
      coefficients   183
9.3   OLS regression results of the top ten business groups in 1995
      on various characteristics of nine emerging countries, 1995   184
9.4   OLS regression results of the top ten business groups in 1995
      on various characteristics of nine emerging countries, 1990   185
9.5   The top 100 non-financial firms in South Korea, Spain, and
      Argentina in 1975 and 1995, by organizational form   187
9.6   Saturated log-linear model of the largest 100 non-financial
      firms in South Korea, Spain, and Argentina by form of control
      and year   189
10.1 International sales and growth patterns among leaders in the
      appliance industry, 1986–98   216
10.2 Relationship between industry environment and firm-level
      globalization initiatives   217
12.1 Correlations among dimensions of supplier influence   253

Boxes

1.1   Shift in international business research   2

Contributors

Preet S. Aulakh is Washburn Research Fellow and Associate Professor of Strategy and International Business at the Fox School of Business and Management, Temple University. He received his PhD from the University of Texas at Austin. Prior to joining Temple University, he taught at Michigan State University and Memorial University in Canada. He is the editor of *Journal of International Management*. His co-edited book, *Rethinking Globalization(s): From Corporate Transnationalism to Local Interventions* (with Michael Schechter) was published by Macmillan Press in 2000. In addition, he has published numerous articles on foreign entry modes, international alliances, technology licensing, and international strategies of emerging economy firms in journals such as *Academy of Management Journal, Journal of International Business Studies, Journal of Marketing, Journal of the Academy of Marketing Science, Industrial Marketing Management, Journal of World Business, Journal of International Marketing*, among others.

Jongmoo Jay Choi is Laura H. Carnell Professor of Finance and International Business, a former chair of finance and currently the director of the doctoral program in international business at Temple University. He received his PhD from New York University. He previously served on the faculty at Columbia Business School and as an international treasury economist at Chase Manhattan Bank. He has been a visiting professor at the University of Hawaii, University of Pennsylvania (Wharton), NYU (Stern), International University of Japan and the Korea Advanced Institute of Science and Technology. He is a former president of the Korea–America Finance Association, and a trustee of the Multinational Finance Society. As an author of over 50 books and articles, he is an internationally renowned scholar in the area of international finance and investments, exchange risk management, and emerging market finance. He is an editor of a book series, *International Finance Review* (JAI/Elsevier), a section editor of *Journal of Economics and Business*, and editorial board member for five other journals. He is a recipient of the Musser Award for Excellence in Leadership and Distinguished Faculty Research Fellowship at Temple.

Michael R. Czinkota is Professor of Marketing and International Business Strategy at the School of Business, Georgetown University. He received his

PhD from Ohio State University. Prior to joining Georgetown he was a deputy assistant secretary at the Department of Commerce. He served as head of the US delegation to the OECD industry committee and as senior trade advisor for export controls. Professor Czinkota has consulted with AT&T, IBM, General Electric and Nestlé, and has assisted various governmental organizations in effective trade promotion policies. He is the senior author of two college textbooks, *International Marketing* (2001) and *International Business* (1999). His other publications include *Export Policy (1982), Unlocking Japan's Market* (with J. Woronoff, 1991) and *The Global Marketing Imperative* (with I. Ronkainen and J. Tarrant, 1995). He was listed in the *Journal of International Business Studies* (1994) as one of the three most productive contributors to international business research.

Lorraine Eden is Associate Professor of Management at Texas A&M University. Her research on multinational enterprises centers on transfer pricing and international taxation, regional integration, and MNE–state relations. Recent honors include a Texas A&M University Former Students Association Award for Excellence in Faculty Teaching (2000), Who's Who in International Business Education and Research (1999), US–Canada Fulbright Research Fellowship (1992–93), and Pew Faculty Fellowship in International Affairs (1991–92). She founded the Women Economists Network in Canada, has been Vice President of the Canadian Economics Association, and President and Program Chair of the International Political Economy Section of the International Studies Association. She is currently Vice President and 2002 Program Chair for the Academy of International Business. She has authored and/or edited five scholarly books: *Multinationals and Transfer Pricing* (with Alan Rugman, 1985); *Retrospectives on Public Finance* (1991); *Multinationals in the Global Political Economy* (with Evan Potter, 1993); *Multinationals in North America* (1994); and *Taxing Multinationals: Transfer Pricing and Corporate Income Taxation in North America* (1998). In addition, she has published more than 50 refereed journal articles and book chapters, including articles in *Academy of Management Journal, Accounting, Organizations and Society, Asian Survey, Canadian Journal of Economics, Government and Policy, International Executive, International Trade Journal, Journal of International Business Studies, Journal of International Management, Millennium*, and *Transnational Corporations*.

Mauro F. Guillén is on the faculty at the Wharton School and Department of Sociology of the University of Pennsylvania, where he teaches multinational management. He previously taught at the MIT Sloan School of Management. He received a PhD in sociology from Yale University and a doctorate in political economy from the University of Oviedo in his native Spain. His latest book is *The Limits of Convergence: Globalization and Organizational*

Change in Argentina, South Korea, and Spain (2001). He is also the author of *Models of Management* (University of Chicago Press, 1994), and, with Charles Perrow, *The AIDS Disaster* (Yale University Press, 1990). In Spanish, he has published *La Profesión de Economista* (Ariel, 1989), *and Análisis de Regresión Múltiple* (CIS, 1992). His research has appeared in *Academy of Management Journal, American Sociological Review, Annual Review of Sociology, Administrative Science Quarterly, East Asian Economic Perspectives, Industrial & Corporate Change, Industrial & Labor Relations Review, Journal of Latin American Studies, Management Science, Trends in Organizational Behavior*, and *Sloan Management Review*. He has been quoted in the *Los Angeles Times, International Herald Tribune*, and *Journal of Commerce*, as well as in several Argentine and Spanish newspapers and magazines. He is a former Guggenheim Fellow and Member in the Institute for Advanced Study in Princeton.

Yaniv Gvili is a doctoral student of marketing at the Fox School of Business and Management, Temple University. He received his BSc in industrial engineering and management from Ben Gurion University, Beer Sheva, Israel, and an MBA from Bar Ilan University, Ramat Gan, Israel. His areas of interest are e-commerce, distribution of online information services, and communications networks for application service providers (ASPs). Prior to joining the doctoral program at Temple University, he held the position of manager of research and information system analysis in a major advertising agency. In addition, Yaniv Gvili has consulted with Spacenet, Inc. (a Gilat–General Electric company) in the areas of CRM-SFA information systems, and business development in the field of satellite communications networks.

Michael A. Hitt is a Professor of Management and holds the Weatherup/Overby Chair in Executive Leadership at Arizona State University. He received his PhD from the University of Colorado. He has authored or co-authored several books and book chapters and numerous journal articles in such journals as the *Academy of Management Journal, Academy of Management Review, Strategic Management Journal, Journal of Applied Psychology, Organization Studies, Journal of Management Studies*, and *Journal of Management*, among others. His recent publications include three books, *Downscoping: How to Tame the Diversified Firm* (1994), *Strategic Management: Competitiveness and Globalization* (2001), and *Mergers and Acquisitions* (2001). He is co-editor of four recent books, *Managing Strategically in an Interconnected World* (1998), *New Managerial Mindsets: Organizational Transformation* and *Strategy Implementation* (1999), *Dynamic Strategic Resources: Development, Diffusion and Integration* (2000), *and Winning Strategies in a Deconstructing World* (2001). He has served on the editorial review boards of multiple journals including the *Academy of Management Journal*, *Academy of Management Executive*, *Journal of Applied Psychology*, *Journal of World Business*, and *Journal of Applied Behavioral Sciences*. Furthermore, he has served as consulting editor (1988–90) and editor (1991–93) of the *Academy of Management Journal*.

Bryan W. Husted currently holds a joint appointment as Professor of Management at the Instituto Tecnológico y de Estudios Superiores de Monterrey (Mexico) and Alumni Association Chair of Business Ethics at the Instituto de Empresa (Spain). He received a PhD from the University of California at Berkeley and a JD from Brigham Young University. He serves as Executive Secretary of the Business Association for Latin American Studies. He is an active member of the Academy of Management, International Association for Business and Society, the European Business Ethics Networks, the Society for Business Ethics, and the International Society for Business, Economics, and Ethics. He is also a member of the editorial board of the *Journal of International Management*. He is a national researcher of the National System of Researchers of Mexico. His research focuses on cross-cultural business ethics and corporate social and environmental performance. His work has appeared in such journals as the *Journal of International Business Studies*, *Business Ethics Quarterly*, *Business and Society*, *Journal of Business Ethics*, *Growth and Change*, and *Journal of Environment and Development*.

Subhash C. Jain is Professor of Marketing, Director, Center for International Business Education and Research (CIBER) and Director, GE Capital Global Learning Center (GECGLC) at the University of Connecticut, School of Business Administration. He received his PhD from the University of Oregon. Dr Jain is the author of more than 100 publications, including articles in the *Journal of Marketing Research*, *Journal of Marketing*, *Journal of Economic Abstracts*, *Long Range Planning*, *Journal of Applied Psychology*, *Columbia Journal of World Business*, *Journal of International Marketing*, *International Business Review*, and others. He is the author of several books including *Marketing Planning and Strategy*, 6th edition (2000), *International Marketing Management*, 6th edition (2000), *Export Strategy*, and *Market Evolution in Developing Countries* (1989). He has been a member of the editorial review boards of the *Journal of Marketing*, *Journal of the Academy of Marketing Science*, *Journal of International Marketing*, *Journal of Global Marketing*, and others. He also offers seminars for the International Trade Center (WTO/UNCTAD) in Geneva. He serves as a visiting faculty at the Graduate School of Business Administration in Zurich in their executive MBA program. Dr. Jain has advised government agencies in Malaysia, Chile, India, Pakistan, St. Lucia, Mexico, Iran, Kenya, and Indonesia on their trade problems.

Masaaki Kotabe holds the Washburn Chair of International Business and Marketing, and is Director of Research at the Institute of Global Management Studies at the Fox School of Business and Management at Temple University. He received his PhD from Michigan State University. Dr Kotabe also served as the Vice President of the Academy of International Business in the 1997–98 period. His research work has appeared in such journals as the *Journal of Marketing*, *Journal of International Business Studies*, and *Strategic Management Journal*. His books include *Global Sourcing Strategy: R&D, Manufacturing, Marketing Interfaces* (1992), *Japanese Distribution System* (with Michael R. Czinkota, 1993), *Anticompetitive Practices in Japan* (with Kent W. Wheiler, 1996), *MERCOSUR and beyond* (1997), *Trends in International Business: Critical Perspectives* (with Michael R. Czinkota, 1998), *Japanese Distribution Strategy* (with Michael R. Czinkota, 2000), and *Global Marketing Management* (with Kristiaan Helsen, 2001). He serves on the editorial boards of the *Journal of Marketing*, *Journal of International Business Studies*, *Journal of International Marketing*, *Journal of World Business*, *Journal of Business Research*, *Latin American Economic Abstracts*, and *Thunderbird International Business Review*. In the 1997 issue of *Journal of Teaching in International Business*, Dr Kotabe was ranked the most prolific international marketing researcher in the world in the last ten years. He has recently been elected a Fellow of the Academy of International Business for his significant contribution to international business research and education. He is also an elected member of the New York Academy of Sciences.

Yadong Luo is Associate Professor of Strategy and International Business at the University of Miami. Prior to joining UM, he was Associate Professor of International Management at the University of Hawaii where he was the recipient of the University of Hawaii Regents' Medal for Excellence in Research. Before coming to the United States, he served as a government official in China in charge of international business. He received his PhD from Temple University. He is the author of over ten books that address international strategies, international joint ventures, *guanxi*, and business, and MNEs in emerging markets. He has also published about 80 journal articles, in journals including *Academy of Management Journal*, *Journal of Applied Psychology*, *Strategic Management Journal*, *Journal of Management*, *Journal of Management Studies*, *Organization Science*, and *Journal of International Business Studies*.

Xavier Martin is Assistant Professor of Management and International Business at Stern School of Business, New York University. He received his PhD from the University of Michigan. Parts of his chapter were written while he was on the visiting faculty of the Graduate School of Business at Columbia

University. His research has appeared in leading publications in management and international business including *Administrative Science Quarterly*, *Strategic Management Journal*, *Research Policy*, and *Advances in Strategic Management*. His current research addresses the antecedents and consequences of hybrid interfirm arrangements, including buyer–supplier partnerships and collaborative alliances. His research also addresses international entry modes and new product introduction strategies. Among his recent honors and awards are the Richard N. Farmer Dissertation Competition Award for the best dissertation from the Academy of International Business; the Best International Paper Award from the Academy of Management; and the Teacher of the Year Award from the undergraduate division of Stern School of Business at NYU. Xavier also serves as a reviewer or board member for various scholarly journals in strategic management and international business.

Ravi Ramamurti is Patrick F. and Helen C. Walsh Research Professor in the College of Business Administration at Northeastern University and is a visiting professor, in summertime at IMD, Lausanne. He obtained his PhD from Harvard Business School. He has served on the faculties of Harvard Business School and MIT's Sloan School and has been a consultant to several firms, governments, and international agencies such as the World Bank and the United Nations. Prior to joining Northeastern University, he served as a consultant to the planning commission of the government of India, and as executive assistant to the CEO of a large engineering company. His most recent book, *Privatizing Monopolies*, was published by Johns Hopkins University Press (1996). His articles have been published in a number of journals, including *Academy of Management Executive*, *Academy of Management Review*, *California Management Review*, *Harvard Business History Review*, *International Executive*, *International Trade Journal*, *Journal of General Management*, *Journal of International Business Studies*, *Management Science*, and *World Development*.

Saeed Samiee is the Collins Professor of Marketing and International Business at the College of Business Administration, the University of Tulsa. He is the Project Director for the Institute of International Business Education (IBE), a joint project between the University of Tulsa and Moscow State Institute of Electronics Technology. He received his PhD from the Ohio State University. Professor Samiee has conducted research and lectured executives and academics in the US, Europe, the Middle East, and in the Asia-Pacific countries. He has also assisted such firms as AT&T, IBM, Merck, NCR, Sonoco, and Toyota, as well as such non-profit and educational institutions as the American Dental Association, and Small Business Development Centers in New Jersey and South Carolina. He has published extensively in several scholarly journals and serves on the editorial review boards of the leading journals in his areas of expertise. Professor Samiee was the sixth most prolific author in international marketing during the 1987–93 period according to the ranking developed by the *Journal of Teaching in International Business*. He is listed among the 10 and the top 30 most prolific authors in the *Journal of the Academy of Marketing Science* and *Journal of International Business Studies*, respectively. He was named Outstanding Professor at The University of South Carolina, selected as an outstanding reviewer by *Journal of the Academy of Marketing Science* (1997–2000) and for the *Journal of International Business Studies*, and is a member of Beta Gamma Sigma, National Business Honor Society.

Indrajit (Jay) Sinha is Washburn Research Fellow and Assistant Professor of Marketing at the Fox School of Business and Management, Temple University. He earned his PhD from the University of Michigan. He has served as Staff Consultant, Management Consulting, Deloitte & Touche and consulted to organizations in the local area (including AAMCO and Philadelphia Chamber of Commerce). His articles have appeared or are forthcoming in such journals as *Harvard Business Review*, *Journal of Marketing Research*, *International Journal of Research in Marketing*, *Journal of Retailing*, and *Psychometrika*. He has been quoted in major national newspapers and magazines on topics relating to e-commerce and the Internet. He has received several recent honors and awards including the Fox School's MBA Student Association Award for Dedication to MBA Student Development and the Marketing Department Outstanding Teaching Award for Excellence in Undergraduate Teaching and Course Development, Temple University.

Klaus Uhlenbruck is Assistant Professor in the Management Department at Texas A&M University. He received his PhD from the University of Colorado. Previously, he was on the faculty of California State University San Marcos and has work experience in the computer and consulting industries. His research focuses on value creation in emerging markets. His scholarly articles have been published in *Academy of Management Journal*, *Journal of Business Venturing*, *Journal of International Business Studies*, *Journal of Management Studies*, *International Journal of Organizational Analysis*, and other periodicals. He published a book in German on service strategies for manufacturers. Professor Uhlenbruck is a member of the Academy of International Business, the Academy of Management, Ciber Cross-Cultural Collegium (UCLA), and the Strategic Management Society. He serves as liaison between the Enterpreneurship and International Management Divisions of the Academy of Management.

Foreword

M. Moshe Porat, Dean, the Fox School of Business and Management, Temple University

It is my pleasure to add a Foreword to this book on emerging issues in international business.

We have witnessed rapid changes worldwide driven by telecommunication, information technology, biotechnology and the forces of enterpreneurship and innovation. These changes are global in nature and therefore the issues and solutions require a global approach. This book is an important contribution in this direction.

I am very proud of the team of researchers assembled in the Fox School of Business and Management under the umbrella of the Institute of Global Management Studies. Our goal is to help them to become the forefront for thought and scholarship in international business education within the school and across the nation. The *Journal of International Management*, the Annual Research Forum, the Annual Spring Conference and other academic and practitioner-oriented efforts are just a sample of such activities.

I commend Professors Kotabe and Aulakh for their foresight and Professor Phatak for spearheading this effort.

Foreword

Arvind Phatak, Executive Director, The Institute of Global Management Studies, Temple University

The Institute of Global Management Studies (IGMS) at the Fox School of Business and Management, Temple University sponsored the Inaugural International Business Research Forum on 'Emerging Issues in International Business Research' during 7–8 April 2000. The purpose of this annual forum was to bring together leading scholars of international business at the Fox School in order to open a dialogue as to the current status and future direction of the discipline. The inauguration of an international business forum of this nature is quite timely, because new international business structures and strategies are bound to emerge as the new millennium dawns upon us with opposing forces of market globalization and re-emergence of nation-states shaping the world economy. Traditional international business paradigms lose their power, displaced by emerging ones. International business research is at a historic turning point.

I would like to congratulate Professors Masaaki Kotabe and Preet Aulakh of Temple University for organizing such an important forum at the Fox School. At this forum, key international business researchers engaged in a candid, non-confrontational discussion on the status and future of international business research. The output of this forum was thoughts and guidelines for future developments in international business research.

I am sure that the reader will find chapters in this book rigorous yet insightful and useful for better understanding of various issues facing international business researchers.

A primary mission of the IGMS is to promote cutting edge international business research, which we hope to achieve in some measure by annually hosting the International Business Research Forum. I thank all eminent scholars who presented and contributed papers at the inaugural research forum, and for their dedication to the pursuit of new insights into the dynamic nature of international business. I hope that the papers in this book will stimulate new avenues for research in the international business field. It is the passion of Dean Moshe Porat for international business education and research that led to the establishment of the IGMS and of the Annual International Business

Research Forum. I speak for all international business faculty in the Fox School in thanking him for his generous support.

Preface

The phenomenon of globalization has captured the popular imagination in the last decade or so. This is reflected in numerous books published on this topic from various academic disciplines and across philosophical discourses. In discussing the various facets of globalization, almost all discourses consider the role of business and/or multinational corporations to be very salient in either enhancing this phenomenon or managing the process of globalization. Thus, to international business scholars, globalization poses unique challenges in terms of analyzing the appropriateness of existing models and paradigms to the new external reality as well as incorporating the changes due to the integrated world economy into new theoretical and normative frameworks.

In light of this challenge, the Institute of Global Management Studies at the Fox School of Business and Management, Temple University, sponsored an International Business Forum during 7–8 April 2000, under the title, 'Emerging Issues in International Business Research'. The purpose of this forum was to bring together both leading scholars and young rising stars in international business studies in order to open a dialogue as to the current status and future direction of the discipline as it confronts the challenges of globalization. Three broad themes (macro-environment, business–institution interfaces, and strategy and competition) provided the framework of this research forum, and thus that of this book.

Each invited scholar was asked to prepare a paper on one topic within the broad theme that not only discusses the state of the current knowledge on that topic but also provides insights into the specific emerging aspects within that topic that need to be researched. After the research forum, the authors were asked to revise their papers to incorporate the issues emanating from forum discussions. The 12 chapters in this book, organized in three parts, are a result of the research forum and the subsequent revisions. It was our desire that the set of papers in this book collectively provide a new research agenda for the discipline as a whole as well as to individual researchers in the field of international business.

We would like to thank a number of people who were instrumental in the success of the research forum as well as this book. First, we acknowledge the initiatives of Dean Mosche Porat and Senior Associate Dean Rajan Chandran in making the study of globalization one of the three strategic areas of focus at the Fox School of Business and Management at Temple University as well as providing the financial resources to initiate the research forum on which this book is based. Their support was critical in bringing together leading scholars in international business to the forum. We also thank Arvind Phatak, Executive Director of the Institute of Global Management Studies (IGMS) under whose aegis this forum was organized, for his enthusiastic support for this initiative as well as his active participation in organizing the forum. The forum could not have been possible without the organizational skills of Melissa Wieczorek, Associate Director IGMS, and Amanda Brennan, Administrative Coordinator IGMS. We sincerely thank both of them for making all the operational arrangements for the research forum. The research forum and this book would not have been possible without the active involvement and enthusiasm of the authors. We thank them for bringing their expertise to the research forum and revising their papers to ensure that the objectives of this initiative were achieved. Finally, we would like to thank Alan Sturmer, our editor at Edward Elgar Publishing, for his enthusiasm for this project.

Masaaki Kotabe
Preet S. Aulakh
Philadelphia, USA

F23

1. International business research: from functional to issue–based focus

Masaaki Kotabe and Preet S. Aulakh

International business (IB) research as a formal academic discipline has completed 40 years of existence. In this relatively short life span, IB research has made important strides as evidenced in the membership of the Academy of International Business as well as the recognition of the academy's flagship journal, *Journal of International Business Studies*. However, during much of the period, the discipline has had to confront its very existence as most of the effort was expended in internationalizing the traditional functional business areas and examining the application of concepts and theories of individual functional areas in cross-national settings. As we begin a new century, due to advancements in information technologies, changes in institutional structures around the world, inter-country economic, political, and social linkages, and the internalization of the term 'globalization' at both popular and political levels, international business activities are no longer considered peripheral to corporations around the world. Given this state of affairs, there are some who argue that there is no need for international business studies since, by default, all business is international.

We believe that although there is some logic to this argument and, in fact, individual functional areas have become internationalized to incorporate this new reality in developing or refining concepts and theories, international business studies will continue to confront unique issues not incorporated into functional disciplines. That is, IB research has to move away from the *international dimensions of functional areas* focus to that of *issue-oriented learning that transcends national boundaries* (see Box 1.1 below). As we progress into the new millennium, the challenge to the international business discipline is to make this transition.[1]

IB research has been gaining in significance in the last two decades. There are several articles and books (for example, Caves 1998; Douglas and Craig 1992; Dunning 1989; Ricks et al. 1990; Toyne and Nigh 1997) that provide the state-of-the-art review of IB research conducted in the past. Although these articles and books present a nice review of an existing stock of IB research of the time and suggest future research directions, they all suffer

---

BOX 1.1   SHIFT IN INTERNATIONAL BUSINESS RESEARCH

Traditional: International dimensions of a functional area

Emerging: Issue-oriented learning that transcends national boundaries

1.   Function-specific research that has appeal across functions and disciplines, and/or

2.   Interdisciplinary research that challenges the paradigms and assumptions of individual functions or disciplines

---

from the traditional functional boundary bias. Recently, there has been a flurry of healthy attempts either to stockpile IB research streams for further development or to offer a detailed account of how to conduct IB research (Rugman and Brewer 2001, Toyne et al. 2001). Rugman and Brewer's book (2001) consists of two dozen chapters written by internationally recognized IB researchers. It covers a wide range of topics, including history/theory of the multinational firm, political environment, international strategy, international management, and regional issues. Given the nature of the chapter layout, this book loyally covers the traditional functional line of research and some regional issues. Toyne et al.'s work (2001) is probably the first of its kind with a focus on how to conduct IB research. It takes a hands-on approach to learning the pitfalls and difficulties of conducting empirical research in IB areas as experienced by the contributors to this book. The book covers topics on how to conduct research in the IB context, but it fails to address emerging research venues and research methodology.

Our book takes a third approach and promises to complement the above two new trendsetting books. As we stated in the outset, consistent with the executive policy of the Academy of International Business, IB research has to move away from the *international dimensions of functional areas* focus to that of *issue-oriented learning that transcends national boundaries*. We solicited contributors who have conducted issue-oriented (and oftentimes interdisciplinary) research projects. The rest of this book consists of chapters with research topics developed in such a way as to compile existing research and identify emerging research areas that have a broader appeal beyond a single functional domain or an interdisciplinary application.

In trying to conceptualize the issue-based framework for international business research, we wanted to examine areas that were unique to international business. Accordingly, the first area we identified was the macro-environment. The macro-environment under which businesses operate has been crucial in understanding the constraints and opportunities imposed on the business operations of firms, in both purely domestic and international settings. However, despite the celebration of globalization as breaking traditional national boundaries, we believe that one aspect that is unique to international business research inquiry is the differences in country environments. For, on the one hand, we see that globalization pressures have pushed corporations to aggressively internationalize, but at the same time they have to come to terms with individual country environments (at political, economic, financial, legal, and cultural levels). Thus, despite the presence of liberal trade regimes and the ostensible convergence of institutions and cultures (Levitt 1983), Fayerweather's (1969: 133) observation that 'the central issue that emerges [in examining multinational strategy] ... is the conflict between unification and fragmentation' due to environmental differences continues to be as relevant today as it was more than 30 years ago. Besides the macro-environmental factors that affect international business, another important challenge for firms is their interactions with a host of institutions at international (for example, Word Trade Organization, IMF, World Bank), national (both home and host country governments), and regional levels (for example, European Union, state and local governments). Thus, the second area we identified that requires systematic research inquiry is how international firms interact with different institutions and balance the often conflicting pressures and opportunities of various institutional forces. Within the broad macro-environmental and institutional factors, the third area identified is an examination of how these factors shape competition and strategy for individual industries and firms on a global basis. That is, changes in the macro-environment (for example, liberalization, regional trading blocs, information technology) and the new realities of interactions between businesses and diverse institutions have combined to shape competition in individual countries or regions as well as pushed organizations to re-evaluate their strategic tools in light of these interactions.

Given these three broad areas of focus, we invited leading researchers to evaluate the state of research in some aspect of each area and also provide research directions in light of contemporary and anticipated future realities. This research forum resulted in twelve chapters organized into three parts (the macro-environment, interfaces between business and institutions, and strategy and competition) in this book. These chapters are briefly summarized below along with a synopsis of each of the chapters.

PART I   THE MACRO-ENVIRONMENT

In this part we explore four issues related to the macro-environment, namely regional trading blocs, intellectual property protection, global financial markets, and the debates over cultural homogenization and Balkanization. Along with the adoption of liberal economic policies and the lowering of tariff and non-tariff barriers to trade around the world during the last four decades, in large part due to multilateral progress by the GATT and its successor, WTO, a parallel trend has been the proliferation of regional trade blocs (or regional integration) in all parts of the world. The impact of regional trade agreements on the globalization of world trade has generated tremendous debates in business, academic, and public policy circles. Similarly, the rise in world trade, especially in manufactured goods, along with the fast-changing technologies, has brought the issue of intellectual property protection to the forefront; and rather than being an issue relevant to specialist lawyers, it has become a salient issue in both bilateral and multilateral trade negotiations. Perhaps one of the major impetuses to the increased interdependence of individual economies has been the globalization of financial markets, which has profound implications for foreign direct investment decisions and strategies and thus is likely to provide new challenges for international business researchers in this traditionally core area of research in the discipline. Within the various debates on globalization and the implications of economic, legal, and financial integration, perhaps one area that has generated the greatest controversy has been the issue of cultural homogenization and Balkanization. The issue of cultural convergence and/or divergence has profound implications for international business strategies of firms. The four chapters in Part I individually explore the above mentioned issues.

In Chapter 2, Eden provides an overview of research implications of regional integration and foreign direct investment. One of the strongest worldwide trends in trade policy in the past 20 years has been the rebirth of regional integration schemes, or preferential trading agreements (PTAs), now called the 'new regionalism'. An explosion of research by international economics and international business scholars, on parallel but separate tracks, has documented and analyzed this phenomenon. This chapter reviews the literature on regional integration, focusing on trade and FDI responses to PTAs at both the macro-region and micro-region levels, and suggests new areas for research by international business scholars.

Jain, in Chapter 3, addresses the increased importance of intellectual property rights and their protection in international business. The chief competitive advantage of the United States and other industrialized countries lies in their technological superiority. Prominent among the issues designated as crucial to our continued technological and competitive standing is the international protection of intellectual property rights – copyrights, patents, trademarks, and so on. In many countries, particularly in some developing countries, the international protection of intellectual property rights is uncertain or nonexistent. Much confusion exists over the details of intellectual property law and enforcement in international markets. Furthermore, the constant introduction of new technologies has made traditional protection of intellectual property rights inadequate. This chapter provides an overview of intellectual property rights and their international protection. Insights into trade-related intellectual property rights issues, based on history and economics, are examined. The chapter also offers suggestions for additional research on the subject. More research must be pursued before the matter of international protection of intellectual property rights can be resolved, particularly in such areas as semiconductor chips, computer software, and biotechnology.

In Chapter 4, Choi tackles the financial implications of globalization in international business research. Global markets provide opportunities for firms to go abroad, while global firms induce the markets to globalize. At the same time, globalization entails risk for firms and investors. What then are the implications of global financial markets for firms, and how is globalization achieved for firms and markets? Despite its importance, the nexus between the global financial markets and global firms has not been a core area of research in the mainstream international business or international finance literature. The mainstream research in international finance also has focused on portfolio and asset pricing issues from the standpoint of investors and markets and the advances that incorporate strategic corporate factors have been scant. This chapter identifies potential frontier research issues pertaining to financial implications of globalization for a general international business and finance audience. Five thematic areas that are both important and ripe for research are identified and discussed, including firm valuation and multinationality; financial and strategic factors in foreign direct investment; risk of international operation; profile of firms and markets; and the effect of exchange rate and finance on operation.

Husted, in Chapter 5, deals with these seemingly contradictory forces at work in shaping the nature of global competition. Although culture has formed the core of much research in international business studies, the process of cultural 'Balkanization' or fragmentation that seems to be occurring in response to globalization has not been studied in great detail by international business scholars. Globalization and Balkanization create a complex dynamic that cannot be adequately understood with the cross-sectional studies common in international management research. The chapter begins by looking specifically at the process of globalization and the various manifestations of cultural Balkanization that are occurring as a result of globalization. It describes a complex and dynamic relationship between these two complementary processes and concludes by drawing some implications for cross-cultural management research.

PART II   INTERFACES BETWEEN BUSINESS AND INSTITUTIONS

Within the macro-environmental trends explored in Part I, and despite the favorable overall environment for internationalization, multinational corporations have to interact with individual institutions at different levels. These institutions can be both facilitators as well as inhibitors of firms' attempts successfully to internationalize and develop international strategies. The four chapters in Part II explore the various interactions of multinational corporations (MNCs) with multilateral and national institutions. Collectively they provide insights into bargaining between country governments as well as between businesses and governments, the new challenges faced by national and regional government agencies in promoting domestic firm internationalization, and the impact of industry conditions and industry groups in individual countries for foreign firms entering these markets as well as competitive strategies of domestic firms in an era of liberalization and globalization.

In Chapter 6, Ramamurti explores the relationships between MNCs and host developing countries that changed dramatically in the late 1980s and 1990s, compared to the adversarial relationship that existed between them in prior decades. Most developing countries have turned their foreign direct investment (FDI) screening organizations into FDI *promotion* agencies. Many have vastly liberalized their rules for FDI, removing from the bargaining process most of the issues on which they used to haggle earlier with MNCs. Developing countries have also signed bilateral investment treaties with rich countries that guarantee MNCs better access to host country markets and provide for greater freedom in FDI matters. Has the world changed so much that the bargaining model is no longer a useful paradigm for thinking about MNC–host government relations? In this chapter, it is proposed that MNC–host government relations in developing countries are better understood today in terms of a *two-tier* bargaining process in which the first tier represents bargaining between host (developing) countries and MNCs' home (industrialized) countries, and the second tier consists of the original bargaining model, that is, bargaining between host developing countries and individual MNCs. It produces *macro* rules and principles on FDI that affect *micro* negotiations in the second tier between individual MNCs and host governments.

Czinkota, in Chapter 7, examines the changing role of government export promotion. Exports have occupied a special niche in business and policy considerations. Between the 1970s and the 1990s the goal of governments was to jump start export efforts, remove or combat market inefficiencies, and retaliate against unfair competition. The approach taken by governmental institutions was to lower transaction cost through subsidization, and to lower transaction risk. Today, however, there is a return to market development expenditures – attempting to create an export culture and export capabilities around the world. It is, however, also the result of a greater need by more players in the global business community to participate in international trade, and a growing awareness of living standard differentials and a desire to achieve growth and poverty alleviation around the world. This chapter addresses the rationale for such government involvement in the market place. After summarizing the key export promotion approaches developed by governments during the second half of the twentieth century, an analysis of the changes of the promotional rules, requirements, and activities of governmental export promotion will be offered.

In Chapter 8, Luo addresses how industry endowment affects MNC performance. Industry endowment determines the industrial environment and market demand that a firm faces abroad, which in turn affect its operational and financial outcomes in a host country. When analyzing the environmental endowments of a foreign country, previous studies often emphasize the national level (that is, country-specific or comparative advantage of a nation), and neglect the endowments at the industrial level (that is, industry-specific or structural advantage of an industry). This is an important gap because most economies today in the world, whether developed or developing, are undergoing many structural changes, presenting industry-unique, not necessarily country-unique, opportunities and challenges for international companies. This chapter illuminates four aspects of industrial dynamics, namely structural dimensions (uncertainty, complexity, and deterrence), structural forces (for example, competitor, government, distributor, supplier, and buyer), structural attributes (for example, profitability, sales growth, concentration, asset intensity, and technological intensity), and structural development (embryonic, growth, shakeout, maturity, and decline). Collectively, these factors provide the core of an analytical framework for industry selection during international expansion.

In Chapter 9, Guillén examines the relationships between industrial groups and governments in emerging economies. Business groups in emerging economies result when entrepreneurs and firms accumulate the capability for repeated industry entry. Traditionally, business groups have been explained through three distinct theoretical frameworks. First, from the economist's perspective, business groups arise in the absence of well-functioning markets. Thus, business groups are functional substitutes for production inputs. The second approach, economic sociology, argues that business groups emerge in countries having prevalent vertical relationships based on authority and subordination. The third approach to the study of business groups argues for the importance of autonomous states in fostering business groups. This chapter examines these three approaches to the emergence of business groups. The main thesis of the chapter is that firms and entrepreneurs create diversified business groups when they can accumulate an inimitable capability to combine domestic and foreign resources to enter industries quickly and cost-effectively.

PART III   STRATEGY AND COMPETITION

The third part of the book explicitly moves the analysis from macro- to micro-level. That is, the four chapters in Part III examine firm strategies and competition. However, discussion of global competition and global strategies cannot be devoid of the environmental and institutional factors discussed in the previous chapters. Thus, the four chapters examine the evolution of firm strategies in light of the shifting political, legal, cultural, and technological environments.

Samiee, in Chapter 10, provides a comprehensive survey of the literature addressing the internationalization of firms and global strategy. The body of knowledge in these areas of inquiry addresses the nature, prerequisites or drivers of internationalization and globalization as well as imperatives, planning process, and implementation of global strategy. The main objective of this chapter is to explore the processes that precede globalization in firms (that is, distinction between internationalization and globalization) and the relevant antecedents (that is, environmental factors favoring transformation to a global paradigm). In doing so, globalization attempts by three leading firms in the major appliance industry as well as industry consolidation as a precursor to internationalization and globalization are discussed. The experiences of these firms demonstrate the diversity of patterns used to achieve an international status, while highlighting the complexities and difficulties associated with the pursuit of global strategy. Next, globalization is compared and contrasted with standardization approaches. The final section consists of a discussion pertaining to the outcomes of the globalization experiences of these firms and ways in which firms might become more successful in their globalization drives.

Hitt and Uhlenbruck, in Chapter 11, further elaborate on various forms of international expansion strategies. Business globalization is accompanied by an increasing number of mergers, acquisitions, and alliances between firms from different home countries. This chapter focuses on acquisitions and strategic alliances as a means for international expansion, market entry, and global business integration. Alliances are recognized as providing access to markets, knowledge, and resources of partners as well as an opportunity to share risks. Accordingly, selection of complementary partners is critical in international expansion. Identifying firms for cross-border acquisition adds further concerns because of the higher investment risk involved and the problems created by integrating acquired firms. Numerous advantages and disadvantages of international alliances are compared and contrasted with those of cross-border mergers and acquisitions. Also, this chapter discusses risks associated with either entry mode and identifies firm internal and external conditions that affect the level of risk associated with international alliances and mergers. The acquisition of the British automaker Rover by Germany's BMW in 1994, and the dissolution six years later, is used to illustrate these issues.

In Chapter 12, Martin focuses on the functional interfaces in such partnerships, and examines the extent and purpose of the interfaces between the key business functions as they operate *between* firms engaged in hybrid partnerships. The focus is on the interfaces among three basic functional areas – research and development (R&D), production (for example, manufacturing), and marketing. Past research has mostly discussed functional coordination *within* firms. Past research has also had a lot to say about interfirm relationships, but at the overall corporate level rather than at the functional level. This chapter describes the extent to which the interaction between two firms is limited to one function, or includes multiple functional areas for each partner. An overall framework is described that encompasses horizontal hybrids (alliances between potential rivals) and vertical hybrids (tightly integrated procurement relationships between buyers and suppliers). Some empirical evidence is offered about the nature of interface patterns in two samples of hybrids, one horizontal and the other vertical. This chapter further discusses how this line of research can inform the study of hybrid organizations, adding a functional dimension to an important subject in international and strategic management.

In Chapter 13, Sinha and Gvili explore the implications of the explosive growth of e-commerce in global competition. Web retailing consists of transactions of products and services over the Net to final consumers. The Internet has now become globally pervasive and widely accessible, and, by all estimates, the commercial potential of e-commerce is limitless. Today 373 million people are connected to the Internet and more than 2 million new users get connected each month in North America alone. For them 20 million domain names (Web sites) have been established. The start-up rate of companies is about 3000 per week. Analysts estimate that the online sales to consumers (B2C) reached $45 billion in 2000 while total Web sales reached $190 billion. More generally, the Internet has evolved into an extremely powerful and versatile marketing tool for firms. From an international business perspective, the issue that is of interest is to identify the commonalities and variations in the perceptions of global e-shoppers toward e-commerce. How do consumers from various regions evaluate online shopping as opposed to traditional shopping? Do non-American buyers perceive that their own country e-retailers serve their needs better than foreign ones? While it has been widely reported that American online consumers are highly price conscious on the Internet, do these characteristics extend to other countries as well? These questions form the central focus of this chapter.

Our book is expressly designed for the academic audience, including IB researchers and doctoral students. We hope that our book has a fairly long shelf life, given the nature of the research focus we emphasize that has been officially endorsed by the leading IB academic organization. While, for the sake of organization and classification, each chapter focuses on very narrow issues to provide the state of knowledge of that particular topic, there are nonetheless inherent interdependencies among individual chapters. Our hope is that the reader will combine insights from individual chapters to develop holistic research areas that combine both macro- and micro-level analyses to make the transition from a functional research focus to an issue-based research approach.

NOTE

1. This research direction was also formally endorsed by the Executive Board of the Academy of International Business (of which the first co-editor of this proposed book was a Vice President for the 1997–98 term).

REFERENCES

Caves, Richard E. (1998), 'Research on International Business: Problems and Prospects', *Journal of International Business Studies*, 29 (First Quarter), 5–19.
Douglas, Susan P. and C. Samuel Craig (1992), 'Advances in International Marketing', *International Journal of Research in Marketing*, 9 (4), 291–318.
Dunning, John H. (1989), 'The Study of International Business: A Plea for a More Interdisciplinary Approach', *Journal of International Business Studies*, 20 (Fall), 411–36.
Fayerweather, John (1969), *International Business Management: A Conceptual Framework*, New York: McGraw-Hill.
Levitt, Theodore (1983), 'The Globalization of Markets', *Harvard Business Review*, May–June, 92–102.
Ricks, David, Brian Toyne, and Zaida Martinez (1990), 'Recent Developments in International Management Research', *Journal of Management*, 16 (2), 219–53.
Rugman, Alan and Thomas Brewer (2001), *Oxford Handbook of International Business*, New York and Oxford: Oxford University Press.

Toyne, Brian and Douglas Nigh (eds) (1997), *International Business: An Emerging Vision*, Columbia, SC: University of South Carolina Press.

Toyne, Brian, Zaida L. Martinez, and Richard A. Menger (eds) (2001), *International Business Scholarship: Mastering Intellectual, Institutional, and Research Design Challenges*, Wesport, CT: Quorum.

PART I

The macro-environment

2. Regional integration and foreign direct investment: theory and lessons from NAFTA

Lorraine Eden

INTRODUCTION

One of the strongest worldwide trends in trade policy in the past 20 years has been the rebirth of regional integration schemes, or *preferential trading agreements* (PTAs). These agreements first became fashionable in the 1960s, after the 1957 Treaty of Rome created the European Economic Community (EEC). Many of the 'first wave' of regional integration schemes were started in Latin and South America, but languished in the 1970s. In the mid-1980s, the desire to deepen European integration with the EC1992 project regenerated interest in a 'second wave' of regional integration schemes (Dunning 1997b; Serra and Kallab 1997). By 1996, there were in excess of 100 PTAs around the world, more than double the number in 1985 (Bhagwati and Panagariya 1996). The 'first wave' PTAs (for example, CARICOM) were revitalized; others (for example, MERCOSUR) were newly created.

Regional integration is a topic that has attracted interest from many disciplines: international economics, international politics, international trade law, and more recently, international business. There is a large and rich literature on the economics of regional integration that stretches back to the early 1950s and the work of international trade economists such as Jacob Viner (1950), Richard Lipsey (1960) and Bela Balassa (1961). Much of the early international trade literature focused on types of preferential trading arrangements and their static and dynamic effects on international trade and national welfare.[1]

International business (IB) scholars first became interested in regional integration by examining the impacts of the formation of the EEC on foreign direct investment (FDI) from the United States (Dunning 1988). More generally, IB scholars have been interested in the way that multinational enterprises (MNEs) have responded to the formation of PTAs, and, in turn, how their strategies have influenced the nature and pace of regional integration.[2] Interestingly, the research on regional integration by international economics and international business scholars has proceeded on parallel but separate tracks, possibly because IB researchers have been more focused on firm strategies and FDI patterns, whereas international economics scholars have been more focused on trade patterns.

Where is the IB literature today on MNEs and regional integration? What lessons have we learned? What issues remain unexplored or controversial? In this chapter, we first briefly review the international economics literature on regional integration theory and then move to the IB literature on the strategic responses of MNEs. A review of empirical work on MNEs and regional integration, focusing on North America, follows. The chapter concludes with an outline of several possible new directions in IB research on MNEs and regional integration.

THE THEORY OF REGIONAL INTEGRATION

Regional integration schemes, in theory, have four general economic effects. The first set of effects are the short-run welfare gains that come from improved specialization of resources and greater opportunities for exchange within the region. These are known as the *static gains from trade*. The second set of effects are the long-run welfare gains, the *dynamic gains from trade*, that come from exploiting region-based economies of scale and scope, attracting inflows of foreign direct investment and technology transfers, and greater competition among firms in national markets. The third set of effects are the *transitional costs* that fall, in the short run, on inefficient sectors and immobile factors as firms rationalize and reallocate their activities throughout the region as they respond to regional integration. Lastly, greater *economic interdependence* within the region is likely to occur in response to rising interregional linkages created by trade and investment flows. Greater interdependence means more sensitivity and vulnerability to instabilities, but also creates additional potential gains from the multiplier effects of economic linkages with other member countries.

The size of the effects depends on several factors, the most important of which are probably the scope of the PTA in terms of number of member countries, industries and products covered, the degree of liberalization of tariff and nontariff barriers among the member countries, and the current and potential economic complementarity of the member countries relative to non-members. We explore these below.

Shallow versus Deep Integration

Preferential trading arrangements vary significantly in terms of how shallow or deep is the integration process among the member countries (UNCTC

1993). *Shallow integration* schemes normally involve little more than lowering or removal of tariff barriers among PTA members, whereas *deep integration* schemes involve significant removal and/or harmonization of nontariff barriers in addition to tariffs (UNCTAD 1993: 35). At the 'shallow end' of the PTAs are *free trade areas* (FTAs) where tariffs are removed against member countries, but members keep their own external tariffs against non-members and no removal or harmonization of nontariff barriers is required. Rules of origin, which define the necessary amounts of regional content required to qualify for duty-free entry, are used to prevent non-member country products from coming in through the lowest-tariff country and moving freely inside the FTA afterwards.

Since more coordination among member countries is required for a *customs union*, where a common external tariff against non-member countries is added to the zero internal tariff requirements, a customs union is deeper than a free trade area. A common market is deeper again, since removal and/or harmonization of nontariff barriers that restrict factor mobility (in particular, mobility of labor and capital) is an added requirement. The last regional integration scheme before the 'deep end' (full political union, as in the United States of America) is an economic union, where the member countries, in addition to the requirements of a common market, adopt common monetary and fiscal policies and a common currency.

Effective deep integration removes all intra-regional barriers that discourage the efficient allocation of international production within the PTA. This includes elimination of barriers to trade in business services, right of establishment and fair treatment for foreign direct investment (FDI), and protection of intellectual property. UNCTC (1993) argues that governments press for shallow integration but deep integration comes from the pressures of multinational enterprises to remove intra-regional impediments to the flow of goods, services, intangibles, capital, and people.

Deep integration occurs in two ways; first, through the extension of the GATT norm of *national treatment* (foreign activities performed within a country's borders receive the same treatment as activities of nationals), to intra-regional flows of investment, services, and intellectual property. National treatment means that a country treats foreign activities performed within its borders in the same way as it treats domestic activities. Foreign goods, services, and investments are treated the same as domestic goods, services, and investments, once they have cleared customs and become part of a country's internal market.

However, deep integration requires that countries go further than simply national treatment. Greater *policy coordination and harmonization* in specific areas takes place as governments harmonize and coordinate a variety of domestic policies and adopt common standards in various fields that are not

directly trade related but do affect multinational enterprises. Removal of
internal barriers facilitates the exploitation of economies of scale and scope
at a regional level through the location of MNE plants where they are most
efficiently located.

Macro-regions and Micro-regions

Ethier (1998: 1150) argues that the 'second wave' of regional integration
schemes in the 1980s and 1990s is a 'new regionalism' with specific characteristics that differentiate it from old regional schemes such as the EEC. First,
the new regionalism typically involves differences in country size, as one or
more small countries joins with a large country; NAFTA (North American
Free Trade Area) is an example. Second, before entry, the small countries
have unilaterally reformed their trade regimes, and, after entry, liberalization
is primarily by the small countries. Third, regional integration involves
neighboring countries, creating what Dunning (2000) calls 'macro-regions'.
Lastly, regional integration often involves deep integration as members harmonize and liberalize nontariff barriers among themselves.

The spread of regional integration schemes in the 1980s and 1990s has
meant that cross-border barriers to trade and FDI flows within a PTA have
fallen relative to barriers against non-member countries. As a result, the
movement of capital, people, goods, and services within regions is probably
freer than it has been since the late 1800s. Over the same period, international
institutions have strengthened their regulation of cross-border flows, most
notably international trade flows, with the lowering of tariff and nontariff
barriers (NTBs) and the creation of the World Trade Organization in the
Uruguay Round. The rapid spread of bilateral investment treaties and tax
treaties also suggests that an international regime for investment is forming
around the national treatment standard (Eden 1996).

Dunning (2000) argues that the liberalization of trade and FDI regulations
at the regional level is creating 'macro-regions' as spatial entities. Some
authors (for example, Ohmae 1995) have suggested that the region is replac-
ing the nation state as the key spatial economic unit, while others (Kobrin
1995) see globalization as an offsetting force to regionalism. At the same
time, 'micro-regions' are developing within countries as clustering activities
by firms create 'sticky places within slippery space' (Markusen 1996). How
PTAs affect firms' location decisions, in terms of both macro-regions and
micro-regions, has attracted recent and substantial attention in the IB literature, which I explore later in this chapter.

Trade Creation and Diversion Effects

International trade economists have long studied the welfare impacts of PTAs, generally focusing on the customs union case, where the member countries erect a common external tariff (Lipsey 1960; Bhagwati et al. 1998). Because the benefits of PTAs are restricted to member countries, their formation has two conflicting effects on trade flows. *Trade creation* occurs when the reduction of trade barriers within the PTA causes a shift from higher cost producers to lower cost producers within the PTA. In this case, differences in comparative costs cause shifts in trade, production, and investment patterns that favor the lower cost producers and improve economic efficiency within the PTA. For example, if the lowest cost producer (country Z) of steel plate is a PTA member, then country X will benefit by joining a PTA with Z, even though X's steel plate producers will suffer dislocations and their production will shrink. The gains to consumers in X outweigh the losses to X's producers, so that trade creation causes a net welfare gain for country X.

Trade diversion, on the other hand, occurs when the PTA causes a shift to higher cost internal producers from lower cost external producers because the products of the external producers have become uncompetitive in the internal market. Before the PTA, both inside and outside countries faced the same tariff barriers; after the PTA, only the outside countries face the tariff barriers. Removal of the tariff barriers against the inside countries may give them a competitive advantage that diverts trade and production away from the most efficient producers (the outsiders) towards the less efficient – but inside and therefore advantaged – countries.

These effects work against one another: regional integration creates welfare losses since trade is not with the lowest cost producer, but provides welfare gains because the average level of tariffs has fallen. Whether or not the country contemplating the PTA is actually worse off, in welfare terms, depends on the cost disadvantage between the member and non-member countries as compared to the tariff savings from removal of the tariff within the PTA. Since trade creation and trade diversion effects will vary by product and industry, the net impact of the formation of a PTA on the welfare of member and non-member countries depends on many factors. The general presumption is that the more trade expands between two countries after the formation of a PTA and the less the negative impact on trade with non-member countries, the more likely that trade creation effects have dominated trade diversion effects.

Bhagwati et al. (1998: 1130) argue that 'trade diversion is not necessarily a negligible phenomenon in current PTAs'. Several empirical studies have found significant estimates of trade diversion. In addition, PTAs can lead to endogenous trade diversion as member countries raise trade barriers against non-members.[3] The authors also argue that the proliferation of PTAs has created a 'spaghetti bowl phenomenon' (1998: 1138) whereby numerous crisscrossing PTAs and tariff rates create a 'who is whose' problem that can also raise protectionism and reduce welfare levels.

MNE RESPONSES TO REGIONAL INTEGRATION

Macro-regions and FDI

The formation of a preferential trading area is a policy shock, a change in the environment facing firms inside and outside the PTA (Eaton et al. 1994a). We therefore expect firm strategies to change in response to this policy shock. Dunning (1993) identifies four basic motivations for foreign direct investment: market access, resource seeking, efficiency seeking, and strategic asset seeking FDI. The formation of a preferential trading area should lead to all four types of FDI as firms take advantage of the lower tariff and nontariff barriers within the PTA.

Rugman and Gestrin (1993b) argue that the FDI response depends initially on the country-specific advantages (CSAs) of each of the member countries and the region-specific advantages (RSAs) that will be available once the PTA is fully phased in. They use internalization theory and the concept of CSAs and RSAs to predict how MNEs would react to NAFTA, but their arguments apply to any preferential trading area. They argue that the ability of MNEs to internalize their own firm specific advantages (FSAs) and take advantage of the country and region-specific advantages determines MNE profitability, market share, and growth. Rugman and Gestrin argue that regional integration reduces the transactions costs (for example, tariffs) associated with intra-regional trade and creates more certainty for investment. How regional integration affects CSAs and RSAs, and their interaction with FSAs, should determine trade and investment responses. Where trade and FDI are complements, they predict that regional integration should increase flows in both directions. However, where transactions costs were the main factor driving FDI (that is, tariff jumping FDI), MNEs should substitute trade for investment, closing tariff factories, and centralizing production in the home market. Where strategic considerations, other than tariffs, are the main driver of FDI, the impact should be largely neutral.

Eden (1998: 166–8) argues that the likely reactions of firms to regional integration depend on the type of firm and its activities before the formation of the preferential trading area.[4] Three types of firms are critical:

- *Insiders* – multinationals headquartered inside the region with significant investments across the region.
- *Outsiders* – foreign firms headquartered outside the region. These outsiders may be *traders* that export or import in the region or *investors* that have foreign investments inside the region.
- *Domestics* – local firms that are primarily focused domestically on their local/national market; they may be exporting to or importing from other member countries but do not have any foreign investments across the region.

Firms that are already established within the region and have affiliates in the member countries should view regional integration primarily as an opportunity. Insider firms should see benefits from lower intra-regional barriers and respond by rationalizing product lines (horizontal integration) and/or production processes (vertical integration) better to exploit economies of scale and scope across the region. That is, the primary response of insiders should be *efficiency seeking* FDI. There should be both a short-run response as MNEs engage in locational reshufflings in response to the falling trade barriers, and a long-run response where insiders locate, close and/or expand their plants with the whole regional market in mind. The result should be reduced numbers of product lines in various plants and increased horizontal trade among plants. MNEs are also likely to segment their production process among plants so that more vertical intra-firm trade takes place. Certain product lines, industry segments, and plant functions should shift within the region to the lowest cost location, causing job losses and plant closures in high cost locations.

Because regional integration normally leaves trade and FDI barriers against non-member countries unchanged, outsider firms exporting into the PTA may face trade diversion as insider firms receive preferential treatment. For defensive reasons, outsiders are likely to respond by investing in the region in order to protect their market access; that is, their defensive response is *market seeking (or protecting)* FDI. If privileged access depends on firm nationality, or if insiders hold complementary assets needed by the foreign firms, we also expect *strategic asset seeking (or asset augmenting)* FDI. Asset augmenting FDI is likely to be in the form of joint ventures or strategic alliances with insider firms. Outsiders that already have transplant operations in the region are likely to behave as the insiders, expanding and rationalizing their investments to take advantage of the larger regional market. Where just-in-time production is critical, these locational reshufflings will induce subsequent investments by upstream suppliers.

For local firms without established links to other PTA member countries, regional integration is both an opportunity (new markets, access to lower cost inputs) and a threat (more competition). These firms, with encouragement, may start or increase their exports within the region and possibly open up distributors or offshore plants where market size or costs warrant. They will, however, have to face the difficult task of breaking into established distribution networks of domestics and MNEs already located in the other PTA countries. The key question is whether to 'go regional' and branch outside the home country into other parts of the region, or stay at home and become less competitive. The FDI strategies of domestics are therefore likely to be either *market seeking* or *resource seeking* (*de novo* FDI). If the domestics lack the complementary assets needed to penetrate other member country markets (for example, distribution networks), we also expect *strategic asset seeking* FDI.

When the PTA consists of countries with very different market sizes (in terms of population and income), another useful distinction can be made between firms headquartered in the *hub* economy (the largest market in the region) and in the *spoke* (small) economies (Eden and Molot 1993). If high trade barriers separate these countries prior to the formation of a PTA, one would expect firms to engage in tariff jumping FDI, setting up plants in each country to supply the local market. These so-called tariff factories were common in North America in the 1960s and 1970s, and in Mexico before NAFTA. Regional integration, in this case, is likely to lead MNEs headquartered in the hub economy to engage in *efficiency seeking* FDI, closing tariff factories in the smaller markets and supplying them with exports from large-scale hub plants. The larger, regional market should also be more attractive as an investment location for market seeking FDI. MNEs located in the spoke economies are also likely to expand, both for offensive and defensive reasons, although they may need to change their market focus from the national to the regional market, adapting to what Rugman and D'Cruz (1991) call the 'double diamond' model of competitive advantage. On the other hand, firms located in the spoke economies that have not invested in the hub market (the domestics) are likely to respond to regional integration by moving closer to the border. The move to relocate to border areas and port cities should be more pronounced for firms in small countries due to the relatively stronger pull of the larger market.

Lastly, if the PTA uses rules of origin to determine duty-free status, outsider firms that are unlikely to meet the rules of origin tests are more likely to cluster in the largest country, thus reducing their intra-PTA tariff duties. Large differences in sizes of member countries therefore suggest that the hub economy may reap a disproportionate share of regional FDI flows.

Micro-regions and FDI

Until Krugman published *Geography and Trade* (1991), little attention had been paid to the spatial effects of international trade. Since then, there has been a virtual explosion of work among international trade and international business scholars on clustering.[5] The key tension identified by these authors lies between the pull to centralize activities in one location and the pull to disperse activities closer to factor and product markets.

For example, in deciding where to locate a plant, the firm must first choose whether to centralize the activity by locating it at home (with the parent firm) or decentralize the activity to a foreign location. Eaton et al.'s (1994b) argument explains how the interaction of economies of scale together with transportation and communication costs produce clustering. Essentially, these authors argue that, 'the degree of agglomeration is determined jointly by the interaction of economies of scale at the plant level, which work to create agglomeration by encouraging fewer larger plants, and transportation and communication costs, which work to limit agglomeration by encouraging smaller plants' (1994b: 82). Economies of scale at the plant level encourage centralization of production in one location with exports being used as the mode to supply foreign markets. Transportation and communication costs, on the other hand, raise the costs of exporting and encourage decentralization. High tariffs act like transport costs, discouraging foreign firms from locating production in one central place and exporting to a variety of foreign markets. Tariff jumping FDI is likely to occur as foreign firms set up domestic plants in order to supply the local market, particularly where the market is large and attractive.

While Eaton et al. (1994b) focused on the individual firm's decision to centralize or decentralize its activities, the unit of analysis for other authors such as Markusen (1996), Enright (1998), Porter (1998a,b) and Dunning (2000) has been the formation of spatial clusters, or 'sticky places within slippery space' (Markusen 1996). These authors identify several different types of clusters or micro-regions, depending on their scope, nature of activities, growth potential, innovatory capacity, and governance structures (Enright 1998). Markusen (1996) identifies four types of clusters: (1) Marshallian new industrial district based on flexible specialization, as exemplified by the north Italy garment district; (2) hub-and-spoke district where satellite firms locate around flagship firms in one or a few industries (for example, the Toyota complex near Tokyo); (3) the satellite industrial platform, such as export processing zones, where branch plants cluster together to take advantage of low wages and/or available resources; and (4) state-centered district where a major government institution (for example, military or research facility) anchors the regional economy.

Where firms are likely to locate is partly dependent on the advantages of firms clustering in one location; that is, whether or not to locate near other firms (upstream suppliers, downstream customers, or competitors). External economies and the benefits of information sharing encourage clustering of firms, particularly in knowledge intensive sectors. Access to natural resources or specialized assets and infrastructure will also encourage resource-seeking firms to cluster in one location. The benefits of labor pooling can similarly encourage clustering, for example, where highly specialized workers are needed. *Horizontal clusters*, firms engaged in similar lines of activity, are likely to form under these circumstances.

The shift from mass to lean production methods can also cause clustering. New process technologies have reduced the importance of labor, transport, and communications costs; shortened the minimum efficient scale of production (thus reducing the importance of economies of scale at the plant level); and increased the need for supplier firms to locate close to their downstream customers in order to use just-in-time production and delivery methods. Lean production therefore encourages the formation of *vertical clusters* of suppliers and buyers. In many cases, these clusters may form around one or more flagship firms, with upstream and downstream firms as satellites around them. Head et al. (1995) perform an empirical study testing whether industry-level agglomeration economies influence location decisions. By examining the location decision of Japanese manufacturing plants in the United States, they found that the Japanese ventures do not mimic the geographical pattern of US establishments; instead, they follow initial investments by other Japanese firms in the same industry or industrial group. Therefore, the authors suggest that locational choice supports the theory on agglomeration externalities rather than the theory on differences in factor endowments.

Regional integration can affect the location of economic activity inside countries. Puga and Venables (1997) examine the effects of preferential trading agreements on industrial location. Free trade areas have the pulling effect of attracting industry into the integrating countries. Moreover, when trade barriers fall, agglomeration economies favor centralization of production so some member countries may gain industry at the expense of others. A hub-and-spoke arrangement will favor location in the hub, with better access to the spoke countries.

Eden and Monteils (2000) explore the impacts of regional integration on clustering. They argue that the type of firm – insider, outsider, domestic – influences the firm's location decisions and therefore the creation of micro-regions. For insider firms, as tariff rates fall in a PTA, where plant-level economies of scale are important, firms that had tariff-jumping factories may close down smaller plants and shift production to the largest, most efficient plant, relying on exports to reach the smaller markets. If the PTA is also accompanied by a decline in transportation costs (for example, liberalization of cross-border transport routes is part of the PTA package), this also encourages centralization of production. This suggests that insider MNEs with investments throughout the PTA are more likely to rationalize production by closing inefficient plants and centralizing production, where economies of scale gains are significant and transport costs low. Alternatively, rationalization of product lines between plants and increased intra-industry horizontal trade is an alternative solution for differentiated product industries.

Outsider firms may be induced by the PTA to locate inside the region. Their locational patterns may also cluster if they are following downstream producers (particularly where lean production techniques are prevalent), choose to locate their market seeking FDI in urban centers, or are attracted to knowledge-based clusters for their external economies and information sharing. Such firms may be more likely to see the region as a whole and make decisions from a regionally efficient perspective, thus increasing their competitiveness relative to member firms.[6] On the other hand, outsider firms may be less well equipped to take advantage of clustering, particularly where the advantages are based on knowledge spillovers (Enright 1996: 204).

For domestics, a PTA expands the set of markets available to firms, if they had not previously engaged in exports or FDI to the member countries. In order to access these new markets, these firms are likely to move to locations with good access to the other markets, such as border areas and port cities. As firms move to border locations, a self-reinforcing movement may occur due to agglomeration economies, creating new clusters. Thus, some clusters could expand with a PTA while other micro-regions shrink.

Hanson (1998) argues that border clusters may be encouraged by the formation of a PTA, as firms move to the border in order to be able to access adjoining markets. Small cities along the border may develop into transportation and wholesale trade hubs, facilitating cross-border flows of goods and services liberalized under the PTA. Large cities, on the other hand, may develop into full-sized regional production sharing networks, where firms from both countries specialize their value adding activities along the value chain, engage in sophisticated subcontracting strategies, and establish cross-border alliances.

LESSONS FROM NAFTA[7]

Any review of the IB literature on MNEs and regional integration is incomplete if it only focuses on theoretical contributions to the literature. In this section, we review empirical work on regional integration in North America.

NAFTA shares three characteristics that distinguish the 'new regionalism' from older PTAs.[8] First, NAFTA allows free movement of goods, services, and capital between two developed market economies and a developing country. Opening trade and investment between countries with very different institutional, legal, political, social, and economic profiles not surprisingly should be more difficult than creating a PTA between two rich countries (for example, the Canada–US Free Trade Agreement (CAFTA)). The extension of CAFTA to Mexico had problems similar to those experienced by West Germany in its amalgamation with East Germany, and transaction costs were, and continue to be, large. Second, the major adjustments in terms of reducing tariffs and nontariff barriers fell on Mexico, as the smaller partner with the highest tariff barriers and the largest amount of necessary adjustment. On the other hand, Mexico was expected to make the largest gains in the long run. Third, country sizes are very different with Canada having the smallest population (30 million), followed by Mexico (100 million) compared to the United States (230 million). In addition, North American trade and investment patterns are dominated by US multinationals. North America can therefore be seen as a *hub-and-spoke* relationship, where the US hub is linked through trade and investment to two spokes: Canada and Mexico (Eden and Molot 1993).

In this section, we examine the impacts of the formation of a macro-region – NAFTA – on MNE trade and FDI patterns, separating our review into macro-region and micro-region (clustering) decisions.

Macro-regions, Trade and FDI

Because NAFTA has only been in place for six years, much of the work in the 1990s has looked at the earlier Canada–US Free Trade Agreement (CAFTA). Rugman (1990) surveyed MNEs in Canada and the United States about their anticipated reactions to the 1989 Canada–US Free Trade Agreement (CAFTA). He found that MNEs in both countries supported free trade, anticipated few adjustment problems, and were particularly attuned to competitiveness. Another study, done two years later by the Conference Board of Canada (Krajewski 1992), also posed questions to its members about their reactions to CAFTA. The Conference Board study looked at two groups: Canadian parents with US subsidiaries and Canadian subsidiaries of US parents. CAFTA was seen by the respondents as a primary driver, in addition to globalization of markets in general, pushing multinationals in Canada to rationalize their production and sales for the North American market. The firms had a sense of new opportunities and/or felt the necessity to compete globally to survive. CAFTA provided new business opportunities through a more open door to the US market.

Schwanen (1997), in a C.D. Howe Institute study, compared the trade and FDI growth rates in sectors liberalized by CAFTA, relative to those that were already barrier free, between 1988 and 1995. He found that Canada–US bilateral trade grew more quickly in liberalized sectors than in tariff-free sectors. Intra-industry specialization, as evidenced by rapid growth in two-way trade, occurred in several sectors. On the other hand, North America's share of global FDI fell over the period, as did the importance of Canada and the US in each other's FDI portfolio. Schwanen concluded that external events (for example, liberalization and privatization in South America, rapid growth in Asia) had attracted FDI outside of North America.

In a later study looking at NAFTA, Rugman et al. (1997) argued that NAFTA posed three challenges for Canadian firms. First, NAFTA did not provide secure access to the US market because US anti-dumping and countervailing duties could still be used to harass Canadian firms. Second, Canadian firms were ethnocentric and needed to develop national responsiveness to the whole North American market, not just Canada. Third, the high degree of foreign ownership in certain sectors complicated business–government relations in Canada. Because Canadian firms depend so heavily on the US market, one way to develop a 'North American mindset' was to establish business networks to maintain competitive advantages (D'Cruz and Rugman 1993). Using the chemical industry as an example, Rugman et al. (1997) argued that a business network arrangement, where key partners were coordinated by a flagship firm, provided an effective strategic response to external environmental changes, such as NAFTA.

Eden (1994b) theorized about the locational strategies of US multinationals after NAFTA. She provided detailed statistics about US MNEs in Canada and Mexico in 1990, and argued that US MNEs were best placed to take advantage of the opportunities created by North American economic integration. A follow-up Conference Board study looking at NAFTA (Blank et al. 1994, 1995) focused on the restructuring of US firms and their Canadian subsidiaries and confirmed Eden's hypotheses. Large US MNEs were quickly moving to adopt North American strategies and structures. Canadian subsidiaries were being rapidly integrated into a continental production system, and more rapidly than their Mexican sister affiliates. Driving this reorganization was what the authors termed the emerging 'architecture' of North America – a North American economic space – as well as intensified global competition, the early 1990s recession and technological change. Many Canadian subsidiaries expected a rise in intra-firm trade as fewer goods were produced in Canadian plants, a decrease in subsidiary autonomy, a loss of production capacity and jobs, redefinition of their role within the corporate network, and growing intra-firm competition for product and marketing mandates (Blank et al. 1995).

Johnson et al. (1995) surveyed senior operations executives at 139 North American manufacturers in 1993. The managers were asked to assess how they thought NAFTA would affect their operations strategies and to outline the responses they had undertaken in the past two years. Canadian firms did not expect to meet global competition through low manufacturing costs, but through superior customer service, dependable deliveries and high quality. Their response was to improve capacity in these areas, seek more international customers, and avoid markets where fast deliveries and product proliferation were critical. In the new North American economic space, both Canadian and Mexican firms saw their greatest potential in the US market, but also saw their US competitors as their greatest threat.

The US International Trade Commission (ITC) conducted a major three-year review of the impacts of NAFTA on the US economy in nearly 200 industrial sectors (ITC 1997; see also the analysis in GAO 1997). The ITC concluded that NAFTA has minimal impacts on the US economy in terms of trade, employment or hourly earnings. Maquiladora-related trade expanded sharply, leading the ITC to conclude that production sharing along the US–Mexico border would continue to expand due to the complementaries of the US and Mexican economies. Intra-industry trade, both Canada–US and Mexico–US, increased in sectors characterized by product differentiation and a high percentage of manufactured components. US–Mexico integration is perhaps proceeding fastest in the auto sector, where high Mexican trade barriers (tariffs on autos, domestic content regulations, trade balancing requirements) are being dismantled and the gains from continental integration are large (USTR 1998).

In a later study of NAFTA and MNE strategies, Blank and Haar (1998) surveyed senior managers of US MNEs with Mexican operation in 1994–96. Incorporating the results of two earlier Conference Board studies of US and Canadian managers, the authors analyze MNE strategies from the perspective of all three countries. They find that 'cross-border corporate integration has been deeper and more far-reaching ... than governments ... seem to realize' (1998: 2). Their interviews with North American managers led Blank and Haar to conclude that an integrated corporate system in North America is emerging where MNEs view North America as a single spatial unit when making their configuration and coordination strategies.

Micro-regions, Trade and FDI

So far, there has been little work asking whether regional integration in North America has encouraged clustering, either within a country or along the borders between member countries. In one of the early statistical analyses of Canada–US trade flows post-CAFTA, Little (1996) found that both US and

Canadian firms tended to rely on trade rather than FDI to serve the US–Canadian market. She focused on changes in the industrial composition of trade at the regional level, which were often obscured when national-level data were employed. For example, inward FDI from Canada and geographic shifts in US industry activity significantly affected New England's export performance, because trade activity shifted to the south and west with the implementation of CAFTA.

A second exception is Gordon Hanson who, across several papers, has examined the impact of NAFTA on US–Mexican trade and FDI patterns. Industry responses to NAFTA were expected to be most evident in terms of US–Mexico trade and FDI flows because the major effect of NAFTA was to bring Mexico into CAFTA. Studying economic activity in the US–Mexico border cities, Hanson (1996) found evidence that export manufacturing expansion in these border cities has increased manufacturing employment in the US border cities, suggesting that NAFTA can positively influence the relocation of US manufacturing production to the US–Mexico border region, especially when transport costs are an important consideration for industry location. As is evidenced by such relocation from interior US region to the border cities, Hanson (1996) suggests that this negates the prevailing view that the smaller Mexican economy would not have any significant effects on the US economy.

Parallel to the US manufacturing relocation, there is a similar pattern of relocation in Mexico (Hanson 1998). Manufacturing employment has increased in northern Mexico and decreased in central Mexico, also suggesting manufacturing relocation to the border cities with the US. The author suggests that NAFTA is likely to have more impact on Mexico in industrial location compared to the two larger economies, the US and Canada. This view is in broad agreement with Rugman and Gestrin (1993a,b) who suggested that the impact of NAFTA on the US and Canada would be more neutral, as most effects should already have taken place since CAFTA, while Mexico would also benefit from significant investment diversion away from other LDCs. Therefore, the most significant post-NAFTA changes were likely to take place in Mexico.

Eden and Monteils (2000) develop a theoretical model of MNE strategic responses to regional integration and then provide some evidence of these responses, looking at FDI patterns in North America over 1985–97. They found that North America became less attractive to inward FDI relative to other regions, especially East Asia and the former Soviet Union, over this period. CAFTA and NAFTA did not appear to have resulted in significant increased inward FDI. Although the dollar value of the FDI stock increased among all the NAFTA partners and in both directions, relatively more investments were directed outside of North America.

Looking specifically at inward FDI entries to the United States, they found that Canadian MNEs invested more frequently at the beginning of the CAFTA and engaged in relatively more new FDI entries, primarily through mergers and acquisitions. Insider FDI entries, for Canada, while more clustered in geography and industry than FDI entries from non-NAFTA countries, were overall similar in terms of the top ten destinations for inward FDI. Mexican investors, reflecting Mexico's joining the PTA only in 1994, its higher trade barriers and developing country status, engaged in small numbers of new investments in the US market which were geographically and industrially clustered. Mexico, in particular, invested more heavily along the US–Mexico border and in manufacturing industries relative to all home country entries. Eden and Monteils concluded that North American firms were making their locational decisions from a macro-regional perspective, but that in the 1990s this meant primarily locational reshufflings as firms rationalized investments on a continental basis. Over the longer term, once NAFTA is fully phased in, they expected new investment decisions to be made treating the North American macro-region as the 'home base'.

What is evident from these studies is that, in response to NAFTA, multinationals are engaged in locational reshuffling, as Vernon (1994) predicted, designed to integrate Mexican and Canadian industry into regional production networks. This is proceeding fastest in the automotive, electronic equipment, and textile sectors, as evidenced by the rapid growth in two-way trade in components and finished manufactured goods and the movement of firms to the US–Canada and US–Mexico border regions.

NEW DIRECTIONS IN IB RESEARCH

Based on our outline of the IB literature on MNEs and regional integration, we suggest the following as potential areas for research. First, there continues to be room for statistical analyses of the impact of regional integration schemes on trade and FDI flows, both extra-region and intra-region. For example, the definitive study of the empirical impacts of NAFTA on FDI patterns, at the national and industry levels, has not been completed. Dunning (1997a,b) is a tour de force on FDI patterns in response to first wave and second wave regional integration within the European Union. Similar studies for other regions remain to be explored.

Second, the dynamics of preferential trading arrangements, as they weaken or strengthen over time, pose opportunities and threats for domestic and multinational firms. Change in the structure and strength of PTAs is likely to occur in two dimensions: breadth and depth. The breadth of a regional integration scheme increases when the PTA takes on new member countries, causing further rounds of trade and FDI creation and diversion effects. For example, the 1989 bilateral CAFTA expanded into the 1994 trilateral NAFTA. While Congress did not approve of Chile as a fourth NAFTA member, the governments in North and South America have been discussing a Free Trade Area of the Americas (FTAA) linking both hemispheres, starting in 2005. Our analysis suggests that insider MNEs, with investments in both hemispheres, are most likely to be the beneficiaries of an FTAA. PTAs can also be deepened through the broader application of national treatment legislation and/or the increased harmonization and coordination of internal policies. The adoption of a common currency within the European Union is one such example.

Third, one can study the impacts of PTA deepening or broadening on the cross-border configuration and coordination decisions of multinational firms. The reactions of different types of firms – insiders, outsiders and domestics – to broadening and deepening PTAs is an under-explored topic. Comparative studies exploring firm responses to different types of PTAs (for example, free trade areas versus customs unions, PTAs with similar sized members versus hub-and-spoke PTAs, PTAs with rich country members versus PTAs that include developing countries) have not been done.

Fourth, although little attention (due to space constraints) has been paid in this chapter to the political economy of MNEs and regional integration, an area that begs for further exploration is how firms can affect the dynamic path of regional integration. Two-level bargaining games should be visible as MNEs negotiate with their domestic governments and with the regional apparatus. Different types of PTAs should lead to different configurations of MNE responses, but no work has been done in this area.

Fifth, another area that was not explored in this chapter due to space constraints, and is under-explored in the literature, is the impact of regional integration schemes on the mode of entry decision into member country markets. We briefly discussed the demand for strategic alliances as a way to obtain strategic assets and attain insider status within the PTA.

Lastly, the life cycle of micro-regions or clusters within countries and along border regions within a larger PTA is a new topic in the IB literature. How different types of micro-regions are formed and how they foster firm-level and national competitiveness is not well understood. Some work has been done on follow-the-leader FDI as suppliers follow flagship firms and create vertical clusters; other work has focused on knowledge clusters; however, this remains a relatively new topic in the IB literature.

CONCLUSIONS

Regional integration schemes have been with us since the late 1950s. Early work on understanding these preferential trading arrangements was conducted primarily by economics and political scientists. In this chapter, we have reviewed the international business literature on multinational enterprises and regional integration, focusing on 'the new regionalism' and its impact on MNE location decisions at both the macro-region and micro-region levels. Much work remains to be done, however. IB researchers need to inform their own studies of MNEs and regional integration with parallel research being undertaken in international economics and political science.

NOTES

1. For recent overviews of this literature see Baldwin and Venables (1996), Bhagwati and Panagariya (1996), De Melo and Panagariya (1996), El-Agraa (1997) and Bhagwati et al. (1998).
2. We can distinguish at least two separate strands of IB literature on regional integration. The first strand takes a political economy approach, focusing on MNE attitudes towards regional integration and how firms can affect the nature and speed of regional integration (for example, Dunning 1988, Eden and Molot 1993, Milner 1997; Rugman 1994a,b). The second strand examines the impacts of regional integration on inward and outward FDI patterns and MNE location decisions. In this paper, we focus on the second strand of the literature.
3. For example, Mexico responded to the peso crisis in 1995 by raising more than 500 tariffs against non-member countries while leaving those against its NAFTA partners unchanged.
4. See also Vernon (1994) and Eden and Monteils (2000).
5. See, for example, Dunning (1997a, 2000), Eaton et al. (1994b), Enright (1995, 1996, 1998), Hanson (1998), Krugman (1991), Markusen (1996), Porter (1998a, b), and Puga and Venables (1997).
6. For example, Dunning argues that US multinationals were the major beneficiaries from Mark I regional integration in the European Community because they 'were able to take advantage of the removal of tariff barriers, and surmount the transactions costs of the remaining non-tariff barriers better than their EC equivalents' (1997a: 5).
7. In this paper, we focus on regional integration within North America. On European integration, see for example, Dunning (1994, 1997a, b).
8. On the specifics of NAFTA see Gestrin and Rugman (1994), Rugman and Gestrin (1993a), Eden (1994a, 1996), Globerman and Walker (1993), Hufbauer and Schott (1993), Lipsey et al. (1994), Rugman (1994a) and Weintraub (1997).

REFERENCES

Balassa, B. (1961), *The Theory of Economic Integration*, Homewood, II: Richard D. Irwin, Inc.
Baldwin, R. and A. Venables (1996), 'Regional Economic Integration', in G. Grossman and K. Rogoff (eds), *Handbook of International Economics, Volume 3*, Amsterdam: North Holland.

Bhagwati, J., D. Greenaway, and A. Panagariya (1998), 'Trading Preferentially: Theory and Policy', *Economic Journal*, 108, 1128–48.

Bhagwati, J. and A. Panagariya (1996), *The Economics of Preferential Trade Agreements*, Washington DC: AEI Press.

Blank, S. and J. Haar (1998), *Making NAFTA Work: U.S. Firms and the New North American Business Environment*, Boulder, CO: Lynne Rienner publishers.

Blank, S., S. Krajewski, and H.S. Yu (1994), 'Responding to a New Political and Economic Architecture in North America: Corporate Structure and Strategy', *Northwest Journal of Business and Economics*, Bellingham, WA: Western Washington University, 17–29.

Blank, S., S. Krajewski, and H.S. Yu (1995), 'U.S. Firms and North America: Redefining Structure and Strategy', *North American Outlook*, 5(2), February, 9–23, 60–74.

D'Cruz, J.R. and A.M. Rugman (1993), 'Developing International Competitiveness: The Five Partner Model', *Business Quarterly*, 58, 101–7.

De Melo, J. and A. Panagariya (eds) (1996), *New Dimensions Regional Integration*, Cambridge: Cambridge University Press.

Dunning, J.H. (1988), 'Cross-Border Integration and Regional Integration', in J.H. Dunning (ed.), *Explaining International Production*, London: Unwin Hyman.

Dunning, J.H. (1993), *Multinational Enterprises and the Global Economy*, Reading: Addison-Wesley.

Dunning, J.H. (1994), 'MNE Activity: Comparing the NAFTA and the European Community', in L. Eden (ed.), *Multinationals in North America*, Calgary: University of Calgary Press.

Dunning, J.H. (1997a), 'A Business Analytic Approach to Governments and Globalization', in J.H. Dunning (ed.), *Governments, Globalization and International Business*, Oxford and New York: Oxford University, Press.

Dunning, J.H. (1997b), 'The European Internal Market Programme and Inbound Foreign Direct Investment', *Journal of Common Market Studies*, 35, 1–30 and 189–223.

Dunning, J.H. (2000), *Regions, Globalization and the Knowledge Based Economy*, Oxford: Oxford University, Press.

Eaton, C., R. Lipsey, and A.E. Safarian (1994a), 'The Theory of Multinational Plant Location in a Regional Trading Area', in L. Eden (ed.), *Multinationals in North America*, Calgary: University of Calgary Press.

Eaton, C., R. Lipsey, and A.E. Safarian (1994b), 'The Theory of Multinational Plant Location: Agglomerations and Disagglomerations', in L. Eden (ed.), *Multinationals in North America*, Calgary: University of Calgary Press.

Eden, L. (ed.) (1994a), *Multinationals in North America*, Calgary: University of Calgary Press.

Eden, L. (1994b), 'Who Does What After NAFTA? Location Strategies of US Multinationals', in L. Eden (ed), *Multinationals in North America*, Calgary: University of Calgary Press.

Eden, L. (1996), 'The Emerging North American Investment Regime', *Transnational Corporation*, 5(3), 61–98.

Eden, L. (1998), *Taxing Multinationals: Transfer Pricing and Corporate Income Taxation in North America*, Toronto: University of Toronto Press.

Eden, L. and M.A. Molot (1993), 'Insiders and Outsiders: Defining "Who Is Us?" in the North American Auto Industry', *Transnational Corporations*, 2(3), 31–64.

Eden. L. and A. Monteils (2000), 'Regional Integration and the Location Decisions of Multinational Enterprises', in John Dunning (ed.), *Regions, Globalization and the Knowledge Based Economy*, Oxford: Oxford University Press.

El-Agraa, A.M. (ed.) (1997), *Economic Integration Worldwide*, New York: St. Martin's Press.

Enright, M.J. (1995), 'Organization and Coordination in Geographically Concentrated Industries', in N.R. Lamoreaux and D.M.G. Raff (eds), *Coordination and Information: Historical Perspectives on the Organization of Enterprise*, Chicago and London: The University of Chicago Press.

Enright, M.J. (1996), 'Regional Clusters and Economic Development: A Research Agenda', in U.H. Staber, N.V. Schaefer, and B. Sharma (eds), *Business Networks: Prospects for Regional Development*, Berlin and New York: Walter de Gruyter.

Enright, M.J. (1998), 'Regional Clusters and Firm Strategy', in A.D. Chandler Jr, P. Hagstrom, and O. Solvell (eds), *The Dynamic Firm: The Role of Technology, Strategy, Organization, and Regions*, Oxford and New York: Oxford University Press.

Ethier, W.J. (1998), 'The New Regionalism', *Economic Journal*, 108, 1149–61.

GAO (US General Accounting Office) (1997), *North American Free Trade Agreement: Impacts and Implementation*, Testimony before the Subcommittee on Trade, Committee on Ways and Means, House of Representatives, September 11, Washington DC: USGPO.

Gestrin, M. and A.M. Rugman (1994), 'The North American Free Trade Agreement and Foreign Direct Investment', *Transnational Corporations*, 3(1), 77–95.

Globerman, S. and M. Walker (1993), *Assessing NAFTA: A Trinational Analysis*, Vancouver: The Fraser Institute.

Hanson, G.H. (1996), 'Economic Integration, Intraindustry trade, and Frontier Regions', *European Economic Review*, 40, 941–9.

Hanson, G.H. (1998), 'North American Economic Integration and Industrial Location', *Oxford Review of Economic Policy*, 14, 30–44.

Head, K., J. Ries, and D. Swenson (1995), 'Agglomeration Benefits and Location Choice: Evidence from Japanese Manufacturing Investments in the United States', *Journal of International Economics*, 38, 223–47.

Hufbauer, G. and J. Schott (1993), *NAFTA: An Assessment*, Washington DC: Institute for International Economics.

ITC (US International Trade Commission) (1997), *The Impact of the North American Free Trade Agreement on the US Economies and Industries: A Three-year Review*, Washington DC: US International Trade Commission.

Johnson, F., J. Kamauff, N. Schein, and A. Wood (1995), 'Manufacturing Strategies under NAFTA', *Business Quarterly*, 59(4).

Kobrin, S. (1995), 'Regional Integration in a Globally Networked Economy', *Transnational Corporations*, 4(2) (August), 15–33.

Krajewski, S. (1992), *Intrafirm Trade and the New North American Business Dynamic*, Ottawa: Conference Board of Canada.

Krugman, P. (1991), *Geography and Trade*, Cambridge, MA: MIT Press.

Lipsey, R.G. (1960), 'The Theory of Customs Unions: A General Survey', *Economic Journal*, 70(279), 496–513.

Lipsey, R., D. Schwanen, and R. Wonnacott (1994), *The NAFTA: What's In, What's Out, What's Next*, Toronto: C.D. Howe Institute.

Little, J.S. (1996), 'U.S. Regional Trade with Canada during the Transition to Free Trade', *New England Economic Review*, Jan–Feb, 3–21.

Litvak, I. (1991), 'Evolving Corporate Strategies: Adjusting to the PTA', in F.O. Hampson and C.J. Maule (eds), *After the Cold War: Canada among Nations 1990–91*, Ottawa: Carleton University Press.

Markusen, A. (1996), 'Sticky Places in Slippery Space: A Typology of Industrial Districts', *Economic Geography*, 72, 293–313.

Milner, H. (1997), 'Industries, Governments and Regional Trade Blocs', in E.D. Mansfield and H.V. Milner (eds), *The Political Economy of Regionalism*, New York: Columbia University Press.

Ohmae, K. (1995), *The End of the Nation State: The Rise of Regional Economies*, London: Harper Collins.

Porter, M.F. (1998a), 'Clusters and the New Economics of Competition', *Harvard Business Review*, November (1), 77–89.

Porter, M.F. (1998b), 'The Adam Smith Address: Location, Clusters, and the "New" Microeconomics of Competition', *Business Economics*, 33, 7–13.

Puga, D. and A.J. Venables (1997), 'Preferential Trading Arrangements and Industrial Location', *Journal of International Economics*, 43, 347–68.

Rugman, A. (1990), *Multinationals and the Canada–U.S. Free Trade Agreement*, Columbia, SC: University of South Carolina Press.

Rugman, A. (ed.) (1994a), *Foreign Direct Investment and NAFTA*, Columbia, SC: University of South Carolina Press.

Rugman, A. (1994b), 'Strategic Management and Canadian Multinationals', in S. Globerman (ed.), *Canadian-based Multinationals*, Calgary: University of Calgary Press.

Rugman, A. and J. D'Cruz (1991), 'The Double Diamond Model of International Competitiveness: Canada's Experience', *Management International Review*, 33, special issue, pp. 17–39.

Rugman, A. and M. Gestrin (1993a), 'The Investment Provisions of NAFTA', in S. Globerman and M. Walker (eds), *Assessing NAFTA: A Trinational Analysis*, Vancouver: The Fraser Institute.

Rugman, A. and M. Gestrin (1993b), 'The Strategic Response of Multinational Enterprises to NAFTA', *Columbia Journal of World Business*, 28 (Winter), 318–29.

Rugman, A.M., J. Kirton, and J.A. Soloway (1997), 'Canadian Corporate Strategy in a North American Region', paper presented at the Annual Meeting of the Academy of International Business, Monterrey, Mexico.

Schwanen, D. (1997), 'Trading Up: The Impact of Increased Continental Integration on Trade, Investment, and Jobs in Canada', *C.D. Howe Institute Commentary*, 89 (March).

Serra, J. and V. Kallab (1997), *Reflections on Regionalism: Report of the Study Group on International Trade*, Washington DC: Carnegie Endowment for International Peace.

UNCTC (United Nations Centre for Transnational Corporations) (1993), *World Investment Report 1993: Transnational Corporations and Integrated International Production*, New York: United Nations.

USTR (1998), Study on the Operation and Effect of the North American Free Trade Agreement, Washington DC: USGPO.

Vernon, R. (1994), 'Multinationals and Governments: Key Actors in NAFTA', in L. Eden (ed.), *Multinationals in North America*, Calgary: University of Calgary Press.

Viner, Jacob (1950), *The Customs Union Issue*, New York: Carnegie Endowment for International Peace.

Weintraub, S. (1997), *NAFTA at Three: A Progress Report*, Washington DC: Center for Strategic and International Studies.

3.   Intellectual property rights and international business

Subhash C. Jain

Intellectual property is defined as the ideas and technologies which are the fruits of human creativity. It refers to a broad collection of innovations relating to things such as works of authorship, inventions, trademarks, designs, and trade secrets. Its two main branches are: (a) *industrial property*, covering inventions, trademarks, industrial design, and protection against unfair competition, including protection of trade secrets; and (b) *copyrights*, which concern literary, musical, artistic, photographic, and cinematographic works. No international treaty completely defines these types of intellectual property, and the laws of various countries differ from each other in significant respects. National intellectual property laws create, confirm, or regulate a property right without which others could use or copy a trade secret, an expression, a design, a product or its mark and packaging.

As far as international protection of intellectual property rights is concerned, it was held as a legal matter to be dealt with by lawyers. In the 1980s, however, international protection of intellectual property became an important trade-related policy issue for the US. While US competitiveness in manufacturing industries has been declining, America is ahead of the rest of the world on its trade in ideas (Spero 1990). For example, in 1991, America ran a $15 billion surplus on its trade in ideas (*The Economist* 1992a). Most other developed countries, by contrast, pay more for technology licenses and copyrights than they earn from them. American companies apply for many more foreign patents than any of their competitors.

Competitive advantage of the United States and that of other industrialized countries rests on their technological superiority. Thus, technological innovation must not only be encouraged but be duly protected. Considered in this light, the concern for the protection of intellectual property rights is closely related to the larger concern over the ability to innovate and compete in the increasingly competitive global market.

Despite the importance of the subject of international protection of intellectual property rights, it has not received the emphasis it deserves among international business scholars. Confusion prevails on many fronts. While it is widely accepted that world intellectual property rights need to be strengthened, questions are raised about exactly what should be protected, what should be the mechanism for protection, and who should monitor the working of the mechanism. In addition, confusion stems from the extremely diverse views held by developing countries on the protection of intellectual property rights.

Companies in the industrialized world are severely penalized when their intellectual property rights are violated. The US government has adopted *ad hoc* measures to resolve the problem. Often a case is made against countries for the infringement of intellectual property rights of US companies. Selected countries are threatened with retaliatory action if they fall to punish their businesses responsible for the infringements. These short-term measures do not go far. The problem persists. The matter of intellectual property rights protection requires probing at the grassroot level. A variety of new information is needed to find a lasting solution to the problem.

The purpose of this chapter is to examine critically the current state of intellectual property rights protection, and identify issues that need to be debated and resolved. Views of developing countries on the subject are clarified. Suggestions are made for finding a permanent solution to the problem. Finally, ideas are given for stimulating additional research into intellectual property protection issues that are of fundamental importance to the competitive strength of the United States, as well as to the well-being of the developing countries.

LITERATURE REVIEW

In 1991, according to *Business Week* (1992), some of the most competitive US industries lost sales in world markets, estimated at $17 billion, because of weak protection granted to their intellectual properties. These industries included pharmaceuticals, software, movies, sound recordings, and books. Goldman (1992) estimated that 80 percent of the software used in Spain is illegal, and it is much worse in many countries of Latin America, the Middle East, and Asia. According to a Software Piracy Report, over 40 percent of business application software is pirated globally, resulting in over $10 billion losses. Losses in the United States for business application software in 1996 amounted to $2.3 billion. Putting it differently, in 1997 the worldwide revenue of business-based software applications was $172 billion, but global revenue losses due to piracy amounted to $11.4 billion (Gopal and Sanders 2000).

Different countries have varying laws and conventions to protect their intellectual properties. Culturally, the patent systems of the US and Japan are different. The Japanese system emphasizes industrial development as the ultimate objective of patent protection, while the US system stresses promotion of useful arts (Helfgott 1990). Further, Japanese patent practices discriminate against foreign applicants with longer pendency periods than for domestic applicants. At the same time, the US, German and British patent practices appear to discriminate against foreign applicants with lower grant ratios than for domestic applicants (Kotabe 1991).

While the direct effect of weak international intellectual property protection in terms of lost business is often mentioned, some scholars argue that the effect may not be as negative as is held. For example, Conner and Rumelt (1991) point out that software piracy may not be harmful for certain types of software, where the value a user derives from the software depends on the user base. The utility of the software increases with piracy because it increases the number of other individuals using it. Gopal and Sanders (1998) suggest that alliances between foreign and domestic software publishers through product relationships can be mutually beneficial and provide an environment of increased copyright enforcement. Glass argues that strengthening of IPR protection makes R&D more difficult, and thus causes firms to waste scarce resources reinventing the wheel. From the perspective that stronger IPR protection increases the cost of R&D it can be demonstrated how weak IPR protection can aid a country's development by enabling its firms to make efficient use of scarce resources and thus further advance the country's technology frontier.

A number of studies have concluded that foreign counterfeiting has ambiguous welfare effects on the world economy (Higgins and Rubin 1986). The most obvious benefit to domestic consumers is an increase in consumer surplus associated with lower priced imports that are acceptable substitutes for 'original' goods. Potential costs to domestic consumers encompass losses associated with buying inferior copies of legitimate products. Some domestic consumers of original products may feel worse off as a result of a loss in 'status', as formerly exclusive goods become increasingly commonplace. Analyzing the United States International Trade Commission data, Feinberg and Rousslang (1990) have developed a framework for measuring the static welfare changes caused by infringement of intellectual property rights. They conclude that profit losses of legitimate US suppliers are significant compared to their total profits, that they are larger than the profits gained by infringers, but that they might well be smaller than the static benefits to consumers and infringers combined.

Firms look to their governments to resolve problems associated with weak protection accorded to their intellectual properties overseas. For example, the United States International Trade Commission (ITC) is responsible for regulating trade regulations between and among US and foreign competitors.

Foreign firms that infringe run a risk of being caught and excluded from US markets, and US firms contemplating the use of the ITC to defend markets strategically from foreign competitors run a risk of losing their patents or being reprimanded. A substantial portion of cases referred to the ITC are settled through agreements (Thomas 1989). Some scholars suggest that foreign aid to developing countries be tied to programs that promise to enhance the intellectual property protection system in those countries (Harvey and Ronkainen 1985). Globerman (1988) cautions that while product piracy has net costs, widespread retaliation through trade protectionism could also prove costly. He argues for a policy that facilitates 'private' protection of property rights.

Often governments revise their laws to keep up with changing times. The US trademark law, for example, has recently been revised to bring it up to date with present day business practices, to increase the value of the federal registration system for US companies, and to remove the current preference for foreign companies applying to register trademarks in the United States (Cohen 1991). Japan has introduced one of the world's most sophisticated electronic patent systems. The computer system permits instant filing of patent applications and quick retrieval of any one of 30 million filings (*Business Week* 1991).

Piracy of mask works embodied within computer chips has been costly to United States high-tech commerce, internationally and domestically. The Semiconductor Chip Protection Act was passed by the Congress in 1984 to provide remedies for such infringement (Bonham 1986). It permits a ten-year *sui generis* (in a class by itself) form of intellectual property protection, which is distinguished from traditional copyright and patent laws. Furthermore, in order to improve the state of the art, reverse engineering is permitted under the act.

The above studies clearly suggest that piracy of intellectual properties is harmful for the firms owning these properties. By losing sales they forgo potential profits. By not knowing the users of pirated goods they also lose opportunities to cross-sell their other products, market new generations of products, and capitalize on any suggestions from pirates for improving the products or developing new products (Givon et al. 1995; Cervantes 1997). A frustrating question for the firms is how to manage the product when they do not know a significant number of their product users.

PROTECTION OF INTELLECTUAL PROPERTY RIGHTS

Inasmuch as there are no international laws to protect intellectual property rights, each country has its own legislative framework to protect and encourage ideas, inventions and creative expressions developed by its people. This legislative framework in the US consists of patent, trademark, copyright, mask work, and trade secret.

Patent   This is a government grant of certain rights given to an inventor for a limited time in exchange for the disclosure of the invention. Patents are the strongest form of legal protection of all the intellectual properties. On obtaining a patent through registration, the law provides the company with an exclusive monopoly for 17 years by protecting ideas, designs, and inventions against copying. In order for a patent to be granted in the United States, the invention or design must be novel or new, useful, and non-obvious to a person of average skill in the area.

The patent law of the United States differs from the laws of most other countries in several important aspects. It grants a patent to the first inventor even if another person who independently makes the invention files an application first. Most other countries award the patent to the inventor who first files a patent application. The United States also provides a one-year grace period when an inventor is not precluded from obtaining protection after an act that makes the invention public, such as publishing, offering for sale, or using the invention. Most countries have no such grace period (Sherwood 1990). The grace period protects the right of the first inventor and prevents competitors from using protected information in their own R&D effort. In countries with an *absolute novelty* rule, a patent application must be filed before making the invention public anywhere.

The underlying purposes of the patent systems are to protect the property rights of the inventor of a novel and useful product or process; and to encourage society's inventiveness and technical progress. The differences between the patent systems of different countries can be explained by the emphasis placed on these two purposes. For example, the patent system of the US places the greatest emphasis on the rights of the inventor. Japan, on the other hand, stresses the societal benefits of an invention (Kotabe and Cox 1993).

In the US where the 'first-to-invent' principle is followed, a patent is granted to the person who first develops an invention. Therefore, some patents granted by the US Patent Office are revoked and reassigned to the 'real' inventor. Such a system protects the small inventor who may not have the sophistication or resources needed to file for a patent quickly. On the other hand, the first-to-file principle has an advantage over the first-to-invent principle. It avoids many potentially expensive lawsuits by legally declaring the first filer to be the owner of a patent. Additionally, the first-to-file system encourages individuals to file for patents quickly as a means of staking out territory where much technological development is taking place.

Trademark   A trademark is a word, symbol, or device that identifies the source of goods and may serve as an index of quality. It is used in trade to differentiate or distinguish a product or service from another. Trademark laws are used to prevent others from making a product with a confusingly similar mark. Similar rights may be acquired in marks used in the sale of services, called service marks.

Internationally, trademark laws vary. Some allow service trademarks; others do not. Since there are no deadlines for registering a trademark, a company may face problems if it enters a foreign market late in the life of a product. It may find that its trademark has been registered by someone else. Therefore, a trademark should be registered in every country in which protection is desired.

Copyright   Copyrights are more limited in scope than patents. They protect original works of authorship, not the ideas they contain. In the United States, *original works* include literary, dramatic, musical, artistic, and certain other intellectual works. A computer program, for example, is considered a literary work and is protected by copyright.

Copyright gives its owner the exclusive right to reproduce and distribute the material or perform or display it publicly. However, copyright law does permit limited reproduction of copyrighted works without the owner's permission for 'fair use' such as criticism, teaching, and news reporting.

In the United States, a published work must bear a copyright notice, the name of the author, and date of first publication. Registration is required in order to sue for infringement. Many countries offer copyright protection without these formalities, while others offer little or no protection for the works of foreign nationals (Hilts 1992). Before publishing a work anywhere, it is advisable to investigate the scope of protection available as well as the specific legal requirements for copyright protection in countries where copyright protection is desired.

Mask work   A mask work is a relatively new type of intellectual property which is protected by the Semiconductor Chip Protection Act of 1984. This act was created because neither patents nor copyrights gave adequate protection to semiconductor chips. Creators of mask work are given exclusive rights over the reproduction, importation, distribution, and sale of the mask work for a ten-year period. The mask work must be original and must be registered within two years of its creation. The law does permit reverse engineering for the purposes of teaching, evaluation, or demonstration in order to encourage competition.

Trade secret   A trade secret is another means of protecting intellectual property. It is simply information that an organization keeps from being known to its competitors. A trade secret is different from patent, trademark, copyright, and mask work since it is not registered. Thus, it is not legally protected. However, it can be protected in the courts if the company can prove that it took all precautions to protect the idea from outsiders and that infringement occurred illegally. The uniqueness of a trade secret is that it has no time limit and no one has public access to the information, which is not the case in other forms of intellectual property.

ADEQUACY OF INTELLECTUAL PROPERTY PROTECTION

From the viewpoint of the US, international protection of intellectual property is inadequate. The US International Trade Commission (1987) estimates that American companies lose at least $23.8 billion a year from factors relating to intellectual property protection failures. Table 3.1 breaks down these losses by industry groups. The factors responsible for these losses were export losses, including sales never made, sales lost relative to previous sales, export sales at risk, domestic sales displaced by imports of infringing goods, revenue losses from fees or royalties not paid, reduced profit margins, damage to reputation or trade name, research costs not recovered, research or business forgone, increased product liability costs, weakening of sales with concurrent damage to other product lines, enforced reductions in plant efficiency (for example, those resulting from decreased sales), and intentional reductions in efficiency (for example, use of older technology in overseas plants to safeguard protected technology). Further, foreign piracy has cost the US some 131 000 jobs (Delmar 1991). Among the industrial sectors where counterfeiting is particularly serious are wearing apparel and footwear, transportation equipment parts and accessories, computer hardware/software, chemicals, records and tapes, supporting goods, toys, video games, and machinery and electrical products.

Literary and artistic work, and scientific developments constitute one of America's major exports. The 1600 large and middle-sized companies that belong to the trade groups making up the International Intellectual Property Alliance amount to a $270 billion industry. A great deal of that revenue is generated abroad: 40 percent for the film industry, about 50 percent for the music makers, and 60 percent of the $110 billion global software market (*The Economist*, 1992b). Pirated and counterfeit products distort international trade. In 1984, for example, Pharmaceutical Manufacturers Association members with new products protected by patents in countries such as the US sold $29 million worth of those products in Korea. Patent pirates, on the other hand, sold $70 million in unauthorized copies of these same drugs in Korea. In five

Table 3.1   Losses suffered by US industries resulting from intellectual property inadequacies, 1986[a]

Industry	Loss (thousands of dollars)	Number of firms reporting		
		No loss	Some loss	Total
Aerospace	119 800	2	5	7
Building materials	738 550	0	6	6
Chemicals	1 334 250	3	18	21
Computers and software	4 130 164	6	25	31
Electronics	2 287 805	6	11	17
Entertainment	2 060 450	0	12	12
Food and beverages	86 300	2	8	10
Forest products	664 755	0	7	7
Industrial and farm equipment	621 700	1	9	10
Metals and metal products	291 500	1	6	7
Motor vehicles and parts	2 194 490	0	4	4
Petroleum refining and related products	1 295 000	3	6	9
Pharmaceutical	1 908 660	0	10	10
Publishing and printing	127 790	0	11	11
Rubber products	511 200	1	4	5
Scientific and photographic	5 090 100	1	6	7
Textiles and apparel	251 489	0	11	11
All other	151 200	0	8	8
Total	23 845 223	26	167	193

Note: [a] Based on a sample of 193 companies.

Source: *Foreign Protection of Intellectual Property Rights and the Effect on US Industry and Trade* (Washington DC: United States International Trade Commission, 1987), pp. 3–4.

countries (Argentina, Brazil, Korea, Mexico, Taiwan), sales of new pharmaceutical products by patent owners in 1984 totaled $162 million, while sales of unauthorized copies of the same products totaled $192 million (Rozek 1990).

In addition, pirates can tarnish valuable trademarks and destroy carefully created images. Pirated goods cheapen the image and dilute the prestige of real products. Furthermore, the product's creator is blamed when a fake breaks or malfunctions and the company refuses to fix it.

Unfortunately, new technologies are making pirating a lot easier, which is likely to increase and thus affect many more businesses around the world

(Bush et al. 1989). Inexpensive personal computers, desktop copiers, and video cassette recorders have made it simpler to steal hours of creativity and research from the innovators. Many pirates work out of basements and garages, moving from location to location. They use relatively portable and inexpensive machinery to sew logos on clothes, silk-screen characters on shirts, copy videos and computer software, and duplicate music cassettes. Obviously, their mobile, decentralized operations make enforcement difficult. They are also highly efficient. Pirates can copy a design or prototype so quickly they sometimes beat the product's creator to market (Alster 1988).

The deficiency in the protection of intellectual property rights is well illustrated by European experience. In the early 1970s, 16 European nations signed a convention to establish a European patent office (EPO). Under this convention, the patent office makes one grant for all the member countries under a single European patent law. Thus, for patent applications in Europe, companies have a choice: to take a national route or opt for a 'European' solution. The first entails the process of applying for a patent in each member state – a drawn-out, expensive process requiring separate translations, procedures, lawyers, agents, and fees for each state. On completion, the company will have a number of patents, each of which varies in scope and conditions, and each open to separate interpretations in each national court.

The 'European' route involves filing an application at the European Patent Office (EPO). However, the EPO does not grant an EU patent but only a bundle of national patent rights whose terms and conditions differ according to the respective national laws of the contracting countries – the 15 EU member states plus Switzerland, Liechtenstein, Monaco and six Eastern European states. Once the grant is made, a 'national phase' follows that entails a full translation of the filing for each state in which a firm has applied for patent rights. The applicant has to pay for translations, filings, and attorney fees.

According to Zeneca, the UK drugmaker, the average cost of translating an 80-page filing for ten states is $80 000. A major 150-page filing for all EPO states would cost $240 000. To that is added the lawyers' and agents' fees for each state and national filing fees. By comparison, the total cost of a patent application (including all fees) in the US is under $7000, and in Japan $19 000. Moreover, it often takes five to ten years to grant a patent. Some critics argue that the EPO is essentially a 'machine for granting patents', more interested in fee income than reliable decisions (*Crossborder Monitor* 1998b).

Protection deficiencies may be divided into two major groups: *regime deficiencies* that is, inadequacies in the protection provision for particular types of intellectual property and *enforcement inadequacies*. The regime deficiencies vary from one type of property to another. They are summa-

Table 3.2 International intellectual property rights protection: regime deficiencies

Copyright	Patents	Trademarks	Mask works	Trade secrets
US works are not protected	Patentability precluded by statute	Scope of what constitutes infringement is too narrow	Short time limits on confidentiality	No legal protection
Laws do not protect all traditional and new work	Term is too short	Renewal proof of use is difficult	No protection against third parties.	Inadequate *sui generis* coverage
Inadequate exclusive rights	Early lapse	No protection of 'well-known' marks		
	Compulsory licensing	Narrow spectrum of class protection		
Exceptions to exclusive rights are overly broad	Paris convention nonadherence			
	Patent claims are narrowed too much	Unreasonable licensing requirements		
Terms of protection are too short	Unrealistic working requirements			
Burdensome substantive or procedural formalities		Circumscribed usage or linking		

rized in Table 3.2. As far as enforcement is concerned, it is one thing to have a law on the books, but it is another thing to have cultural values and views changed in order to accommodate, particularly, the interests of people who are from outside the country or region. For example, Indonesia in 1993 beefed up antipiracy laws and policies because of pressures by the US and other countries. The new law did away with the country's previous trademark approval process, under which the first company to file for a trademark received it – even if it was already used by another company. Yet, businessmen in the country continue to ignore the law and the courts rule in their favor (Woo and Borsuk 1994). For another example, Brazil is a signatory to the Pan's Convention, an intellectual property rights protection agreement. Most of the country's statutes on intellectual property rights are consistent with Western standards. In practice, however, the government often discounts existing statutes and enforcement mechanisms in its quest for rapid economic growth, annual trade surpluses, and advanced technology (Turner 1988).

Major enforcement deficiencies in the protection of intellectual property rights are listed in Table 3.3.

Table 3.3   Major enforcement deficiencies

(a)	No preliminary or final injunctive relief,
(b)	Lack of seizure and impoundment relief,
(c)	Lack of exclusion of infringing imports;
(d)	Lack of compulsory court process and/or discovery;
(e)	Inadequate civil remedies, usually in monetary damages; limits on recoveries preclude deterrent effects;
(f)	Fine or other criminal penalties inadequate;
(g)	Unreasonably slow enforcement process during which illegal activity continues;
(h)	Enforcement officials systematically discriminate against foreigners;
(i)	Training and resources for enforcement inadequate;
(j)	Court decisions biased or political; and
(k)	Corruption.

The types of deficiencies do vary by country. Comparatively speaking, the industrialized countries have stronger protection regimes and more workable enforcement arrangements. At the other extreme, the developing countries (with a few exceptions) are deficient both in regime and enforcement. The middle-level countries have more or less 'acceptable' protection regimes but badly lack enforcement.

Consider Brazil. In 1996 it passed a modern patent law and has vowed to address software piracy. But the International Intellectual Property Association (IIPA) complains that Latin America's largest market has failed to impose adequate criminal penalties or to make any serious attempt to prevent pirated and counterfeit goods from entering from Paraguay. Moreover, the association wrote in recent comments to the US government that there 'seems to be a lack of interest in effective enforcement of the copyright law throughout the enforcement system, including judges, prosecutors and custom officials' (*Crossborder Monitor* 1998a, b).

The law of trade secrets covers things like the formula for Coca-Cola, which the inventor protects simply by keeping them secret. The law of trademark helps companies ensure that only they can use their own identities. Copyright covers songs, writings, and other creations whose creators are typically interested in spreading the underlying ideas freely but wish to charge for the privilege of copying their exact expression of those ideas. A patent, by contrast, covers the very idea of a particular product or a given process. It is the most powerful form of intellectual property right. It is also the most problematic and the most in need of reform.

Patenting has always been an imperfect process. Patent offices cannot be certain of what is truly new and 'non-obvious', particularly in fast-moving fields like electronics and biotechnology. The recent developments in American law have expanded the scope for confusion. American courts are now freer to interpret patents as applying more broadly than the specific claims made in their texts. Mounting complications arise from a longstanding American policy of striving to identify the first person or company to invent something, rather than accepting, like the rest of the world, the first credible claim filed. Worst of all, America keeps patent applications secret until it can decide whether they should be granted – sometimes a decade or two later. Such perfectionist uncertainty leads to high legal costs (*The Economist* 1992a).

International cooperation on intellectual property is overdue. What is needed is a simpler system that would work in practice. It might involve defining the scope of patents narrowly; granting them to the first inventor to apply; making applications public immediately; and encouraging arbitration before litigation.

DIFFERING VIEWS

The US and other industrialized countries argue that technological superiority is the cornerstone of their competitiveness. Because intellectual property rights foster creativity in high technology, strengthening its protection has been a priority for these nations. Advocates of stronger protection argue that without protection, businesses will not be willing or able to invest adequate resources in the development of new products. Consequently, US competitiveness would decrease (Duvall 1992). Furthermore, with adequate protection, companies will be willing and able to transfer technology to foreign countries, both developed and developing. This will result in higher economic growth around the world.

Developing nations oppose strong intellectual property rights protection for both philosophical and economic reasons. They favor shorter patent periods and other measures of weakening protection of intellectual property. They consider 'free riding' as a necessary precursor to advancement. Western intellectual property rights protection is based on the twin premises that individuals can originate and own ideas. However, these premises are not universally accepted (Mittelstaedt and Mittelstaedt 1997).

Developing countries argue that intellectual property rights raise prices and profits for one country or company at the expense of the well-being of a developing nation. One example of this is in the area of pharmaceuticals. By temporarily creating a monopoly on new pharmaceutical products, intellectual property creates higher prices which profit the industrialized nations. The international community loses the opportunity to benefit from the products because it cannot afford them. In this respect, intellectual property protection restricts the widespread use of new technology (Subramanian 1991). In a way, intellectual property is a state-granted monopoly provided to creators to encourage intellectual goods. It is not an intrinsic moral night, but a necessary intervention in the economic system. Such a monopoly or intervention is only a good thing so long as it is truly necessary to promote the creation of new work. If enough profit can be made without such protection, then the monopoly need not be granted (Berman 2000).

Developing nations feel that without free use of technology and information, they will always be worse off than industrialized nations. Weaker protection of intellectual property nights is seen as a means to increased access to information and technology which is needed for economic growth. They submit that it is in the industrialized nations' best interests to allow free use of information. This way they will need less financial support and can provide a larger market of consumers to multinational corporations (MNCs) (Higgins and Rubin 1986). Developing countries take the position that Western technology is unjustly expensive. Intellectual property rights give innovators a monopoly on information that is used to exact unreasonably high prices for their knowledge and to impose severe and unwarranted restrictions on its use. These restrictions hinder the efforts of the developing countries to modernize and thereby perpetuate and strengthen the split between them and the developed nations (Feinberg and Rousslang 1990). Some of these nations argue that Third World development is in the interests of all nations and that technological information should be provided readily, at low cost, and with a minimum of restrictions on its use. Others maintain that knowledge is the common heritage of mankind and should be made available at low cost. As has been said:

> Copying is pervasive in China because it is so easy to get away with it. Laws protecting intellectual property are unclear and sporadically enforced. Even when they are applied, sanctions are minimal, typically consisting of confiscation, a warning, a public apology, and perhaps a fine. Moreover, copying enjoys a long tradition in China and does not carry a stigma. Copying a masterpiece was historically considered an art form in its own right, while Chinese students have been taught for centuries to copy their teachers as accurately as possible before attempting to create. (Yatsko 2000: 213)

The differing views of industrialized and developing countries on the subject are depicted in Figure 3.1.

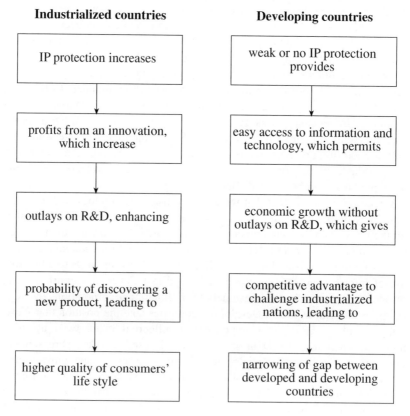

Figure 3.1   Differing views on intellectual property protection

To summarize, developing countries think of intellectual property – the results of science and technology – as a public good. On the other hand, industrialized countries view intellectual property primarily as a means of maintaining a competitive edge in the marketplace as well as providing monetary returns to the individual investor.

On balance, economic growth is a common goal pursued both by developed and developing countries. Historically, technology played the central role in achieving economic growth among all factors of production. Mansfield (1990) refers to a study that found that 90 percent of the increase in output per capita during 1909–49 was attributable to technological change. Since then, the role of technology as an engine of growth has increased much more rapidly. Briefly, the development of technology should be an important aim of a society desirous of economic growth. Public policy should encourage the development of technology through providing incentives for engaging in knowledge generation and in creating innovations. Thus, adequate intellectual property protection is essential. Mansfield (2000) determined that a substantial proportion of innovations would never have taken place if it were not for patent protection. As shown in Table 3.4, 60 percent of inventions in pharmaceuticals and 38 percent in chemicals would not be developed if there were no patent protection. In the same two industries, in the absence of protection, 65 percent and 30 percent of inventions, respectively, would not be commercially introduced.

Certainly, innovations help companies that invest money and effort in developing them. But the rewards of their investments are shared by the society in general as well. As a matter of fact, an empirical study by Mansfield and his colleagues (1977) showed that the rate of social return from investment in innovation far exceeded the private return (see Table 3.5).

The benefits of protecting intellectual property evolve from the level of innovative output available to a country. Innovative output may consist of new products, new processes, or new literary works. Both direct and indirect benefits to the country result from this innovative output even if the intellectual property protection mechanism is used primarily by foreigners. Direct employment and investment benefits accrue from R&D laboratories, new manufacturing plants, or import facilities for creating, producing, or processing the output associated with the innovative effort. Indirect benefits accrue from an increase in local market activity (Rozek 1990). For example, foreigners use many local services such as banks, insurance firms, and legal experts. If the innovative output is a book, movie, painting, or scientific chapter, the cultural and educational levels of the entire population increase. Furthermore, demand for this type of output in other countries with strong protection of intellectual property will generate returns for innovators in the home country and provide resources for additional expansion. This improves the prospects for economic growth of the country.

The macro-environment

Table 3.4   *Effect of patent protection on inventions, 1981–83*[a]

Industry	% of inventions that would not be introduced	% of inventions that would not be developed
Pharmaceuticals	65	60
Chemicals	30	38
Petroleum	18	25
Machinery	15	17
Fabricated metals	12	12
Primary metals	8	1
Electrical equipment	4	11
Instruments	1	1
Office equipment	0	0
Motor vehicles	0	0
Rubber	0	0
Textiles	0	0

Note: [a] Based on random sample of 100 US firms. Some inventions that were developed in this time period were not introduced then, and some inventions that were introduced then were not developed then. Thus, the left-hand column of the table may refer to different inventions than the right-hand column.

Source: Edwin Mansfield (1986), 'Patents and Innovation: An Empirical Study', *Management Science*, 32(2), February.

Some developing countries recognize the benefits of protecting indigenous ideas through an intellectual property protection mechanism. Several recent trends illustrate this point. Sun (1986) summarizes a meeting of the Food and Agriculture Organization (FAO) at which participants considered a resolution that all germ plasm be made freely available to all countries. In 1983, developing countries voted as a block to support such a resolution. By 1985, however, many of these same countries wanted to protect the new crop varieties developed from their own research. At the 1985 FAO meeting, these countries joined the US in expressing reservations about free access to the germ plasm, and the resolution did not pass.

Briefly, a country has two broad choices regarding intellectual property: allowing free access (free rider) or providing protection. The free access solution yields short-term benefits at best while it imposes long-term costs. The protection solution enhances the prospects for economic growth to produce long-term benefits in exchange for a grant of monopoly power to the innovator (Blass 1992). Protecting intellectual property improves the size, quality, and efficiency of both the labor force and the capital stock within a

Table 3.5 Social and private rates of return from investment in innovation

Innovation	Rate of return	
	Social	Private
Primary metals innovation	17	18
Machine tool	83	35
Component for control system	29	7
Construction material	96	9
Drilling material	54	16
Drafting innovation	92	47
Paper innovation	82	42
Thread innovation	307	27
Door control innovation	27	37
New electronic device	neg.	neg.
Chemical product	71	9
Chemical process	32	25
Chemical innovation	13	4
Major chemical process	56	31
Household cleaning device	209	214
Stain remover	116	4
Dishwashing liquid	45	46
Median	56	25

Source: Edwin Mansfield et al., 'Social and Private Rate of Return from Industrial Innovations', *Quarterly Journal of Economics*, May 1977.

country (Mansfield 2000). In other words, strong protection of intellectual property tends to: (1) create jobs in primary industries as well as in supporting industries; (2) create a higher-quality labor force through on-the-job training; (3) shift jobs to higher-productivity areas; (4) increase the capital stock of the country; (5) improve the quality of the capital stock through innovation; (6) improve the allocation of the capital stock; (7) expand those activities subject to economies of scale; (8) improve efficiency through a reduction in local monopoly elements; (9) provide lower-cost methods of production for existing products; and (10) provide new products.

Both developed and developing countries agree that innovation is a good thing and that innovators should be rewarded. But the problem is to find the best way to encourage the former and reward the later.

PROTECTING INTELLECTUAL PROPERTY ABROAD: INTERNATIONAL REGIME

The international regime for the protection of intellectual property rights consists of a number of regional and bilateral agreements. These agreements are governed by an institutionally fragmented network of organizations. The agreements vary widely in their effect depending on the number of member countries. The governing organizations lack authority to enforce intellectual property rights or to settle disputes.

Essentially, the international regime for the protection of intellectual property can be split into two areas: industrial property agreements, and copyright agreements.

Industrial Property Agreements

Industrial property agreements are mainly developed to harmonize divergent national laws. In other words, internationally, efforts have been made to adapt industrial laws common to each specific country into a framework for agreement among these countries.

Paris Convention The primary agreement for the protection of industrial property is the Paris Convention. It covers such properties as patents, trademarks, service marks, trade names, utility models, industrial designs, and inventions. Established in 1883, the Pan's Convention is the oldest agreement and it secured early participation from most industrialized countries. The US joined in 1887. The most recent signatory was the former Soviet Union which endorsed the Paris Convention in 1968. The current membership of the convention is 92 including 51 developing countries. From its inception, the Pan's Convention has been based on reciprocity: (a) the people from member states have the same rights that the state grants to its own nationals, and (b) foreigners have equal access to local courts to pursue infringement remedies. In addition, the convention establishes rights of priority which stipulate that once an application for protection is filed in one member country, the applicant has twelve months to file in any other contracting state, which should consider such an application as if it were filed on the same date as the original application.

Other conventions There are 11 other conventions that deal with different aspects of industrial property protection: Madrid Agreement, Source of Goods (1891); Madrid Agreement, Registration of Marks (1891); Hague Agreement (1925); Nice Agreement (1957); Lisbon Agreement (1958); International Convention for the Protection of New Varieties of Plants (1961); Locarno

Agreement (1968); Patent Cooperation Treaty (1970); Trademark Registration Treaty (1973); Budapest Treaty (1977); and Nairobi Treaty (1981).

Copyright Agreements

There are no international laws that specify explicit rules for worldwide copyright protection. Protection is available only in a particular country based on its national laws.

Berne Convention　　The oldest and most comprehensive international copyright agreement is the Berne Convention. This treaty provides reciprocal copyright protection in each of the 15 signatory countries. Until recently, the US was not a member of the Berne Convention (the US joined with effect from 1 March 1989). The Berne Convention establishes the principle of national treatment and provides for protection without formalities, for the independence of protection, and for certain minimum rights.

Other conventions　　The other major international copyright agreements comprise the Rome Convention (1961), Geneva Convention (1971), Brussels Convention (1974), and Madrid Multilateral Convention (1979).

Administration of Agreements

All the above agreements, both for the protection of industrial property and copyrights, fall under the jurisdiction of the World Intellectual Property Organization (WIPO). In other words, WIPO facilitates international agreements regulating intellectual property. WIPO was created in 1967, came into force in 1970, and was made a specialized agency of the United Nations in December 1974. WIPO pursues the following objectives: (a) promote the protection of intellectual property rights by encouraging new treaties; (b) assist in the modernization of domestic laws; (c) collect and provide information and technical assistance; and (d) ensure cooperation among member countries through centralizing administration of the agreements. However, WIPO is a policy-making body only, with no delegated authority to make binding decisions or to impose sanctions. Its membership consists of most European countries, the United States, Japan, and other major countries. Overall, 101 countries hold membership in WIPO.

There are a number of conventions relative to industrial property and copyright that do not fall under the jurisdiction of WIPO. Important among them are the European Patent Convention (1973) for the protection of industrial property as discussed above, and the Universal Copyright Convention (1952) for copyrights. The former is administered by the European Patent

Office (EPO) in Munich, and the latter by the United Nations Educational, Scientific, and Cultural Organization (UNESCO).

GATT and Intellectual Property Rights Protection

In the Uruguay Round of the GATT negotiations, concluded in December 1993, intellectual property rights was a new issue deliberated by the nations. When the Uruguay Round talks started in 1986, GATT members were apprehensive about including intellectual property rights as a subject for multilateral trade negotiations, but in April 1989, at the insistence of the United States GATT members agreed to a negotiating framework which allowed for conclusion of a comprehensive agreement to govern the Trade Related Aspects of Intellectual Properties (TRIPS).

Under the new rules, new inventions will enjoy 20 years of protection. During this time, about half of which is usually taken up by development and testing, a patent holder will have sole control over who is allowed to manufacture an invention (*The Economist* 1994). The agreement requires that most nations should be in compliance with the minimum standards for IPR protection by the year 2006 (Sherwood 2000).

CURRENT PROBLEMS

Efforts to protect intellectual property rights suffer from three major problems: *institutional issues*, *philosophical issues*, and *handling of new technologies*. The institutional issues refer to the shortcomings of existing regimes and their enforcement. To begin with, the signatories to specific agreements are limited. Thus, countries that are not a part of the agreement do not have to subscribe to the provisions of the agreement. Further, the agreements lack enforcement powers. In addition, the agreements *per se* are limited in scope, leaving many crucial areas unprotected. Above all, the focus of most agreements is on national treatment as the basis for international protection. Since there is no common set of rules or guidelines, countries follow a wide variety of protection measures. Thus, national treatment provides insufficient guarantees for international protection.

The enforcement of agreements is a difficult issue in itself. Currently, most major agreements are administered through WIPO. The developing countries would like WIPO to continue playing the key role. According to them, WIPO should be equipped with enforcement powers and thus made more effective. The industrialized countries, on the other hand, would like the World Trade Organization (WTO) to enforce worldwide intellectual property protection. WTO carries the leverage necessary to enforce the protection of intellectual property via the threat of modifications in the *most favored nation* and *generalized system of preferences* tariff control programs. The Uruguay Round talks left the matter of administering intellectual property rights protection uncertain. Debate continues on the best strategy to ensure international intellectual property rights protection. Each alternative involves costs and benefits, many of them political, which must be assessed.

There are philosophical issues related to differences between industrialized nations and developing countries (Berenbeim 1989). Developing countries, for good reason, are interested in fast development, which requires adoption of the latest technology. Such technology is only available in the advanced countries and at a high price, which prevents them from acquiring it. They, therefore, seek access to technology through unauthorized sources. But advanced countries cannot allow such unauthorized use, since in the absence of adequate compensation and reward, future research and development and their outcomes will be jeopardized.

Industrialized countries claim that adequate intellectual property rights protection makes a developing country attractive for foreign investors. In addition, the protection spurs indigenous technology development. Some countries like Singapore and China, under pressure from the United States, have begun to strengthen intellectual property rights to facilitate greater foreign investment and inflows of Western technology. But the pervading trend in the developing world toward weaker protection of intellectual property rights will continue until the benefits of adequate protection can be established through empirical work and case studies.

The third problem area relates to new technologies, especially the innovations in communications and information technologies. These innovations have eroded national borders and have reduced individual governments' ability to forge independent macroeconomic policies. As a matter of fact, these technologies are altering the foundation of a modern nation state (*US News and World Report* 1988).

The emerging importance of information raises questions about traditional intellectual property laws, particularly copyright laws. US copyright laws as well as international copyright agreements by and large deny protection for information or ideas. They concentrate on the expression of ideas. In the context of interconnected information networks, this approach is ineffective.

Computers have further complicated the situation. Consider databases. Databases such as dictionaries and encyclopedias have been eligible for copyright protection under US law. Presumably, databases stored in computers are equally protected. But that is not so. Copyright law protects the format of the information, but not the information *per se*. Minor variations or manipulations of data-sets may be sufficient to negate copyright protection.

An additional problem is the fact that a number of new technologies do not fit clearly into any of the existing categories of intellectual property; for example, computer software. In many countries (including the US), software is protected through copyright law. These nations argue that software creation is analogous to other copyright works, that is, by placing symbols in a medium (Whiting 1992). As Benko (1987: 40) has said: 'Software is simply another form of writing brought about by technical change, as were sound recordings and motion pictures, and copyright should be extended as it was in those cases.' But many nations reject the applicability of copyright law to software. They submit that only the source code, written in eye-legible form is predictable. Software, that is, the object code, is addressed to machines, not to human beings. Thus it differs from writing and cannot be copyright (Menell 1990).

Similarly, traditional intellectual property laws are inadequate to protect semiconductor chips. The basic technology for constructing chips is well established. Thus, patents are inappropriate for chip protection. A patent could protect the technology of a new microprocessor but could not protect the layouts and artwork necessary to adapt the technology to industrial uses, which are more expensive and most susceptible to piracy. The problem created by the piracy of semiconductor chips is enormous. The cost of designing and preparing masks for chip manufacturing can reach $100 million. Photocopying each layer of the chip and reproducing it, however, are fairly simple and can be done for less than $50 000. Thus, chip makers need adequate safeguards against piracy.

Finally, advances in biotechnology have created protection problems (Eisenberg 1987). The US approach in the matter differs from the one followed by the Europeans and the Japanese. The US prefers a broad protection for an invention while the Europeans and the Japanese provide patents for specific aspects of the invention. Further, recent developments in genetic research have heightened conflict over European treatment of property rights in biotechnology.

SUGGESTIONS FOR RESEARCH

Protection of intellectual property internationally is a complex subject. US companies have a great stake in it. Yet business academics have taken little interest in it. Most scholarly studies on intellectual property protection have come out of the legal profession. They have examined it very broadly with the result that many fundamental questions remain unanswered (*Chemical and Engineering News* 1992). Literature review suggests the following areas for exploration by international business scholars.

Economic Rationale of Protection

Studies are needed to examine the cost–benefit aspects of intellectual property rights protection (Landes and Posner 1987). For example, what is the worth of a trademark, copyright or patent? A firm is less likely to expend resources on developing a new product if competing firms that have not borne the expense of development can duplicate the product and produce it at the same marginal cost as the innovator; competition will drive the price down to marginal cost, and the sunk cost of invention will not be recouped.

An information base should be established to determine the cost of violations of intellectual property. How are the violations related to social welfare? How are the social welfare implications of intellectual property rights protection related to trade dimensions? Will society eventually be better served through increased trade than violations?

The importance of protection needs to be probed from the viewpoint of developing countries as well. How do they, in the long run, benefit from providing adequate protection? What do they give up in return? Longitudinal studies covering different geographic regions are needed to convince developing countries of their interest in greater international protection (Kuttner 1992).

Organizational Arrangements for Administration and Enforcement

Studies are needed to determine the most effective way of administering intellectual property rights internationally. Should WIPO be restructured? If yes, what are the dimensions of such restructuring? Should the administration of intellectual property rights be entrusted to the WTO? If WIPO were to continue, what relation, if any, should it maintain with the WTO? What role, if any, should other multilateral institutions such as the OECD play? Will it be more effective to create a new organization? What should be its structure? Such questions need to be probed and analyzed in both technical and political contexts.

Another area where research insights are needed is the enforcement issue. Dimensions of enforcement need to be examined, which requires information on and analysis of enforcement practices from different governments (Ostergard 2000). Two aspects of enforcement need to be considered: institutional capacity (that is, statutes, judiciary, technical expertise, and public policy); and institutional will (that is, behavior aspects of carrying out the enforcement of laws). What enforcement powers should be given to the administering organizations? What arrangements are required for resolving conflicts between countries, and between a multinational firm and a country? Should provisions be made for arbitration? Can arbitration be binding on the conflicting parties? The implications of such arrangements need to be examined in light of developed–developing country controversies which may pose a major hurdle in finalizing any organizational arrangement.

Further research is needed to develop criteria for assessing the strength of IPR protection in different countries. For example, which laws must be examined to gauge protection?

Weak Protection and Product Diffusion

The impact of weak intellectual property protection on product diffusion needs to be examined. Conner and Rumelt (1991) argue that under certain circumstances software piracy may not be bad since it might help in fast diffusion. Studies are needed to verify this argument in different settings; especially on the impact of weak protection on the shape and form of the legal life cycle of a product.

Weak Protection and Marketing Mix Strategies

A central question from the marketing viewpoint is what firms may do if their intellectual properties are stolen. To answer this question, research should be focused on changes that may be made in marketing mix strategies under different conditions to resolve the problem. For example, examination of marketing mix mechanisms that can facilitate the conversion of illegal use into legal use would be useful. These mechanisms may include differentiated pricing strategies, bundling of product offerings, exclusive distribution arrangements, and so on. These examples are primarily provided to highlight the point that instead of using punitive mechanisms (for example, lawsuits, raids, or protection strategies) that might destroy demand, firms can use creative marketing mechanisms to convert illegal use to their advantage. Consider exclusive distribution arrangements. This strategy facilitates identification of counterfeit products by effectively shifting the 'certification' process from the upstream stage (that is, the trademark holder) to the downstream stage (that is, the exclusive distributor or retailer). Studies are needed to indicate under what circumstances this strategy will be effective.

Price is always an important factor to consider. Prices of innovations are set at the US or another industrialized country level, which are significantly higher than individuals in most developing countries can afford. Thus, buyers in developing countries, particularly where per capita GNP is less than $1000, do not have the option of, for example, purchasing software legitimately.

Research is needed to determine the extent of price discounts that might be granted to wage an effective campaign against piracy of such products as music tapes and software. As a matter of fact, prices may have to varied from one nation/region to another to entice governments across the world to be more willing participants in the enforcement of intellectual property rights. Studies must be conducted to develop a worldwide price schedule.

Harmonization of National Laws

Even in the industrialized world, nations have different rules for protection of intellectual property rights. The underlying principle of the existing system is the *national treatment*, which at best provides a minimum standard (Berenbeim 1989). Is it feasible to establish common international rules to strengthen the effects of national treatment? Can basic laws be harmonized globally? A beginning in this matter has already been made via the Uruguay Round of the GATT talks, providing 20-year protection of patents, trademarks, and copyrights for books, software, film, and the pharmaceutical industries.

Another area of research is the pursuit of a multifaceted strategy. Should the United States use both bilateral and multilateral avenues simultaneously to seek intellectual property rights protection? Studies are needed to delineate the pros and cons of each strategy, and the areas where they complement and conflict with each other. Finally, is it politically wise and trade-wise effective for the United States to force intellectual property protection through its own laws, for example, Super 301?

Protection of New Technologies

New technologies raise new concerns for intellectual property rights protection. Many new technologies (for example, computer software, semiconductor chips, and biotechnology products), which are extremely important, do not clearly fit into any existing categories of intellectual properties. For example, current copyright law offers no protection for information *per se*. It only protects its packaging. The research in this area will deal with the re-evaluation and redefinition of existing intellectual property classifications so that new and emerging technologies can be accommodated.

Should current laws, for example, copyright law, be changed to accommodate new forms of protection? Should new kinds of intellectual properties and laws be created for that purpose? Should the United States take the lead in working out new categories, and then seek the cooperation of major trading partners to internationalize them? As an alternative, will it be more effective to seek multilateral solutions from the outset to avoid future disputes?

The above areas of research need thorough examination and debate. Data must be gathered and analyzed. Pros and cons of different alternatives must be delineated. Only through reliable information can the complicated questions related to the international protection of intellectual property rights be addressed.

REFERENCES

Alster, Norm (1988), 'New Profits from Patents', *Fortune*, 25 April, 187.
Benko, Robert P. (1987), *Protecting Intellectual Property Rights*, Washington DC: American Enterprise Institute for Public Policy Research, p. 40.
Berenbeim, Ronald E. (1989), *Safeguarding Intellectual Property*, New York: The Conference Board, p. 4.
Berman, Paul S. (2000), 'Ease Up on MP3', *Hartford Courant*, 10 September: C1.
Blass, Anthony (1992), 'Learning the Soft Way', *Far Eastern Economic Review*, 84 (25), 3 December, p. 6.
Bonham, Yeaman (1986), 'The United States Leadership in Global Protection for Computer Chip Designs', *Columbia Journal of World Business*, 21, 81–8.
Bush, Ronald F., Peter H. Bloch, and Scott Dawson (1989), 'Remedies for Product Counterfeiting', *Business Horizons*, 32(1), January–February, 18–26.
Business Week (1991), 'Is it Time to Reinvent the Patent System?', 2 December, 110–15.
Business Week (1992), 'The Patent Pirates are Finally Walking the Plank', 17 February, 125–7.
Cervantes, Mario (1997), 'Diffusing Technology to Industry', *OECD Observer*, August/September, 20–23.
Chemical and Engineering News (1992), 'Impact of Intellectual Property Violations', 27 January, 29–30.
Cohen, Dorothy (1991), 'Trademark Strategy Revisited', *Journal of Marketing*, 55, 46–59.
Conner, Kathleen Reavis and Richard P. Rumelt (1991), 'Software Piracy: An Analysis of Protection Strategies', *Management Science*, 37, 125–39.
Crossborder Monitor (1998a), 'Grey Market Blues', 29 April, 2.
Crossborder Monitor (1998b), 'Wanted: One Patent for One Market', 9 September, 1.
Delmar, John (1991), 'Are Pirates Cutting into Your Sales?', *International Business*, July, 31–3.
Duvall, Donald K. (1992), 'Import Relief or Risk? Protection is a Double-edged Sword', *Industry Week*, 16 November, 46–51.
The Economist (1992a), 'Policy Thoughts', 1 August, 55–6.
The Economist (1992b), 'The Harm of Patents', 22 August, 17.
The Economist (1994), 'Intellectual Property … Is Theft', 22 January, 72–3.
Eisenberg, Rebecca S. (1987), 'Proprietary Rights and the Norms of Science in Biotechnology Research', *The Yale Law Journal*, December, 177–231.
Feinberg, Robert M. and Donald J. Rousslang (1990), 'The Economic Effects of Intellectual Property Right Infringements', *Journal of Business*, 63(1), 79–90.
Givon, Moshe, Vijay Mahajan, and Eiton Muller (1995), 'Software Piracy: Estimation of Lost Sales and the Impact on Software Diffusion', *Journal of Marketing*, 59, January, 29–37.
Globerman, Steven (1988), 'Addressing International Product Piracy', *Journal of International Business Studies*, 19(3), 497–504.

Goldman, Neal D. (1992), 'Software Theft: A \$4.5 Billion Headache', *Business Forum*, Spring, 10–12.

Gopal, Ram D. and G. Lawrence Sanders (1998), 'International Software Piracy: Analysis of Key Issues and Impacts', *Information Systems Research*, 9, December, 380–97.

Gopal, Ram D. and G. Lawrence Sanders (2000), 'Global Software Piracy: You Can't Get Blood Out of a Turnip', Working Paper, University of Connecticut, CIBER.

Harvey, Michael and Ilkka Ronkainen (1985), 'International Counterfeiters: Marketing Success Without the Cost or Risk', *Columbia Journal of World Business*, 20, Fall, 37–46.

Helfgott, Samson (1990), 'Cultural Differences Between US and Japanese Patent Systems', *Journal of Patent and Trademark Societies*, 72, March, 231–8.

Higgins, Richard S. and Paul H. Rubin (1986), 'Counterfeit Goods', *Journal of Law and Economics*, 29, October, 211–30.

Hilts, Paul (1992), 'Through the Electronic Copyright Maze', *Publishers Weekly*, 8 June, 35–7.

Kotabe, Masaaki (1991), 'A Comparative Study of US and Japanese Patent Systems', *Journal of International Business Studies*, 23(1), 147–68.

Kotabe, Masaaki and Eli P. Cox III (1993), 'Assessment of Shifting Global Competitiveness: Patent Applications and Grants in Four Major Trading Countries', *Business Horizons*, January–February, 57–64.

Kuttner, Robert (1992), 'Without Ground Rules it will be Open Season on Open Markets', *Business Week*, 16 March, 22.

Landes, William M. and Richard A. Posner (1987), 'Trademark Law: An Economic Perspective', *Journal of Law and Economics*, 30(10), October, 265–309.

Mansfield, Edwin et al. (1977), 'Social and Private Rate of Return from Industrial Innovations', *Quarterly Journal of Economics*, 56, May, 18–39.

Mansfield, Edwin (1990), 'Intellectual Property, Technology and Economic Growth', in F.W. Rushing and C.G. Brown (eds), *Intellectual Property Rights in Science, Technology, and Economic Performance*, Boulder, CO: Westview Press, pp. 17–30.

Mansfield, Edwin (2000), 'Intellectual Property Protection: Direct Investment and Technology, Transfer – Germany, Japan and the US', *International Journal of Technology Management*, 19(2), 3–21.

Menell, Peter S. (1990), 'Tailoring Legal Protection for Computer Software', *Stanford Law Review*, 39(6), 1329–72.

Mittelstaedt, John D. and Robert A. Mittelstaedt (1997), 'The Protection of Intellectual Property: Issues of Origination and Ownership', *Journal of Public Policy and Marketing*, 16, Spring, 14–23.

Ostergard, Robert L. Jr (2000), 'The Measurement of Intellectual Property Rights Protection', *Journal of International Business Studies*, 31(2), 349–60.

Rozek, Richard P. (1990), 'Protection of Intellectual Property Rights', in Francis W. Rushing and Carole Granz Brown (eds), *Intellectual Property Rights in Science, Technology, and Economic Performance*, Boulder, CO: Westview Press, pp. 31–46.

Sherwood, Robert M. (1990), *Intellectual Property and Economic Development*, Boulder, CO: Westview Press.

Sherwood, Robert M. (2000), 'The TRIPS Agreement: Benefits and Costs for Developing Countries', *International Journal of Technology Management*, 19(2), 57–76.

Spero, Donald M. (1990), 'Patent Protection or Piracy – A CEO Views Japan', *Harvard Business Review*, 68(5), September–October, 58–67.

Subramanian, Arvind (1991), 'The International Economics of Intellectual Property

Right Protection: A Welfare-theoretic Trade Policy Analysis', *World Development*, 19(8), 945–56.

Sun, M. (1986), 'The Global Fight over Plant Genes', *Science*, 31 January, 445–7.

Thomas, Robert J. (1989), 'Patent Infringement of Innovations by Foreign Competitors: The Role of the International Trade Commission', *Journal of Marketing*, 53, October, 63–75.

Turner, Roger (1988), 'Brazil: A Practical Guide to Intellectual Property Protection', *Business America*, 18 January, 14.

United States International Trade Commission (1987), *Foreign Protection of Intellectual Property Rights and the Effect on US Industry and Trade*, Washington DC: ITC.

US News and World Report (1988), 'Whose Property Is This Anyway?', 14 November, 50.

Whiting, Rick (1992), 'Power of the Idea', *Electronic Business*, 24 February.

Woo, Junda and Richard Borsuk (1994), 'Asian Trademark Litigation Continues', *Wall Street Journal*, 16 February, A8.

Yatsko, Pamela (2000), 'Knocking Out The Knockoffs', *Fortune*, 2 October, 213.

F23
G32
632

4. Global financial markets and global firms: implications for international business research

Jongmoo Jay Choi

Concomitant with the globalization of firms, there has been a rapid globalization of markets. In fact, global markets are necessary and sufficient conditions for global firms. Global markets provide opportunities for firms to go abroad, while global firms induce the markets to globalize. At the same time, globalization entails risk, as well as opportunity, for firms and investors. What then are the implications of global financial markets for firms, and how is globalization achieved for firms and markets?

Despite its importance, the nexus between global financial markets and global firms has not been a core area of research in mainstream international business literature. In international business literature, the major emphasis has been on the strategic, cultural, and behavioral dimensions of firms. For instance, although the original industrial organization view of foreign direct investments (FDIs) of Caves (1971), Hymer (1976), and Kindleberger (1969) does include imperfect financial markets as one of the necessary assumptions for multinational firms and FDIs, most empirical work in the tradition of Dunning (1980) makes little reference to financial or market variables.

Mainstream research in international finance, on the other hand, has focused on portfolio and asset pricing issues from the standpoint of investors and markets, or those that 'internationalize' a particular domestic finance topic. Advances that incorporate strategic factors in corporate financial decisions in a global context have been scant. To some extent, this reflects the development of international finance as a functional discipline. International finance has matured from the early stage of 'foreign' or 'comparative' analysis of finance functions to that which internalizes issues that are unique for cross-boundary transactions, such as political and currency risks. However, it has yet to offer an integrated model of corporate financial strategy that includes both strategic and financial factors in a global setting.

This chapter identifies potential frontier research issues pertaining to the financial implications of globalization for the general international business

and finance audience as well as for specialists in international finance interested in extensions to international business. To this end, it will first outline
the conceptual valuation framework for a multinational firm on the grounds
that all major corporate decisions must be based on, and geared to, value
enhancement. Existing work will be discussed within such a framework. Five
thematic areas that are both important and ripe for research will then be
identified and discussed:

1. Firm valuation and multinationality
2. Strategic and financial factors in corporate international investments
3. Risk and cost of capital for international firms
4. The effects of exchange rate and finance on operations
5. Profile of firms and markets

It is hoped that the chapter will help stimulate research towards the integration of financial and strategic factors in the mainstream international business
literature.

CONCEPTUAL FRAMEWORK FOR INTERNATIONAL FIRM VALUATION

A conventional model of multinational firms and foreign direct investments
in the industrial organization tradition of Caves (1971, 1982), Kindleberger
(1969), Hymer (1976), Buckley and Casson (1985), and Dunning (1980)
assumes market failure of some kind. Multinational corporations (MNCs)
have oligopolistic advantages that can be exploited profitably by FDIs in the
host country that offers abnormal profit opportunities because of market
imperfections. Market imperfections include taxes, transaction costs, informational inefficiency, imperfect competition, imperfect factor mobility,
institutional rigidity, government restrictions, and other factors contributing
to sub-optimal pricing of financial and real assets. MNCs are formed to
facilitate internalization of transactions within the corporate network to
reduce transaction costs and pricing uncertainty that exist in the external
open market. That is, MNCs benefit from superior appropriability of
oligopolistic (or information-intensive) benefits by internalization (Magee
1981). An open question, at the theoretical level, is determination of the
conditions under which internal markets formed by multinational firms are
more beneficial than external markets.[1]

Much of the empirical work on FDIs in the international business literature
has focused on firm-specific technological or operational advantages such as
research and development or advertising expenditures, but does not include

financial, market, or decision variables. As has been pointed out by Itaki (1991) in his criticism of the eclectic theory of Dunning (1980), this is a glaring omission, which reduces the applicability of the eclectic theory.

From the standpoint of international finance, two questions are in order. First, to the extent that all corporate decisions are (or should be) motivated by value enhancement, how are the valuation effects of a firm's operational decisions incorporated in the model of MNCs or their primary modus operandi, FDI decisions? Second, how would financial or market variables influence the value of multinational firms in the context of a firm's international investment decisions?

A point of departure for the corporate valuation framework is simple recognition that corporations make strategic (investment or otherwise) *decisions* in the presence of particular *market* conditions. Market variables include asset prices such as stock prices, interest rates, exchange rates, default risk premium and commodity prices, market structure variables such as liquidity, and government policy and institutional factors, as well as the wage rate and other real market prices. Corporate variables relevant for the current discussion would include those that describe decisions pertaining to domestic versus international investment, expansion versus contraction, greenfield versus mergers and acquisitions, domestic versus offshore financing, as well as issues pertaining to spin-offs and restructuring, international operations management, and risk management. To the extent that these decisions significantly influence the firm, their valuation impacts should be incorporated in a model of MNCs. In addition, the extent to which the financial markets influence a choice of strategic or operational decisions, or vice versa, must be recognized.

Summary I: The conventional model of MNCs or FDIs does not specifically address issues related to global financial markets or the choice of alternative corporate strategies. A model of firm valuation in a global context must include financial–market–decision variables, in addition to the ownership–location–internalization (OLI) variables used in the eclectic FDI model.

Consider a valuation framework where the effect of multinationality on the firm's value depends, sequentially, on the assessment of benefits and costs/ risks of various options in light of market conditions, as well as on the subsequent choice of the appropriate strategic decisions. Note that the analysis of benefits and costs/risks in Step II in Table 4.1 depends on conditions in financial and real markets, while corporate decisions in Step III depicts a choice of various strategic, operational, and financial decisions of the firm. The value of the firm also depends on conditions in both financial and real markets, as the present value of a given cash flow stream, for instance, would

Table 4.1   A valuation framework

Step I	Step II[a]	Step III	Step IV[a]
Multinationality	Benefits Costs/risks	Corporate decisions[b]	Value

Notes:
a. The markets partially determine II and IV: financial markets; real markets; national and international markets.
b. Corporate decisions in III include: strategic, restructuring, operational, financial, and risk management decisions.

be valued differently depending on the interest rate and risk premium determined in the market. Dunning's OLI model does not consider Step II and Step III variables, nor the market valuation aspect of Step IV explicitly.

The framework in Table 4.1 also identifies currency exchange rate changes and political risk as two uniquely international variables that may influence the valuation of the firm in an international context. For instance, international operation of a firm (Step I) is evaluated in terms of benefits and risks of operating in the host country (Step II), which can be altered by the firm's strategic, restructuring, operational, financial, and risk management strategies (Step III), with a resulting impact on valuation (Step IV). However, given the imperfect and incomplete global financial markets, the degree of risk reduction by risk management may not be complete, in which case the residual risks must be weighed against the diversification benefits of international operation to determine the overall impacts on the value of a multinational firm.

Summary II: A model of the multinational firm should reflect the extent to which corporate decisions and market conditions affect its valuation, in addition to strategic considerations.

THEMATIC RESEARCH AREAS

Having considered the valuation framework of a multinational firm, five thematic areas will be identified and discussed that are likely to be frontier research areas in international business as it relates to global financial markets.

Firm Valuation and Multinationality

Portfolio theory suggests that international operations, compared to otherwise identical domestic operations, would entail lower risk to the firm because of diversification benefits (for example, Rugman 1976). However, it is less clear that multinational firms would have superior performance. Since valuation is a function of both return and risk, the question is whether a greater degree of multinationality will increase value. Despite the work of Fatemi (1984), Errunza and Senbet (1981) and others in finance literature, the empirical evidence on this is mixed.[2]

While no theoretical work can be found on the optimality of multinational operations, it is reasonable to expect that the multinational operation is a double-edged sword, and has both merits and demerits. Merits of international operations include the usual reasons of going abroad (access to resources, access to markets, and access to lower cost, in search of better profit opportunities overall), and demerits include additional risk due to currency and political risks, as well as the cost of operating in complex, unfamiliar environments. This implies that an optimal level of multinationality is an interior solution, with a quadratic schedule where the net benefits of international operation first increase and then decrease after a certain point.

Morck and Yeung (1991) tested the industrial organization view of multinational firms by estimating the following regression:

$$\text{Firm value} = f(\text{multinationality, R\&D, control})$$

The research and development expense (R&D) variable measures the oligopolistic advantages of MNCs relative to local indigenous firms, which may interact with the multinationality variable in terms of their joint impacts on firm value. However, consistent with agency cost (Jensen and Meckling 1976) in corporate finance literature, which recognizes the ulterior motive for management, Christophe (1997) relates the desire to go multinational to hysteresis and corporate ego rather than sound economic analysis.

From a methodological standpoint, the unaltered inclusion of firm values or stock prices in ordinary regressions may be problematic because these variables may not be stationary. A unit roots test should be performed prior to regressions to see whether the variables are stationary (note that the regressions assume stationary variables). If stock prices or firm values are not stationary as indicated in several studies (for example, Bachman et al. 1996), then differences in stock prices or rate of returns must be used to ensure the stationarity of variables included in regressions. Alternatively, a cointegration analysis of non-stationary variables would be in order to determine the extent to which non-stationary variables become stationary in a linear combination, which depicts a long-run equilibrium relationship (Engle and Granger 1987).

Substantively, an important issue is how the impacts of international operations are distinguished from other factors such as industry factors. Industry factors are well recognized in a multi-factor model in the investment literature.[3] However, interactions between the industry and international factors – to what extent they are complements or substitutes, for instance – need to be examined more formally.

Another question pertains to firm valuation in the presence of exchange and political risk. Choi (1986) develops a model of firm valuation under exchange risk focusing on cash flows from domestic and foreign operations, while Hodder (1982) analyzes the impact of exchange rate changes on the basis of the assets and liabilities of the firm. However, there remains an open issue as to how a firm's exposure to contingent contracts can be valued, or how political risk can be incorporated in a formal model of firm valuation.

A basic issue that has not been well recognized in the literature is the fact that the diversity of international operations – like other forms of diversified operations across products, industries, or divisions – entails extra costs because of complexity of operations, monitoring and controls. These costs may outweigh the benefits of diversity. Rajan et al. (2000) develop a model of diversity of operations which recognizes these costs. A model of this kind is potentially extendible to international firms, subject to modifications necessary to incorporate the impacts of uniquely international factors such as currency risk, political risk, and market segmentation.

Finally, the decisions on international investments – a key ingredient of an MNC – are made under uncertainty and on the basis of comparative analysis of alternative strategic options. As such, corporate international investments can be viewed as a choice of real options. The real option theory, developed in corporate finance, assigns value to management flexibility under uncertainty and is potentially applicable to such important strategic decisions as FDIs.[4] Before discussing FDIs specifically, we summarize our discussion on valuation thus far as follows:

Summary III: The value of a multinational firm can be stated generally as:

*Firm value = f(multinationality, oligopolistic strategic real factors,
              financial factors, market and/or location variables)*

where the valuation scheme, f denotes both the standard net present value (NPV) valuation of domestic and international operations and the value of real options:

*Firm value = NPV (domestic and international operations) + real
              option value.*

Financial Factors in Foreign Direct Investments

The traditional FDI literature in international business focuses on owner-ship or internalization variables such as research and development or advertising expenditures, on the grounds that these variables capture the oligopolistic, ownership-specific advantages of MNCs. However, non-traditional FDIs are made by emerging market firms, even when they do not possess clear oligopolistic advantages vis-à-vis indigenous or competing firms (Choi et al. 1995). It has been argued that a low interest rate at home, or a strong yen, gave an advantage to Japanese firms because they were able to create a lower cost of capital or more investable wealth.[5] More impor-tantly, the fact of the matter is that, in the real world, corporate investment decisions are rarely made without taking account of both financial and strategic factors.

Despite the neglect of financial variables in the empirical literature, the industrial organization theory actually embraces imperfections in global financial markets as one of the plausible conditions for FDIs. The advantages of MNCs may be defined in terms of financial variables, as well as strategic ones. The financial advantages of MNCs include superior access to financing, lower cost of capital, access to favorable currency markets, or superior ability to manage risk. Incorporation of financial variables in a model of FDIs presupposes that international capital markets are partially segmented. The risk-adjusted cost of financing would be equal for all firms in perfect, fully-integrated international capital markets.[6] Multinational firms may also possess superior resources to manage risk operationally beyond what can be achieved financially in capital markets.

Aliber (1970) was the first to propose a theory of FDIs based on financial factors. His currency premium theory indicates that multinational firms can raise funds in a strong currency in international financial markets, while the indigenous firms would be confined to local financing in weak currency units. This gives an advantage to MNCs because they face a lower currency pre-mium and hence a lower cost of capital vis-à-vis a local firm. A project in the host country thus can result in a higher valuation for MNCs than for local firms and is likely to be taken up by MNCs rather than by local firms.

Froot and Stein (1991) argue that FDIs can take place because of the increase in wealth due to exchange rate changes. Stulz (1983) analyzes the effects of portfolio and wealth changes. Choi (1989) defines the source of wealth and portfolio effects from real exchange rate changes in terms of the firm's output and input choices. FDIs, in this model, take place as a result of interactions of diversification gains and the firm's production and sourcing decisions under output and input price uncertainty caused by real exchange rate changes.

Clearly FDI is one decision among many alternative strategic options: growth versus contraction or no growth, internal growth versus external growth, domestic versus international growth, greenfield in the form of FDIs versus acquisitions, solo versus joint venture, licensing versus FDIs, and so on. The real option theory provides a framework for valuing these decisions under uncertainty, with applications in capital budgeting, project valuation, abandonment, and interactions among multiple options. The real option can be viewed as an addition to the value computed in the usual static NPV valuation based on cash flow projections. Although little work has been done in international applications, real option theory appears to be well suited as a theoretical framework for extensions to FDIs and other international strategies.

Summary IV: FDIs can be viewed as a result of considering both strategic and financial factors and can be modeled by real option theory:

$$FDIs = f(strategic\ factors,\ financial\ factors,\ real\ option)$$
$$= f(static\ NPV\ analysis) + f(real\ option)$$

Beyond these general theoretical or conceptual issues, the following specific issues appear to be interesting topics for research in this area:

- How are FDIs different – in terms of behavioral profiles, motivations, and determinants – from mergers and acquisitions?
- How are FDIs different from international portfolio investments?
- When do expansions or contractions add value?
- How do financial and strategic variables interact in FDI decisions?

Risk and Cost of Capital of International Firms

Ever since Solnik (1974a,b), it is well known that a firm's systematic risk is lower in a global context than it is in a domestic context. However, that is so only in terms of market risk. The question is whether the currency risk and political risk – the two international risks that can potentially increase the risk of investing abroad overall – can be diversified or hedged away in a global market in such a way that the firm's overall risk is lower. Elimination of these international risks assumes that appropriate financial instruments are available for all contingencies and durations, that different cash flow contingencies are well defined, and that hedging and diversification can be done in a costless way. Clearly, these assumptions are not realistic, especially when the risk exposures are operational in nature, long term in duration, or political in origin. In addition, complete risk elimination may not be optimal in a risk–return trade-off sense.

Regarding currency risk, there is a growing realization that a portion of exchange risk is systematic due to the empirical work of Dumas and Solnik (1995), and Choi et al. (1988). However, little work has been done with regard to the systematic nature of political risk.

A more basic question is whether the non-systematic risk, or total risk, of a firm is relevant in addition to its systematic risk. Non-systematic risk is diversified away in efficient, perfect markets. However, if the capital markets are partially segmented and imperfect, then firm-specific, non-systematic risk becomes relevant as well in corporate financial and investment decisions. An empirical issue is (a) to sort out the degree of importance and relevance of firm-specific or total risks of multinational firms (in addition to the systematic risk), and (b) to estimate the determinants of a firm's systematic risk in an international context.

For the latter, Kwok and Reeb (2000) estimate the systematic risk of a firm in a multi-factor model. The systematic risk of a firm can be stated as:

Systematic risk = *cov* (firm return, market return)/ *var* (market return)

which includes both firm and market return factors. We can extend this equation by including separate components of the firm's operations (domestic and global operational factors), as well as by recognizing global market environments in which the firm is operating (domestic and global market factors). Firm-specific factors can include both operational and financial variables. The inclusion of domestic and global market factors is necessary in partially segmented global capital markets.

Summary V: The systematic risk of a firm can be stated as a function of domestic and foreign market and firm-specific factors in partially segmented international capital markets, in the absence of currency and political risks:

Systematic risk = f(domestic and international, firm-specific and market factors)

The formulation of systematic risk thus far incorporates dual domestic and international market factors due to partial integration of international capital markets, but it does not incorporate systematic risks due to currency and political risks. With proper currency adjustments, the systematic currency risk factor can be included in the above framework. Alternatively, it can be estimated separately as:

Systematic exchange risk = *cov* (firm return, exchange rate changes)/ *var* (exchange rate changes) or by estimating the exchange risk exposure coefficients in the factor model:

$$R_i = \alpha + \beta_1 R_m + \beta_2 R_e$$

where R_i is the return of firm i's stock, R_m is the market return, and R_e is the rate of changes in exchange rates. A model of this kind has been estimated by Jorion (1990), Bodnar and Gentry (1993), Choi and Prasad (1995) and others.

Political risk is more discrete in nature and is not easily quantifiable in an asset pricing framework. However, Stulz (1981), Eun and Janakiramanan (1986), and Errunza and Losq (1985) introduce the impacts of location-related factors (including the impacts of 'political risk') in a 'tax' term, which drives a wedge between domestic and international asset pricing in a discrete way. However, it remains an open question as to how political events influence corporate strategies and firm valuation.

In a multi-factor model, the market factor can be traced further back into such macroeconomic fundamentals as changes in interest rates, exchange rates, inflation, balance of payments, industrial production, and others, as well as firm-specific fundamentals such as firm size, price–earnings ratios, and others. A challenge in this investigation is the selection of fundamental variables in a way that is not arbitrary, as well as the incorporation of non-linear and simultaneous relationships.

A parallel literature concerns the management of international risks. Standard textbooks in international finance provide the framework for analyzing accounting, economic, and operational measurement of risks faced by MNCs. The value-at-risk model is well suited to implement the risk measurement at the level of the firm, although issues are still open with regard to assumptions on statistical distributions and the like.

A more difficult issue concerns the management of risk. That is, when operational strategies are appropriate as opposed to financial hedging, how do we combine operational and financial hedging in a value-enhancing way? Or more basically, how do we determine the optimal level of hedging for multinational firms that have both accounting and economic exchange exposures? These are some of the thorny issues in this area that still await formal answers. I should also indicate that the issue of accounting treatment for hedging transactions is still open, with regard to both theory and design of proper accounting methods. Finally, the strategic responses of firms in the face of major crises, such as the Asian financial crisis of 1997, also need to be studied not only as a topic in crisis management but also for their implications for the relationship between financial crisis and strategic decisions.[7]

The Effects of Exchange Rate and Finance on Operations

The general issue here is how financial variables such as funds availability, cost of capital, and exchange rates would affect the operational side of the firm. Of course, the reverse is true as well, as operational decisions affect the financing in terms of level and mix. The idea that financial and operational decisions are interdependent is recognized in corporate finance and is predicated on the assumption that the capital markets are not 'perfect' in the textbook sense. Myers and Majluf (1984), for instance, show that a firm's investment decisions are likely to be sub-optimal because of constraints on financing due to market imperfections or moral hazard problems stemming from informational uncertainty.

A variable of particular interest for international application is the exchange rate. Changes in nominal exchange rates can influence interest rates and inflation, and hence the firm's choice on the source of financing in international markets. However, exchange rate changes in real terms would affect the firm's operational and investment decisions. Thus, real exchange rate changes affect the cost of operation and hiring, influencing the pattern of a firm's sourcing and human resource staffing. International marketing also depends on exchange rates because the relative cost of advertising (as well as the image it creates) is affected by exchange rate changes. Real exchange rate changes also influence the firm's decisions on international investment and contraction (Kim, 1997; Miller and Reuer, 1998). The whole area of interactions between finance and operation for global firms is open and is an excellent area for interdisciplinary international business research.

Another interesting area concerns corporate ownership. How does a firm's equity ownership structure affects its operational decisions, or how would different international stockholder profiles affect the relationship between financing and operation within the firm? A related issue is how the firm's capital structure (the debt–equity mix) at both local and corporate levels affects its pattern of global operations, or vice versa. An issue in comparative analysis is how the governance structure in each country influences corporate strategies and behaviors.

Profile of Firms and Markets

I now turn to the most basic and in a sense the most important issue. In principle, a point of departure in any scientific investigation is the observation and profiling of reality. It is surprising that, despite significant progress in international business and finance research, efforts to establish a profile of firms and markets are relatively lagging.

A new sub-area of finance, called the 'micro market structure', investigates the micro-structure of a particular financial market. In a similar vein, a profiling of international differences of a given market, as well as the differences across different kinds of financial markets, would be a useful prerequisite for serious research in international finance.

More specific to international business research is the profiling of national firms.[8] For instance, how do US, Japanese, and European firms differ, and how do the firms from emerging market countries behave differently from traditional multinationals? More directly relevant to the theory of MNCs, what are the behavioral, operational, and financial differences between domestic and multinational firms?

The comparative analysis of different classes of firms can begin with comparison of valuation (after adjustment for size and industry). The differences in valuation can then be traced to differences in financial structure, asset structure, ownership structure, government structure, and control structure, as well as behavioral differences, operational profiles, and risk characteristics. The difficulty is how the properties of firms can be disentangled from those of nations. Factual information regarding these would provide a basis for serious comparative analysis from various perspectives: cultural, institutional, and economic. As such, the comparative study of firms and market characteristics would provide a useful point of departure for research on multinational firms.

CONCLUDING REMARKS

It is generally true that there exist greater potential gains from global operations or investments than domestic ones if the markets are globalized. Globalization of financial markets provides an opportunity for firms and investors, and makes it easier for potential gains from international investments to be realized. However, it does not follow that, for any given investor or firm, the gains from international investments would increase with an increasing internationalization of markets. In fact, portfolio theory suggests the reverse: the potential gains from international investments in fact decrease the more closely the international markets are correlated. To the extent that high correlation depicts highly integrated markets, the potential gains actually decrease with greater integration of markets.

The key to resolving the apparent conflict is the realization that the portfolio theory only indicates the *potential* gains, while the popular notion regarding the benefit of globalization points to the *realized* gains. That is, the more integrated the markets are, the lower would be the potential benefits from international diversification. However, integrated markets also make the realization of potential gains easier. This suggests an interior solution for the optimal level of international diversification. Since the potential gains decrease but their realization rate increases with an increased integration of global capital markets, the actual gains – which are the product of potential gains and realization rate – should initially increase with market integration and then, after a while, decrease.

A paradigm in traditional finance is that of perfect, efficient markets. To the extent that international markets are partially segmented and hence less than perfect and efficient, there exist gains to be made for investors and firms from investing or operating globally.

A challenge in international business research is to formulate a holistic perspective not just in terms of viewing corporate operations globally, but also in the sense of integrating operational and financial considerations as a whole in the theory of multinational firms and international investments. Beyond sounding the holistic note, I have also attempted to highlight some of the potential frontier research issues in international business that are brought about by global firms and integrated global financial markets. I have also suggested that some of the financial concepts, such as real option theory, are potentially applicable as conceptual devices towards the integrated theory of operational and financial strategies in the holistic theory of multinational firms.

NOTES

1. Stein (1997) discusses the conditions for internal markets in a domestic context. No work has been published to analyze the issue in the international context.
2. Lins and Servaes (1999) provide international evidence on the value of corporate diversification. This is useful but is not evidence on the value of international corporate diversification.
3. For an earlier work on industry factors, see Lessard (1974).
4. For exposition of real option theory, see Trigeorgis (1996).
5. Blonigen (1997) shows the linkage between the yen and Japanese investments in the US.
6. There is ample evidence that international capital markets are partially segmented. See Choi and Rajan (1997) for evidence, or Stulz (1994) or Choi and Severn (1991) for the survey of the literature.
7. See various articles in an edited volume on the Asian financial crisis by Choi (2000).
8. Michel and Shaked (1986) examine the differences in financial ratios of US domestic and multinational firms.

REFERENCES

Aliber, R.A. (1970), 'A Theory of Foreign Direct Investment', in C.P. Kindleberger (ed.), *The International Corporation*. Cambridge, MA: MIT Press, pp. 17–34.
Bachman, D., J.J. Choi, B.N. Jeon, and K.J. Kopecky (1996), 'Common Factors in

International Stock Prices: Evidence from a Cointegration Study', *International Review of Financial Analysis*, 5(1), 39–53.

Blonigen, B.C. (1997), 'Firm-specific Assets and the Link between Exchange Rates and Foreign Direct Investments', *American Economic Review*, 87, 447–65.

Bodnar, G.M. and W.M. Gentry (1993), 'Exchange Rate Exposure and Industry Characteristics: Evidence from Canada, Japan and U.S.', *Journal of International Money and Finance*, 12(1), February, 29–45.

Buckley, P.J. and M.C. Casson (1985), *The Economic Theory of the Multinational Enterprise*, London: Macmillan.

Caves, R.E. (1971), 'International Corporations: the Industrial Economics of Foreign Investment', *Econometrica*, 38, 1–27.

Caves, R.E. (1982), *Multinational Enterprise and Economic Analysis*, New York: Cambridge University Press.

Choi, J.J. (1986), 'A Model of Firm Valuation with Exchange Exposure', *Journal of International Business Studies*, 17(2), Summer, 153–9.

Choi, J.J. (1989), 'Diversification, Exchange Risk and Corporate International Investment', *Journal of International Business Studies*, 20(1), Spring, 145–55.

Choi, J.J. (ed.) (2000), *Asian Financial Crisis: Financial, Structural and International Dimensions*, Volume 1 of International Finance Review, New York: JAI and Elsevier Science.

Choi, J.J., T. Hiraki, and N. Takezawa (1988), 'Is the Foreign Exchange Risk Priced in the Japanese Stock Market?', *Journal of Financial and Quantitative Analysis*, 33(3), 361–82.

Choi, J.J., K. Kim, and R. Chandran (1995), 'Foreign Direct Investments by Firms from Developing and Developed Countries: Stylized Facts and Theoretical Interpretations', in Y. Kim and K. Oh (eds), *The US–Korea Economic Partnership*, London and New York: Avebury Publishing.

Choi, J.J. and A.M. Prasad (1995), 'Exchange Risk Sensitivity and Its Determinants: A Firm and Industry Analysis of U.S. Multinationals', *Financial Management*, 24(3), 77–88.

Choi, J.J. and M. Rajan (1997), 'A Joint Test of Market Segmentation and Exchange Risk Factor in International Capital Markets', *Journal of International Business Studies*, 28(1), 29–49.

Choi, J.J. and A.K. Severn (1991), 'On the Effects of International Risk, Segmentation and Diversification on the Cost of Equity Capital: A Critical Review and Synthesis', *Journal of Multinational Financial Management*, 1(3), 1–19.

Christophe, S.E. (1997), 'Hysteresis and the Value of the U.S. Multinational Corporation', *Journal of Business*, 70(3), 435–62.

Dumas, B. and B. Solnik (1995), 'The World Price of Foreign Exchange Risk', *Journal of Finance*, 50, 445–79.

Dunning, J.H. (1980), 'Toward a Eclectic Theory of International Production: Some Empirical Results', *Journal of International Business Studies*, Spring/Summer, 11(1), 9–31.

Engle, R.T. and C.W.J. Granger (1987), 'Cointegration and Error Correction: Representation, Estimation and Testing', *Econometrica*, 55, 251–76.

Errunza, V. and E. Losq (1985), 'International Asset Pricing under Mild Segmentation: Theory and Evidence', *Journal of Finance*, 41, 105–24.

Errunza, V. and L. Senbet (1981), 'The Effects of International Operations on Market Value of the Firm: Theory and Evidence', *Journal of Finance*, 36, 401–17.

Eun, C.S. and S. Janakiramanan (1986), 'A Model of International Asset Pricing with a Constraint on Foreign Equity Ownership', *Journal of Finance*, 41(4), 897–914.

Fatemi, A. (1984), 'Shareholder Benefits from Corporate Industrial Diversification', *Journal of Finance*, 39, 1325–44.

Froot, K.A. and J.C. Stein (1991), 'Exchange Rates and Foreign Direct Investment: An Imperfect Capital Markets Approach', *Quarterly Journal of Economics*, 106, November 1191–217.

Hodder, J.E. (1982), 'Exposure to Exchange-rate Movements', *Journal of International Economics*, 13, November, 375–86.

Hymer, S. (1976), *The International Operation of National Firms: A Study of Direct Foreign Investment* (MIT dissertation 1960), Cambridge, MA: MIT Press.

Itaki, M. (1991), 'A Critical Assessment of the Eclectic Theory of the Multinational Enterprise', *Journal of International Business Studies*, 22(3), 445–60.

Jensen, M.C. and W.H. Meckling (1976), 'Theory of the Firm: Managerial Behavior, Agency Costs and Capital Structure', *Journal of Financial Economics*, 3, 305–60.

Jorion, P. (1990), 'The Exchange Rate Exposure of U.S. Multinationals', *Journal of Business*, 63(3), July, 331–45.

Kim, Y.C. (1997), 'Stock Price Reactions to International Investment and Divestiture and Management of Currency Operating Exposure', *Journal of Economics and Business*, 49, 419–37.

Kindleberger, C. (1969), *American Business Abroad: Six Lectures on Direct Investment*, New Haven: Yale University Press.

Kwok, C.C.Y. and D.M. Reeb (2000), 'Internationalization and Firm Risk: An Upstream and Downstream Hypothesis', *Journal of International Business Studies*, 31(4), 611–29.

Lessard, D. (1974), 'World, National, and Industry Factors in Equity Returns', *Journal of Finance*, 29(2), 379–91.

Lins, K. and H. Servaes (1999), 'International Evidence on the Value of Corporate Diversification', *Journal of Finance*, 54, 2215–39.

Magee, S.P. (1981), 'Information and the Multinational Corporation: An Appropriability Theory of Foreign Direct Investment', in J.N. Bhagwati (ed.), *The New International Economic Order*, Cambridge, MA: MIT Press.

Michel, A. and I. Shaked (1986), 'Multinational Corporations vs. Domestic Corporations: Financial Performance and Characteristics', *Journal of International Business Studies*, 18, 89–100.

Miller, K.D. and J.J. Reuer (1998), 'Firm Strategy and Economic Exposure to Foreign Exchange Rate Movements', *Journal of International Business Studies*, 29(3), 493–513.

Morck, R. and B. Yeung (1991), 'Why Investors Value Multinationality', *Journal of Business*, 64, 165–87.

Myers, S.C. and N.S. Majluf (1984), 'Corporate Financing and Investment Decisions when Firms Have Information that Investors Do Not Have', *Journal of Financial Economics*, 13, 187–221.

Rajan, R., H. Servaes, and L. Zingales (2000), 'The Cost of Diversity: The Diversification Discount and Inefficient Investment', *Journal of Finance*, 55(1), 35–80.

Rugman, A. (1976), 'Risk Reduction by International Diversification', *Journal of International Business Studies*, 7, 75–80.

Solnik, B. (1974a), 'An Equilibrium Model of the International Capital Markets', *Journal of Economic Theory*, 8(4), 500–24.

Solnik, B. (1974b), 'Why Not Diversify Internationally Rather Than Domestically', *Financial Analysts Journal*, 30(4), July/August, 48–54.

Stein, J. (1997), 'Internal Capital Market and the Competition for Corporate Resources', *Journal of Finance*, 52, 111–33.

Stulz, R.M. (1981), 'On the Effects of Barriers to International Investment', *Journal of Finance*, 36, 923–34.

Stulz, R.M. (1983), 'On the Determinants of Net Foreign Investments', *Journal of Finance*, 38(2), 459–68.

Stulz, R.M. (1994), 'International Portfolio Choice and Asset Pricing: An Integrative Survey', NBER Working Paper Series No. 4645, Cambridge, MA.

Trigeorgis, L. (1996), *Real Options: Managing Flexibility and Strategy in Resource Allocation*, Boston, MA: MIT Press.

5. Cultural balkanization and hybridization in an era of globalization: implications for international business research

Bryan W. Husted

In August 1999, José Bové was arrested for ransacking a McDonald's restaurant in Millau, France. He was seen as a hero fighting against the pollution of French culture by the Big Mac. Fear of an impending McWorld and the globalization it represents has unleashed an increasingly strong backlash against the possibility of cultural homogenization. Indeed, some evidence of the loss of cultural variety can be found in the fact that while 6000 distinct languages are spoken today experts estimate that only about 3000 languages will be spoken by 2100 (Davis 1999). However, at the same time, the very processes leading to a reduction in variety also foster an increase in such variety as evidenced by the backlash of cultural balkanization and new cultural syntheses that are being created through hybridization.

Although culture has formed the core of much research in international business (IB) studies, the process of cultural 'balkanization' or fragmentation that seems to be occurring in response to globalization has not been studied in great detail by IB scholars. This chapter looks at the parallel processes of globalization and cultural balkanization to determine the current state of knowledge regarding these processes, and develops directions for future IB research. It begins by defining the concept of globalization and reviewing the different schools of thought that explain this process. It then defines cultural balkanization as a consequence of and response to globalization. Next, it describes the complex and dynamic relationship between these two dialectical processes and discusses how these issues have been treated in the IB literature. Finally, it concludes by briefly developing some implications of this dynamic relationship for IB research in three areas: management, marketing, and business ethics.

GLOBALIZATION

Globalization refers to many related processes in the economic, political, and social spheres. However, it is within the cultural arena where the popular idea of globalization takes root and either horrifies or delights the imaginations of most people. Unfortunately, it is difficult to determine precisely what scholars mean by globalization, and even more difficult to understand the processes by which it occurs. In general, Robertson's (1990: 20) reference to globalization as 'a particular series of developments concerning the concrete structuration of the world as a whole' is a useful place to begin understanding globalization as a cultural phenomenon because it captures the idea that human ways of seeing the world are becoming more similar. As Boli and Thomas (1997: 173) explain, through globalization 'definitions, principles, and purposes are cognitively constructed in similar ways throughout the world'.

Scholars have developed a number of different perspectives to explain the forces driving globalization. In Sklair's (1995) Marxian analysis of globalization, the principal forces behind the adoption of global practices are the multinational corporations and national elites attuned to global trends. The multinational corporation promotes a culture of consumerism that in turn creates a need for its products by the elite. According to this view, globalization creates contradictory processes – the generation of wealth and 'globalized' marginality that stimulates migration within and between countries toward global cities (Sassen and Appiah 1998). These processes will provide the basis for conflict and violence now and in the near future.

Keohane and Nye (1989) modify the realist school of international relations, which originally focused on the power of nation-states as the source of structure in the world, to focus on multiple international actors, including multinational business enterprises and non-governmental organizations, as sources of structure. Globalization leads to a complex interdependence among these actors who pursue their own interests on a global playing field. Military security no longer dominates international politics as economic and social issues play an increasingly important role in international relations.

Reacting to the rationalism implicit in both the Marxist and neo-realist approaches, world polity theorists such as Meyer et al. (1997) understand the adoption of transnational practices to be caused by forces of mimetic isomorphism. Mimetic isomorphism refers to the tendency of organizations to imitate the structures and practices of other organizations and institutions in the face of environments characterized by great uncertainty (DiMaggio and Powell 1983). World polity theorists argue that the adoption of organizational practices by international and local actors depends upon a world culture to which they conform. Among the elements of this world culture, Boli and Thomas

(1997) identify five values: universalism, individualism, rational voluntaristic authority, human purposes of rationalizing progress, and world citizenship.

Finally, for world culture theorists, a world culture does exist, but is much less homogeneous than suggested by the world polity theorists. Instead, globalization is best characterized by processes, alternatively called hybridization (Pieterse 1994), 'creolization' (Hannerz 2000), or 'glocalization' (Kraidy 1999), in which different cultural elements are joined in new and sometimes unexpected ways as they come into contact with each other as a result of different cultural flows.

Appadurai (1990) postulates that cultures come into contact with each other through five specific kinds of global cultural flows: 'ethnoscapes' (tourists, immigrants, refugees, and so on), 'mediascapes' (radio, television, and so on), 'technoscapes' (low- and high-technology transfers), 'finanscapes' (capital flows), and 'ideoscapes' (ideologies). These cultural flows occur in all directions between north and south and east and west. In each case, these flows bring people into contact with new ideas that serve as catalysts for the creation of new cultural forms.

According to Hannerz (2000), culture flows occur in four ways. First, the market causes cultural commodities to move across borders. Second, the state as a manager of meaning implants cultural norms and categories to standardize practices as well as to accentuate some differences in order to aid the creation of national identity. The third pattern or process involves the everyday activities involved in production whether at home, work, or school, which may or may not be subject to considerable global influence. The fourth deals with movements (women's, environmental, peace, and so on) that transcend national borders and often deliberately transmit new values. These four processes contribute to the flow of cultural products from the north (or the center) to the south (or the periphery) (Hannerz 2000). But this flow is not one-way. Rather, actors at the periphery take cultural products from the center, modify them to local conditions and tastes, and develop new syntheses or hybrids.

CULTURAL BALKANIZATION

Cultural balkanization is a term used in the US to describe the tendency to assert local identities over national identity. William Bennett (1998: 19) speaks of cultural balkanization as an 'erosion of our national self-understanding'. It refers to the cultural and ethnic fragmentation that is part of the same reality that constitutes globalization (Friedman 1990). In opposition to the thesis of cultural imperialism and global homogenization (Tomlinson 1991), Barton (1998) uses cultural balkanization as a negative label for the increased pluralism that accompanies globalization. Ger and Belk (1996) find that globalization creates division by 'increasing social inequality, class polarization, consumer frustrations, stress, materialism, and threats to health and environment'. These divisions serve as the impetus for the reassertion of local identities. Cultural balkanization is also evidenced by the resurgence of fundamentalist groups and the development of new religious movements (Robertson and Chirico 1985; Lechner 1993; Dawson 1998). Thus cultural balkanization is a return to the 'particular' after a great deal of interest in the 'universal'.

Interestingly, both cultural balkanization and globalization can be understood as undermining national identity and, at the same time, as existing in tension with one another. On the one hand, globalization attacks national identity by emphasizing cultural elements that transcend national boundaries. On the other hand, cultural balkanization reasserts local identities at the expense of national identities, which have often been created as the result of unstable political compromises.

Although the connotation of cultural balkanization is negative, the process it describes has been experienced both negatively and positively. Negatively, it raises images of jihad, nationalisms, and the resurgence of religious, ethnic, and racial strife (Barber 1995; Huntington 1993). Religious orthodoxy and fundamentalism often arise as a rejection of modernity and globalization. Despite this rejection, fundamentalisms are themselves inherently modern projects, which offer a particularistic identity within a global universalism (Robertson and Chirico 1985; Lechner 1993; Dawson 1998). Fundamentalism is not free of the processes of hybridization as it often adopts bureaucratic organizational structures similar to those in the wider environment as well as using the same means provided to advance globalization such as the Internet (Dawson 1998; Lechner 1993).

Perhaps cultural balkanization reaches its most terrifying form in the clash of civilizations that Huntington (1993) sees as the defining feature of conflict in the future. Further, the major civilizations (Western, Confucian, Japanese, Islamic, Hindu, Slavic-Orthodox, Latin American, and African) are largely, although not entirely, differentiated by religion. Given the process of globalization and the separation of people from traditional sources of identity, the gap is being filled by religious fundamentalism.

Despite these problems, Lin (1998) argues that a revalorization of the local is occurring in large, global cities. Ger (1999) shows how the particular can be a source of competitive advantage for local firms. Barton (1998) views the pluralism arising from cultural fragmentation as benign and even beneficial if it is channeled through appropriate plural legal systems designed to accommodate multicultural states and value communities. In fact, he sees this diversity as one of the defining characteristics and strengths of the postmodern world. Pluralism can be either a source of conflict or a source of creativity and innovation that benefits all people. The management of this diversity is the key to determining whether pluralism will yield to order or chaos.

What then are the processes by which cultural balkanization is occurring? Marxists emphasize the different economic impacts of advanced capitalism on global elites and on local, marginalized groups. These impacts create an inherent struggle between the global and the local. However, according to cultural theory, both globalization and cultural balkanization are the products of hybridization. Cultural change has been the rule, rather than the exception, throughout history. Globalization has never been monolithic, but is an inherently plural concept that should be conceived of as 'globalizations'. Similarly, cultural balkanization is always a product of hybridization, often between traditional, local elements and global ones.

Increasing communication and transportation due to technological advances and economic reforms have made an increasing range of organizational structures and cultural practices available to a larger population. However, separated from their origins, these options and practices recombine under new conditions in a hybrid form (Pieterse 1994). In the case of globalization, multinational corporations are important actors in a multicentric world in their role as transmitters of cultural forms and as creative agents recombining old forms into new hybrids. In the case of cultural balkanization, a hybridization of local and global elements usually occurs as groups fostering local or traditional values absorb elements of globalization.

'Glocalization' has been used by Robertson (1995) and Kraidy (1999) to refer to the interface between the processes of globalization and localization (or cultural balkanization). The term emphasizes that both global and local culture are inherently hybrid and that both globalization and localization involve processes of hybridization. Food provides an interesting example of how hybridization occurs (Wilk 1999). Mexican food is hybridized in the US to create Mexican-American food. Along with Italian-American, Chinese-American, and other hybridized cuisines, these new combinations may be unrecognizable and even unpalatable in the originating society, but are highly appreciated in the hybridizing society by both the immigrant groups that seek to assert their local identity and the dominant culture. When Mexican food goes to Spain, it becomes Mexican-Spanish food, different from either the Mexican-American kind or its Mexican parent. Thus, although the local may reassert itself, it is inevitably changed by the new contexts in which it arises. Cultural balkanization must be understood as a product of globalization as well as a reaction to it.

INTERNATIONAL BUSINESS RESEARCH

The convergence–divergence–cross-vergence literature developed by IB researchers deals with some of the same issues regarding globalization and cultural balkanization discussed by anthropologists, sociologists, and political scientists (Ralston et al. 1997; Ralston et al. 1993; Ricks et al. 1990). The convergency theorists argue that the economic ideology of capitalism has a relentless impact upon managerial practice and values that is stronger than national culture. Divergency theorists, on the contrary, say that national culture is too strong and that economic ideology will have little impact on managerial practice and values.

The cross-vergence framework argues that a kind of hybridization of local culture and global practice takes place. Ralston et al. (1997) found evidence of cross-vergence by comparing Japan and China. Both countries are low on the individualism dimension, although Japan is less so than China. In China, collectivism is a traditional kind of collectivism with the family as the main in-group. In Japan, the company has replaced the family as the principal in-group. Thus, although Japan has been affected by the economic ideology of capitalism with its emphasis on individualism, it has manifested this impact in a unique form of collectivism oriented toward the company.

Ralston et al. (1999) made a very interesting study of work values among northern and southern Vietnamese managers. There they found that northern Vietnamese managers had a more Western orientation toward individualism, while southern Vietnamese managers had a more traditional Confucian orientation toward collectivism. They also compared cosmopolitan Chinese respondents and traditional Chinese respondents. The cosmopolitan Chinese had the most Western orientation on individualism of the four Asian groups. They were followed by the northern Vietnamese, who had been very influenced by cosmopolitan Chinese because of trade, then the traditional Chinese, and finally the southern Vietnamese. In terms of collectivism, the cosmopolitan Chinese scored the lowest, followed by the traditional Chinese, while both groups of Vietnamese scored the highest.

The study suggests that it is easier to adopt individualistic values than to leave collectivistic values. The authors speculate that the influence of the cosmopolitan Chinese in Vietnam is greater than that of the traditional Chinese because the northern Vietnamese have greater contact with the cosmopolitan Chinese through trade than with the more traditional Chinese who arrive as poor immigrants. As a result of this contact, the northern Vietnamese have moved closer toward individualistic, market-oriented values than their southern compatriots, while maintaining their collectivist orientation derived from Vietnam's traditional culture (Ralston et al. 1999).

Probably the most prolific generator of practices and customs that are consumed in other parts of the world is the United States. However, when those practices and customs are uprooted from the cultural context that gave them meaning, the imitation of the practice without that context creates new meanings as the adopting culture does not use the practice or understand the practice in the same way. As a result, hybridization not only occurs, it is inevitable. The work of anthropologists would lead us to believe that in fact, cultural convergence will never occur. In other words, cross-vergence is not a transitional stage, but the very nature of globalization.

Part of the problem in understanding globalization and cultural balkanization is deciding what we mean by culture. Nath (1986) observed that culture could be defined ideationally in terms of value orientations or comprehensively in terms of both artifacts and entities (tribes, groups, nations, and so on) having common cultural elements. Much of the discussion of globalization seems to revolve around culture as products of consumption (food, clothing, music, and so on), which can be observed easily. However, if culture refers to value orientations, as found in the work of Hofstede (1997), Rokeach (1973) and others, suddenly cultural globalization becomes much more difficult to observe, except with respect to the cultural value of individualism, which does seem to be experiencing more widespread acceptance (Hofstede 1984). IB research on cross-vergence has focused largely on the value-based orientation to culture, and supports in part the thesis that cultural homogenization is not occurring.

Several factors may explain the resistance to globalization as homogenization. First, the transmission of values is usually two-way (Ralston et al. 1997). So while the peripheral culture is influenced by the dominant culture, the reverse also happens. Second, the transmission of values is not easy. Husted et al. (1996) found that attitudes toward questionable business practices were much more susceptible to the influences of globalization than was the form of moral reasoning among Mexican, Spanish, and US students. Despite the widespread occurrence of tourism around the world, the limited access of tourists to the local population limits their cultural impact to the communication of consumption patterns rather than the transmission of 'deep inter-cultural learning' (Ger and Belk 1996). Without deep inter-cultural learning, values are unlikely to change easily. Finally, some values, like individualism, appear to be adopted more quickly than others (Ralston et al. 1999). The end result is that the direction and form of cultural change are difficult to predict.

Unfortunately, many of the methods used by IB scholars fail to really capture the complexity of hybridization processes. Studies typically compare values or attitudes using survey instruments that are ill equipped to probe the processes by which culture is transmitted and hybridized (Lenartowicz and

Roth 1999). Most of the international business studies cited involve the application of surveys measuring values, attitudes, or moral reasoning to different groups at a single point in time. Generally, they lack a longitudinal element in the research design, and thus these studies fail to explain the processes by which these changes are occurring. More ethnographic studies will be necessary in order to understand these processes from the perspective of the people who are engaged in them (Spradley 1979).

IMPLICATIONS

International Management

Globalization and cultural balkanization significantly affect management processes in global companies. There has been great interest in the possibility of creating a global organization with a global organizational culture (Ralston et al. 1997). Yet, if cross-vergence is not just a temporary phase, but rather a permanent condition, it may be that such a global organizational culture will never be possible or, if possible, will only occur under very special conditions. Hofstede's (1984) original study of IBM managers indicates that important cultural differences persist, even in an organization known for its strong organizational culture.

Similarly, there exists evidence that although some attributes of charismatic/transformational leadership are universal, others are culturally specific (Den Hartog et al. 1999; Pillai et al. 1999). In addition, leadership attributes do not stand independently, but in configurations of attributes that create an overall style. Given processes of cultural balkanization or fragmentation, it is likely that despite certain generalizable attributes of leadership, acceptable configurations of leadership will continue to be different and continue to hybridize, making a universal leadership philosophy, beyond certain core attributes, unlikely even in global companies.

The challenge of international management research is to determine to what extent a universal leadership style and organizational culture may be possible, given the dynamics of globalization, cultural balkanization, and hybridization. Scholars should continue to direct efforts toward developing theories that will enable managers to evaluate, instruct, negotiate, and work with people of diverse cultural backgrounds that are in a state of permanent hybridization. Since hybridization is a biological term, and ecological models have been useful in explaining such social phenomena as the birth and death of firms and organizational structures, such models may also be helpful in understanding cultural hybridization as new cultural traits are born and others are discarded (Hannan and Freeman 1977).

International Marketing

Cultural balkanization and hybridization also present special challenges for the area of international marketing. Alden et al. (1999) speak of the role of global consumer culture in brand positioning. They argue that high-technology products represent this global consumer culture and are often positioned as such, while food is usually part of a local consumer culture and is usually positioned as a local product. Yet even food cannot be so neatly defined as a local product. For example, when Belize was isolated as a British colony, no such local cuisine developed (Wilk 1999). Belizean cuisine only developed when the country was opened to world trade and the global community, which demanded a local identity and cuisine from Belize. It appears that one of the elements of global culture is local identity. Thus, the strengthening of local identities is part of the same process driving global capitalism. In a sense, to be part of the global marketplace, it is necessary to have a local culture.

Clearly, one of the impacts of globalization has been an increased appreciation for the local and the ethnic. Ethnic entrepreneurs have sprung up throughout the major cities of the world, each selling their unique cultural products, whether food, music, dance, or martial arts, adapted to local tastes (Lin 1998). In addition, local companies may try to position their products within the global consumer culture (Alden et al. 1999). Conversely, positioning a product with respect to local consumer culture is not the sole domain of local companies. Take Johnson & Johnson, which Brazilians perceive as a Brazilian company (Nash 1988). These complex relations between global and local are just beginning to be examined in cross-cultural research.

Ger and Belk (1996) have studied extensively the reactions of consumers to globalization. They find that global consumption patterns frequently produce frustration and stress among consumers. As a result, a backlash to the globalization of consumption patterns is occurring. Many consumers are interested in returning to their local roots. Consumer resistance and movements of voluntary simplicity are arising, especially in the developed parts of the world. A more common response involves the 'local appropriation of global consumer goods and reconfiguration of their meaning to better fit local culture' (Ger and Belk 1996: 288). For example, Ger and Belk (1996) describe how Turkish women use dishwashers to wash their dirty spinach. But the most likely response appears to be creolization or hybridization (Hannerz 2000). In this case, people do not ascribe local meanings to global products, but create new synthesized meanings from local and global sources. Consumer responses to global consumption patterns clearly need to be studied in terms of their consequences for product positioning, publicity, and promotion.

One area that needs greater study is the role that cultural brokers play in the processes of globalization and balkanization. Cultural brokers are those who 'trade in popular culture at a national/international level' (Peace 1998: 274). They include television, radio, newspapers, sports organizers, pop concert organizers, travel and tourism agencies, and so on. Unfortunately, their role has rarely been studied in IB research. These organizations and their agents help to define the meaning of culture in a society. But we know little about how cultural brokers create markets for local or global products. For example, why are products of local culture being so rapidly produced in Belize (Wilk 1999), while Australia is importing US cultural products so rapidly that its people sometimes jokingly refer to it as the 51st state (Peace 1998)? The role of these cultural brokers and the factors that affect their decisions to import or export cultural products need to be examined more deeply.

Business Ethics

The tension between the universal and the particular goes to the heart of current debates over international business ethics. There has been a long-standing concern in ethics regarding moral absolutism versus relativism. Absolutists state that there are universal ethical principles that transcend the particularities of time and space. The relativists respond that ethical princi-ples are dependent upon local culture. Hans Kung (1997) has argued that a global ethic is possible, citing the work of the Parliament of the World's Religions (1993). That meeting concluded that there are three ethical princi-ples that are shared by all of the world's religions: respect for the intrinsic dignity of the human person, the fundamental equality and liberty of all people, and the necessary solidarity and interdependence of all human beings. But finding a common religious basis for international ethics is far from developing a global ethical practice for business.

In addition, although we may be converging on universal ethical princi-ples, it is not clear that this convergence is due to the existence of objectively universal principles rather than to globalization, which may be moving us toward common ethical beliefs and expectations. Levinson (1998) has found that the critical attitudes of Mexican secondary school students about their teachers regarding their arbitrary use of power, formality of teaching style, and favoritism, is informed by the discourses of empowerment and rights that permeate much of the mass media (television, film, music, and so on). These students are influenced by global norms of human rights through exposure to such media as well as to compatriots returning from extended periods of work in the United States. But if this universalism is emerging from the forces of globalization, rather than from a universal human impulse toward dignity as suggested by the agreement of the Parliament of World Religions, ethical divergence and cross-vergence may also occur as a result of cultural balkanization and hybridization.

Despite the forces of globalization, we know that moral reasoning is culture-dependent (Ma 1988) and it appears that moral reasoning is less susceptible to the influence of globalizing cultural agents than are attitudes toward unethical practices (Husted et al. 1996). Thus it appears that the arena of business ethics will also be subject to processes of hybridization as global attitudes are transmitted to cultures with fundamentally different ways of reasoning about moral issues. Careful research should be able to shed light on these issues.

Integrative social contracts theory is a new approach to business ethics that addresses the problem of conflicts among local ethical norms and between local norms and global norms (Donaldson and Dunfee 1994). This kind of situation can arise in multinational corporations with global policies against discrimination based on gender, for example, that may conflict with local customs. Donaldson and Dunfee (1994) argue that from an ethical point of view, local divisions of corporations may observe rules based on local custom as long as they do not contradict 'hypernorms' or universal ethical principles. The key is to determine what the universal principles are. Mayer and Cava (1995) note that in some work, social contract theory includes gender discrimination as a hypernorm (Donaldson 1989), but in other work, it is subsumed within a more general respect for the dignity of the individual (Donaldson and Dunfee 1994). Thus, the identification of what is or is not a universal principle is itself a significant problem.

Given the possibility of ethical hybridization, the determination of hypernorms is difficult at best and the application of integrative social contracts theory becomes nearly impossible in many concrete cases. Kung's (1997) hope for a global ethic, as summarized in the conclusions of the Parliament of the World's Religions, may be realized only at the most general of levels of agreement. In addition, given different ways of reasoning about moral problems, which seem resistant to forces of globalization, shared attitudes will still lead to different applications. Research into the interaction between globalization, cultural balkanization, and the formation of ethical norms and attitudes is sorely needed.

The dynamic between the global and the local also has an impact on expectations of corporate citizenship. For example, in the area of corporate environmental responsibility, the work of Greenpeace and international advocacy networks has sensitized both business and government to the environmental problems that are occurring around the world as well as to their possible impacts on people at home (Wapner 1996; Keck and Sikkink 1998). Many segments of the public now see corporate citizenship as an important responsibility of the business firm (Tichy et al. 1997). Yet in many ways multinational firms are only beginning to realize that they must not only be good global citizens, but good local citizens as well, responding to local problems and issues. The environmental movement has allied itself with local, indigenous groups in order to fight the economic dangers wrought by globalization (Brosius 1999). Corporate social responsibility and environmental sustainability may be reflected in universal concerns and global movements, but the concrete application usually remains local and may even operate against globalization. For example, the protesters at the 1999 World Trade Organization meetings in Seattle were motivated by diverse local causes to attack globalization, while being enabled to organize because of the development, not only of new technologies like the Internet, but also because of the emergence of a global awareness and concern about the impacts of business activity. IB needs to study how global technologies and tendencies change local issues into new hybrid forms, even as those local issues provide the basis for opposition to globalization.

CONCLUSIONS

Clearly, the twin processes of cultural balkanization and globalization provide much grist for the IB researcher's mill. These related processes seem to mean that concepts of global organizational culture, global leadership, global consumer markets, and global ethics are somewhat inaccurate as the tension between these two processes continues to generate new variation, which makes a truly 'global' anything somewhat elusive. Global culture would seem to be possible only under conditions where all barriers in time and space are broken. Given the impossibility, at least for now, of such a scenario, cultural variability may actually be increasing as a result of hybridization.

Globalization and cultural balkanization create a complex dynamic that cannot be adequately understood with the cross-sectional studies common in international management research. We need theory, probably based on ecological models, not only to understand culture and its impact on managerial practice at a given point in time, but also to explain how cultural change, especially hybridization, occurs and how it will affect managerial practice in the future. Clearly, the opportunities for IB research are enormous.

REFERENCES

Alden, Dana L., Jan-Benedict E.M. Steenkamp, and Rajeev Batra (1999), 'Brand Positioning in Asia, North America, and Europe: The Role of Global Consumer Culture', *Journal of Marketing*, 63, 75–87.

Appadurai, Arjun (1990), 'Disjuncture and Difference in the Global Economy', in Mike Featherstone (ed.), *Global Culture: Nationalism, Globalization and Modernity*, London: Sage Publications.

Barber, Benjamin (1995), *Jihad vs. McWorld*, New York: Times Books.

Barton, Thomas D. (1998), 'Troublesome Connections: The Law and Post-enlightenment Culture', *Emory Law Journal*, 47(1), 163–236.

Bennett, William J. (1998), 'Is Affirmative Action on the Way Out? Should It Be? A Symposium', *Commentary*, 105(3), March, 18–57.

Boli, John and George M. Thomas (1997), 'World Culture in the World Polity: A Century of International Non-governmental Organization', *American Sociological Review*, 62, 171–90.

Brosius, J. Peter (1999), 'Anthropological Engagements with Environmentalism', *Current Anthropology*, 40(1), 277–309.

Davis, Wade (1999), 'Vanishing Cultures', *National Geographic*, 196 (August), 62–89.

Dawson, Lorne L. (1998), 'The Cultural Significance of New Religious Movements and Globalization: A Theoretical Prolegomenon', *Journal for the Scientific Study of Religion*, 37(4), 580–95.

Den Hartog, N. Deanne, Robert J. House, Paul J. Hanges, and Antonio S. Ruiz-Quintanilla (1999), 'Culture Specific and Cross-culturally Generalizable Implicit Leadership Theories: Are Attributes of Charismatic/Transformational Leadership Universally Endorsed?', *Leadership Quarterly*, 10(2), 219–56.

DiMaggio, P.J. and W.W. Powell (1983), 'The Iron Cage Revisited: Institutional Isomorphism and Collective Rationality in Organizational Fields', *American Sociological Review*, 48, 147–60.

Donaldson, Thomas (1989), *The Ethics of International Business*, New York: Oxford University Press.

Donaldson, Thomas and Thomas W. Dunfee (1994), 'Toward a Unified Conception of Business Ethics: Integrative Social Contracts Theory', *Academy of Management Review*, 19(2), 252–84.

Friedman, Jonathan (1990), 'Being in the World: Globalization and Localization', in Mike Featherstone (ed.), *Global Culture*, London: Sage Publications, pp. 311–28.

Ger, Güliz (1999), 'Localizing in the Global Village: Local Firms Competing in Global Markets', *California Management Review*, 41(4), 64–83.

Ger, Güliz and Russell W. Belk (1996), 'I'd Like to Buy the World a Coke: Consumptionscapes of the "Less Affluent World"', *Journal of Consumer Policy*, 19, 271–304.

Hannan, Michael T. and John Freeman (1977), 'The Population Ecology of Organizations', *American Journal of Sociology*, 82 (March), 929–64.

Hannerz, Ulf (2000), 'Scenarios for Peripheral Cultures', in Frank J. Lechner and John Boli (eds), *The Globalization Reader*, Malden, MA: Blackwell Publishers, pp. 331–7.

Hofstede, Geert (1984), *Culture's Consequences: International Differences in Work-related Values*, Beverly Hills, CA: Sage Publications.

Hofstede. Geert (1997), *Cultures and Organizations: Software of the Mind*, New York: McGraw-Hill.

Huntington, Samuel P. (1993), 'The Clash of Civilizations', *Foreign Affairs*, 72(3), 22–49.

Husted, Bryan W., Janelle B. Dozier, Timothy J. McMahon, and Michael W. Kattan (1996), 'The Impact of Cross-national Carriers of Business Ethics on Attitudes about Questionable Practices and Moral Reasoning', *Journal of International Business Studies*, 27(2), 391–411.

Keck, Margaret E. and Kathryn Sikkink (1998), *Activists beyond Borders: Advocacy Networks in International Politics*, Ithaca, NY: Cornell University Press.

Keohane, Robert O. and S. Joseph Nye (1989), *Power and Interdependence*, Reading, MA: Addison-Wesley Publishing.

Kraidy, Marwan M. (1999), 'The Global, the Local, and the Hybrid: A Native Ethnography of Glocalization', *Critical Studies in Mass Communication*, 16, 456–76.

Kung, Hans (1997), 'A Global Ethic in an Age of Globalization', *Business Ethics Quarterly*, 7, 17–31.

Lechner, Frank J. (1993), 'Global Fundamentalism', in William H. Swatos (ed.), *A Future for Religion*, Newbury Park, CA: Sage Publications, pp. 27–32.

Lenartowicz, Tomasz and Kendall Roth (1999), 'A Framework for Cultural Assessment', *Journal of International Business Studies*, 30(4), 781–98.

Levinson, Bradley, A. (1998), 'The Moral Construction of Student Rights: Discourse and Judgment among Mexican Secondary School Students', *Journal of Contemporary Ethnography*, 27(1), 45–84.

Lin, Jan (1998), 'Globalization and the Revalorizing of Ethnic Places in Immigration Gateway Cities', *Urban Affairs Review*, 34(2), 313–39.

Ma, H.K. (1988), 'The Chinese Perspectives on Moral Judgment Development', *International Journal of Psychology*, 23, 201–27.

Mayer, Don and Anita Cava (1995), 'Social Contract Theory, and Gender Discrimination', *Business Ethics Quarterly*, 5(2), 257–70.

Meyer, John, John Boli, George M. Thomas, and Francis O. Ramirez (1997), 'World Society and the Nation State', *American Journal of Sociology*, 103, 144–81.

Nash, Laura (1988), 'Johnson & Johnson's Credo', in James Keogh (ed.), *Corporate Ethics: A Prime Business Asset*, New York: the Business Roundtable, pp. 77–104.

Nath, Raghu (1986), 'Role of Culture in Cross-cultural and Organizational Research', in Richard N. Farmer (ed.), *Advances in International Comparative Management*, 2, Greenwich, CT: JAI Press, pp. 249–67.

Peace, Ada (1998), 'Anthropology in the Postmodern Landscape: The Importance of Cultural Brokers and their Trade', *Australian Journal of Anthropology*, 9(3), 274–84.

Pieterse, Jan Nederveen (1994), 'Globalisation as Hybridisation', *International Sociology*, 9(2), 161–84.

Pillai, Rajnandini, Terri A. Scandura, and Ethlyn A. Williams (1999), 'Leadership and Organizational Justice: Similarities and Differences across Cultures', *Journal of International Business Studies*, 30(4), 763–79.

Ralston, David A., David J. Gustafson, Fanny M. Cheung, and Robert H. Terpstra (1993), 'Differences in Managerial Values: A Study of U.S., Hong Kong, and PRC Managers', *Journal of International Business Studies*, 24(2), 249–75.

Ralston, David A., David H. Holt, Robert H. Terpstra, and Yu Kai-Cheng (1997), 'The Impact of National Culture and Economic Ideology, on Managerial Work Values: A Study of the United States, Russia, Japan, and China', *Journal of International Business Studies*, 28, 177–207.

Ralston, David A., Nguyen Van Thang, and Nancy K. Napier (1999), 'A Comparative Study of the Work Values of North and South Vietnamese Managers', *Journal of International Business Studies*, 30(4), 655–72.

Ricks, David A., Brian Toyne, and Zaida Martinez (1990), 'Recent Developments in International Management Research', *Journal of Management*, 16(2), 219–53.

Robertson, Roland (1990), 'Mapping the Global Condition: Globalization as the Central Concept', in Mike Featherstone (ed.), *Global Culture*, London: Sage Publications, pp. 15–30.

Robertson, Roland (1995), 'Glocalization: Time–Space and Homogeneity–Heterogeneity', in M. Featherstone, S. Lash and R. Robertson (eds), *Global Modernities*, London: Sage Publications, pp. 25–44.

Robertson, Roland and JoAnn Chirico (1985), 'Humanity, Globalization, and Worldwide Religious Resurgence', *Sociological Analysis*, 46, 219–42.

Rokeach, Milton (1973), *The Nature of Human Values*, New York: The Free Press.

Sassen, Saskia and Kwame Anthony Appiah (1998), *Globalization and its Discontents*, New York: The New Press.

Sklair, Leslie (1995), *Sociology of the Global System*, Baltimore, MD: Johns Hopkins University Press.

Spradley, James P. (1979), *The Ethnographic Interview*, Fort Worth, TX: Harcourt Brace Jovanovich.

Tichy, Noel M., Andrew R. McGill, and Lynda St. Clair (eds) (1997), *Corporate Global Citizenship: Doing Business in the Public Eye*, San Francisco, CA: The New Lexington Press.

Tomlinson, John (1991), *Cultural Imperialism: A Critical Introduction*, Baltimore, MD: Johns Hopkins University Press.

Wapner, Paul (1996), *Environmental Activism and World Civic Politics*, Binghampton, NY: State University of New York Press.

Wilk, Richard R. (1999), '"Real Belizean food": Building Local Identity in the Transnational Caribbean', *American Anthropologist*, 101(2), 244–55.

PART II

Interfaces between business and institutions

6. Emerging issues in MNC–host government relations in developing countries[1]

Ravi Ramamurti

One important issue in international business research has been the relationship between multinational corporations (MNCs) and host governments, especially in developing countries. Historically, that relationship has been fraught with conflict. In the 1960s and 1970s, host governments in many developing countries – with a few exceptions like Hong Kong or Singapore – feared the power of MNCs and their capacity to inflict costs on host countries in the course of optimizing global operations. To guard against these risks, many governments engaged in case-by-case bargaining with MNCs on the conditions under which they would operate in the host country. Typically, these conditions covered such things as the extent of foreign ownership in the host country subsidiary, technology transfer from parent to subsidiary, export requirements, local content requirements, constraints on profit and capital repatriation, or the role of expatriate staff.

However, in the 1980s and 1990s, relations between MNCs and host countries changed dramatically. As Dunning (1998: 280) notes, they changed from being 'predominantly adversarial and confrontational to being non-adversarial and cooperative'. Raymond Vernon, who drew attention (Vernon 1977) to the conflicts between MNCs and host governments, noted in *In the Hurricane's Eye* (Vernon 1998) that many developing countries had begun actively to court MNCs and foreign direct investment rather than to block or screen them out. Similar sentiment is echoed in Weigel et al. (1997) and in official publications like the United Nations' *World Investment Report*.

The new environment for FDI in developing countries presents a number of challenges for international business (IB) scholars, including raising the following questions:

1. Why did so many developing countries shift in the 1980s and 1990s from restrictive FDI policies to MNC-friendly policies?
2. Has that shift rendered host government policies irrelevant to MNCs, and does it mean that MNCs now face few restrictions on which developing countries they can enter and on how they operate in those countries?
3. What does the changing nature of MNC–host developing country relations mean for traditional bargaining models of the Fagre and Wells (1982) type that helped explain MNC–host government relationships in the 1960s and 1970s? Can the changes in MNC–host government relations be explained within those frameworks, with or without modifications, or has the world changed so much that traditional bargaining models are no longer a useful paradigm?

These emerging research issues are addressed in this chapter. I start by documenting the fact that developing countries have become more MNC-friendly in the 1990s. Scanning the international business literature suggests that bargaining models of the past have indeed become obsolete in today's environment. First, the old models had only two parties to the negotiation – the MNC and the host government – but in today's environment a number of additional actors are relevant, including the MNC's home government and international institutions, such as the International Monetary Fund (IMF) and the World Bank. Second, as a corollary, traditional bargaining models considered only microeconomic variables, such as the MNC's competitive advantages or the size and rate of growth of the host country's market for the products or services offered by the MNC. In today's more complex environment, macroeconomic and macro-political factors pertaining to home and host country are also relevant considerations. Finally, traditional bargaining models were static, in the sense that the parameters of the models were assumed to be fixed over time. However, today reality is better understood as a dynamic, evolving process.

A dynamic, two-tier, multi-party bargaining model is proposed here as a general scheme for understanding MNC–host developing country relations. Tier-1 bargaining occurs between host developing countries and home (industrialized) countries, and takes place bilaterally or through multilateral institutions like the IMF, World Bank, and WTO. These negotiations produce *macro* rules or principles governing FDI, anchored in bilateral or multilateral agreements, which then affect *micro* negotiations in tier 2 between individual MNCs and host governments. I argue further that all countries and sectors are not equally affected by tier-1 bargaining. Therefore, the old bargaining model is more relevant in countries that have made fewer concessions in tier-1 bargaining (for example, China) than those that have made deeper concessions (for example, Argentina). Similarly, it is more relevant in service sectors or natural resources, where FDI liberalization has been slower than in the case of goods. Ideas of this sort can be used to test the merits empirically of the two-tier bargaining model.

In the long run, FDI in more and more sectors and countries is likely to be determined by rules-based regimes anchored in multilateral and bilateral agreements, and the bargaining model will become less and less irrelevant. However, in the transitory period, the two-tier bargaining model is a more accurate and useful way of thinking about MNC–host government relations in the developing world than the old bargaining model.

At the outset, let me clarify what I mean by 'developing countries'. I use the term to include both mixed economy developing countries on which past bargaining models have tended to focus (Fagre and Wells 1982; Lecraw 1984; Kobrin 1987; Gomes-Casseres 1990), as well as transitional economies that became important recipients of FDI in the 1990s, following the collapse of communism.

ABOUT-TURN IN FDI POLICIES IN DEVELOPING COUNTRIES

Data on FDI flows into developing countries had a discontinuity in the 1990s. From only $20 billion in 1980 and $23.7 billion in 1990, FDI inflows rose to $120 billion in 1997, a five-fold increase in a six-year period. Between 1980 and 1996, the stock of inward and outward FDI in developing countries rose from 5 percent of GDP to 20.5 percent of GDP. This increase was more dramatic than the increase in exports and imports as a share of GDP, which rose only slightly from 51.5 percent in 1980–82 to 56.6 percent in 1994–96 (United Nations 1998: 8).

To be sure, the explosion of FDI inflows to developing countries does not imply that these countries have become FDI-friendly, since the growth could conceivably have occurred despite restrictive FDI policies. But, in fact, there is ample evidence that developing countries did liberalize their FDI policies. Wells and Wint (1990) found that even in the 1980s many countries had shifted from screening FDI to attracting it. In many countries, FDI screening and review agencies became FDI *promotion* agencies. More systematic evidence comes from the UNCTAD, which reports that from 1991 to 1997, 94 percent of the 750 regulatory changes made in FDI policies by governments were in the direction of being more favorable to FDI and only 6 percent were unfavorable (United Nations 1998: 57). In 1997, for instance, 76 countries introduced 151 changes to their FDI regulations, of which 135 were favorable to FDI, ranging from more liberal entry conditions, fewer performance requirements, more incentives, more sectoral liberalization, and more guarantees and protection for investors. Only 16 regulatory changes were unfavorable to FDI: in these instances, countries either exercised more control over FDI or reduced the incentives offered. Describing the FDI climate in 1998, this report states:

> the number of activities in which FDI is barred or restricted has been considerably reduced, especially in the manufacturing sector but also increasingly in natural resources and services, as most countries have moved to open traditionally closed industries ... Fade-out requirements have virtually disappeared. Most countries have eliminated authorization requirements for the entry of greenfield FDI, replacing them with registration, although some authorization requirements and restrictions on the number of foreign firms allowed remain in many countries ... for some 'strategic' industries ... There are also indications that certain operational conditions – such as performance requirements or those relating to the hiring of foreign managerial personnel – are becoming less significant. Certain types of performance requirements have been reduced or have become more transparent as a result of international commitments ... Exchange restrictions on repatriation of profits and capital have become exceptional measures reserved for cases of serious balance-of-payments difficulties in most countries. (United Nations 1998: 96)

As the quote shows, the scope of FDI liberalization is very broad, covering most of the issues on which negotiations used to take place earlier between MNCs and host countries. The more open climate for FDI is also highlighted in a 1997 study on the subject by the International Finance Corporation (Weigel et al. 1997). Presumably, a survey of MNCs would confirm that their perceived freedom from government controls in various functional areas is higher now than it was earlier, for example, when Lecraw (1984) surveyed manufacturing subsidiaries of US, European, and Japanese MNCs in five ASEAN countries. To our knowledge, no such comparative survey has been conducted. However, US data on parent corporations' equity share in foreign subsidiaries – a popular proxy for the relative bargaining power of MNCs – shows a slightly upward trend in developing countries.

Developing countries have also taken many other initiatives to improve the climate for foreign investment. Most of the new Double Taxation Treaties signed in the 1990s involved either an Asian country or a transitional economy as one of the signatories. There has also been an explosion of bilateral investment treaties (BITs) in the 1980s and 1990s, making for a total of 1513 BITs in 1997; every BIT involved a developing or transitional economy as one of the signatories since there are no BITs between developed countries (United Nations 1998: 85). Similarly, the membership of the Multilateral Investment Guarantee Agency (MIGA) rose from 52 in 1989 to 134 in 1996, of which 115 were developing countries (Iida 1997:100). Correspondingly, the number of applications for guarantee received by MIGA rose from 91 in

1989 to 2892 in 1996 (ibid: 108). A growing number of countries also allow MNCs to refer disputes with host governments to international conciliation and arbitration, for example through the International Center for the Settlement of Investment Disputes (ICSID). Finally, instances of expropriations in developing countries have virtually disappeared. Minor (1994: 180) could identify only 11 cases from 1981 to 1992, while he identified 83 cases in 1975 alone.

Taken together, these facts show that the governments of developing countries have begun to give MNCs greater freedom in market entry and operations and greater protection from arbitrary government interventions. How is one to reconcile these new developments with the bargaining models of the past?

TRADITIONAL BARGAINING MODELS REVISITED

Bargaining models of MNC–host government relations assume that MNC entry into developing countries involves negotiations on a case-by-case basis, with the actual entry conditions depending on the bargaining power of the two sides, which, in turn, depends on their respective strengths. This kind of scheme was used by Fagre and Wells (1982), Lecraw (1984), Kobrin (1987), and Gomes-Casseres (1990). Figure 6.1 depicts this approach by showing the two sides' sources of bargaining power and the main elements of the resulting bargain on the MNCs' terms of entry and operations.

According to previous studies, the bargaining power of MNCs is derived from their sophisticated technology, product differentiation (including strong brand names), their ability to contribute to exports, especially through intrafirm transactions, their better access to or lower cost of capital, and their product diversity. Each of these variables has been discussed extensively in the literature and therefore does not require further elaboration here. Fagre and Wells (1982) confirmed empirically that US MNCs with these strengths had higher ownership shares in their subsidiaries in Latin America. Lecraw (1984: 30) proposed one more source of bargaining power for MNCs, namely, their overall size (as measured by total assets), because larger MNCs would be more likely to have the managerial and financial resources to invest in majority-owned subsidiaries and also to undertake long drawn out negotiations with host governments. Finally, Lecraw argued that the bargaining power of MNCs would weaken if other MNCs could offer comparable advantages, that is, if host countries could play MNCs off against each other.

Several authors have identified host countries' sources of bargaining power. Root and Ahmed (1978) proposed a long list of economic, social, political, and policy variables that determined a country's attractiveness as a destination for FDI. It has been argued that countries with large, rapidly growing

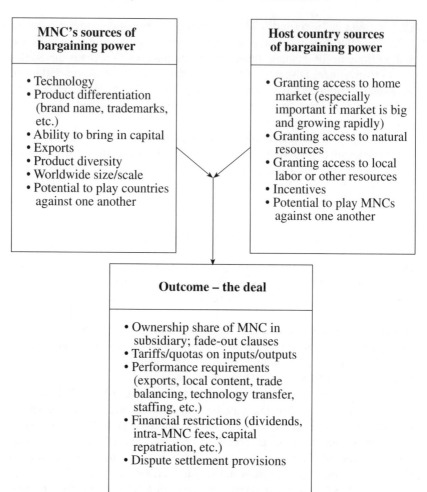

Figure 6.1   Bargaining model of MNC–host government relations

markets should enjoy higher bargaining power with MNCs (Gomes-Casseres 1990). Lecraw argued, like others before him, that the bargaining power of countries arose from their ability to limit MNCs' access to host country resources, such as local markets, labor, or raw materials. In addition, host countries could use tax and other incentives to attract MNCs or to influence their strategic decisions. Finally, the bargaining power of host countries would weaken to the extent that MNCs could play one country off against other, for example, by making them compete for FDI.

The main elements of the deal emerging from MNC–host government negotiations include the MNC's ownership share in the subsidiary, protection through tariffs and quotas, fade-out provisions, performance requirements in terms of technology transfer, local content, exports, trade balancing, or staffing, financial restrictions, such as dividend payments, capital repatriation, intra-MNC fees, transfer pricing, and so on, and dispute settlement provisions (see Figure 6.1).

Can the changes in the FDI climate in developing countries discussed in the previous section be explained within the framework of the bargaining model? Can they be explained better by incorporating new actors and variables into the bargaining model? Or has the world changed so much that the bargaining model is no longer a useful paradigm for thinking about MNC–host government relations? One can find in the IB literature at least some evidence to answer each of these questions in the affirmative. But a complete answer has to admit all of these possibilities.

ALTERNATIVE EXPLANATIONS FOR THE POLICY SHIFT

There is much evidence that developing countries have voluntarily adopted a more open stance towards FDI because of a change in development strategy. Disillusioned with closed, import-substituting industrialization, many countries turned in the 1980s and 1990s to a more open, market-friendly development strategy. As part of this shift, countries lowered tariffs, eliminated quotas, freed up exchange rates, relaxed price controls and deregulated domestic markets. With economic distortions thus reduced, private profit corresponded more closely with social profit, obviating the need for FDI screening on a case-by-case basis as was necessary when distortions were high (Wells 1998: 104). Entry strategies chosen by profit-maximizing MNCs, subject to undistorted competition in a globalizing economy, would automatically also be in the host country's interest.

Vernon (1998: 70–71) argues in the Latin American context that the liberalization of FDI was also triggered by the presence of a new generation of well-trained, often US-educated, civil service with more faith in markets and private ownership than its predecessors had. It has also been suggested that as policy makers in developing countries gained experience dealing with MNCs, their confidence in negotiating with such firms has grown. Another positive factor has been the increased diversity of MNCs, because European, Japanese, and Third World multinationals have joined American multinationals in many industries. Finally, the local private sector in many developing countries is stronger today than in the 1980s, which may also have made host governments less fearful of MNCs. In addition, some of these local firms have themselves become multinational in scope. In 1997, countries like Singapore, Korea, Taiwan, Brazil, and Mexico were registering outward FDI flows that were 10–30 percent of their inward FDI flows, and were therefore developing a vested interest in liberal FDI policies. As more developing countries turn from being only hosts to FDI to also being exporters of FDI, the forces favoring liberal FDI regimes should gather strength.

All of these arguments question the soundness of the bargaining model's premise that host governments are intent on improving the terms of MNC entry from the country's point of view by bargaining with them. If FDI screening and case-by-case negotiation with MNCs are no longer desirable or necessary from the host country's point of view, the bargaining model ceases to be a useful paradigm for thinking about MNC–host government relations. MNC entry strategies will then be determined solely by MNC preferences, transaction costs, market signals, and competition (Gomes-Casseres 1990; Buckley and Casson 1985).

We believe it would erroneous to carry this line of reasoning to the point of rejecting the bargaining model out of hand – at least as yet. First, although FDI policies in developing countries have changed from being restrictive to being more liberal, there are still significant barriers to trade and inward FDI in developing countries. A developing country that has liberalized FDI may still review projects above some cut-off size or in particular sectors, for example, services, or it may use non-traditional means to squeeze concessions out of MNCs. Besides, at any given time, the FDI policies of some developing countries will be less liberal than those of others, China being the prime example of a country that successfully courted FDI in the 1980s and 1990s despite quite restrictive FDI policies.

It is therefore more helpful to view the FDI policies of developing countries as being in various transitory stages between the highly restrictive FDI regimes of the past and the highly liberal FDI regimes that may emerge in the future (see Figure 6.2). FDI policies of a few emerging economies like Hong Kong (China) or Singapore may already be at the liberal levels one finds in the European Union or the United States, in the sense that the host country imposes few restrictions on ownership, performance requirements, or financial transfers (admittedly, the representation in Figure 6.2 is highly subjective and arbitrary; it is intended to illustrate the point rather than to compare countries' openness to FDI precisely). Most developing countries, however, may take another decade or two to adopt highly liberal FDI policies. The pace at which developing countries will liberalize FDI policies in the future is uncertain, and one cannot rule out the possibility that from time to time they may even move in the restrictive direction. This takes us to the second reason why it is premature to discard the bargaining model. Although the shift toward liberal FDI policies has been partly voluntary, to some extent the

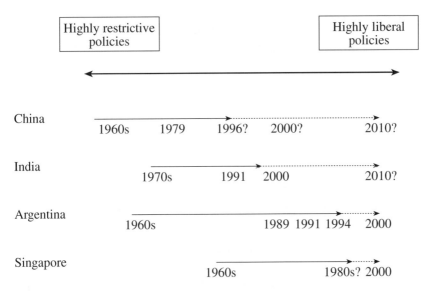

*Figure 6.2   Liberalization of FDI policies of developing countries:
subjective characterization of trends*

pace has been forced along by powerful international actors, institutions, and
agreements that have systematically strengthened the bargaining power of
MNCs and weakened that of host countries. Most of these forces will continue to push developing countries toward liberal FDI policies, but some of
them could conceivably lose steam or reverse course, giving developing
countries the opportunity to backslide toward restrictive FDI policies (see, for
example, Kennedy 1993). At any rate, our understanding of the forces that
shape MNC–host government relations in developing countries *in the transitory phase* will be richer if bargaining models of the past are modified to
include additional actors and variables that have become important now but
were relatively unimportant in the 1960s or 1970s.

A NEW BARGAINING MODEL

Figure 6.3 presents a two-tier bargaining model that retains the original bargaining model as one tier of the negotiating process but adds another tier in
which host developing countries bargain bilaterally with industrialized countries or with multilateral institutions like the IMF, World Bank, and the WTO
on various matters including FDI. Since there is no 'GATT for FDI', industrialized countries have tried to liberalize FDI either through bilateral negotiations

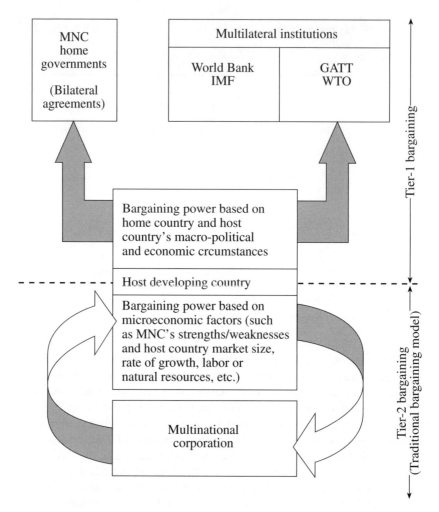

Figure 6.3   Two-tier bargaining model

or by linking FDI to the agendas of multilateral institutions meant for other purposes, such as ones providing development finance (for example, The World Bank), financing balance-of-payments crises (that is, the IMF), or negotiating trade deals (that is, the WTO). In addition, they have slowed or reduced official capital flows, including aid and multilateral lending, to developing countries, as a result of which developing countries have had to rely more on private capital flows, including FDI. The United States has been particularly aggressive in using these means to liberalize trade and FDI in developing countries.

Tier-1 bargaining became much more important in the 1980s and 1990s than in previous decades. For instance, of the 41 Bilateral Investment Treaties signed by the United States with developing countries through the end of 1998, seven were signed in the 1980s and 34 in the 1990s. Prior to 1980, 95 percent of all World Bank lending was for investment projects and only 5 percent was for adjustment lending, but by 1992 those percentages had changed to 75 percent and 25 percent, respectively; economic liberalization, including some degree of FDI liberalization, was usually a condition for disbursing structural adjustment loans (World Bank 1992: 33). Previous GATT rounds mostly affected trade in goods, but the Uruguay Round touched on issues such as intellectual property rights, local content, and services – all of which had implications for FDI. Similarly, while regional trade agreements were limited traditionally to trade issues, recent agreements like NAFTA and Mercosur have also covered FDI and dispute settlement issues. And, although home governments have rallied to the support of their beleaguered MNCs in the past, in the 1980s and 1990s, such support was proactive rather than reactive and much more widespread.

While tier-2 bargaining is driven by micro variables, such as the uniqueness of an MNC's technology or the size of the host country market for a particular product, tier-1 bargaining is driven by macroeconomic and political variables. Bilateral bargaining may be driven by the magnitude of bilateral trade between the countries, which side enjoys the bilateral trade surplus, how much aid the developing country is receiving, historical and cultural ties between the two countries, geopolitics, and so on (Bayard and Elliott 1994; Vandevelde 1993). Bargaining with multilateral institutions like the IMF and the World Bank is shaped by the severity of the borrowing country's economic crisis, its relationship with industrialized countries, its size, its dependence on bilateral or multilateral aid, and so on (Babai 1988). Finally, negotiations in multilateral forums like GATT or its successor, the World Trade Organization, are complex because of the number of parties and interlinked issues involved (Winham 1998). It is beyond the scope of this chapter to model comprehensively the tier-1 bargaining process, including its several sub-processes. We hope future research will do more justice to this topic than is attempted here.

In what follows we lay out the impact of tier-1 bargaining on the tier-2 bargaining process. Where possible that impact is pinpointed by indicating how a tier-1 actor or institution affects a particular source of bargaining power for MNCs or host governments. In this way, we try to show how tier-1 bargaining alters the context for tier-2 bargaining.

The liberalization of FDI policies in the developing world may have been partly voluntary, but the tier-1 bargaining process has also been a factor. It is not possible to separate the voluntary element from that which was forced upon developing countries, and so we make no claim that the one or the other was more important. Our only point is that FDI liberalization in developing countries is not simply the result of a unilateral shift in developmental strategy but also the result of tier-1 bargaining, and is anchored in a patchwork of bilateral, plurilateral, and multilateral agreements.

DETERMINANTS OF TIER-1 BARGAINING

We begin the discussion of Tier-1 bargaining by looking at concessions made in bilateral negotiations.

Bilateral Negotiations

Two developments in bilateral relations between developing countries and industrialized countries have profoundly affected FDI policies in the former. One is the cutback in aid offered by industrialized countries to developing countries, and the other is the more aggressive approach taken by industrialized countries, particularly the United States, to liberalize FDI policies in developing countries through unilateral actions and bilateral negotiations.

In the 1980s and 1990s, official capital flows to developing countries either stagnated or declined. Grants from rich countries to developing countries fell in real terms, and their share in capital flows to developing countries fell from 30 percent in 1990 to 8.3 percent in 1997 (all statistics in this paragraph are derived from the World Bank 1998). There was also a sharp decline in official bilateral loans to developing countries, from $11.6 billion in 1990 to a net *outflow* of $7.2 billion in 1996 and an inflow of only 1.8 billion in 1997. At the same time, multilateral development finance (consisting mainly of IMF and World Bank loans) stagnated at $10–15 billion, and their share in capital flows to developing countries fell from 16 percent in 1990 to less than 6 percent in 1997. One reason for this was that World Bank lending declined for sectors that had been privatized. In all, official development finance fell from $56 billion in 1990 to $44 billion in 1997, making developing countries more dependent on private capital flows. Following the debt crisis of 1982, commercial bank lending to developing countries almost ground to a halt. Developing countries then turned increasingly to other sources of private capital, including FDI and portfolio flows. By 1997, private capital accounted for 85 percent of capital flows into developing countries, about half of which was FDI. Thus, MNCs once again became important as sources of not only technology or marketing skills but also of capital, as had been the case in the 1950s and 1960s.

The other important development on the bilateral front was the signing of bilateral investment treaties (BITs) that pried away FDI restrictions in developing countries 'BIT by BIT', as one observer put it (Salacuse 1990). We will illustrate this using the example of the United States, an important economic actor and an aggressive user of this approach. A government document describes unabashedly the objectives of the US BIT program as 'promoting US exports and enhancing the international competitiveness of US companies' (US Trade Representative's Office 1999). US BITs were more comprehensive than most BITs in furthering the interests of MNCs. They assured US MNCs the better of national or MFN (Most Favored Nations) treatment at the time of entry and thereafter, they established clear limits on expropriation and called for prompt and fair compensation, and they guaranteed that US investors would have the right to transfer funds into and out of the country at market exchange rates. Unlike BITs signed by other countries, US treaties also prohibited performance requirements, such as local content or export quotas. They ensured that US investors would have the right to submit investment disputes to international arbitration, with no requirement to use domestic courts. And, finally, they gave US investors the right to engage top managerial personnel of their choice. In other words, US BITs removed from the negotiation agenda most of the issues on which MNCs and host governments used to haggle (see Figure 6.1).

Among the top ten recipients of FDI in the developing world in 1997, Argentina and Poland had signed BITs with the United States, while Mexico was covered through the provisions of NAFTA. But the following top ten hosts to FDI in 1997 had *not* signed BITs with the US: Brazil, China, Chile, Hungary, Indonesia, Singapore, and Venezuela. The US seems to have been more successful at persuading smaller mixed economies and transitional economies to sign BITs than larger mixed economies (Vandevelde 1993).

But the bilateral investment treaty was only one tool in the US armory to open foreign markets to US products and MNCs. Other tools included the use of Section 301 and Super-301 provisions of US trade laws to pry open particular sectors in countries like Brazil, China, India, Indonesia, and Korea – a practice that Bhagwati and Patrick (1990) called 'aggressive unilateralism'. US actions under Section 301 not only pertained to trade matters but to FDI restrictions as well. In addition, the US can impose unilateral sanctions on host governments that are hostile to US investors. A report by the US International Trade Commission identified 42 separate laws that authorize economic sanctions by the US, including 142 statutory provisions pertaining to unilateral economic sanctions (USITC 1998: ix–x). Although most of these pertained to terrorism or nuclear proliferation, some provisions applied to expropriation of US investors' assets. The sanctions are applied through US trade, aid, or finance policies. For instance, the terms of the Generalized System of Preferences call for withdrawal of benefits from a host country that expropriates US investors' properties without prompt and adequate compensation. The Hickenlooper Amendment calls for the withholding of US aid from countries that act similarly, while the Gonzales Amendment demands that US representatives in multilateral financial institutions vote against loans to offending countries (Wells 1998: 38).

Other exporters of FDI also signed bilateral treaties with developing and transitional economies for the same reasons. In this manner, FDI policies were liberalized in the developing world, one bilateral relationship at a time.

Multilateral Negotiations

We include under this category both multilateral negotiations, like those conducted under GATT or WTO auspices, and negotiations with multilateral institutions, like the IMF and the World Bank.

Multilateral financial institutions

Although multilateral lending became less important as a source of finance for developing countries in the 1980s and 1990s, the influence of the IMF and the World Bank over policy-making in developing countries increased in this period as they engaged in structural adjustment lending. The 'conditionalities' attached to these loans required the liberalization of not only fiscal, trade, exchange rate, and industrial policy, but also FDI policy. In addition, the privatization of state-owned enterprises was expected.

To encourage FDI and portfolio inflows, developing countries were required to relax rules on foreign ownership, performance requirements, taxation of dividends or capital gains, guarantee convertibility, and so on. Highly indebted countries like Argentina, Chile, Mexico, the Philippines, Peru, and Venezuela, that sought debt relief in the 1980s under a Brady work-out usually agreed to deeper liberalization in all areas including FDI. Later, similar conditionalities were imposed by the IMF and the World Bank on other borrowers, including transition economies (after the collapse of communism), and the Asian economies (after the 1997 financial crisis).

Not only have the Bretton Woods' sister institutions coordinated their programs tightly in recent years, they have also begun to work more closely with the G-7 countries as the size and complexity of rescue packages have increased. For instance, in the case of the Brady Plan, IMF and World Bank money was combined with debt write-down by US commercial banks and backed by zero-coupon bonds issued by the US Treasury. The United States provided almost half the funds for the Mexican bail-out in 1995, while the money for the Asian bail-outs in 1997–98 and the Brazilian bail-out in 1999 came from several rich countries as well as the IMF and the World Bank. FDI liberalization was invariably a condition of these rescue packages.

The extent of FDI liberalization expected by multilateral institutions as a condition for emergency financing is illustrated by the experience of Asian countries after the financial crisis of 1997–98. For instance, between June 1997 and July 1998, Korea liberalized fully the hostile takeover of Korean firms by foreign investors, waived government approval of such takeovers except when national security was involved, allowed foreign banks and securities to enter the market, and abolished the ceiling on individual or aggregate foreign ownership of listed Korean companies. A Foreign Investment Promotion Act was passed that opened up all types of businesses to foreign investors in principle, allowed foreigners to participate in the privatization of large public enterprises in key industries, liberalized the real-estate market and offered tax and other incentives to foreign investors (United Nations 1998: 341). FDI was similarly liberalized after the Asian financial crisis in Indonesia, Malaysia, the Philippines, and Thailand (see ibid. for details).

The cumulative effect of the IMF and World Bank's one-by-one approach to FDI liberalization was substantial. Each of the following countries, which were among the top ten recipients of FDI in the developing world in 1997, sought emergency financing from the IMF/World Bank in the last decade: Argentina, Brazil, Chile, Hungary, Indonesia, Mexico, Poland, and Venezuela. The only countries among the top ten recipients that had not signed BITs with the United States nor sought emergency financing from the multilateral institutions were China and Singapore.

One might wonder if countries that liberalized FDI following a structural adjustment loan reverted to restrictive policies after the economic crisis passed; after all, conditions imposed by multilateral agencies do not have the permanency of bilateral or multilateral agreements. The evidence shows, at least until 1999, that there was not much backsliding to restrictive FDI. One reason was that when FDI was liberalized, the new rules had a multi-year or indefinite validity. But the more important reason was that many of these countries went back for a second or third round of emergency funding from the IMF and the World Bank (for example, Argentina, Brazil, Mexico, Venezuela), in which case they had to liberalize FDI policies even further. In the case of Mexico, for instance, after the 1994 peso crisis, additional sectors, such as financial services and electricity, were opened up to FDI. In Argentina, the tequila crisis saw FDI policies even further liberalized, especially in banking and financial services.

The other important factor promoting liberalization of FDI policies in these countries was the privatization of state-owned enterprises. Since many SOEs were too big to be purchased by local investors, foreign investors had to be attracted. Between 1989–93, 30 per cent of the privatization revenues in Latin America and 57 per cent of the privatization revenues in Europe and Central Asia were raised from foreign investors, two-thirds of which came as direct investment and one-third of which came as portfolio investment (Sader 1995: 34, 42). In the transition economies, FDI linked to privatization accounted for 43.4 percent of total FDI inflows into the bloc from 1988–93, while the corresponding number for Latin America was 14.9 percent (Sader 1995: 17). A particularly important consequence of the privatization trend was that sectors in which FDI had previously been highly restricted, such as public utilities and other services, were suddenly opened up to foreign investment.

As a result of the country-by-country approach to FDI liberalization, implemented bilaterally or multilaterally, competition among host countries for FDI was progressively increased, with each host trying to be more FDI-friendly than the others. From the MNCs' point of view, it was wonderful that FDI liberalization occurred simultaneously in so many countries, because it enhanced their bargaining power. One thus saw in the 1980s and 1990s that despite incentives and liberal FDI policies, competition among host countries for FDI was fierce. For instance, many of the early privatizations in developing and transitional economies often attracted only one or two qualified foreign bidders each, and sometimes not even that (for examples from airlines and telecommunications in Latin America, see Ramamurti 1996). The heightened competition among host countries for FDI is confirmed by the reduction in the share of the top ten developing country hosts of FDI (excluding China) – from 82 percent in 1984–89 to 73 percent in 1997 (calculated from data in United Nations 1998: 361–5; United Nations 1996: 227–31). In the same period, five new countries joined the list of top ten hosts of FDI in the developing world, of whom three were transition economies – the Czech Republic, Hungary, and Poland.

Multilateral trade agreements/institutions

We turn finally to FDI liberalization brought about through the Uruguay Round of trade talks. On the one hand, this round saw a cut in tariffs imposed by developing countries, which at the margin reduced the incentive for MNCs to undertake market-seeking FDI. But, more importantly, the Uruguay Round included for the first time several provisions that affected developing countries' FDI policies, although always in the guise of addressing some trade-related issues. These covered intellectual property rights through the TRIPS (Trade-related Aspects of Intellectual Property Rights) agreement, performance requirements through the TRIMS (Trade-related Investment Measures) agreement, and services, through the General Agreement on Trade in Services (GATS).

Since the Uruguay Round deal was concluded only in December 1994 and developing countries did not have to be in full compliance with many provisions until 2000 or later, this agreement cannot explain the changes in

MNC–host government relations that occurred in the past. But it will increase the bargaining power of MNCs in the years to come, and, more importantly, it has set important precedents for raising and negotiating FDI issues within the WTO framework.

The TRIPS agreement   The TRIPS provisions, which came into effect in January 1995, covered all forms of intellectual property, including copyrights, trademarks, industrial designs, process and product patents, including new varieties of plants, the layout of integrated circuits, trade secrets, and test data. In each case, minimum standards of protection similar to those in the US were agreed upon (50 years protection for copyrighted works and 20 years from filing for patents). Developing countries were given five years to change their laws to comply with these requirements, while the least developed countries were given ten years, or until 2005, to comply.

Collectively, these provisions strengthen the ability of MNCs to leverage their traditional strengths, that is, intangible assets like technology, know-how, brand names, and trademarks. Copyright provisions will help MNCs in sectors such as software, entertainment, and publishing, while the patent provisions will help MNCs in pharmaceuticals.

The TRIMS agreement   For the first time in multilateral trade negotiations, the Uruguay Round restricted host countries' rights to impose local content or trade-balancing requirements. The rationale was that such policies were trade-restricting or trade-distorting and therefore inconsistent with GATT's guarantee of national treatment for imported goods (Article III) and prohibition of quantitative restrictions on imports and exports (Article XI). Countries had to notify the WTO of instances in which they were in violation of TRIMS, and end those practices within two years, in the case of industrialized countries, and within 5–7 years, in the case of developing countries. By August 1998, 25 developing countries had submitted notifications per this requirement.

The TRIMS agreement did not prohibit export performance requirements, export incentives, or technology transfer requirements. Nor did it question the right of countries to screen FDI. But the provisions included took away the right to impose local content requirements, and they created a committee on TRIMs under WTO's Council for Trade in Goods. Most importantly, the Council for Trade in Goods was required to 'consider whether the Agreement should be complemented with provisions on investment policy and competition policy' (Article IX, TRIMS). In September 1996, working groups were formed to study these questions.

At the same time, the OECD began negotiations on the Multilateral Agreement on Investment (MAI), which developing countries were to be free to join if they wished. Some observers saw in this the risk that developing countries might join MAI on the 'apprehension that a non-signatory developing country will be at a disadvantage in competing for FDI as compared to a signatory one' (Ganesan 1998: 2). Although the MAI negotiations ran aground in late 1998, developing countries' FDI policies came under renewed scrutiny in trade talks, including at the December 1999 WTO meeting held in Seattle.

Other WTO provisions   The agreement leading to the creation of the WTO also included a multilateral agreement on trade in services (GATS), an understanding on the rules for settling disputes, and a plurilateral agreement liberalizing government services. The only developing countries to sign the agreement on government services were Korea, Hong Kong, and Singapore, and therefore other developing countries can still use access to government markets as a bargaining chip with MNCs. The dispute settlement provisions will require developing countries to live up to the promises they have made on TRIMS and TRIPS or risk facing WTO-approved sanctions. The agreement on services has potentially important ramifications for developing countries, inasmuch as these sectors have typically been closed to imports and often require direct investment to serve local markets. But GATS only requires countries to extend MFN treatment, adopt transparent policies, and agree to progressive liberalization of services. It provides the framework for signing more substantive plurilateral deals in individual sectors but does not by itself require countries to provide market access or guarantee national treatment in services.

GATS' definition of services included not only cross-border services like telecommunications and tourism but also services that might be provided 'through commercial presence in the territory' of another country (Article I) or by 'natural persons' working in another member's country. It allows countries to offer different degrees of market access and national treatment in each mode of service delivery. But an important footnote to Article XVI of GATS notes that 'if a member undertakes a market-access commitment in relation to the supply of a service [requiring commercial presence] and if the cross-border movement of capital is an essential part of the service itself, that member is thereby committed to allow such movement of capital' (WTO, GATS, Part III, footnote 8). The same clarification is made with respect to services provided by natural persons. Thus, the thin edge of the FDI wedge was introduced into the GATS deal. By 1999, 'specific commitments' agreements had been signed under the GATS framework by 72 countries for telecommunications and by several countries for financial services.

TIER-2 BARGAINING

As shown in Figure 6.3 , tier-1 bargaining has mostly weakened the bargaining power of host governments and strengthened that of MNCs. Looking ahead, there are many reasons to expect that tier-1 bargaining will continue to chip away at the FDI policy discretion of developing countries. With trade deficits continuing to be high and support for free trade waning in Congress and among the public, the US is likely to press forward unilaterally and bilaterally to loosen trade and FDI restrictions in developing countries. At the same time, developing countries are likely to become even more dependent on private capital flows, including FDI, to supplement domestic savings and finance investments in manufacturing and infrastructure. This growing dependence on foreign capital, coupled with the volatility in exchange rates, may well produce more balance-of-payments crises like the ones in 1997–99, and each crisis will bring pressure from multilateral agencies to liberalize FDI policies. At the international level, if MAI negotiations are revived, some developing countries may become signatories, thereby taking the competition for FDI among developing countries to a new level. Even without MAI, the next round of WTO talks is likely to give more prominence to services and FDI issues than past rounds. Finally, the relative bargaining power of MNCs over host governments is likely to increase in the future because of the global mega-mergers that have taken place in many industries, including automobiles, banking, computers, petroleum, pharmaceuticals, software, and telecommunications. Host countries will find that there are fewer MNCs in each industry that can be pitted against one another.

On the other hand, there could conceivably be some backlash in developing countries against the cumulative effects of FDI liberalization. Host countries must be convinced that FDI liberalization has served their interests, or else local opponents of MNCs may try to move policies in the opposite direction. However, international agreements will make backsliding difficult. It is certainly possible that developing countries may try to slow the pace of FDI liberalization in the future, if not reverse it. The attempt in 1999 by some countries to push their own candidate for Director-General of the WTO in open opposition to the candidate favored by the US may have been motivated by the desire to slow the pace of future trade and investment liberalization.

SOME IMPLICATIONS

We conclude this section with two implications of the two-tier bargaining model that can be used to test it empirically. The basic argument is that, through tier-1 bargaining, home governments of MNCs have systematically weakened the ability of host developing countries to extract concessions from individual MNCs in tier-2 bargaining, and that the concessions made in tier-1 bargaining vary across countries and sectors in predictable ways.

Country Variations

Countries with the following characteristics are likely to have made fewer concessions in tier-1 bargaining and therefore to enjoy greater bargaining power with individual MNCs in tier-2 bargaining:

- those that are big enough or otherwise powerful enough to resist pressure from countries like the US to sign BITs or to make concessions on FDI policy in bilateral bargaining;
- those whose emergency borrowings from the IMF/World Bank have been small rather than large in relation to exports or GDP;
- those that are not members of WTO or parties to all of its agreements.

China is probably the best example of a developing country that meets all of these criteria; it is a large, important, and powerful player in the world economy, and therefore cannot easily be forced even by the United States to liberalize FDI; as late as 1999 it had not signed a BIT with the United States, nor had it sought structural adjustment loans from the IMF/World Bank, nor was it a member of the WTO. Therefore, it had made minimal concessions through tier-1 bargaining, and its FDI policies in the 1980s and early 1990s were similar to those of developing countries in the 1960s and 1970s. By all accounts, MNCs have accepted ownership, performance requirements, staffing, and dispute settlement conditions in China that they might not have accepted elsewhere, including in other large countries like Brazil or India. We expect the traditional bargaining model used by Fagre and Wells (1982) or Gomes-Casseres (1990) to hold up well in China in the 1980s and early 1990s. Conversely, we expect it not to hold up well in countries like Argentina or Mexico that greatly liberalized FDI in the 1990s as a result of tier-1 bargaining.

Proposition 1: Developing countries with large home markets, that have not been highly dependent on emergency financing from multilateral lending agencies, and that are not parties to WTO agreements, are more likely to use tier-2 bargaining to extract concessions from individual MNCs on foreign ownership, performance requirements, financial restrictions, and dispute settlement provisions. Conversely, countries with opposite characteristics will have yielded most of their bargaining power in tier-1 negotiations and therefore have little room for tier-2 bargaining.

Sector Variations

Just as the scope for tier-2 bargaining varies across countries, so too it varies across type of foreign investment, because the constraints imposed by tier-1 bargaining are more severe in some sectors than others. For example, host governments have enjoyed greater flexibility in FDI policy in natural resource or service sectors than in manufacturing sectors, especially in multilateral agreements like GATT or WTO. However, in the 1990s host governments have liberalized FDI policies even in natural resource and service sectors in response to bilateral pressures or to commitments made to multilateral agencies (United Nations 1998). For example, large private capital inflows into developing countries in the 1990s have occurred in telecommunications, electricity, roads, ports, banking, and other infrastructure or service sectors, as these sectors were deregulated and privatized (World Bank 1995). But FDI in these sectors was still heavily regulated and subject to case-by-case negotiation, covering matters such as foreign ownership and, to a lesser extent, performance requirements (see, for example, Wells and Gleason 1995). Foreign investors receiving special incentives and tax breaks have also been subject to case-by-case negotiations with host governments (United Nations 1996; Guisinger and Associates 1985). The WTO has set limits on the extent of export incentives that host governments can offer, but it will be a while before WTO agreements prohibit other kinds of incentives.

Proposition 2: All else being equal, case-by-case tier-2 bargaining will be more relevant in developing countries in sectors such as mining or infrastructure, where concession agreements and regulation are involved, and whenever special incentives are offered to foreign investors. Tier-2 bargaining will be less prevalent in manufacturing and non-regulated sectors.

AVENUES FOR FURTHER RESEARCH

To recapitulate, I have argued that relations between MNCs and host governments in developing countries in the 1960s and 1970s could be analyzed in terms of each side's bargaining power. But that static two-party bargaining model has become less relevant today, because another level of bargaining – between host governments and the home governments of MNCs – has become far more important in shaping host developing countries' FDI policies. Accordingly, in this essay I have proposed a two-tier bargaining model, whose lower tier is the original bargaining model and whose first tier involves country-to-country bargaining via bilateral or multilateral negotiations. Our understanding of the forces shaping MNC–host government relations in developing countries in the 1990s and beyond will be richer and more accurate if analyzed through this kind of two-tier model. Eventually, MNC–host government relations may be governed largely by a rules-based system negotiated through tier-1 bargaining and anchored in multilateral and bilateral agreements, while tier-2 bargaining will become less and less important. But until then, case-by-case bargaining between MNCs and host governments will continue to be relevant, especially in some countries and sectors. I have also advanced some propositions about the countries or sectors in which tier-2 bargaining is likely to be more important.

Returning, then, to the three questions with which this essay began, the answer to the first question is that voluntary liberalization of FDI policies by host developing countries is only a partial explanation of the MNC-friendly policies of these nations. Externally-driven tier-1 bargaining has to be recognized as another important factor driving FDI liberalization by these countries. The answer to the second research question follows directly from the fact that tier-1 bargaining is not equally important in all countries or sectors. Therefore, host governments are more important players in some countries and sectors than others, although, on average, they are less interventionist today in FDI matters than in the 1980s. Finally, as argued earlier, the traditional bargaining model is incapable of explaining by itself MNC–host developing country relations in the new millennium. It must be augmented, as proposed here, by another layer of country-to-country bargaining that circumscribes the traditional (tier-2) bargaining process.

The ideas proposed here can be extended empirically and theoretically in future work. On the empirical front, the propositions presented here and in Ramamurti (2001) can be formally tested. Such studies will confirm or reject the two-tier model. Alternatively, the two-tier model could be enriched through case studies of the FDI policy-making process in developing countries. On the theoretical front, the two-tier model can be improved by including other important actors that shape host and home country FDI policies, for example, non-governmental organizations. It would also be useful to explore whether countries are offsetting greater openness to FDI at the entry stage with greater intervention in the operational phase – similar to what has been observed in the realm of trade, that is, where the lowering of tariff barriers is offset by the erection of non-tariff barriers. Further research on these issues will add greatly to our understanding of the causes and consequences of FDI liberalization in developing countries.

NOTE

1. A shorter version of this chapter first appeared as 'The Obsolescing Bargaining Model? MNC–Host Developing Country Relations Revisited', *Journal of International Business Studies*, 32(1), First quarter 2001, 23–39.

REFERENCES

Babai, Don (1988), 'The World Bank and the IMF: Rolling Back the State or Backing its Role?' in Raymond Vernon (ed.), *The Promise of Privatization*, New York: The Council on Foreign Relations, pp. 254–85.

Bayard, Thomas O. and Kimberly Ann Elliott (1994), *Reciprocity and Retaliation in U.S. Trade Policy*, Washington DC: Institute for International Economics.

Bhagwati, Jagdish and Hugh T. Patrick (eds) (1990), *Aggressive Unilateralism: America's 301 Trade Policy and the World Trading System*, Ann Arbor: University of Michigan Press, Summer, 27–43.

Buckley, Peter J. and Mark Casson (1985), *The Economic Theory of the Multinational Enterprise: Selected Papers*, New York: St. Martin's Press.

Dunning, John H. (1998), 'An Overview of Relations with National Governments', *New Political Economy*, 3(2), 280–84.

Fagre, Nathan and Louis T. Wells Jr (1982), 'Bargaining Power of Multinationals and Host Governments', *Journal of International Business Studies*, 13(2), Fall, 9–23.

Ganesan, A.V. (1998), *Strategic Options Available to Developing Countries with Regard to a Multilateral Agreement on Investment*, Geneva: UNCTAD Discussion Paper 134.

Gomes-Casseres, Benjamin (1990), 'Firm Ownership Preferences and Host Government Restrictions: An Integrated Approach', *Journal of International Business Studies*, 21(1), 1–22.

Guisinger, Stephen E. and Associates (1985), *Investment Incentives and Performance Requirements: Patterns of International Trade, Production, and Investment*, New York: Praeger.

Iida, Akira (1997), *MIGA: The Standard-setter*, Washington DC: Multilateral Investment Guarantee Agency.

International Center for Settlement of Investment Disputes (1997), *ICSID 1997 Annual Report*, Washington DC: ICSID.

Kennedy, Charles R. Jr (1993), 'Multinational Corporations and Expropriation Risk', *Multinational Business Review*, 1(1), 44–55.

Kobrin, Stephen J. (1987), 'Testing the Bargaining Hypothesis in the Manufacturing Sector in Developing Countries', *International Organization*, Autumn, 609–38.

Lecraw, Donald J. (1984), 'Bargaining Power, Ownership, and Profitability of Transnational Corporations in Developing Countries', *Journal of International Business Studies*, 15(1), Spring/Summer, 27–43.

Minor, M.S. (1994), 'Demise of Expropriation as an instrument of LDC Policy, 1980–1992', *Journal of International Business Studies*, 25(1), 177–88.

Ramamurti, R. (ed.) (1996), *Privatizing Monopolies: Lessons from the Telecommunications and Transport Sectors in Latin America*, Baltimore, MD: Johns Hopkins University Press.

Ramamurti, R. (2001), 'The Obsolescing "Bargaining Model"? MNC–Host Developing Country Relations Revisited', *Journal of International Business Studies*, 32(1), First Quarter, 23–39.

Root, F.R. and Ahmed A. Ahmed (1978), 'The Influence of Policy Instruments on Manufacturing Foreign Direct Investment in Developing Countries', *Journal of International Business Studies*, 9(3), 81–93.

Sader, Frank (1995), *Privatizing Public Enterprises and Foreign Investment in Developing Countries, 1988–93*, Occasional Paper No. 5, World Bank: Foreign Investment Advisory Service.

Salacuse, Jeswald W. (1990), 'BIT by BIT: The Growth of Bilateral Investment Treaties and their Impact on Foreign Direct Investment in Developing Countries', *International Law Review*, 24, 655–63.

United Nations (1996), *Incentives and Foreign Direct Investment*, New York and Geneva: UNCTAD.

United Nations (1998), *World Investment Report 1998: Trends and Determinants*, New York and Geneva: UNCTAD.

USITC (United States International Trade Commission) (1998), 'Overview and Analysis of Current U.S. Unilateral Economic Sanctions', Investigation No. 332–391, August.

United States Trade Representative's Office (1999), 'US Bilateral Investment Treaty Program', available at http://www.ustr.gov/agreements/bit.pdf.

Vandevelde, Kenneth J. (1993), 'United States Bilateral Investment Treaties: The Second Wave', *Michigan Journal of International Law*, 11, 1–16.

Vernon, Raymond (1977), *Storm over the Multinationals*, Cambridge, MA: Harvard University Press.

Vernon, Raymond (1998), *In the Hurricane's Eye*, Cambridge, MA: Harvard University Press.

Weigel, Dale R., Neil F. Gregory, and Dileep M. Wagle (1997), *Foreign Direct Investment*, Washington DC: International Finance Corporation.

Wells, Louis T. Jr (1998), 'God and Fair Competition: Does the Foreign Direct Investor Face still other Risks in Emerging Markets?', in Theodore H. Moran (ed.), *Managing International Political Risk*, Malden, MA: Blackwell Publishers Ltd.

Wells, Louis T. Jr and Eric S. Gleason (1995), 'Is Foreign Infrastructure still Risky?', *Harvard Business Review*, 73, Sept.–Oct., 44–55.

Wells, Louis T. Jr and Alvin G. Wint (1990), 'Marketing a Country: Promotion as a Tool for Attracting Foreign Investment', mimeo, Washington DC: FIAS (Foreign Investment Advisory Services) Occasional Paper 1.

Winham, Gilbert R. (1998), 'The World Trade Organization: Institution-building in the Multilateral Trade System', *World Economy*, 21(3), 349–68.

World Bank (1992), *World Bank Structural and Sectoral Adjustment Operations: The Second OED Overview*, Washington DC: Operations Evaluation Department Report No. 10870.

World Bank (1995), *Bureaucrats in Business: The Economics and Politics of Government Ownership*, Oxford and New York: Oxford University Press for the World Bank.

World Bank (1998), *World Debt Tables 1997*, Washington DC: World Bank.

F23
F14
F13

7. National export promotion: a statement of issues, changes, and opportunities

Michael R. Czinkota

INTRODUCTION

Exports represent one of many market expansion alternatives. The fact that the new customers do not live in the next town or next province, but rather in another country, however, has motivated governments to devise policy instruments designed to encourage exports. This chapter will address the rationale for such government involvement in the market place. After summarizing the key export promotion approaches developed by governments during the second half of last century, an analysis of the changes in rules, requirements, and activities of governmental export promotion will be offered. The chapter concludes by presenting thoughts on why and how export promotion should be restructured in the new millennium.

WHAT MAKES EXPORTS SPECIAL?

For much of recorded history, governments have treated international trade as a special dimension of economic activity. Early on, imports received most attention. In particular during times when imports represented the rapacious capabilities of a nation, their accumulation, and thus contribution to 'national' wealth were prized. Later on, 'exchange' became the more acceptable form of wealth accumulation, which increased the importance of voluntary exports. Work by Smith (1776) and Ricardo (1819) subsequently offered theoretical insights into absolute and comparative advantage, which helped to identify export industries whose activities would be of particular benefit to a nation and its citizens.

In more recent times, the special status of exports has continued. From a governmental perspective, exports are seen as special because they can affect currency values, fiscal, and monetary policies. Since the introduction of floating exchange rates, economic theory sees exports as a key balancing beam of international economic performance. Exports also shape public perception of the competitiveness of a nation, and determine (at least in the long run) the level of imports that a country can afford. Therefore, exports are crucial for the degree of choice and quality of life experienced by consumers.

For the firm, exports offer the opportunity for economies of scale. With a broader market reach and many customers abroad, a firm can produce more, and, particularly in the manufacturing sector, produce more efficiently. As a result, exporting can lead to lower costs and higher profits both at home and abroad. This important impact of exporting on the firm has been particularly tantalizing during the past 30 years, when the value of global exports has risen from $200 billion to more than $6.8 trillion (WTO 2001) and the growth rate of exports has consistently exceeded average domestic growth rates (IMF 2000).

Exporting also brings market diversification, due to different growth rates and market conditions around the world, and provides stability by not making the firm overly dependent on any particular market. Exporting lets the firm learn from the competition, makes it sensitive to different demand structures and lets it appreciate divergent cultural environments. Exporting means that the firm has to bridge distances in transportation, communication, and financing, overcome market and customer unfamiliarity, and outperform often well entrenched domestic competitors. To do so takes courage, commitment and capability, all of which tend to affect corporate performance positively.

Research in the United States has shown that exporters of all sizes and in all industries outperform their strictly domestic counterparts – they grow more than twice as fast in sales and earn significantly higher returns on equity and assets (Taylor and Henisz 1994). Workers also benefit from export activities. Exporting firms of all sizes pay significantly higher wages than non-exporters (*Business America* 1996), and workplace stability is significantly greater for exporting plants (Richardson and Rindal 1996)

Successful exporting is therefore often proof of a firm's special talents that enable it to prosper in spite of higher transaction costs. Such a display of economic strength of the firm is, on an aggregate level, also a manifestation of the economic success and security of a nation.

WHY GOVERNMENT PROMOTION OF EXPORTS?

Given the positive effects of exports on both the nation and the firm, one could expect, in a market-driven economy that exports will take place on their own, and that export profitability will be suitable reward for the successful exporter. Nonetheless, most governments maintain an export policy that regulates, stimulates, directs, and protects exports (Czinkota 2000), thus interfering with unfettered market forces. Key reasons for this intervention are:

- Overcoming market barriers abroad
- Bridging market gaps
- Alleviating a trade deficit

These reasons and their implications for export promotion are examined below.

Overcoming Obstacles Abroad

International business practices differ on a country, regional, or even firm-specific basis. Such differences can easily result in market access barriers for an outside firm. For example, the fact that most people in France use French as their language of choice in business transactions may represent an important impediment to British managers. Their government can facilitate the circumvention or overcoming of such barriers by offering English courses in France or French courses in England. However, specific sovereign action is not required to address the problem since the private sector can find its own solution.

Conditions are different, however, when market actors, with the active or tacit support by government, devise ways specifically to harm exporting firms from other nations. In such instances, market barriers turn into unfair trade impediments, be it due to exclusionary practices or due to subsidies that provide the recipients with an unassailable competitive advantage. Such barriers are often only visible when analyzed on a systematic, cross-industry, and longitudinal basis. Often, only government may possess the confidence of firms, and the stamina and the funding to conduct such an analytical effort. Due to the imbalance of power between firms and governments, only government may be able to address the issue with its counterpart, the foreign government, and cause a change in existing practices. If there is no resolution to an unfair practice, it is principally government that can provide for other remedies and achieve change either through coercion, or through punishment. Finally, if there is inappropriate support abroad, it is typically government that has the resources to annul deleterious foreign practices. Even if the practice of public support for exports is frowned upon, such support is still seen as preferable to leaving the field to the opposition.

Bridging Market Gaps

Market gaps tend to be export barriers grounded at home. Exports require substantial investment by the firm. Such private sector investment, while helpful in areas such as product adaptation or market research, may not be sufficient when it comes to infrastructure challenges faced by the firm intending to go international. Take, for example, a comparison between Russia and the United States on the distribution dimension. For the US economy, the total cost of distribution is close to 11 percent of GDP (Bowersox et al. 1992). By contrast, Russia is only beginning to learn about the rhythm of demand and the need to bring supply in line. The country is battling warehousing space constraints, poor lines of supply, non-existent distribution and service centers, limited rolling stock, and insufficient transportation systems. Producers in the supply chain are mostly uninformed about issues such as inventory carrying cost, store assortment efficiencies, and replenishment techniques. The need for information development and exchange systems for integrated supplier–distributor alliances and for efficient communications systems is only poorly understood. As a result, distribution costs remain well above 30 percent of GDP (Czinkota 1998). Therefore, any firm intending to export from Russia is handicapped to a substantial degree by domestic infrastructural shortcomings. Overcoming such an international performance gap requires investments that can only be addressed with government involvement.

Market gaps can also exist within firms. This is particularly the case for firms that are new to the export effort. In light of the gradual development of export experience, the existence of barriers to exporting, and a firm's uncertainty with the new environment it is about to enter, management's perception of risk exposure grows. In its previous domestic expansion, the firm has gradually learned about the market, and therefore seen its risk decline. In the course of international expansion, the firm now encounters new factors such as variable currency exchange rates, greater distances, new modes of transportation, new government regulations, new legal and financial systems, and new languages. As a result, the firm is exposed to increased risk. At the same time, due to the investment needs of the exporting effort in areas such as information acquisition, market research, and trade financing, the immediate profit performance may deteriorate. Eventually international market familiarity and diversification effects are likely to reduce the risk below the previous 'domestic only' level, and increase profitability. In the short and medium term, however, managers may face an unusual and perhaps unacceptable situation – rising risk accompanied by decreasing profitability. In light of this reality, and not knowing whether there will be a pot of gold at the end of the rainbow, many executives either do not initiate export activities or discontinue them when adversity arises. Such an interruption in the working of rational economic market forces, due to human shortsightedness, may be bridged by government export assistance that helps firms over this rough patch to the point where profits again increase with stable or downward risk. (Czinkota 1994). Particularly for firms too small to be on the radar screen of consulting firms, government can lead efforts to help firms appreciate that they are ready for export or learn what they need to do to get ready. These efforts allow a better understanding of market forces and increase market transparency, which therefore contributes to the better functioning of markets (Deutsches Institut 1991).

Governmental efforts can therefore either help overcome large macro-market gaps, where export promotion offers public solutions serving the common good, or they can assist firms in overcoming temporary shortcomings and thus jump start a corporate export effort.

Alleviating a Trade Deficit

A third major rationale for export promotion consists of a government's perceived need to overcome a persistent trade deficit. The currency crises in Asia, Russia, and Latin America have shown the deleterious effects of large trade deficits on national economies. In the United States, the large and growing trade deficit that, in 2000, reached 4.3 percent of GDP (Federal Reserve 2000), gave rise to substantial concerns about its long-term sustainability (Blecker 1999; Mann 2001). Given the economic and political repercussions of such a deficit, governments often consider an increase in exports to be more benign than a forcible decrease in imports. In addition, the job creation effects of exports are economically and politically expedient. In the United States, $1 billion of exports supports the creation, on average, of 15 500 jobs (International Trade Administration 1996). Due to a greater labor intensity of exports in many other countries, the job creation effects there will be even larger. Overall, export promotion enthusiasm rides high when it is seen to overcome trade deficits and generate desirable new jobs.

These three key reasons account for the fact that governments have consistently given a place of special importance to exports, have championed the performance of exporting firms, and have, in turn, been encouraged to do so by many of their corporate constituents.

TRADITIONAL EXPORT PROMOTION APPROACHES

Governments have developed various approaches towards export promotion. One focuses on knowledge transfer to enable greater competence within firms and offers either export service programs or market development programs.

Service programs typically consist of seminars for potential exporters, export counseling, and how to export handbooks. Market development programs provide sales leads to local firms, offer participation in foreign trade shows, preparation of market analyses and export news letters (Lesch et al.

1990). Within each category, program efforts can be differentiated as to whether the intent is to provide informational knowledge (of the how-to nature) or experiential knowledge – which provides hands-on exposure (Singer 1990).

Export researchers have been able to segment exporting firms based on a wide variety of variables, and have offered the stage theory of gradual export development (Bilkey 1978; Cavusgil 1980; Czinkota 1982). From this, governments have learned that firms have different types of export support needs, depending on their level of export experience. Therefore, promotional assistance varies, depending on whether it is provided to firms that are new to exports, firms with some export experience, small exporters, or large, successful exporters.

A second export promotion approach deals with subsidization of export activities. Such government support can be direct or indirect. For example, low-cost export financing which mixes development aid monies with commercial credit funds can produce an attractive package deal, particularly for large sales which are paid for over time, such as airplanes, or power plants. Exports are also subsidized with lower tax rates for export earnings, preferential access to governmental resources and favorable insurance rates.

Governments have also been known to offer special licenses for imports if export obligations are fulfilled, or to impose offset export requirements, thus providing a firm with the opportunity to earn additional export rents. The overall focus of these subsidized activities is to increase the profitability of exporting to the firm, either by reducing the risks or by increasing the rewards.

A third approach to export promotion consists of reducing governmental red tape for exporters. For example, the requirements for multiple export licenses or permits issued by various government agencies, the imposition of technology export controls, or a confiscatory approach to export earnings are all impediments to exporting which government can remove, thus stimulating an increase in exports. Similarly, the reduction of anti-trust concerns in the export arena has led to the formation of (export) trading firms that are able to share facilities and expertise without the threat of government intervention.

Common to all these export promotion activities is the fact that they are focused on the domestic firms. Typically, governments ask their firms what support they need in order to do more or better in their export effort. The answers then determine the type of resources allocated – leading over time to substantial subsidized programs. Such a result is not entirely unexpected, since corporations the world over tend to be willing recipients of government funding.

CHANGES IN THE EXPORT PROMOTION ENVIRONMENT

The trade environment has changed, and with it the need for and capabilities of export promotion. Several rounds of trade negotiations have successfully lowered barriers to exports. High tariffs have been reduced. Non-tariff barriers have been identified and, in many instances, have been lowered. Market gaps continue, with many firms in many countries still highly reluctant to participate in exporting. In some regions, firms have benefited from an increased stability of currencies. At the same time, firms in many developing countries have been exposed to increased economic volatility and to the vicissitudes of global competition without the benefit of enhancing their own ability to compete. For them, the market gaps have grown in many instances. Their plight is now more public, due to the involvement of many concerned groups, institutions, and individuals. Yet, firms and managers in these developing countries find that it is easy for outsiders to argue for the self-actualization level in Maslow's hierarchy of needs since they do not have to worry about basic needs and since such recommendations typically are not accompanied by resources or plans.

Trade imbalances continue, particularly on the part of the United States. Given the large absorptive capacity of the US market and the important market that the US represents for many exporters, all parties will soon, if they are not already – be economic hostages to each other. Nonetheless, the continuing trade deficit tends to ensure export promotion will continue to be viewed favorably by US firms and policy makers.

The regulatory aspects of the trade environment have also changed. Decades ago governments were virtually unrestrained in their export promotion activities. Today, bilateral, plurilateral, and multilateral international accords are substantially restrictive when it comes to such government intervention. NAFTA (North American Free Trade Agreement), for example, sharply limits the extent to which governments can encourage their exports, and provides for very specific and rapid remedies when violations are suspected. The government procurement code, though limited in participation, restricts the exclusionary practices which can be used by its signatories and threatens quick retaliation if agreed upon practices are not implemented.

Most importantly, the World Trade Organization has taken a much closer look at export promotion activities, has identified trade distorting practices and has devised rules which permit the countervailing of prohibited export promotion practices. The WTO is, in particular, opposed to export subsidization measures. This opposition applies to virtually all countries and conditions. The exceptions for developing countries with a GDP of less than $1000 is likely to be of only limited impact (Laird 1997). Furthermore, the WTO's clarification of anti-dumping rules, has made it easier for any country actively to combat exporters which are believed to operate with a comparatively lower cost structure, thus making export pricing a much more sensitive issue (Schott 1994).

Additional restrictions emanate from international institutions such as the Organization for Economic Cooperation and Development (OECD) and the World Bank. The OECD has long sponsored the gentlemen's agreement on export credits, which limits the availability of below cost financing for exporters. Increasingly, this agreement is being expanded to previously sacrosanct areas such as agricultural exports and project finance (Cutts and West 1998). The World Bank, in a turnabout from earlier days, has moved away from its support of export promotion, particularly subsidization and trade promotion organizations. Bank staff claim to be disillusioned by past poor allocation of funds, weak leadership, lack of imagination and innovation, bureaucratically-oriented staff, and debilitating intervention and control by the government. As a result, there is, within the Bank, an unwillingness to support new export promotion activities (Pursell 1999).

Institutionally, it appears to many that export promotion organizations over time have become bureaucratized and politicized. Export promotion authorities have often become the grazing grounds for retired officials and have served as havens for job generation. Governments are accused of using export promotion events such as trade missions merely as tools to reward political friends. Goals have become blurred and efficiency is low. Just like the creation of state-controlled firms, export promotion institutions, in many instances, are said to have become a good idea gone bad.

Even more critically, lead countries that, for generations, have been the spear carriers for an increase in global free trade, and for an encouragement of exports, have gradually become less enthusiastic when it comes to exports. For example, in the United States, Congress has, since the mid-1990s, no longer provided the President with 'fast-track' (now known as 'trade promotion') authority to facilitate the negotiation of international trade agreements. In spite of the passage of a limited number of trade agreements, liberalizing legislation to encourage foreign exports (and domestic imports) has become very scarce.

There is one additional difficulty that confronts export promotion programs: high subsidization and large export promotion expenditures tend not to show linkage to export success! Among industrialized countries, those with particularly large exports typically are not the leaders in relative or even absolute promotion expenditures. For example, the United States – the world's leading exporter, spends 3 cents per $1000 of GDP on export promotion. This level of expenditure is followed closely by Germany's and Japan's expenditure of 5 cents per $1000 (US Department of Commerce 1996).

By contrast, the highest level of relative export promotion expenditures occurs in Burkina Faso, where a record 1.03 percent of all exports are supported by governmental promotional expenditures. However, Burkina Faso is not yet a household word in terms of export success. Overall, it appears that developing countries that have used export subsidies have not expanded their exports faster than those that have pursued less interventionist policies (*The Economist* 2000).

Research has also indicated that firms are typically less than satisfied with governmental export promotion. Czinkota and Ricks (1981) found that with increasing export experience, firms rated governmental assistance to be of decreasing use. More than a decade later, researchers showed that the needs of exporting firms and the corresponding supportive government activities were very different from each other (Kotabe and Czinkota 1992). When investigating governmental export promotion in a different country, Crick and Czinkota (1995) determined that UK firms were even less desirous of government support than US firms.

It also appears that government export promotion efforts are often conducted without much regard for industry. Take the promotion of US wood exports to Japan as an example. In its report on the US–Japan wood products initiative, the US General Accounting Office (1993) reports that trade negotiations were conducted for more than a decade, so that more US solid wood products could enter the Japanese market. High-level meetings, ongoing negotiations, government financial support, and industry demonstration projects were to achieve that goal. Japanese building codes and product certification procedures were changed and tariffs were lowered. The Foreign Agricultural Service spent more than $17 million to promote US wood product sales to Japan. The result? Canadian lumber companies are the leading wood exporters to the Japanese market. There were only marginal increases in US exports and export-related jobs. A well-intended approach did not achieve its deserved success since the focus rested on the wrong opportunities, the needs of customers were not sufficiently taken into account, and firms were unable or unwilling to adjust to market requirements.

Overall, while perhaps planned with plenty of enthusiasm and goodwill, and initiated with involvement of firms, export promotion has suffered from significant shortcomings in the more recent past.

EXPORT PROMOTION – DEAD END OR CROSSROADS?

Might one then end all export promotion and perhaps leave it all to the market? This author does not believe so. Shortcomings, if they can be remedied, highlight the need for improvement, not for abolition. New thinking needs to clarify the purpose of export promotion, and a new business environment enables and requires a new approach. However, the fact that much of traditional export promotion is becoming prohibited and restricted under WTO rules should not drive the activity underground. Doing so will only lead to even greater biases and inefficiencies. Rather, export promotion should be carried out in the open, for the right reasons and in the right way. Export promotion must be seen as offering the latest thinking and the most recent tools to bring efficiency and effectiveness to an important component of governmental policy aimed at international business.

Developing countries are likely to remain key users of export promotion. Sweeping policy reforms dominated the international trade policy debate in the 1990s, but figuring out how to help developing countries capitalize on these staggering changes is more important today. As the tide, which is to lift all boats, keeps on rising, thoughts must go to readying the boats, training the crews, and setting the sails of the developing economies. These countries must find practical ways to execute a quantum leap in terms of their economies, thus enabling them to catch up with industrialized nations. It will be instrumental to find ways to lower production costs, extend product life cycles, reduce costs of importing components, services, and manufactured goods and improve market performance (Belisle and Czinkota 1999). Export promotion will be a key aspect of translating these internal accomplishments into success on a global level.

But export promotion will also be useful for industrialized nations. Every day, new firms are being formed, are beginning to learn about the international market, and are running into barriers to international trade. The population of exporting firms does not remain stable. For example, in the US it has been found that in any given year, 15 percent of exporters will stop exporting by the next year, while 10 percent of non-exporters will enter the global market. The most critical juncture for firms is when they begin or cease exporting (Bernard and Jensen 1997), which is where export promotion may have its greatest impact.

Determinants of Export Performance

An inward look

The key determinant of export performance is the increased competitiveness of firms. Ironically, this means that rather than through international negotiations, it is mostly through down-to-earth domestic measures that firms receive their greatest opportunity to be part of the export playing field. Export promotion then must have a decidedly inward looking component, which makes the production of goods and services cheaper, faster, and better. It has to permit domestic producers to measure levels of competitiveness in comparison to firms in other nations, and allow them to correct weaknesses.

Concurrent with such an inward look, governmental efforts also need to pay heed to the financial environment, particularly the variations in exchange rates. There is little benefit to the development of competitive products if, due to currency gyrations, carefully developed business plans fall apart and entire markets disappear. Therefore, global collaboration to find a financial architecture, which, although flexible, does offer some stability to firms with a reasonably foreseeable international financial outcome, is an important second pillar of the international launching pad.

The outward perspective

The outward looking portion of export promotion is built upon this foundation. Even though the institutional ties of an export promotion authority are often either with a trade or a commerce ministry, it should be recognized that its activities and focus are cutting across typical policy delineations. Therefore, a stand-alone authority, if endowed with sufficient bureaucratic influence, may work well here. This also brings into focus the issue of budgeting. Since the task of export promotion greatly affects commerce, labor, economics, transportation, and foreign policy, just to name a few traditional government departments, its funding and support should also come from a variety of government ministries. Such an approach will not only provide for more than the traditional funding but will also encourage more intergovernmental collaboration, which is beneficial to overall export progress.

A key limitation

Here, one also has to recognize one key limitation: outward export promotion will always only comprise a small fraction of any national budget and directly support only a minute portion of national exports. Given such a limitation, it must then be recognized that it cannot be the only role of export promotion directly to support specific export activities. Rather, export promotion needs to initiate activities, to blaze trails with new approaches and experimentation, to highlight new ways of overcoming hurdles, to be the venture capital of an economic activity. Particularly in industrialized nations, export promotion should not necessarily be placing the safe bet – why have government compete against market forces? Such a perspective may make it difficult to evaluate export promotion activities with traditional return on investment criteria. However, it develops an entire new focus and burden on export promotion efforts – concentrating a large portion of them 'outside the box.'

Some Program Considerations

Here are some considerations for researchers and policy makers interested in structuring effective outward export promotion programs.

Captive export trade

Trade theoreticians often complain about the lackluster responsiveness of trade flows to traditional trade models. One key lament has been that trade flows no longer quickly adjust to shifts in currency values. What has perhaps not received sufficient attention are intra-firm trade and other captive exports. In an era of massive foreign direct investment flows, the relationship between multinational firms and their subsidiaries has a major impact on their internal trading activities, which, in turn, greatly affects export performance.

For example, in the United States, over 25 percent of overall exports are from US multinationals to their affiliates. An additional 10 percent of US exports come from foreign affiliates in the United States sending products to their parent firms. (Zeile 1999) Furthermore, many firms are likely to have developed long-term supplier relationships, which leads to another large set of 'captive' exports. All these types of exports are much less subject to short-term changes in policy or the environment, since considerations beyond export concerns enter corporate decision making.

With more than one half of exports so affected in many countries, export promotion needs to reflect several new dimensions of these relationship-influenced exports. Key questions are: how can these intra-firm flows be identified and segmented into specific niches? What promotional tools can be brought to bear to specifically assist in increasing these captive export flows? Are there investment promotion strategies that can influence the corporate strategic sourcing choice How can the affiliates of foreign multinationals be made part of a domestic export promotion effort?

Demand-oriented focus

Traditionally, export promotion has aimed to please the local customer, the constituent – the exporting firm. Given the intent to increase exports, how-ever, it may make sense to devote promotional funds to develop a better understanding of the actual buyer of exports, namely the customer abroad. Any promotion of exporting will fall short, if no one in the market is buying.

While there may be fewer political points to collect on that score, such a demand-oriented customer focus would require substantial research activities abroad. Findings could tell us about the weaknesses of export activities. In what areas does an industry or a firm need to improve its export product or export processes? How can it be more responsive to changing demand pat-terns? For example, is better/faster/safer transportation required? How can transport tracking systems be linked to facilitate better global supply chain management? A better understanding and meeting of such customer-driven needs can help propel the potential exporter to become the winning bidder.

Making accidents happen

Many firms become exporters by accident. Managers often receive unsolicited orders over the transom from abroad, and then have to make a choice as to whether or not to fill them. Such unsolicited orders were found to account for more than half of all cases of export initiation by small and medium-sized firms in the United States (Czinkota 1982). More recently, due to the growth of corporate Web sites, firms can become unplanned participants in the international market even more quickly. For example, customers from abroad can visit a Web site and place an international order. Of course, the firm can choose to ignore foreign interest and lose out on new markets. Alternatively, it can find itself unexpectedly an exporter. In the services area, specialty retailers such as bookstores and fitness equipment are examples of firms that have become international in this way (Grönroos 1999). Regional research found that two-thirds of small exporting firms started to do so because of unsolicited approaches from buyers or third parties (McAuley 1999).

While some have bemoaned the lack of planning reflected by such a serendipitous internationalization process, outward export promotion can focus on such unsolicited orders. In which ways can the offering of a firm be disseminated globally so that interested parties learn about the existence of a product? How can such parties then be guided in order to make easy, unsolicited inquiries about such product? How can both the buyer and seller exchange information and develop a trust level to such a degree that order placement and order fulfillment becomes possible?

Using and disseminating new technologies

It is assumed by many that the emergence of electronic commerce has opened up new opportunities to exporters. While this may be true conceptually, the actual understanding and use of e-commerce lags far behind its potential even in highly industrialized nations. For example, in the United States, most e-tailers do not accept orders from outside their home market. More than 55 percent of US Web merchants are not even shipping to Canada (Putzger 2000). The problem must be more severe in nations where the penetration of the Internet is much lower. In these countries use of the Internet could be most critical to exporters, who may need to circumvent infrastructural shortcomings. It is also in the interest of industrialized exporters to encourage greater e-commerce acceptance there, since such an achievement will also help ensure greater exports to these countries.

It is not just the access to the new technology that export promoters need to consider. Of key importance is also the content within and the approach to the technology. Export Web site content must not only be available, it must be appropriate if export performance is to be enhanced! This may mean translation of the content, but it also refers to content localization. For example, sentences in Japanese need to be formal, whereas an informal tone may be more appropriate for the United States. Length of text plays a role – a page of English may need up to two pages in German. Characters may vary in size, and may read in different directions (for example left to right or right to left) (MacLeod 2000).

The supply chain dimension also needs to be incorporated into e-commerce approaches. Domestically there is a good understanding that companies are embedded in linkages with direct and indirect suppliers and customers. Internationally, however, most Web sites still represent companies rather than networks, thus missing out on an important cooperative perspective (Wilkinson et al. 2000).

Finally, there is the issue of technology power, which can both help and hurt the exporter. For example, the availability of e-mail can inform more customers more quickly about new opportunities. However it also brings new risks to firms. Today, one complaint can easily be developed into millions of complaints by e-mail (Makihara 2001).

Export promotion endeavors have a rich choice of activities with this new technology. The use of electronic commerce in international marketing can redefine traditional trade shows and missions, alter payment structure and flows, re-cast distribution and customer complaint systems, to name but a few. It is here where the greatest potential lies for export promotion to become a venture capital tool of innovation and creativity.

A resource-sharing paradigm

In today's rapidly changing business environment, few resources are needed permanently. A shift is moving us all from 'possession' towards 'usage'. Jobs are only held temporarily, cars are leased rather than purchased, and stocks are acquired through mutual funds rather than bought directly. Much of the ideological conflict of the twentieth century centered around the issue of ownership – be it of the means of production or of the fruits of production. In the new millennium, ownership has become less important, giving way to the use of things.

In an export context, this shift is giving rise to a resource-sharing paradigm. Companies have more opportunities to collaborate by, for example, sharing warehousing, transportation, or even assembly facilities abroad, thus making exports easier and cheaper. Governments can encourage such export collaboration and alliances within or even across their borders in order to make their firms more competitive. For example, an accumulation and subsequent sharing of benchmarking information on industry-specific performance dimensions can make a major difference in letting firms learn how and where to compete. One successful performance example for other export promotion organizations to emulate is the automotive equipment benchmarking already offered by the International Trade Centre in Geneva. It provides comparative performance data across countries and firms for one global industry and informs firms about their strengths and weaknesses (International Trade Centre 1999). Other alternatives include risk sharing opportunities between governments and exporters – approaches that are already used in the foreign direct investment promotion field (Mudambi 1999). Actual financial exposure of government to its own advice may also reduce the frequency with which export promotion counseling reflects the wishful thinking of government policy rather than economic reality.

CONCLUSIONS

Export promotion must take new approaches to remain viable. The business environment has made old tactics obsolete and calls for new strategies. The focus of export promotion can no longer be on subsidization. Quite apart from the dangers that tend to accompany the distribution of 'free monies', subsidization places the smaller players at an unfair disadvantage compared to larger countries that they cannot overcome. How would one expect a small developing nation to compete in the amount of available subsidy funding against, say, Canada? Therefore, it is best for all parties to abstain from such practices.

Much of export promotion has to become domestically oriented, aiming to develop a competitive platform that permits a successful launch of exports. Even though perhaps accompanied by too little political credit from the export community, the streamlining of regulations, the tight focusing of export controls, and the development of infrastructure and information systems can be crucial in enhancing the competitive capability of firms.

It is also important to recognize the limits of export promotion efforts. Rather than see them as changing the economic climate or supporting the entire trade activities of a country, they should be seen as a supplement to, not as a substitute for market forces. Therefore, export promotion expenditures should be evaluated using criteria such as innovativeness, identification and use of new technology, and the filling of temporary market gaps.

Finally, export promotion needs to be seen in a spirit of international collaboration – after all, every export has to be someone's import. Therefore, export promotion needs to recognize the nexus between trade and investment, as well as the links between economic and national security.

REFERENCES

Belisle, Denis J. and Michael R. Czinkota (1999), 'Trade Must Extend to Poorer Countries', *The Japan Times*, 31 May, 19.

Bernard, Andrew B. and J. Bradford Jensen (1997), *Exceptional Exporter Performance: Cause, Effect or Both*, Census Research Data Center, Pittsburgh: Carnegie Mellon University.

Bilkey, Warren J. (1978), 'An Attempted Integration of the Literature on the Export Behavior of Firms', *Journal of International Business Studies*, 9, Spring/Summer, 33–46.

Blecker, Robert A. (1999), 'The Ticking Debt Bomb: Why the U.S. International Financial Position is not Sustainable', Washington DC: Economic Policy Institute, 29 June.

Bowersox, Donald J., Patricia J. Daugherty, Cornelia L. Droege, Richard N. Germain, and Dale S. Rogers (1992), *Logistical Excellence*, Burlington, MA: Digital Press.

Business America (1996), 117, September, 9.

Cavusgil, Tamer S. (1980), 'On the Internationalization Process of Firms', *European Research*, 8, November, 273–9.

Crick, Dave and Michael R. Czinkota (1995), 'Export Assistance: Another Look at Whether We Are Supporting the Best Programmes', *International Marketing Review*, 12(3), 61–72.

Cutts, Steve and Janet West (1998), 'The Arrangement on Export Credits', *The OECD Observer*, April/May, 12–14.

Czinkota, Michael R. (1982), *Export Development Strategies: U.S. Promotion Policy*, New York: Praeger.

Czinkota, Michael R. (1994), 'A National Export Assistance Policy for New and Growing Businesses', *Journal of International Marketing*, 2(1), 91–101.

Czinkota, Michael R. (1998), 'Global Neighbors, Poor Relations', in M. Czinkota and M. Kotabe (eds), *Trends in International Business: Critical Perspectives*, Oxford: Blackwell, 20–27.

Czinkota, Michael R. (2000), 'The Policy Gap in International Marketing', *Journal of International Marketing*, 8(1), 99–111.

Czinkota, Michael R. and David Ricks (1981), 'Export Assistance: Are We Supporting the Best Programs?', *Columbia Journal of World Business*, 16, Summer, 73–8.

Deutsches Institut für Wirtschaftsförderung (1991), 'Die Aussenwirtschaftsförderung der wichtigsten Konkurrenzländer der Bundesrepublik Deutschland – Ein internationaler Vergleich' (The export promotion of the most important countries competing with the Federal Republic of Germany – An international comparison), Berlin, June.

The Economist (2000), 'Going Too Far in Support of Trade', 14 December, www.economist.com, accessed 27 March 2001.

Federal Reserve Board (2000), 'Monetary Policy Report to the Congress', *Federal Reserve Bulletin*, August, 550–51.

Grönroos, Christian (1999), 'Internationalization Strategies for Services', *Journal of Services Marketing*, 13(4/5), 290–97.

IMF (International Monetary Fund) (2000), *International Financial Statistics*, Washington DC: IMF.

International Trade Administration (1996), 'U.S. Jobs Supported by Exports of Goods and Services', US Department of Commerce, Washington DC, 17 June.

International Trade Centre (1999), 'Redefining Trade Promotion', *International Trade Forum*, April.

Kotabe, Masaaki and Michael R. Czinkota (1992), 'State Government Promotion of Manufacturing Exports: A Gap Analysis', *Journal of International Business Studies*, 23, 4th quarter, 637–58.

Laird, Sam (1997), 'WTO Rules and Good Practice on Export Policy', Geneva, World Trade Organization, 20 March.

Lesch, William C., Abdolreza Eshghi, and Golpira S. Eshghi (1990), 'A Review of Export Promotion Programs in the then Largest Industrial States', in T. Cavusgil and M. Czinkota (eds), *International Perspectives on Trade Promotion and Assistance*, New York: Quorum Books, 25–37.

MacLeod, Marcia (2000), 'Language Barriers', *Supply Management*, 5(14), 37–8.

Makihara Minoru (Co-Chairman of the Annual Meeting of the World Economic Forum) (2001), Davos, www.worldeconomicforum.org.

Mann, Catherine L. (2001), 'Is the US Trade Deficit still Sustainable?', The Institute for International Economics, Washington DC, 1 March.

McAuley, Andrew (1999), 'Entrepreneurial Instant Exports in the Scottish Arts and Crafts Sector', *Journal of International Marketing* 4 July, 67–82.

Mudambi, Ram (1999), 'Multinational Investment Attraction: Principal–Agent Consideration', *International Journal of the Economics of Business*, 6(1), 65–79.

Pursell, Gary (1999), *Export Policies and Institutions in Developing Countries. The Role of the World Bank*, Washington DC: World Bank, Development Economics Research Group.

Putzger, Ian (2000), 'On-line and International', *Journal of Commerce Weekly*, 11/13–19, 27–8.

Ricardo, David (1819), *On the Principles of Political Economy and Taxation*, Port Jervis, NY: Lubrecht and Cramer Ltd.

Richardson. J. David and Karin Rindal (1996), 'Why Exports Matter: More!', The Institute for International Economics and the Manufacturing Institute. Washington DC, February.

Schott, Jeffrey (1994), *The Uruguay Round: An Assessment*, Washington DC: Institute for International Economics.

Singer, Thomas O. (1990), 'The Role of Export Promotion in Export Management: The Case of the Minnesota Trade Office', Doctoral dissertation, George Washington University, Washington DC.

Smith, Adam (1776), *An Inquiry into the Nature and Causes of the Wealth of Nations*, Chicago: University of Chicago Press.

Taylor, Charles and Witold Henisz (1994), 'U.S. Manufacturers in the Global Market Place', Report 1058, New York: The Conference Board.

US Department of Commerce (1996), *National Export Strategy*, Washington DC: US Government Printing Office, October.

US General Accounting Office (1993), *Agricultural Marketing: Export Opportunities for Wood Products in Japan Call for Customer Focus*, Washington DC: Government Printing Office, May.

Wilkinson I.F., L.G. Mattson, and G. Easton (2000), 'International Competitiveness and Trade Promotion Policy from a Network Perspective', *Journal of World Business*, 35(3), 275–99

WTO (World Trade Organization) (2001), 'International Trade Statistics', wwx.wto.org, 13 February.

Zeile, William J. (1999), 'Foreign Direct Investment in the United States', *Survey of Current Business*, August, 21–44.

8. Industrial endowments in international business: an analytical framework

Yadong Luo

INTRODUCTION

Globalization has become a permanent and irreversible part of economic life. It provides firms with both tremendous opportunities and daunting challenges. International expansion has become a pervasive and prominent strategic response to global economic dynamics for a large array of companies. The need to simultaneously balance the dynamic tension between multiple forces (geographic, product, market, technological) has resulted in firms extending their presence all over the globe for a multitude of purposes and through a multitude of forms. Correspondingly, international expansion decisions and strategies have acquired increasing strategic significance.

International expansion is the process by which a multinational enterprise (MNE) enters and invests in a target foreign country in the pursuit of strategic objectives. Firms often expand internationally because of both 'pull' and 'push' factors. Firms are 'pulled' or attracted by the cost-side and/or revenue-side benefits derived from host country dynamics. Cost-side benefits are generated from low-cost production factors and operational expenses. Revenue-side benefits result from market demand growth in a foreign country. Although facing liabilities of foreignness, an MNE's competitive advantages, manifested in strong technological and organizational skills, may enable the firm to pre-empt emerging investment opportunities and explore market potential. Other revenue-related benefits include accessibility to scarce resources, preferential treatment for foreign direct investment (FDI), and learning or experience accumulation. Unlike 'pull' factors, which are related to the host country, 'push' factors are associated with the home, or source country, environment. Source-country contextual factors act either as stimuli or impediments to the outflow of foreign direct investment.

Whether or not an MNE can attain economic benefits accrued from 'pull' or 'push' factors largely depends upon industry selection. Selecting the right industry enables a firm to benefit from both cost and revenue-related advantages in a host country as it affects the extent to which the firm can take advantage of factor endowments and market demand. Home country conditions may also influence this decision by offering a frame of reference by which MNEs judge and evaluate the industrial dynamics of a host country. More importantly, strategic choices and outcomes of globalization are significantly determined by industrial conditions manifested in such areas as market, cost, competition, and governmental policy (Yip 1994, 1995). These conditions, which vary in strength from industry to industry (Porter 1986), include globally common customer needs (Yip 1994), cost determinants such as economies of scale or technological and advertising intensity (Porter 1986), international trade agreements which affect governmental policies (Willmore 1994), and conditions such as cross-border subsidization which drive up competition (Teece 1985). A global strategy must be formed in light of these factors if a firm is to gain such benefits as cost reduction, improved product quality, enhanced customer loyalty, or an increased competitive edge (Yip 1995).

When analyzing environmental or factor endowments of a foreign country, previous studies in international business often emphasize the national level (that is, country-specific or comparative advantage of a nation), and inadequately address the endowments at the industrial level (that is, industry-specific or structural advantage of an industry). This is an important gap because most economies today, whether developed or developing, are undergoing many structural changes, presenting industry-unique, not necessarily country-unique, opportunities and challenges for international companies. MNEs entering a particular country today are more likely to face different opportunities or hazards in different industries than in the 1990s. Technological change, increasing globalization, and the transformation of emerging economies are the three major reasons for this international phenomenon. Technological change (especially information technology) has created many emerging industries characterized by enormous opportunities while making other industries, many of them labor-intensive, less attractive in the international market. Increasing globalization facilitates the link between an individual nation's industry structure and international market structure. This convergence magnifies the changes of an individual nation's industrial competition and accentuates transformation of its industrial structure. Finally, many emerging economies themselves, now important players in the global marketplace and major targets of MNEs, are undergoing industrial transformation and structural changes. In many cases, MNEs investing in different industries within the same emerging market experience fundamentally heterogeneous opportunities and threats as if they operate in different nations. Realizing the importance of industrial endowment and analyzing the industrial structure of a foreign country are therefore critical for MNEs to expand internationally.

FDI and MNE theories have shed some light on the importance of industry selection during internationalization. The existence of differences in industrial and market structures between countries influences an MNE's profitability (Caves 1971; Hymer 1976). Particular industries are more attractive to the degree that they contain structural impediments to competition, thus allowing participating firms to sustain competitive advantages once their positions in the industry are obtained (Porter 1991; Teece et al. 1991). MNEs can achieve higher performance than firms which only operate domestically because they benefit from the structural variance of industries between host and home countries. When the industrial structure of a host country is imperfect and entry barriers are low, FDI will flow in as a direct response (Hymer 1976). Structural imperfection in a foreign market constitutes a dominant factor which not only makes FDI preferable to trade or licensing (Contractor and Lorange 1988) but also determines the relative attractiveness of one host country over any other countries (Dunning 1979). Firms in oligopolistic industries enjoy the advantages of economies of scale and other characteristics that give them market power. This power allows them to overcome the disadvantages of being foreign to compete with local rivals (Caves and Mehra 1986; Porter 1986). Focusing on competition and life cycle stages, Porter (1991) also asserts that competition is a major driving force underlying international expansion. Firms in a harsh, competitive, domestic sector may expand overseas to regions where competition is low, an industry is at the growing or shakeout stage, or a competitive position would be more readily attained and sustained.

While the above theories explain *why* industry selection is important, our understanding of *how* to choose an appropriate industry in a host country is incomplete. Although international diversification strategy has been addressed by several researchers (for example, Geringer et al. 1989; Kim et al. 1993; Tallman and Li 1996), they focus on the performance implications of individual or joint effects of the product portfolio (that is, related versus unrelated) and transnationality. This line of research does not address how to select the proper industry in a foreign context to fit an MNE's strategic goals and dynamic capabilities and to create the maximum risk-adjusted premium from international expansion. Similarly, the industrial structure-based view in the strategy literature sheds light on whether industrial structure matters to firm performance (Rumelt 1991). This research suggests that particular industries are more attractive when they contain structural impediments to competitive forces which allow participating firms to sustain a competitive advantage once obtained (Porter, 1986; Teece et al. 1991). These studies do not, however, address how to choose an industry that will enhance a firm's competitive advantage initially in an international setting.

This chapter will illuminate this issue by providing an integrated framework for selecting an appropriate industry in a host country. The desired industry may not necessarily be the same as the firm's core domestic business. Both related (vertical or horizontal) and unrelated FDI diversification can engender abnormal rates of return if the selected industry presents distinct pre-emptive opportunities and industrial dynamics align properly with a firm's competencies. The following paragraphs present the framework which is the primary focus of this chapter analyzing industrial dynamics comprised of structural dimensions, structural forces, structural attributes, and structural evolution. The next section elaborates on the integrated framework by linking structural dynamics with other important contingencies.

ANALYZING STRUCTURAL DYNAMICS

A major challenge for today's multinational corporations is how to become competent and attain sustained superior performance in the global marketplace. International expansion through foreign direct investment tends to involve market conduct that extends the recognition of mutual market dependence – the essence of oligopoly – beyond national boundaries (Teece 1985). Likewise, it tends to broadly equalize the rate of return on capital (equity) throughout a given industry in all the countries where production actually takes place. This common profit rate, however, may exceed a normal or competitive one since a persistent oligopoly, nation- or worldwide, is marked by barriers to entry of new firms and, perforce, to the inflow of capital (Caves 1971; Teece 1985). International competition and expansion reduce structural imperfections in a host country. In practice, however, this effect differs according to industry and country. The structure of some industries may be more exogenous than others, as reflected by higher entry barriers, more governmental regulations, greater asset intensity, and the like. Structural imperfections are even more exogenous in transitional markets than in advanced economies. Such imperfections partially result from a paradox wherein governments aim to alleviate structural distortions by injecting more competition and assimilating more foreign capital yet simultaneously impose policies which present new obstacles to the mitigation of imperfection. Some policies may increase rather than reduce structural distortions when a government attaches a high value to social stability, infant sector protection, and pillar industry subsidies. In sum, structural dynamics in a host country are complex, exogenous, and often heterogeneous across both industries and countries. The analysis of such dynamics should reveal not only structural dimensions such as complexity and uncertainty but also the impact of structural forces (for example, suppliers and buyers), attributes (for example, sales growth and asset intensity), and evolution (that is, life cycle), as detailed below.

Structural Dimensions

Structural dimensions include structural uncertainty, complexity, and deterrence. These dimensions may affect an MNE's profitability, stability, and sustainability in a host industry. International managers need to diagnose these dimensions in order to opt for a host industry that will result in maximum economic benefits without imposing uncontrollable hostilities and risks.

Structural uncertainty

Strictly speaking, uncertainty means unpredictable variability whereas dynamism is comprised of both predictable and unpredictable elements. Both dynamism and uncertainty in an industry carry opportunities and challenges. Uncertainty may arise due to market force fluctuations or changes in industrial policies in the host country. Structural uncertainty often results from high fluctuations in prices, sales, and material supplies. Under these circumstances, foreign companies confront more operational risks. If they intend to avoid these risks, they should reduce their reliance on local settings. In an effort to do this, foreign investors can decrease local sourcing and marketing while increasing exports. Many Asian MNEs investing in neighboring countries used this strategy to respond to the financial chaos which occurred in Asia in the late 1990s. Generally, MNEs interested in entering an industry characterized by structural uncertainty should consider whether their ability to offset risks is sufficient to enable them to realize their international expansion goals.

Structural complexity

Structural complexity refers to the diversity and heterogeneity of environmental factors (for example, competitors, customers, and suppliers). Structural diversity means how many different factors and issues a firm must deal with. Structural heterogeneity refers to how different each factor is from the others. High complexity in an industry reinforces the difficulty of using standardization and cost efficiency strategies. It also increases an MNE's operational uncertainties and production instabilities. As a strategic response to structural complexity, strategic and operational flexibility is imperative. A more focused strategy with respect to the scope of both products and markets appears to be the proper solution in this environment for those firms with little experience of a specific host country or having only a short presence in the market. When a foreign firm has gained more diverse experience in dealing with competitors, customers, and suppliers, and has thus reduced the liabilities of foreignness, the firm may consider extending its line of business in an attempt to explore more opportunities. In deciding on a product portfolio for a complex foreign industry, using related diversification in the area of a firm's core competency seems a better choice than an unrelated strategy. Nevertheless, the firm's length of operations, the diversity of its host country experience, and the contribution of its local partner (if in a joint venture) may moderate this relationship.

Structural deterrence

Structural deterrence refers to the availability of resources from a specific industry and its support industries. A foreign industry may not be complex or uncertain, but still be hostile. In this situation, the foreign business will be constrained in implementing its business- and operational-level strategies, deploying internal resources contributed to local operations, and participating in indigenous markets. Resource munificence, on the other hand, helps firms achieve operational and financial synergies from the interactions between internal resources (competitive advantages) and external resources (comparative advantages). Reliance on external resources in a host country comes from either the firm's strategic needs or the host government's requirement that product components must be localized. In general, structural resources include: (i) natural resources, raw materials, parts, and components; (ii) investment infrastructure such as power supplies, telecommunications, and transportation; (iii) product factors such as land, capital, labor, information, technology, and management; and (iv) governmental treatment, assistance, and efficiency. MNEs need to ensure that all of these resources are available in the industry within which they will operate as well as in related or support industries.

Structural Forces

Structural forces are composed of new entrants, suppliers, buyers, rivals, substitutes, distributors, and government authorities. These forces individually and jointly affect the level of competitive threat and bargaining pressure facing an MNE sub-unit in a host industry. They determine an industry's competitive pattern, which influences a firm's competitive position, market power, financial returns, and growth potential. International managers need to identify the strength of each of these seven forces in a target market and choose an industry in which an MNE will confront the fewest competitive threats so it can maintain a superior competitive position.

Although Michael Porter's five forces model (1980) was designed for domestic settings, it can be revised to apply to industry selection in a foreign context. Selecting the right industry overseas largely determines an MNE's profitability and competitive position in the host country market. The intensity of industrial competition and profit potential is a function of five competitive forces, whether in a domestic or host market: threat of new entrants, suppliers, buyers, product substitutes, and intensity of rivalry among competitors. A foreign company should analyze each of these five forces, identify possible opportunities or threats generated by each, and then select an industry in the target country that best fits its organizational competencies and strategic goals.

In recent years, global industrial boundaries have become blurred. As a result, competition is no longer viewed as limited to direct business rivals. Instead, it is seen as coming from all avenues by which customers seek value. Porter argues that the stronger each of these forces, the more limited the ability of established companies to raise prices and earn greater profits. A strong competitive force is regarded as a threat since it depresses financial returns. A weak competitive force is viewed as an opportunity, for it allows a firm to earn more profit. Firms that constitute a competitive force include local companies as well as foreign investors or marketers that may influence each of the five forces.

It is also important to recognize the industrial evolution and dynamism of each force. When operating in a foreign market, an MNE often confronts greater operational uncertainty and risks derived from the industrial or macro-national environment than in its home country. The strength and source of the each of the five forces can change through time. For instance, suppliers could become competitors (by integrating forward), or buyers (by integrating backward). The task facing international managers is to choose the industry that will allow them to seize opportunities while overcoming threats from these forces.

MNEs need to verify the threat of new entrants, whether local or foreign, to their subsequent operations. New competitors can threaten existing businesses by bringing in additional production capacity. Unless product demand is also increasing, the additional capacity will hold consumer costs down, resulting in less sales revenue and lower returns for all firms in the industry. The likelihood that firms will enter an industry is a function of two factors: barriers to entry and the expected retaliation from incumbents. Entry barriers clearly exist if firms find entry into a new industry difficult or competitively disadvantaged. Normally, incumbents develop such barriers so that potential entrants will seek other markets where entry barriers are relatively insignificant. The absence of high entry barriers increases the probability that a new entrant facing relatively less barriers in comparison with other entrants will be able to operate profitably, at the expense of incumbent profits. Therefore, competent MNEs should opt for industries where entry barriers are reasonably high in order to keep out competitors.

International expansion often necessitates an extension of the value chain and reliance on external resources. The relationship with local suppliers affects an MNE's processes and quality of production, which in turn influences operational success in a host market. Increasing prices and reducing product quality are means by which suppliers can exert power over firms competing within an industry. If unable to recover cost increases through its pricing structure, a firm's profitability will be reduced. The likelihood of forward integration is enhanced when suppliers have substantial resources and provide the industry's firms with highly differentiated products. In the process of internationalization, MNEs should choose industries in which the bargaining power of suppliers is relatively low or does not have a critical effect on firm operations.

The prominent objective of most MNEs in expanding into foreign markets is to enhance their overall market power while improving their competitive position in the target market. The relationship with local buyers plays a large part in determining organizational reputation, customer loyalty, and gross profit margin. In general, buyers (customers of the focal industry or firm) prefer to purchase products at the lowest possible price, which means the industry earns the lowest acceptable rate of return on its invested capital. Buyers bargain for higher quality, greater levels of service, and lower prices by encouraging competitive battles among firms in an industry. When MNEs invest in a host industry in which they have greater bargaining power than the buyers, they can manipulate transactions and increase sales prices. Product differentiation and customer responsiveness in coping with demand changes and utility functions of segmented markets are important levers for enhancing MNE bargaining power over customers.

As a result of rapid technological change and reduction of entry barriers across borders, MNEs face increasingly greater competitive pressure from substitutes. The ongoing development of information technology is creating more and more new industries over time, further reinforcing threats of substitution. Substitute products are different goods or services that can perform similar or the same functions as the focal product. Functional substitutes place an upper limit on the prices firms can charge. In general, the threat of substitute products is strong when customers face few, if any, switching costs and when the substitute product's price is lower and/or its quality and performance capabilities are equal to or greater than established products. To reduce the attractiveness of substitution, firms must differentiate their offerings along dimensions that are important to their customers (for example, price, product quality, delivery, after-sales service, and customer responsiveness). In selecting a target industry abroad, MNEs should assess the possible threat from substitute products manufactured by local firms or other foreign companies. The risk of substitutes directly influences the sustainability of a firm's competitive advantages and, consequently, its competitive position in the foreign market. If MNEs have to choose an industry involving high risks of substitutes, the firm must at least maintain production and operation flexibility.

The vigor of competition among existing firms in an industry is undoubtedly the foremost factor to be considered. Competition has the most direct impact on a firm's entry, operations, marketing, and investment success. In many industries, firms compete actively with one another to achieve strategic competitiveness and earn above-average returns. To analyze the intensity of existing rivalry, MNEs may use such indicators as concentration ratio, entry barriers, capital commitment, and minimum economy of scale. Competition among rivals is further stimulated when one or more firms identify an opportunity to improve their market position, usually by differentiating products/services or reducing costs/prices. Competitive pressure is particularly strong when an MNE is a late entrant into a foreign market. In this situation, the organizational capabilities of the firm are crucial in determining whether it will survive or not. Strategic responses and adaptability to changes in the external environment are also important in heightening its competitive position. While it is natural that MNEs prefer less competitive industries in foreign markets, *ceteris paribus*, this choice is strongly influenced by strategic goals. For instance, if an MNE pursues cost minimization or exploits product factor advantages in the host country via production–export or global vertical integration, fierce competition in the host market will not constitute a major threat to the firm.

The competitive threat or munificence from distributors is another important force in international expansion. The supportiveness of indigenous distributors influences an MNE's profit margin, delivery efficiency, and customer responsiveness. As it is costly to establish a firm's own distribution system and less effective to use such a system to market products, MNEs often have to rely upon local distributors such as wholesalers, large retailers, exclusive agents, distribution centers, and even some host government-instituted distribution channels. Establishing a distribution network can be such a long process that foreign companies may be unable to seize market opportunities or align with contextual changes in a timely fashion. Building distribution networks in a foreign market (for example, in Japan or China) can also be a complicated social investment. If the interpersonal or inter-organizational relationship is constructed inappropriately, such networks will be unreliable. To overcome this liability of foreignness, MNEs therefore should verify that they will be able to collaborate with appropriate local distributors. Although a well-established distributor may possess greater bargaining power against the foreign company, its networks are essential for MNEs seeking market share and long-term profitability in the host country. Arranging long-term distribution agreements is advisable for MNEs that wish to mitigate possible threats from distributor bargaining power while benefiting from distributor competencies.

The host country government is a critical structural force that MNEs must not overlook. Structural interference by the local government is generally based on two types of governmental policies, one relating to industrial regulations, the other to FDI. In fact, most national governments have utilized these two sets of policies to manipulate and oversee foreign direct investment inflow. Although each nation may have country-specific policies, some typical industrial policies include:

1. Classification of industries as prohibited, restricted, permitted, or encouraged. Each category is treated differently in terms of taxation, financing, land rent, infrastructure access, and the like.
2. Ratification of projects in certain industries. In general, these industries are state monopolies or controlled.
3. Preferential treatment for those MNEs which bring in more advanced technology, managerial skills, foreign exchange via export, or substitute imported products.

Discriminatory treatment is often designed by a government to rationalize its industrial structure, alleviate resource or price distortions across industries, create foreign exchange earnings, and modernize pillar industries.

In general, most developed countries provide foreign investors with national treatment, meaning that foreign companies enjoy the same treatment as local enterprises. Nevertheless, there are still some economies that treat local and foreign investments differently at the national (federal) level (for example, Ireland, Spain, Canada, and Japan) or the local (state) government level (for example, Alabama in the US). Some of the following FDI policies, typically used by governments of developing countries, may also be adopted in developed countries:

1. Entry mode control, that is, MNEs are allowed to enter into certain industries only through certain entry modes (for example, joint ventures, co-production, technology transfers via international licensing or franchising, or build-operate-transfer). Generally, the host country government requires at least one state-owned enterprise to participate in the venture or collaboration.
2. Equity control, that is, foreign investors are restricted from holding a certain percentage of equity in the joint venture. For instance, MNEs entering Chinese auto assembly industries can only maintain up to 49 percent of equity in the venture.
3. Location control, that is, the host government requires MNEs to locate projects in certain geographical regions. This requirement is expected to help boost regional economies by launching heavy investment in certain industries as planned by the central or federal government. Projects in different locations are also taxed differently. Even within the same city,

ventures in different locations can be subject to different treatment. For example, the Chinese Economic and Technological Development Zones (ETDZs) provide more tax breaks than non-ETDZs within the same city or county.

4.   Duration control, that is, each FDI project should specify a term (number of years) in its joint venture contract. Although this term can be renewed, such renewal is not automatic but usually subject to a new round of approval by relevant governmental authorities.

5.   Partner control, that is, certain big projects must include local firms assigned by the government. These firms may or may not have a previous cooperative history with the foreign investors.

6.   Timing control, that is, the host government may delay the approval of certain FDI projects for certain periods of time. This often occurs when the government and its agencies have over-approved new projects, surpassing the actual need for economic development. Major FDI policies may also be changed for a variety of economic and political reasons.

7.   Project orientation control, that is, each project must be identified in its application and confirmed by the government as belonging to one orientation category: export, technologically advanced, infrastructure, import substitution, or local market. Each of these orientations is offered different treatment and support by the government. In general, the first three enjoy preferential treatment, including lower income tax and tariff rates, refund of value-added taxes, lower financing costs, better infrastructure access, governmental support, and cheaper land rent.

8.   Size control, that is, projects with different investment sizes have to be ratified by different levels of the government. The greater the size, the higher the rank of the authority in charge. When a project plans to increase its investment size, it usually has to get approval by the same authority that initially ratified the project.

Structural Attributes

Major structural attributes that are particularly important in international expansion include industry profitability, sales growth, concentration level, asset intensity, growth of number of firms in an industry, capital requirements, and technological intensity. Within an industry, each attribute may have a different influence on firm operations. For instance, a growing industry may show sales growth but not necessarily profitability growth because of the heavy burden of classified or accumulated corporate income taxes in a host country. The important task of international managers, therefore, is to select a foreign industry that has structural characteristics best matched to the firm's strategic goals for expansion. Each individual attribute may have a different effect on the various aspects of international expansion success.

Inter-industrial variance in profitability has been an enduring characteristic of many economies in the world. In developing countries, the breadth and depth of the removal of government-induced asymmetries in an industry during economic reform depend largely upon that industry's profit level. In high profit industries, although competitive entry from both domestic and foreign firms can gradually erode supra-normal profits on invested capital, continued government involvement in the structural adjustment process can result in appreciable barriers to entry which enable established firms to maintain market power and competitive position for some time. Additionally, foreign companies are more likely to confront governmental constraints on materials supplies and product distribution, latent competitive pressure, and market fluctuations in high-profit industries. These risks can be even greater when MNEs invest in emerging economies, since the objective of economic reform is normally to orient the industrial structure towards greater equilibrium and market force determination.

Industry sales growth is a key component of market attractiveness for both local firms and foreign businesses. Growth serves as an indicator of disequilibrium (a condition favorably associated with entry) and as an indicator of industrial evolution. Porter (1980) argues that rapid industrial growth ensures strong financial performance for incumbents even when new entrants take some market share. In general, when a particular industry is deregulated or freed from governmental control over market supply, rapid initial development ensues. This take-off is reflected in a surge in industry sales growth. In such circumstances, many new firms enter the industry unless start-up costs or other non-government instituted entry barriers are extremely high. Further, when the local market for a particular industry appears to grow dramatically, it is reasonable to expect that foreign companies will pursue local market expansion rather than export growth.

A host industry's concentration level implies the degree of competition or monopoly that an MNE will face. If an MNE is able to invest and operate in a highly concentrated industry, it will more likely achieve abnormal profits. If an MNE can sustain itself in a highly concentrated industry, it is likely to become one of the few oligopolists or monopolists in the industry, as characterized by holding a dominant market share and power. Because high concentration prevents free competition, many host country governments are wary of entry by MNEs into already concentrated local industries. Therefore, MNEs in these industries are likely to encounter high governmental intervention. In order to avoid such interference, MNEs should attain governmental support during entry and maintain good relationships with governmental authorities during operations. Both investment (for example, entry mode, timing of entry, partner selection) and business strategies (for example, sourcing, distribution, market orientation) should align properly with the concentrated industry if a foreign firm is to attenuate its vulnerability to institutional contingencies. Because low concentration implies high competition, MNEs entering such industries should ensure that they have sufficient competitive advantages to compete against rivals and compensate for their liabilities of foreignness.

Asset intensity is an indicator of capital requirements, a proxy for entry barriers, and a determinant of economies of scale. The imperfect capital market argument in industrial organization studies contends that firms in an industry which requires a large initial capital investment can obtain monopolistic profits over the long run because few qualified competitors will enter the industry. Furthermore, exit barriers created by substantial resource commitments may not be fully recoverable (Scherer and Ross 1990). High asset intensity hence discourages the entry of new firms into an industry. According to resource-based theory, the strategic objectives of firms are determined by their core competencies or resources. By contributing their distinctive resources to local capital- or technology-intensive industries, MNEs manifest their long-term commitment to indigenous production and host market expansion.

In examining the degree of competition in an industry in market economies, the most widely used measure is the leading firm concentration ratio (for example, CR4 for the US, CR5 for the UK, and CR3 for Germany). The degree of inequality of firm shares in an industry does not, however, necessarily reflect the vigor of competition. Governmental intervention and the existence of publically owned lead firms also have an influence. While the concentration ratio indicates an existing pattern of competition intensity, growth in the number of firms in an industry implies *ex post* patterns of competition that will eventually occur, depending upon the average length of time needed for a firm to reach full operation after entry in an industry. Therefore, this growth measure can be used as an important proxy for assessing the degree of competition in an industry. When a new industry emerges or the government deregulates or opens up an industry with pent-up demand, the number of firms, whether local or foreign, is expected to grow drastically as long as entry barriers are not too high. Over time, however, the increase in the number of firms in the industry is likely to boost competition, decrease disparities in profitability, and slow down local sales growth rates. Whenever a host country industry appears to be highly competitive as a result of a continuous increase in the number of firms in the industry, MNEs may consider shifting their focus from local market development to production factor exploitation or production rationalization through a globally integrated network.

An industry's capital requirements affects an MNE's international expansion because it determines investment commitment, capital structure, and currency mix. While asset intensity has implications for levels of start-up and exit costs, capital requirements determine the level of dynamic commitment and economic exposure an MNE faces. In contrast to operations in a domestic setting, international investment often requires financing in local currencies from local commercial banks or other financial institutions. Local financing, however, may face more barriers or bear higher costs. It can impact the MNE's capital structure, creating more difficulties for optimizing the capital structure of geographically dispersed businesses. Full reliance on international financing, on the other hand, may increase exchange risks if MNEs are focusing on indigenous markets. It can reduce strategic flexibility if MNEs cannot diversify their sourcing and marketing activities. In recent years, many MNEs have chosen to enter into international joint ventures in order to share the capital requirement with local partners. Risk and cost sharing is becoming increasingly necessary in rapidly changing industries. IBM, Siemens, and Toshiba each had financial strengths, yet still formed an international alliance to reduce their costs and risks in manufacturing computer chips. By keeping the levels of risk commensurate with each party, an international joint venture tends to be more stable and have a more cooperative culture.

Finally, a host industry's technological intensity also influences an MNE's entry decision and operational outcomes. Competitive, innovative MNEs often prefer technologically intensive industries when entering a foreign market as it can help them overcome disadvantages of newness and foreignness. However, selecting this type of industry requires contributions of distinctive knowledge and technological skills. The payoff from such contributions is highly uncertain in a foreign industry because MNEs confront greater risks of imitation by local firms. The challenges of protecting uncompensated leakage of their strategic assets are daunting. It is generally more difficult to maintain organizational control over international operations than over domestic ones. When international joint ventures are used as a vehicle for expansion into a host country's technologically intensive industry, this difficulty is magnified. MNEs thus need to make sure they are capable of achieving maximum payoffs from technological commitments in the course of choosing an industry.

Structural Evolution

In selecting a target industry overseas, an MNE should also identify the stage of its life cycle. This will provide insight into the demand side of the industry. Over time, most industries pass through a series of phases, from growth, through maturity, and eventually to decline. The strength and nature of structural forces and attributes typically change as an industry evolves. This is particularly evident when analyzing existing and potential competition. International managers must be able to identify the current stage of a candidate industry and anticipate how long the industry will remain at that stage before moving to the next phase. The industry life cycle model is used by international managers to assess whether the company is able to take advantage of opportunities and counter emerging threats in light of its strategic goals. In general, the life cycle has a greater impact on those MNEs pursuing long-term market power and a competitive position in a host country market than those seeking short-term profits or using a host country as a manufacturing platform for worldwide export.

Five industrial environments can be identified, each linked to a distinct stage of an industry's life cycle: (1) embryonic; (2) growth; (3) shakeout; (4) mature; and (5) declining. An embryonic industry is one that is just beginning to develop (for example, personal computers in 1980). Growth is slow because of such factors as consumer unfamiliarity with the industry's product, high prices due to the inability of companies to reap any significant economies of scale, and less developed distribution channels. MNEs investing at this stage are generally recognized as first movers or early entrants who face many tradeoffs between pre-emptive opportunities and financial or operational risks. An MNE needs to assess whether it should, and can, capitalize on such opportunities while countering emerging threats if opting for an embryonic industry in a host country.

Once market demand for the product begins to take off, a growth industry develops. First-time demand expands rapidly as many new consumers enter the market. In the internationalization process, investing in a growing industry in a target country is generally an ideal choice. A growth stage can be readily identified by evaluating growth of sales, profitability, output, and capital investments. This information is usually available from the statistical yearbooks or other periodicals. The length of the growth stage differs from industry to industry because it depends on such factors as entry barriers, capital requirements, economies of scale, technological requirements, risk and cost factors, and the openness of the industry to new local and foreign entrants. MNEs often encounter daunting challenges when taking the plunge into a foreign growth industry because host governments are likely to impose more entry or operational barriers on their fastest growing sectors. This is done in order to protect domestic firms or control the speed and pattern of foreign investment.

During the shakeout stage, market demand approaches saturation. Foreign companies may consider entering a shakeout industry if they aim to exploit short-term profitability or establish a presence in the market for exploring product, market, or technological niches in the host country. This stage can be identified by looking at changes in the growth pattern over time. In general, if entry barriers are low to both local and foreign firms, the shakeout stage will not last very long. It is critical for foreign companies to find a market niche or new opportunities from product differentiation when they plunge into a shakeout industry overseas.

An industry enters the mature stage as the shakeout stage ends. Although investing in a mature industry in a foreign market is generally inadvisable, some MNEs may choose to enter anyway if their objective is to shift home manufacturing sites to a target foreign country where production factors cost much less. In other words, when an MNE's foreign operations are not designed to explore the economic benefits of pent-up demand, the impact of an industry's life cycle stage is minimal. In fact, MNEs with this orientation may be able to acquire more benefits from a mature industry by taking advantage of greater bargaining power with suppliers.

An industry enters the decline stage when growth becomes negative for various reasons, including demographic changes, technological substitution, and international competition. Although there is no economic logic for local market-oriented MNEs to enter a declining industry in a host country, MNEs focused on minimizing costs may still benefit from starting production at a host site as a platform for export or vertical integration. Medium and small MNEs may use such sites for export to neighboring countries, the home country market, or other countries. As a result of increasing regionalization and gradual removal of trade barriers worldwide, this strategy will enable medium and small international firms to maximize benefits from their competencies in international distribution, strategic flexibility, and entrepreneurial orientation. Indeed, many Asian MNEs have successfully operated in neighboring countries using this strategy.

It is generally advisable for MNEs to select a growth industry when expanding into a target country. This is particularly true for MNEs seeking long-term market shares and a strong competitive position in the local industry. Today, most Western MNEs use this orientation when investing in emerging foreign markets. An embryonic industry appears to be an appropriate choice if an MNE wants to pursue first mover advantages in a foreign market. It is critical for MNEs to know the industry life cycle stages of both home and foreign industries. A mature industry at home may be embryonic or growing in a foreign country. MNEs pursuing market power should be able pre-empt first mover opportunities not only in a home industry but also in embryonic industries in foreign markets. Firms that aim at cost minimization, transnational distribution, local market niches, or vertical integration within a global network may consider entering mature or declining industries where they can still benefit from cheaper production factors or comparative advantages in the host country. The market orientation (local market versus export market), strategic goals (profit versus market share), distinctive competencies, rival behavior, and host country government policies are all important factors in making a life cycle analysis before selecting an industry.

INTEGRATING STRUCTURAL DYNAMICS WITH OTHER FACTORS

Each set of industrial dynamics presented above, namely structural dimensions, forces, attributes, and evolution, is useful for analyzing and selecting an industry in a foreign country. With a different focus, each set reveals an idiosyncratic, yet complementary, perspective on the industrial dynamics in a host country. Collectively, they serve as the foundation of an industry selection framework. In this core, the structural dimension perspective (structural uncertainty, complexity, and deterrence) mirrors the nature of the target industry, while consideration of structural forces (supplier, buyer, potential or existing rival, distributor, substitute, and government) uncovers the competitive situation of the industry. Meanwhile, the structural attributes analysis (profitability, sales growth, concentration, asset intensity, growth of number of firms, capital requirement, technology intensity) reveals industrial traits and the structural profile, and diagnosis of structural evolution (embryonic, growth, shakeout, maturity, and decline) displays a host industry's life cycle stage and corresponding characteristics of each phase.

The above four perspectives interact with one another. Structural dimensions are associated with all other structural dynamics. Industrial uncertainty, complexity, and deterrence contain dynamics of each structural force. For instance, if structural forces are munificent, structural deterrence will be low. Some structural attributes, such as concentration and growth of number of firms, are interrelated with structural complexity and deterrence. Structural evolution reflects the longitudinality of every structural dimension. In addition, structural forces and structural attributes are linked because the former provide conditions which nourish the latter. For example, favorable conditions in terms of existing rivalry, new entrants, buyer, and government segments may spur industrial growth in profit and sales. Moreover, structural attributes such as sales growth and concentration change over time along with the life cycle of an industry. These attributes are generally more favorable in the early stages of structural evolution. Lastly, the competitive pattern of structural forces alters as structural phases evolve. For instance, the threat of potential rivalry is certainly more fierce in a growth stage than in a decline stage.

Given this complementarity, MNEs should identify and verify structural dynamics in an integrated fashion to assess specific overseas industries. For example, all three sets of structural dynamics were relevant to Motorola's decision to enter the Chinese telecommunications industry. Analysis of structural forces shows that the degree of existing and potential rivalries from both local and foreign firms were low, as was the threat of substitutes. Buyer and supplier bargaining power in the early years after entry was also relatively weak. The life cycle stage of the industry was embryonic in the early 1980s, and Motorola knew that the pent-up demand for its products could create tremendous market opportunities. Finally, although uncertainty was expected to be high, the industry's sales and profitability growth were also high. Moreover, the high asset intensity of the industry decreased the threat of new entrants and increased the company's bargaining power with the local government. By allocating most of its FDI projects on the east coast of China and in major municipalities such as Tianjin and Shanghai, Motorola largely mitigated the risks of structural deterrence.

LONGITUDINAL AND COMPARATIVE PATTERN

Figure 8.1 schematically outlines an integrated framework for industry selection in international expansion. As shown in Figure 8.1, MNEs should take other relevant factors into account during industry selection.

It is crucial for MNEs to analyze the industry and its opportunities and threats both longitudinally and comparatively. Structural dimensions, forces, attributes, and life cycle stages of an industry in a host country are generally

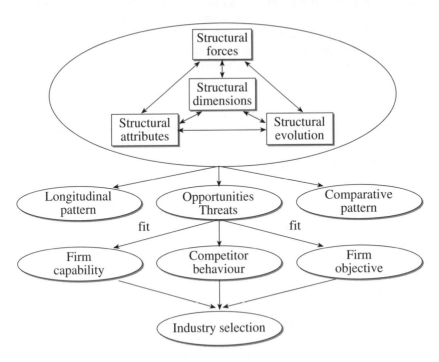

Figure 8.1   An integrated framework of industry selection

different from those at home. In other words, MNEs are often unfamiliar with these segments in a foreign context unless they have already operated there long enough. As most foreign industries are dynamic and most MNEs seek long-term economic benefits from international expansion, MNEs need to scan, analyze, and interpret structural dimensions, forces, attributes, and the life cycle based on longitudinal information as a prerequisite for analyzing target markets where fluctuations frequently occur. This *ex ante* longitudinal assessment of structural dynamics, as well as opportunities and threats identified from such dynamics, solidifies an understanding of industrial characteristics and reduces the likelihood of negative consequences arising from information asymmetry. According to transaction cost theory, this longitudinal appraisal improves bounded rationality in screening a host industry's dynamics, thus reducing transaction costs incurred during international expansion.

In addition, MNEs need to compare the target country's structural dynamics with those of home and other foreign countries. There has been an increasing tendency for industrial changes in one country to partially correlate with those in others as the result of technological advancement, international competition, capital flow, and reduction of entry barriers. Therefore, a firm should use a home or third country as a benchmark for assessing structural dynamics as well as opportunities and threats in a target foreign industry. This comparison helps an MNE find an appropriate industrial setting which will provide maximum economic rents. As seizing opportunities and mitigating threats in a foreign industry depend upon an MNE's distinctive abilities and competitive strategies, this comparison also helps the firm best to match its competence–opportunity configuration and align the strategy–environment relationship. The ultimate leaders in the global marketplace are normally those firms which establish such configurations and alignments.

Capability, Objective and Competitor Behavior

As noted above, evaluating whether or not the firm has the ability to seize these opportunities and counter these threats is important. This match often determines the financial and operational outcomes of international expansion in a dynamic, complex market. Misallocation of distinctive resources will waste not only internal resources but also external opportunities. The ability of an MNE to survive and succeed in today's turbulent international environment largely depends on its dynamic capabilities during international expansion. Dynamic capabilities refer to a firm's ability to diffuse, deploy, and use tacit, organizationally embedded resources in order to attain a sustained competitive advantage. Capability exploration (rent generation) and capability building (organizational learning) are two critical aspects of the dynamic capabilities needed during international expansion. Rent generation, or firm-specific strategic resources are critical both to gaining a competitive advantage and determining firm-level strategies which can exploit such advantages. Without such firm-specific capabilities (financial, technological, operational, and organizational), it is difficult for an MNE to explore and exploit pre-emptive, rent-yielding opportunities in a target foreign industry.

Dynamic learning capabilities are also critical. They ensure the evolutionary development of sustainable advantages and generate new bundles of resources. International expansion always calls for organizational learning to overcome the liability of foreignness. On the one hand, international expansion provides learning opportunities through exposure to new markets, internalization of new concepts, ideas from new cultures, access to new resources, and exposure to new competitors and terms of competition. On the other hand, learning does not take place in a vacuum, but rather results from coping with specific industrial environments. While rent-generating resources are necessary for MNEs exploring market opportunities, learning capabilities are imperative for trying to reduce vulnerability to contextual variabilities. Combining capabilities by integrating and synthesizing internal resources and external learning and applying both to the competitive environment is vital to an MNE's survival and growth in a foreign industry.

Another match lies between a firm's objectives and the emergence of opportunities or threats in a foreign market. Needless to say, every foreign market has opportunities that MNEs can explore or exploit. However, it is not realistic for an MNE to plunge into every market because its distinctive resources and competitive edge are limited. Therefore, in international competition an MNE's industry selection should be linked to its strategic goals. These goals include not only its objectives in operating in a foreign country (for example, local market share, risk reduction, financial returns) but also its aims for overall global expansion. For example, if an MNE seeks horizontal FDI (that is, FDI in the same industry abroad as a firm operates in at home) or forward vertical FDI (that is, FDI in an industry abroad that sells the output of a firm's domestic production processes), the firm should opt for a fast-growing, low-risk, less competitive industry in the host country. By contrast, if an MNE seeks backward vertical FDI (that is, FDI into an industry abroad that provides input for production at a firm's domestic or other foreign sub-units), it should attach more value to the comparative advantages of production factors of the host country. In principle, this decision should be made in such a way that the company can optimize goal fulfillment while using limited resources.

When promising opportunities emerge in a foreign market, other MNEs are expected to move in as well. If a firm enters a promising industry overseas, it will face competition from local businesses and other foreign rivals. Thus, before making the final decision on industry selection, an MNE should analyze the behavior of its major rivals. This means that it should ask such questions as whether the firm should go if its rival does, and when and how. If an MNE enters a target industry as a first mover, managers need to make sure that the first mover advantages outweigh the disadvantages. It should be able to seize first-mover opportunities in products, markets, and technologies, and sustain the first-mover position by driving out late competitors. If an MNE enters the target industry as a follower or late mover, managers should probe whether it can earn risk-adjusted net profits from the industrial environment, achieve benefits from the first mover's experience and learning curve, and develop competitive advantages in the industry against other rivals.

CONCLUDING REMARKS

The selection of a foreign industry is a system project in which the firm must analyze structural dimensions, forces, attributes, and evolution, employ an interactive and integrated approach to appraising all structural dynamics, and identify opportunities and threats longitudinally and comparatively. Moreover, the industry selection decision should be coupled with the firm's strategic objectives and organizational capabilities and analysis of competitor behavior. International managers need to ensure that the firm has the ability to enter the target industry successfully, efficiently explore market opportunities and over-come threats, and compete against major rivals in the industry. If these are probable, then the firm's goals will most likely be accomplished.

MNEs should configure their market and strategic orientations as well as other entry strategies such as entry mode, timing, location, and partner selection with structural dynamics of a foreign industry. Market orientation choices include local, export, and dual market foci. In principle, an MNE's orientation should be structured such that it can not only achieve its goals but also keep a certain degree of flexibility in responding to structural changes in a host industry and beyond. Similarly, strategic orientation (pros-pector, analyzer, defender, and reactor) must be arranged in such a way that an MNE will be innovative enough to maximize benefits from structural dynamics without assuming risks it cannot control. Entry mode should be arranged to facilitate rent-yielding from industrial dynamics. When a host industry is undergoing growth, the wholly-owned entry mode seems a bet-ter choice than the joint venture. Because timing of entry always involves trade-offs between economic returns and investment risks, whether an MNE should pursue early-mover advantages by entering an embryonic industry or seek niche benefits as a late mover depends on the firm's experience, competency, and strategic goals behind internationalization. When an MNE enters an economically and socio-culturally diverse country, different locations may present heterogeneous structural dynamics. Therefore, industry selection and location selection decisions should be coupled properly so as to maximize risk-adjusted net wealth from international expansion. Further, partnering with a competent local firm can assist an MNE in accessing an ideal industry, escalating its competitive edge, and alleviating operational uncertainties and financial risks. Thus, industry selection should align with decisions such as whether to collaborate with a local partner and what organizational attributes the partner firm should possess. In closing, this chapter presents an analytical framework on industry selection for MNEs, an important international business and strategy issue for both academics and practitioners alike.

REFERENCES

Caves, R.E. (1971), 'International Corporation: The Industrial Economies of Foreign Investment', *Economica*, 38, 1–27.
Caves, R.E. and K. Mehra (1986), 'Entry of Foreign Multinationals into US Manufacturing Industries', in M.E. Porter (ed.), *Competition in Global Industries*, Boston, MA: Harvard Business School Press.
Contractor, F.J. and P. Lorange (1988), 'The Strategy and Economic Basis for Cooperative Venture', in F.J. Contractor and P. Lorange (eds), *Cooperative Strategies in International Business*, Toronto: Lexington.
Dunning. J.H. (1979), 'Explaining Changing Patterns of International Production: In Defense of the Eclectic Theory', *Oxford Bulletin of Economics and Statistics*, 41, 269–96.
Geringer, J.M., P.W. Beamish, and R.C. da Costa (1989), 'Diversification Strategy and Internationalization: Implications for MNE Performance', *Strategic Management Journal*, 10, 109–19.
Hymer, S.H. (1976), *The International Operations of National Firms: A Study of Direct Foreign Investment*, Cambridge, MA: MIT Press.
Kim, W.C., P. Hwang, and W.P. Burgers (1993), 'Multinationals' Diversification and the Risk–Return Trade-off', *Strategic Management Journal*, 14, 275–86.
Porter. M.E. (1980), *Competitive Advantage*, New York: Free Press.
Porter, M.E. (1986), *Competition in Global Industries*, Boston, MA: Harvard Business School Press.
Porter, M.E. (1991), 'Towards a Dynamic Theory of Strategy', *Strategic Management Journal*, 12, 95–117.
Rumelt, R.P. (1991), 'How Much Does Industry Matter?', *Strategic Management Journal*, 12, 167–85.
Scherer, F.M. and D. Ross (1990), *Industrial Market Structure and Economic Performance*, third edition, Boston: Houghton Mifflin.
Tallman, S. and J. Li (1996), 'Effects of International Diversity and Product Diversity on the Performance of Multinational Firms', *Academy of Management Journal*, 39, 179–96.
Teece, D.J. (1985), 'Multinational Enterprises, Internal Governance, and Industrial Organization', *American Economic Review Papers and Proceedings*, 75, 233–8.

Teece, D.J., G. Pisano, and A. Shuen (1991), 'Dynamic Capabilities and Strategic Management', Working paper, University of California at Berkeley.

Willmore, L. (1994), 'Determinants of Industrial Structure: A Brazilian Case Study', in J.H. Dunning (ed.), *Transnational Corporations: Market Structure and Industrial Performance*, The United Nations Library on Transnational Corporations, 15, 96–129.

Yip, G.S. (1994), 'Industry Drivers of Global Strategy and Organization', *The International Executive*, 36(5), 529–56.

Yip, G.S. (1995), *Total Global Strategy: Managing for Worldwide Competitive Advantage*, Englewood Cliffs, NJ: Prentice Hall.

9. Business groups and economic development: a resource-based view*

Mauro F. Guillén

This chapter provides a resource-based explanation of why the importance of diversified business groups in emerging economies differs across countries and over time. Business groups result when entrepreneurs and firms accumulate the capability to combine the necessary domestic and foreign resources for repeated industry entry. Such a capability, however, can be developed and maintained as a valuable, rare, and inimitable skill only as long as asymmetric foreign trade and investment conditions prevail. Cross-sectional and longitudinal data on a variety of emerging economies are used to test this hypothesis simultaneously with three other competing explanations drawn from the existing literature. The importance of business groups is found to grow with foreign trade and investment asymmetries. The managerial problems and opportunities surrounding the rise and decline of business groups are discussed especially in the context of the current turmoil in emerging economies.

WHY DIVERSIFIED BUSINESS GROUPS?

The rise of large, diversified business groups in newly industrialized countries has captured the imagination of academics, journalists, and policy makers. Students of organization and management have long been fascinated by the questions of why firms diversify into new product lines, and what forms of control are best suited to manage such diversified businesses (Hoskisson and Hitt 1990; Ramanujam and Varadarajan 1989). Historically, the rise of the large modern corporation in the United States and Western Europe followed a pattern of specialization in a core technology family and subsequent related diversification (Chandler 1990). By contrast, diversified business groups operating in a collection of unrelated activities are typical of the capitalist countries that industrialized after World War II, that is, the emerging economies of southern Europe, Latin America, and East and South Asia (Amsden and Hikino 1994; Granovetter 1995. Khanna and Palepu, 1997).

In this chapter I argue that the rise of business groups is best approached from a resource-based perspective, that is, by looking at the distinctive capabilities, strengths, and weaknesses of this form of organization under different development circumstances. While the resource-based view has offered a compelling theory of diversification in the advanced countries (Markides and Williamson 1996; Peteraf 1993), little effort has been devoted to understanding the rise of business groups in emerging economies in terms of resources and capabilities. Yet, business groups are becoming major players in the world economy. Organization and management theory and practice would be enhanced by an understanding of the political–economic conditions accounting for differences in the importance of business groups across countries and over time (Granovetter 1995: 122; Orrù et al. 1997). Research has addressed how multinational companies are influenced by different political–economic contexts (Murtha and Lenway 1994), but neglected their effects on business groups. While in the more advanced economies government antitrust and tax policies are important to understand diversification (Hoskisson and Hitt 1990: 472–3), in emerging economies foreign trade and investment policies are far more momentous because they affect the interactions between local and foreign entrepreneurs and firms. The key contribution of this chapter is to conceptualize a resource-based view of business groups in emerging economies and to test empirically whether it surmounts the shortcomings of existing explanations. This chapter, therefore, offers a framework to think about the new political–economic realities of the turn of the century, and the resources and capabilities that facilitate diversification.

The notion of what exactly constitutes a business group requires clarification. A business group is a 'collection of firms bound together in some formal and/or informal ways' (Granovetter 1995: 95). Given its focus on the question of diversification, this chapter only considers groups that (1) are active in a wide variety of industries, (2) operate under somewhat unified entrepreneurial guidance, that is, that go beyond alliances among otherwise independent firms, and (3) fall short of constituting a fully integrated organizational structure. The Korean *chaebol*, the Indian *business houses*, the Turkish family holdings, or the Latin American and Spanish *grupos* come to mind as examples of such business groups. By contrast, the inter-organizational alliances exemplified by the Japanese *keiretsu* or the Chinese *guanxiqiye* networks in Taiwan and among the overseas Chinese throughout South East Asia (Orrù et al. 1997) lack the entrepreneurial coordination proposed in the above definition. Diversified business groups in emerging economies are also different from the conglomerates of the advanced countries in that they grew not in search of financial diversification but thanks to their ability to set up new business ventures across a variety of industries quickly and at low cost based on proprietary resources and coordination skills (Amsden and Hikino 1994;

Miller and Shamsie 1996). Business groups are more diversified than the Chandlerian modern industrial enterprise, but less coordinated (Amsden 1989: 125).

ALTERNATIVE THEORIES

The existence of diversified business groups in emerging economies long after the conglomerate form fell from grace in the most advanced countries has generated a considerable theoretical and empirical literature (Amsden and Hikino 1984; Granovetter 1995). This section reviews the assumptions, logic, and pitfalls of three existing theories of business groups in emerging economies, and proposes an alternative approach following the resource-based view. Each of the four perspectives provides a different answer to the question of why the importance of business groups in the economy differs across countries rather than to the question of which entrepreneurs or firms create a business group or whether they do it through organic growth or through mergers and acquisitions. This section develops four testable hypotheses that will be contrasted in the empirical section using information on the importance of business groups in a cross-sectional sample of nine emerging economies. The empirical section also compares longitudinal data drawn from three country case-studies – South Korea, Spain, and Argentina – to evaluate the effect of resource-related state policies at two points in time.

Existing Theories of Business Groups

Economists, economic sociologists, and development scholars have proposed three different ways to study business groups in emerging economies. They have made different assumptions and predictions as to the conditions under which business groups become an important factor in the economy. Each of the theories emphasizes a different domestic factor to account for the importance of business groups: market failure, social structure, or state activity.

Economics assumes that diversified business groups can only exist in the absence of a well-functioning market. Thus, it regards business groups as functional substitutes for allocation failures in the markets for production inputs (Leff 1978). Business groups step in where the market does not work or is not allowed to work by 'information problems', 'misguided regulations', or 'inefficient judicial systems' (Khanna and Palepu 1997). Business groups are but the internalization of market failure by entrepreneurs seeking to overcome the difficulties of obtaining capital, labor, raw materials, components, and technology in emerging economies. Groups step in where the market does not work or is not allowed to work by institutionalizing an alternative allocation mechanism so that production can take place (Khanna and Palepu 1997). An example helps to clarify the logic of the economic argument. If the capital market is underdeveloped or does not work efficiently, economists predict that the firm will tend to withhold earnings and develop internal capital allocation mechanisms to guide funds to their best economic use within the firm itself, either in an existing business or in a new one. Business groups grow in an economy to the extent that the failure of its capital market invites firms to invest retained earnings in new businesses as the rate of return in existing businesses drops with further additions of capital. The main prediction of the market failure view of business groups is:

Hypothesis 1:   The greater the market imperfections, the greater the importance of business groups in the economy.

The second approach, economic sociology, underlines how social and cultural patterns spawn different types of organizations. The argument revolves around the concept of authority as developed by the Weberian sociological tradition. It assumes that firms are isomorphic with the social structure surrounding them, and seeks to identify how vertical, horizontal, and reciprocal authority patterns affect organization at firm and interfirm levels. Economic sociologists have intensively analyzed East Asian countries, finding that business groups guided by a single entrepreneur proliferate in countries with vertical social relationships (Korea), though not when reciprocal (Japan) or horizontal ones (Taiwan) are the norm. These patterns of authority are assumed to be relatively stable over time and resilient to foreign pressure (Orrù et al. 1997).

A social order characterized by vertical relationships is based on a patrimonial concept of authority and on inheritance rules that favor the eldest son (Fields 1995: 38–44). Members of the firm owe obedience and personal loyalty to the patrimonial figurehead. New activities or businesses are integrated into the patrimonial household as subordinate units, and every effort is made not to lose control as the household turns into a collection of businesses of greater size and complexity. Moreover, patrimonial entrepreneurs compete with each other without ever collaborating on projects of mutual interest, unlike in social settings characterized by reciprocal relationships (the Japanese *keiretsu*) or horizontal ones (the Taiwanese *guanxiqiye*). The argument that social and authority relationships of a vertical kind are associated with groupings of firms under the guidance of a single entrepreneur leads to:

Hypothesis 2:   The more vertical the pattern of relationships in the society, the greater the importance of business groups in the economy.

The third approach to the study of business groups focuses on late economic development as a process driven by the state and/or the banks. In a first version of this theory, scholars of East Asian development have observed that 'autonomous' states with the ability to allocate capital and other resources at will encourage a few entrepreneurs to enter new industries, thus facilitating the proliferation of business groups. Autonomous states are those free from socially rooted demands and from struggles among class or group interests. Autonomous policy makers are in a position to formulate their own economic agendas ahead of social demands or even against those demands. For control and accountability reasons autonomous states generally prefer to deal with only a few entrepreneurs as their private-sector agents (Amsden 1989).

The second version of late development theory also attributes a key role for the state in the growth of business groups even when it cannot act autonomously. The argument is that when the state falls prey to special interests or lacks control over the financial system, business groups will become important as the 'non-autonomous' state uses its budget to secure the political support of entrepreneurs by enabling them to exploit rent-seeking opportunities (Evans 1979). Thus:

Hypothesis 3:   The greater the autonomy and size of the state, the greater the importance of business groups in the economy.

The three existing theoretical perspectives, however, do not consider how entrepreneurs and firms build rare, valuable, inimitable, and excess *capabilities* that allow them to diversify into unrelated product-market areas. This omission is very difficult to justify because a sound theory ought to explain how entrepreneurs and firms diversify in the face of competition from non-diversified firms and/or foreign multinationals. Existing theories are fairly deterministic in their approach, leaving very little room, if any, for entrepreneurial or firm choice and capability building. Market failure theory focuses entirely on factor markets to the exclusion of product markets in which the business group as an organizational form competes against other types of domestic and foreign producers. Economic sociology only takes into account capabilities embedded in social structure and not those that entrepreneurs can appropriate as their own. Like market failure theory and economic sociology, late development theory falls to explain why diversification is sustainable in the face of competition from other domestic and foreign firms. The importance of providing an explanation of how business groups can sustain their diversification requires an alternative view based on resources and capabilities.

A Resource-based View of Diversified Business Groups

The resource-based view advanced in this chapter seeks to surmount the limitations of previous approaches. Its main assumption is that entrepreneurs and firms in emerging economies create business groups if political–economic conditions allow them to acquire and maintain the capability of combining foreign and domestic resources – inputs, processes, and market access – to repeatedly enter new industries. Given that the logic of diversification is to access both domestic and foreign resources rather than to reap scope economies and minimize transaction costs, diversifying entrepreneurs or firms will rarely bother to build integrated organizational structures to capture cross-industry synergies (for example, Kock and Guillén 2001; Chandler 1990; Hoskisson 1987; Hill and Hoskisson 1987). They will rely on the looser arrangement of the business group.

Entrepreneurs and firms need to gain access to three types of resources when entering an industry: (1) *inputs* such as labor, capital and raw materials; (2) process-related *knowledge*, including technology and operational know-how; and (3) *markets*, including distribution channels and contracts with foreign and domestic customers or with the state (Markides and Williamson 1996). Those who learn to combine these resources quickly and effectively will be best able to create a business group by repeatedly entering a variety of industries. This capability for repeated industry entry consists of a bundle of skills that facilitate conducting feasibility studies, obtaining licenses from the state, arranging financial packages, securing technology and know-how, setting up plants, hiring and training the workforce, and establishing supply and distribution channels (Amsden and Hikino 1994; Evans 1979: 281). The capability is generic precisely because it is not industry specific, and difficult to trade because it is embodied in the organization's owners, managers, and routines. It is in excess supply immediately after the entrepreneur or firm consummates entry into a new industry. Once the new plant has been set up and is running, the capability to enter new industries becomes idle. Therefore, it encourages those who possess it to diversify across industries rather than become specialists in one industry or product line. In terms of Miller and Shamsie's (1996) categories, the capability for repeated industry entry is related to both discrete property-based resources (exclusive access to production factors, technology and distribution channels), and systemic knowledge-based resources (coordination skills). It also contains two of Barney's (1991: 101–2) and Hoskisson and Hitt's (1990: 464–5) excess capabilities. First, intangible resources such as contacts, access to subsidized finance, and the know-how to set up a plant and absorb foreign technology (see also Amsden and Hikino 1994). And second, tangible resources such as group-affiliated general trading units that can be used to import a variety of needed inputs and/or export a diversified portfolio of products (Fields 1995).

A generic and non-tradable capability to combine foreign and domestic resources for industry entry, however, is not enough for a business group to sustain its competitive advantage over time. Per the resource-based view, it is imperative that certain *limits* to competition exist so that the capability can be accumulated through learning-by-doing, and maintained over time as a rare, valuable, and inimitable asset (Barney 1991; Peteraf 1993). The inimitability requirement is especially important. Limits preventing the imitation of the strategy of rapid industry entry by competitors – whether domestic or foreign – may result from causal ambiguity, time lags, size advantages, superior foresight, sheer luck, or preferential access to resources (Barney 1991: 105). In an emerging economy, access to resources is very sensitive to the kinds of policies that the state implements to promote economic development (Haggard 1990).

Development Strategies and Limits to Resource Access

Among the various development policies and strategies, those having to do with *foreign trade* and *foreign direct investment* tend to have a momentous impact on resource accessibility by entrepreneurs and firms in emerging economies. The reason lies in the fact that some of the resources for new industry entry are domestic (labor, access to home market) while others are situated, at least in part, beyond the country's borders (raw materials, capital, technology, know-how, access to foreign markets). If foreign trade and investment policies are such that only certain local entrepreneurs and firms can combine the required domestic and foreign resources, they will be able to accumulate the capability of repeatedly entering new industries, and build a diversified business group. Thus, the resource-based view needs to be complemented with an understanding of the political and economic context in which entrepreneurs and firms accumulate capabilities.

Research on the political economy of development suggests that it is crucial to distinguish between *outward* and *inward* foreign trade and investment flows because they need not be correlated with each other. While many of the advanced economies have balanced outward and inward foreign investment flows, the reverse is true for most emerging economies (Haggard 1990). Unbalanced outward and inward flows may affect the access to resources by different domestic and foreign actors. Outward flows will remain at a low level if the emphasis is on inward-looking development, that is, 'populist' policies that promote short-term compromise and income redistribution among interest groups frequently at the expense of productivity growth and long-term prosperity. Outward flows will reach higher levels when 'modernizing' policies encourage firms to sell and invest abroad (Kaufman and Stallings, 1991). Similarly, inward flows will remain at a low level when policies are 'nationalist', that is when there is protectionism and subsidization of domestic firms (trade) or if there is a preference for national private and state ownership of firms (foreign investment). Policies that allow for high levels of inward flows are generally labeled 'pragmatic' or 'liberal' (Haggard 1990).

Inward and outward flows appear cross-classified in Table 9.1. The low–low configuration follows from a 'nationalist–populist' development strategy. This is a situation in which most developing countries found themselves at mid-twentieth century. It was a fairly unstable predicament because acute balance-of-payments crises and rampant inflation tend to cripple the economy if the government perseveres in keeping low levels of both inward and outward flows (Kaufman and Stallings 1991; Haggard 1990). When faced with such crises, one frequent option is to selectively allow imports and inward investment, that is, to relax nationalist policies without abandoning populism. These changes, however, frequently produce economic and political problems for the government as the domestic interests affected by the opening of inward flows mobilize against it. Thus, it is common to observe populist countries oscillating between the two cells on the right side of Table 9.1 unless they adopt a modernizing strategy characterized by high levels of outward flows. Argentina, Venezuela, Brazil, and India provide examples of this 'erratic' populist strategy during much of the post World War II period (Haggard 1990).

The 'nationalist–modernizing' or low–high cell in Table 9.1 is exemplified in the political economy literature by the East Asian 'tigers' (Haggard 1990). It is a situation in which the country combines low levels of imports and inward investment with high levels of exports and outward investment. By contrast, the 'pragmatic–modernizing' cell implies high levels of both imports and exports and of inward and outward investment, and has been recently adopted by emerging economies adjacent to developed areas – Mexico, Ireland, or the southern European countries – as well as by the commercial enclaves of Singapore and Hong Kong.

The Impact of Development Strategies on Business Groups

The impact of different development strategies on the proliferation of business groups and other organizational forms can be directly derived from the characteristics of each of the four cells in Table 9.1. Subsidiaries of foreign multinational enterprises (MNEs) are more likely to proliferate in the two upper cells characterized by permissive policies toward inward investment, while state-owned enterprises should be more likely in the two lower cells with restricted inward flows resulting from nationalist policies such as pro-

Table 9.1 The effect of foreign trade and investment flows on business groups in emerging economies

	Level of outward flows	
Level of inward flows	High (Modernizing)	Low (Populist)
High (Pragmatic)	HIGH: Allow imports & inward investment HIGH: Export-led growth & outward investment *Context conducive to:* Foreign MNEs & unaffiliated firms	HIGH: Allow imports & inward investment LOW: Import substitution & local investment *Context conducive to:* Foreign MNEs & **business groups**
Low (Nationalist)	LOW: Protectionism & local ownership HIGH: Export-led growth & outward investment *Context conducive to:* State firms & **business groups**	LOW: Protectionism & local ownership LOW: Import substitution & local investment *Context conducive to:* State firms & unaffiliated firms

tectionism and a preference for domestic ownership. A more interesting theoretical problem is to predict which cells are expected to contain more business groups. The core conceptual idea is that the circumstances associated with the two cells on the diagonal of Table 9.1 (high–high or low–low cells) do not produce cross-border limits to resource access by entrepreneurs and firms. By contrast, *the cells off the diagonal describe asymmetric situations in which only some (local) entrepreneurs and firms have access to domestic and foreign resources simultaneously.* Business groups will become more important in the economy when such asymmetries persist long enough to allow entrepreneurs and firms to develop and maintain an inimitable capability to combine foreign and domestic resources that encourages them to enter multiple industries. Let us analyze each cell of Table 9.1 in turn.

The low–high cell

The two off-diagonal cells in Table 9.1 are characterized by asymmetric foreign trade and investment. First, the low–high configuration of nationalist–modernizing countries offers the well-connected entrepreneur or firm the possibility of contributing to export-led development by combining domestic and foreign resources under the protective umbrella of policies restricting imports and inward foreign investment. Preferential access to resources, however, constitutes a competitive capability only if it allows diversification that is beyond the reach of other actors (Markides and Williamson 1996; Peteraf 1993). When inward investment is restricted, such local inputs as labor, physical resources or loans will only be available to domestic actors and not to foreign MNEs. Process-related knowledge will only be available to the few trustworthy entrepreneurs with connections to foreign MNEs. Entrepreneurs and firms who manage to repeatedly obtain operating permits from the government and technology licenses from foreign MNEs will be in a position to reduce the cost of entering new industries (Amsden and Hikino 1994). Over time, this experience effect will advantage diversified business groups over non-diversified firms. Finally, access to markets can be allocated in discriminating ways by the government (licenses, contracts with the state) or by foreign MNEs (original equipment manufacturing contracts for export). The capability to combine resources for industry entry will remain valuable as long as nationalist–modernizing policies do not shift.

The case of the South Korean Hyundai group illustrates the dynamics of diversification and business group formation in the asymmetric low–high cell. South Korea is a country in which foreign trade and investment flows have been asymmetric since the 1960s (see the Appendix). In 1947 entrepreneur Chung Ju Yung founded a construction company that grew quickly thanks to three important contracts with the state: the first bridge over the Han river, Kimp'o international airport, and the Seoul–Pusan highway. The first unrelated diversifications took place in the mid-1960s when Hyundai entered steel manufacturing and oil refining, two industries protected by the government. During the 1970s Hyundai was among the fastest growing *chaebol*, achieving a stunning 38 percent cumulative annual asset growth rate with new entries into automobiles, aluminum, shipbuilding, and heavy engineering. It was one of a handful of *chaebol* allowed to create a trading company and a merchant marine in the mid-1970s, two key tangible resources to support further diversification into new fields. Hyundai's diversification projects were undertaken with subsidized credit, government trade protection, and foreign technology. For example, Hyundai Motor Co. assembled Ford Escorts for export. During the 1970s the company obtained technology from Japanese, British, Italian, and American auto companies. In shipbuilding, Hyundai acted as a subcontractor to Kawasaki Shipbuilding, and later obtained technology from several European companies as well as from Japan. In each of these industries the state committed itself to protect the domestic market and to prevent MNEs from operating freely in Korea. Thus, Hyundai could use domestic sales to subsidize exports using borrowed capital, technology, and market access. A similar blueprint of diversification was followed during the 1980s and 1990s when entering electronics, elevators, robotics, software, broadcasting, and publishing (Amsden 1989: 175–9, 269–90; Kim 1997: 131, 155–6).

A second example of a South Korean group which thrived on the basis of contacts inside and outside Korea is Samsung ('three stars'). Its origins date back to 1938, when entrepreneur I Pyong Ch'ol founded a trading company. After the Korean War, under the asymmetric populist–modernizing conditions created by President Rhee, the company moved into sugar refining and textiles, and then into insurance and banking. As Korea started to pursue an asymmetric export-led, nationalist–modernizing path to development during the 1960s, Samsung found new opportunities for diversification in industries with a potential for export sales. In 1965 Samsung entered the manufacturing of fertilizers first for the domestic market and later for the international one. Further diversification into electronics, shipbuilding, chemicals, petrochemicals, industrial engineering, construction, and aerospace took place during the 1970s and 1980s as the government emphasized heavy industry. While Samsung grew slower than Hyundai and Daewoo during the 1970s because it did not benefit nearly as much as them from the government's heavy industry drive (Kim 1997: 157), it did take advantage of the protection of the domestic market. In 2001, Samsung is the world's largest manufacturer of semiconductors, having taken the world by storm with its 4-megabyte dynamic random-access memory chip. In 1997 Samsung Electronics obtained some 1300 patents in the US, ranking sixth in the world after IBM, Canon, NEC, Motorola, and Sony. In defiance of the government's efforts to curb the power of the *chaebol* and overcome chronic overcapacity problems during the 1990s, Samsung entered the auto industry in collaboration with Nissan.

Samsung's consumer electronics diversification is the most interesting from the point of view of understanding how business groups rise in an asymmetric nationalist–modernizing context. The Samsung Electronics Company was created in the early 1970s to make audio and video equipment, household appliances, and electronics products. It was only as late as 1981 that Samsung and another of the *chaebol*, Goldstar, licensed the video cassette recorder (VCR) technology and trademark from the Victor Company of Japan, a Matsushita affiliate. Samsung learned the manufacturing technology swiftly and – thanks to subsidized loans – became a low-cost VCR manufacturer, exporting as much as 70 percent of production. In the late 1980s Korean-made VCRs represented one fifth of the US market. By 1992, a mere decade after entering the industry, Samsung was the second largest VCR manufacturer in the world, with a worldwide market share of about 10 percent. The company has only recently started to establish its own brand name. It still relies on original equipment manufacturing contracts with foreign MNEs for two-third of its sales. In 1999 it signed the largest ever contract to supply displays to Dell. As predicted by the resource-based theory of business groups furthered in this chapter, Samsung leveraged its contacts both with the government and with foreign technology and market providers so as to enter mature industries with the intention of engaging in exports.

The high-low cell
The second off-diagonal cell in Table 9.1 represents the high–low or pragmatic–populist development strategy. Entrepreneurs and firms with inimitable ties to the state, foreign MNEs, and moneylenders will benefit in a way that mirrors the low–high cell. Pragmatic–populist policies loosen regulations concerning foreign equity investment, especially when import-substitution efforts escalate from consumer non-durable goods to intermediate, durable, and capital goods. But this is an asymmetric strategy because exports and outward foreign investment are low (Haggard 1990; Evans 1979). In an import-substitution environment MNEs prefer to manufacture or distribute their products in collaboration with local entrepreneurs who know how to navigate through the treacherous conditions created by economic and political populism, including powerful labor unions, import-competing interests, and idiosyncratic credit allocation practices. MNEs may also choose to sell manufacturing licenses to local entrepreneurs either because attaining minimally efficient plant scales is difficult inside the domestic market or because access to natural resources and distribution channels is hard for a foreigner to obtain. As long as asymmetric pragmatic–populist policies remain in place, entrepreneurs and firms with a combinative capability will continue utilizing

it to enter new industries in association with MNEs, forming business groups in the process.

The dynamics of diversification in the high–low cell can be illustrated by looking at the evolution of Pérez Companc. This is the second largest group in Argentina, a country in which business groups have alternately thrived during periods of asymmetric, pragmatic–populist development, and contracted under symmetric nationalist populism (see the Appendix). Pérez Companc was founded as a shipping company in 1946. It grew slowly during the 1950s and 1960s as a general subcontractor to the state-owned oil and coal companies, and the few foreign oil firms allowed to operate in the country. A period of much faster diversification and growth started under the military juntas in the mid-1970s, which pursued policies that resulted in an asymmetric situation of high imports and inward investment but low exports and outward investment. In 1973 the group controlled only ten firms, but by 1983 it included 53 firms in such diverse industries as mining, oil, petrochemicals, fertilizers, appliances, machinery, nuclear engineering, agribusiness, food processing, fishing, cement, metals, construction, tourism, and financial services. In each of these businesses the group combined local and foreign resources. Pérez Companc resumed its diversification under the asymmetric conditions following the Latin American debt crisis of 1982. By 1987 it controlled 84 companies, with new entries into fields in which it had little or no expertise, obtaining it from abroad: electronics, data processing, biotechnology, and retailing (Acevedo et al. 1990: 78–81). The group grew inside the protected domestic market, never exporting more than 5 percent of production. After the impasse caused by hyperinflation during the late 1980s, Pérez Companc divested from several industries, but at the same time entered new ones, especially services, so as to take advantage of privatizations of state-owned companies. In 1995 the group comprised 69 companies in oil, petrochemicals, agribusiness, food processing, metals, gas transportation and distribution, electrical utilities, telecommunications, railways, and construction. In most of these businesses Pérez Companc relies on the state for concessions and on MNEs for technology.

While Pérez Companc has not developed any proprietary technological or manufacturing capabilities and has largely failed to make a dent in international competition, other Argentine groups have not only diversified into a variety of manufacturing and service activities but also demonstrated they excel at some activity on a global scale. The best two examples are Industrias Metalúrgicas Pescarmona (IMPSA) – a major player in the world markets for turbines and cranes – and Techint, whose DST firm (Dalmine-Siderca-Tamsa) is the world's largest manufacturer of seamless steel pipe (2.4 million tons), accounting for over 18 percent of total world production and 26 percent of world exports. Over the last 52 years, companies affiliated to Techint have made more than 26 000 miles of pipelines, enough to circle the globe.[1] In 1999, Techint's Tamsa subsidiary tied with Steel Dynamics of the US and POSCO of South Korea in Morgan Stanley's ranking of the world's most competitive maker of steel products (*Korea Times*, 4 May 1999).

Techint comprises over 100 firms in steel, machinery, engineering, construction, turnkey plant design and construction, oil and gas exploration and production, flat and pressed glass, paper, cement and ceramic tiles, and a bewildering assortment of privatized firms, namely, sanitary services, railways, toll highways, telecommunications, gas transportation and distribution, power generation, and even correctional facilities. Total group sales totaled $5.6 billion in 1997, making it the largest in the country. It exports about 40 percent of its production in Argentina. Sixty percent of its 50 000 employees are located in Latin America, Europe, and Asia, unlike the case of Pérez Companc, which is mostly a domestic group.

The historical origins of Techint go back to fascist Italy. During the Great Depression, bankrupt steel company Dalmine was taken over by the state. Mussolini appointed engineer Agostino Rocca as its chairman. At the end of the war, Rocca exiled himself first in Mexico and then in Argentina, where he opened a branch of Dalmine with capital of Italian and US origin. In 1954 he built the first South American seamless pipe facility some 50 miles outside Buenos Aires. In 1962 he spun off Propulsora Siderúrgica, a firm making flat steel. Rocca organized his businesses under the Techint holding company, which was also the group's engineering and construction arm. He was well-connected both internationally and in Argentina. In fact, most of Techint's early contracts came from the state-owned oil, gas, water, and sanitation companies, and the technology from foreign sources. By 1973 Techint included 30 different companies, and 46 by the end of the period of military juntas in 1983, benefiting from asymmetric pragmatic–populist conditions to diversify into textiles, cellulose fibers, paper, nuclear power equipment, insurance, and banking as well as steel, engineering and construction. Rocca also had interests in the Argentine subsidiary of Italian tire maker Pirelli (Acevedo et al. 1990: 111–13; Lewis 1992: 266–7, 346–7, 356, 470; Toulan 1997). After the difficult period of decline and hyperinflation during the late 1980s, Techint resumed its growth as a result of liberalization and privatization during the 1990s. By 1997 Techint was the fifth largest business group in Argentina. As in the cases of Hyundai and Samsung, Pérez Companc and Techint have reacted to their country's asymmetric pattern of insertion in the global economy by establishing ties within and across borders.

The low–low cell

The generic capability of repeated industry entry is not useful in the presence of symmetrical circumstances. In the low–low cell, diversification is tricky for two reasons. First, import substitution without direct foreign activity typically results in a variety of bottlenecks that slow down the growth of new industries due to the scarcity of equity or loan capital, and technology. Thus, opportunities for diversification will be rare. Second, maintaining a 'low profile' is politically more advantageous in a nationalist–populist context because of heavy government regulation (Haggard 1990; Kaufman and Stallings 1991). The evolution of the Pérez Companc group when Argentine foreign trade and investment flows were low in both directions illustrates this situation. The group shrank during the mid-1960s, early 1970s, and late 1980s, precisely when foreign MNEs reduced imports, investments, technology transfers, or simply left the country (Acevedo et al. 1990; Lewis 1992).

The high–high cell

Under high–high conditions foreign MNEs, for example, can freely operate inside the country and across its borders in either direction, and they will find it profitable to locate certain activities in the country so as to engage in exports. Freedom to operate across borders will facilitate international sourcing and organizational integration, thus making MNEs more competitive than domestic business groups. Local knowledge will become less important because MNEs are interested not only in selling domestically but also internationally. Moreover, a non-diversified local firm may also be at an advantage over a business group as long as it develops product-focused expertise. Hence, one would expect the capability to combine domestic and foreign resources to lose its inimitable character when inward and outward flows are both high.

The fall and demise of business groups when inward and outward foreign trade and investment flows become more balanced can be illustrated with the case of the Spanish groups (see the Appendix). The groups' once useful capability to enter multiple industries lost its inimitable character once the protection awarded by asymmetric development disappeared, forcing them to focus on other capabilities that they may or may not have developed. Unión Explosivos Río Tinto (UERT) was originally founded as a mining company with the participation of British capital. The firm grew via diversification during the 1960s when Spain implemented asymmetric policies similar to those of Korea. Given its contacts with the government, local banks, and foreign MNEs, UERT diversified into fertilizers, chemicals, oil, plastics, engineering, pharmaceuticals, cosmetics, real estate, and consulting services. By the mid-1970s it was the largest diversified conglomerate in the country (Muñoz et al. 1978: 428–33). The economic crisis of the 1970s forced many of its companies into bankruptcy. Subsequently, Spain's bid to become a member of the European Union meant that trade and investment protectionism had to be abandoned. Like many of the other

Spanish groups, UERT collapsed during the 1980s, with its various companies being sold to foreigners.

There is a noteworthy case of a business group in Spain that – although
originating in the asymmetric conditions of the 1950s and 1960s – has managed not only to survive but to thrive under the less auspicious symmetric
circumstances of the 1980s and 1990s. Intriguingly, it is not a family-controlled
business group, but the world's most famous system of worker-owned
manufacturing and service cooperatives: the Mondragón group. Mondragón
is the largest cooperative group in the world, with over 25 000 employees,
$3.5 billion in revenues, and a surplus of 7 percent of sales, making it one of
the ten largest companies in Spain, and among the 500 largest groups in
Europe. Unbelievable as it may be, Mondragón has become a multinational
enterprise with production and distribution investments in Europe, the Americas, Northern Africa, and Asia. Cooperatives belonging to the group are
engaged in everything from chips, appliances, autoparts, and furniture to
machine-tools, robotics, elevators, heavy machinery, and large construction
projects. It is the world's largest manufacturer of digital readouts. Mondragón
also includes a savings bank (Caja Laboral Popular), and Spain's fifth largest
retailer (Eroski). About a dozen books and monographs, as well as a myriad
of articles, published in English or in Spanish testify to the economic and
sociological significance of this worker-owned group of cooperatives. The
Mondragón cooperatives expanded over the years in response to the reigning
conditions inside a country that was attempting to industrialize and, later, to
develop a service economy (Guillén 2001).

The first cooperative of the Mondragón group was founded in 1956 with
the capital raised by five workers under the leadership of a Catholic priest
interested in promoting the ideas of self-management, worker ownership, and
capital–labor harmony. This northern Basque town, located close to the Franco-
Spanish border, was home to the large foundry and metalworking firm of
Unión Cerrajera. The area had long been known for its skilled craftsmen and
the manufacturing of a variety of high-quality metal products, including
swords and firearms. In order to secure the required governmental authoriza-
tions to enter new industries, the founders purchased a bankrupt firm that
used to make electrical and mechanical household appliances. In subsequent
years new cooperatives were created to manufacture machine tools, electro-
mechanical components, and metallic products. In 1959 a Workers' Savings
Bank was founded to provide funds for social security, cultural and educational activities, and new cooperatives (Whyte and Whyte 1991: 10–11, 25–87).
The economic crisis of the mid-1970s and the subsequent pursuit of symmetric pragmatic–modernizing policies by the Spanish government created both
the pressure and the opportunity to reorganize the system of diversified
independent cooperatives as a multidivisional group, with a strategic plan-

ning department on top staffed by professional managers. The culmination of these efforts was the creation in the early 1990s of Mondragón Corporación Cooperativa, including financial, distribution, and industrial divisions. Simultaneously, the group's multiple brands were consolidated and export growth was emphasized over the domestic market. Between the early 1970s and the early 1990s exports of manufactured goods climbed from 10 to 31 percent of total production, mimicking the transformation of the overall Spanish economy (Whyte and Whyte 1991: 195–211).

A rather unusual development during the 1980s has been Mondragón's increasing foreign investments, largely in response to the pragmatic–modernizing policies underpinning the country's accession to the European Union. Mondragón cooperatives have a chip facility in Thailand, refrigerator assembly plants in Morocco and Argentina, a bus body work joint venture and an acquired refrigerator plant in China, auto parts and electric components plants in Mexico, and several stores of the Eroski supermarket chain in southern France. It has purchased a Dutch electro-mechanical components firm (Controls International), an elevator manufacturer in the UK (Cable Lifts and Elevators), two French machine-tool companies (SEI and Cima Robotique), and a Polish household appliances plant. Mondragón is now planning to open an electric appliances assembly line in Egypt, invest in joint-venture auto parts plants in the UK and the US, and acquire Ford's and Volkswagen's auto parts subsidiaries in Brazil and Argentina. As of the mid-1990s, the Fagor cooperative had strategic alliances with Thomson Electroménager, General Domestic Appliances, and Ocean (household appliances), Societé Européenne de Propulsion (Vulcain engine for the Ariane satellite-launching rocket), Baumüller (machine-tool components), and participated in the European Union's ESPRIT and Eureka high-tech programs. Mondragón has managed to survive as a group in the pragmatic–modernizing Spanish context thanks to its ability to develop technology and markets internally and in collaboration with others.

The Resource-based View and the Importance of Business Groups

A resource-based view of business groups adopts a managerially-oriented perspective in arguing that the inimitability of the set of rare resources that enable entrepreneurs to diversify is only guaranteed under certain development circumstances and not others (Barney 1991). It predicts that the importance of business groups will be greater in emerging economies with asymmetric trade and investment conditions (high–low and low–high cells of Table 9.1) because they allow a few entrepreneurs and firms to develop the capability of combining the requisite foreign and domestic resources for repeated industry entry. Such a generic capability remains idle if the group does not prepare to enter a new industry, has multiple uses, and is difficult to

trade, encouraging those who possess it to diversify across unrelated manufacturing and service industries. The advantages associated with this capability
can only be sustained to the extent that asymmetries in trade and investment
persist over time, making it inimitable. Otherwise, any firm or entrepreneur
would be able to enter new industries, including foreign MNEs (the high–
high cell of Table 9.1). As Hoskisson and Hitt (1990) have noted, if the
capability to diversify is tied to government policy, the firm will continue
using it in search of opportunities for cross-subsidization and in order to
become 'too big to be allowed to fall'. Thus, the resource-based view argues
that diversification in the form of a business group is sustainable if there are
limits to the combination of foreign and domestic resources for industry entry
(as in the high–low and low–high cells of Table 9.1), but not in the absence of
such limits (high–high and low–low cells). This argument leads to a single
prediction that captures the fundamental difference between the two off-
diagonal cells of Table 9.1 and the two cells on the diagonal:

Hypothesis 4:   The greater the asymmetries in foreign trade and investment,
the greater the importance of business groups in the economy.

The next section provides empirical tests of the four alternative explanations of business groups summarized in hypotheses 1–4. Both cross-sectional
and longitudinal analyses are used to assess the effects of market failure,
vertical social relationships, state autonomy and size, and foreign trade and
investment asymmetries on the importance of business groups in the economy.

EMPIRICAL TESTS

Comparable data on the importance of business groups relative to the size of
the economy are surprisingly lacking from the extant literature (Amsden and
Hikino 1994; Granovetter 1995). Moreover, existing theories of business
groups have never been tested empirically across a sample of countries. Most
previous research has adopted the form of detailed and very valuable case
studies within countries or between pairs of countries. Accordingly, the
extant literature does not offer empirical measures of either the importance of
business groups in the economy or of the various factors believed to be
causally linked to the phenomenon of business groups.

Two kinds of evidence are used to assess the four hypotheses on business
groups. First, cross-sectional data for a sample of 90 groups in nine emerging
economies will be used to test hypotheses 1–4. Second, comparative longitudinal evidence on the affiliation of the 100 largest firms in each of three
countries – South Korea, Argentina, and Spain – between two points in time,

1975 and 1995, will provide evidence on how various organizational forms, including business groups, fare under changing foreign trade and investment asymmetries.

Business Groups Across Emerging Economies

Data and methods

Information on each of the top ten business groups was collected for the nine emerging economies in South and East Asia, Latin America, and southern Europe for which comparable data exist (N = 90).[2] The total net sales of each of the top ten business groups was divided by the country's Gross Domestic Product (GDP), with a sample mean of 1.77 percent and standard deviation of 2.21. This ratio provides a repeated measure of the importance of business groups relative to the size of the economy that is comparable across countries at each level of the top ten ranking (Cohen and Cohen 1983: 429–35). The goal is to assess which country conditions affect the importance of the top ten business groups relative to the economy.

Because the focus of existing theories and of the resource-based view is on explaining the *importance* of business groups in the economy and not which particular entrepreneurs or firms create a business group, the proxies chosen for each theory capture the conditions that are supposed to foster the proliferation and/or growth of business groups in general. Indicators for existing theories of business groups were as follows. Market failure theories point to underdeveloped financial markets as a reason for the creation of business groups. The most widely used indicator of the development of financial markets, stock market capitalization as a percentage of GDP, was chosen (IFC 1998). Economic sociology's prediction that vertical or hierarchical societies foster business groups was operationalized by Hofstede's (1991: 26–7) power distance index, which captures the extent to which relationships in a society are based on autocratic and paternalistic assumptions. This index is frequently used in the international management literature. Late development theory's predictions about state autonomy and state size were measured with the inverse of Henisz's (2000) index of political constraints based on the Polity III database (Gurr, 1990 and subsequent electronic updates), and with general government consumption as a percentage of GDP, respectively. In addition to these four indicators, measures of corruption and of law and order were also included in the analysis under the assumption that business groups may benefit from corruption or from the lack of sound political and legal institutions, a strong court system or an orderly succession of power. These two variables were obtained from the International Country Risk Guide (PRS 1985–1996).

The resource-based view proposed in this chapter was tested with two indicators, one for trade – calculated as the absolute difference between *z*-

scores (standardized values) for imports of consumer goods and passenger cars and z-scores for total exports – and the other for foreign investment – the absolute difference between z-scores for inward and outward stocks of foreign direct investment.[3] Table 9.2 presents the sample descriptive statistics and bivariate correlation coefficients. The indexes of asymmetry in foreign trade and investment are significantly correlated with each other, which provides additional confidence in their robustness when it comes to capturing the concept of asymmetry. Therefore, they were not entered simultaneously in the analysis. Similarly, the measures for law and order and for corruption are highly negatively related to each other and thus not entered simultaneously as control variables.

Parameter estimates, standard errors, and goodness-of-fit statistics from OLS regressions are reported in Table 9.3 for six different specifications using 1995 values for the independent variables. Table 9.4 presents the same models using lagged 1990 values for the independent variables, following the usual practice in the strategic management field of calculating the effect of five-year lags (Miller and Friesen 1980). All regressions include a set of nine dummy variables accounting for each place in the ranking of the top ten business groups (tenth place omitted). The inclusion of these dummies guarantees that the OLS method produces correct estimates of the standard errors and t-tests in a repeated measures design (Cohen and Cohen 1983: 429–35).

Results

Columns A and B in Table 9.3 report the results without including the indexes of asymmetry. While several of the coefficients are significantly different than zero, they do not bear the expected sign. Power distance and the state autonomy index were expected to increase the importance of business groups. They appear to reduce it in this sample. Columns C and D include the index of asymmetry in trade. When corruption is present as a control variable (column C), asymmetry in trade is not significant, but it is positive and significant when law and order is in the model (column D). Using asymmetry in foreign investment yields positive and significant estimates regardless of whether corruption or law and order are controlled for (columns E and F). Thus, models E and F provide some support for hypothesis 1, which argued that market imperfections increase the importance of business groups in the economy. Stock market capitalization is significant and bears the predicted negative sign, but only when asymmetry in foreign investment is in the equation. Hypothesis 2 predicting that a greater importance of business groups results from hierarchical social relationships receives no backing because power distance consistently has a negative sign. Hypothesis 3 stating that the greater the autonomy and size of the state the greater the importance of business groups receives no support either. However, the control measures of

Table 9.2   Cross-sectional sample descriptive statistics and correlation coefficients (N = 90)

	Mean	Std dev.	1	2	3	4	5	6	7	8	9	10	11	12	13	14	15
1. Sales of business group (% of GDP) 1995	1.77	2.21															
2. Stock market capitalization 1995	38.70	24.00	0.07														
3. Power distance index	66.22	10.44	-0.10	-0.13													
4. State autonomy index 1995	0.49	0.25	0.25*	-0.22*	0.54*												
5. State size 1995	12.75	3.46	-0.32*	0.07	-0.65*	-0.82*											
6. Corruption index 1995	2.33	0.82	-0.19	-0.24*	0.48*	0.49*	-0.36*										
7. Law and order index 1995	3.89	1.38	-0.01	0.42*	-0.41*	-0.26*	0.40*	-0.66*									
8. Asymmetry in foreign trade 1995	0.61	0.44	0.45*	0.05	-0.06	0.54*	-0.41*	-0.28*	0.42*								
9. Asymmetry in foreign direct investment 1995	1.04	0.69	0.31*	0.66*	0.17	0.47*	-0.39*	-0.15	0.38*	0.61							
10. Stock market capitalization 1990	19.12	20.01	0.25*	0.88*	-0.33*	-0.26*	0.08	-0.58*	0.59*	0.29*	0.66*						
11. State autonomy index 1990	0.51	0.25	0.16	-0.23*	0.49*	0.97*	0.75*	0.63*	-0.26*	0.47*	0.38*	-0.32*					
12. State size 1990	12.40	3.23	-0.21*	0.49*	-0.61*	-0.87*	0.84*	-0.45*	0.44*	-0.36*	-0.12	0.43*	-0.83*				
13. Corruption index 1990	3.11	1.29	0.25*	-0.13	0.60*	0.84*	-0.81*	-0.28*	0.06	0.70*	0.48*	-0.14	0.81*	-0.72*			
14. Law and order index 1990	2.89	1.20	-0.26*	0.55*	-0.36*	-0.64*	0.77*	-0.42*	0.53*	-0.34*	0.16	0.47*	-0.64*	0.83*	-0.64*		
15. Asymmetry in foreign trade 1990	0.48	0.45	0.17	-0.18	-0.05	0.14	-0.16	-0.63*	0.48*	0.43*	0.14	0.08	0.00	-0.16	0.27*	-0.08	
16. Asymmetry in foreign direct investment 1990	1.11	1.05	0.20	0.33*	0.28*	0.60*	-0.45*	0.12	0.20	0.60*	0.75*	0.19	0.56*	-0.19	0.72*	-0.08	0.23*

Note: * $p < 0.05$.

183

Table 9.3 OLS regression results of the top ten business groups (net sales as % of GDP) in 1995 on various characteristics of nine emerging countries, 1995 (N = 90)

Variables (hypothesis, predicted sign)	A	B	C	D	E	F
Stock market capitalization (H1: −)	0.00	0.00	0.00	0.01	-0.13***	-0.07***
	0.01	0.01	0.01	0.01	0.03	0.01
Power distance index (H2: +)	-0.09***	-0.11	-0.08**	-0.06**	-0.14***	-0.11***
	0.02	0.02	0.02	0.02	0.02	0.02
State autonomy index (H3: +)	1.35	-0.04	-0.02	-2.08	-15.71***	-7.20***
	1.18	1.23	1.73	1.23	4.16	1.70
State size (H3: +)	-0.36***	-0.43***	-0.36***	-0.22*	-0.81	-0.51
	0.09	0.10	0.09	0.10	0.13	0.09
Corruption index (control variable: +)	-0.71**				1.25*	
	0.23				0.51	
Law and order index (control variable: −)		0.04	-0.46	-0.52**		-0.34*
		0.15	0.32	0.20		0.15
Asymmetry in foreign trade (H4: +)			0.75	2.74***		
			0.69	0.68		
Asymmetry in foreign investment (H4: +)					5.52***	3.29***
					1.30	0.62
Constant	11.92***	13.06***	11.00***	8.54**	24.08***	18.62***
	2.47	2.59	2.61	2.61	3.63	2.45
Model F	9.77***	8.09***	9.22***	10.17***	12.40***	12.23***
R-squared	0.65	0.60	0.65	0.67	0.72	0.71

Notes:
Standard errors shown beneath regression coefficients.
*** $p < 0.001$; ** $p < 0.01$; * $p < 0.05$ (two-tailed tests).
All models include a set of nine dummy variables accounting for each place in the ranking of the top ten business groups (10th place omitted).

Table 9.4   OLS regression results of the top ten business groups (net sales as % of GDP) in 1995 on various characteristics of nine emerging countries, 1990 ($N = 90$)

Variables (hypothesis, predicted sign)	A	B	C	D	E	F
Stock market capitalization (H1: −)	0.04***	0.05***	0.04***	0.05***	0.03**	0.03**
	0.01	0.01	0.01	0.01	0.01	0.01
Power distance index (H2: +)	−0.09***	0.05*	−0.11***	0.05*	−0.10***	−0.09***
	0.02	0.02	0.02	0.02	0.02	0.02
State autonomy index (H3: +)	−2.99*	−0.54	−4.21*	0.35	−5.91**	−5.27**
	1.36	1.13	1.59	1.19	1.76	1.75
State size (H3: +)	−0.43***	−0.26	−0.49***	−0.22	−0.75***	−0.58**
	0.10	0.14	0.11	0.15	0.16	0.16
Corruption index (control variable: +)	0.63**		0.84**			
	0.23		0.27			
Law and order index (control variable: −)		−0.53*		0.56*		−0.36
		0.26		0.26		0.25
Asymmetry in foreign trade (H4: +)			−0.63	0.21		
			0.43	0.39		
Asymmetry in foreign investment (H4: +)					0.98*	0.88**
					0.39	0.26
Constant	11.05***	8.36**	12.96***	7.66*	18.08***	15.84***
	2.40	2.67	2.72	2.97	3.66	3.33
Model F	9.13***	8.60***	8.79***	7.97***	9.53***	9.94***
R-squared	0.63	0.62	0.64	0.62	0.66	0.67

Notes:
Standard errors shown beneath regression coefficients.
*** $p < 0.001$; ** $p < 0.01$; * $p < 0.05$ (two-tailed tests).
All models include a set of nine dummy variables accounting for each place in the ranking of the top ten business groups (10th place omitted).

corruption and law and order behaved in the expected way and were significant. Finally, hypothesis 4 based on the alternative, resource-based view of business groups advanced in this chapter receives strong and robust support when asymmetry in foreign investment is used as the proxy. The greater the asymmetry the larger the importance of the top ten business groups in the sample of nine emerging economies. All models reported in Table 9.3 fit the data well, as reflected in the highly significant F-ratios.

The results reported in Table 9.4 using lagged 1990 values are similar to those in Table 9.3. The indicators used for existing theories of business groups exert the opposite effect from that predicted. By contrast, both corruption and law and order affect the importance of business groups in the direction predicted. The index of asymmetry in trade does not reach significance, but the index of asymmetry in foreign investment is a strong predictor of the importance of business groups. As in Table 9.3, all models fit the data well.

Adding the indexes of asymmetry to the baseline models A or B in Tables 9.3 and 9.4 yields significant increases in explanatory power, except when the asymmetry index itself is not significant. Thus, including asymmetry in trade in model D of Table 9.3 explains a significant additional part of the variance in the dependent variable when compared to model B ($F = 16.28, p < 0.001$), though not when included in model C and compared to model A ($F = 1.17$). Similarly, including asymmetry in foreign investment in models E and F of Table 9.3 yields a significant increase in explanatory power when compared, respectively, to models A ($F = 18.04, p < 0.001$) and B ($F = 28.59, p < 0.001$). In Table 9.4, models E ($F = 6.18, p < 0.05$) and F ($F = 11.63, p < 0.01$) result in significant increases in explanatory power but not models C ($F = 2.13$) and D ($F = 0.29$). Thus, the results reported in Tables 9.3 and 9.4 provide strong and robust support for hypothesis 4 when the index of asymmetry in foreign investment is used, and some inconsistent support when asymmetry in trade is used. No robust support is found for previous theories (hypotheses 1–3).

Longitudinal Analysis

A comparative longitudinal analysis of the importance of business groups relative to other organizational forms can be used to further assess the empirical validity of hypotheses 1–4. As indicated in the Appendix, an analysis of organizational forms in South Korea, Argentina, and Spain over time provides a useful comparison because foreign trade and investment policies have set each country onto a very different development trajectory.

Data and methods

Data on the presence of companies affiliated to business groups among the 100 largest non-financial firms in South Korea, Argentina, and Spain at two points in time provide a useful longitudinal indicator of the importance of business groups relative to other organizational forms such as foreign multinational enterprises (MNEs), state-owned enterprises and non-affiliated (that is, independent) firms. The rankings of the top 100 firms in terms of total sales were obtained from a combination of sources for each country and year, for a sample total of 600 firms. Multiple reference sources and field interviews were used to code whether a firm was affiliated to one of the 30 largest business groups in the country, a foreign MNE, or the state. The residual category includes companies affiliated to a group that was not among the top 30, worker-owned cooperatives, and firms with dispersed control.

Table 9.5 displays the cross-classification of the largest 100 firms by country and form of control in 1975 and 1995. In 1975 South Korea, Argentina,

Table 9.5   *The top 100 non-financial firms in South Korea, Spain and Argentina in 1975 and 1995, by organizational form (N = 600)*

	South Korea		Spain		Argentina	
	1975	1995	1975	1995	1975	1995
Organizational form						
Firms affiliated to a business group[a]	41	79	22	11	21	27
Subsidiaries of foreign multinationals	7	1	28	44	43	46
State-owned enterprises	4	4	24	24	21	2
Other[b]	48	16	26	21	15	25
Total	100	100	100	100	100	100
Explanatory variables						
Stock market capitalization (% GDP)	6.01[c]	39.95	7.85[c]	35.41	5.02[c]	17.05
State autonomy index	1.00	0.59	0.33	0.21	1.00	0.46
Size of the state (% GDP)	11.14	10.36	10.45	16.32	12.59	17.20
Asymmetry in foreign trade	1.15	1.50	1.01	0.43	0.02	0.58
Asymmetry in foreign investment	1.20[c]	1.69	1.67c	0.56	0.45[c]	0.40

Notes:
[a]   Includes firms affiliated to one of the largest 30 business groups in the country.
[b]   Includes unaffiliated firms, worker-owned cooperatives, and firms with dispersed ownership.
[c]   Data for 1980 (not available for 1975).

Sources: South Korea: *1978 Ki Eop Che Yeon Kam* (Yearbook of Korean Company 1978), by Kyung je Tong Shin Sa; *Han Kook Ki Eop Eui Sung Jang Jeon Ryak Kwa Kyung Young Koo Jo* (Growing Strategies and Management Structures of Korean Businesses), by Dai Han Sang Kong Hoi Eui So, 1987, pp. 207–9; Korea Investors Service, *Financial Report of Korean Companies*, several years; Asia-Pacific Infoserv, *Korea Company Yearbook*, several years.
Spain: Fomento de la Producción, *Las mayores 1500 empresas españolas*, several years; Muñoz et al. (1978).
Argentina: *Prensa Económica* no. 1 (1975); Acevedo et al. (1990); www.mercado.com. Sources for the explanatory variables are reported in Table 9.2.

and Spain had proportions of firms affiliated to one of the 30 largest business groups of 41, 22 and 21 percent, respectively. By 1995 the proportion had sharply grown to 79 percent in Korea, increased slightly to 27 percent in Argentina, and plunged to 11 percent in Spain. The growth of the top 30 Korean business groups came at the expense of foreign MNEs and other smaller groups, indicating that increasing asymmetries in foreign trade and investment displace from the top 100 list companies that are not affiliated to one of the 30 largest groups. The distribution of the top 100 firms in Argentina experienced an important change between 1975 and 1995: state-owned enterprises have almost disappeared in the wake of privatization, with business groups and MNEs gaining share albeit modestly. In Spain, by contrast, the same 20-year period witnessed a sharp rise in the presence of MNEs among the top 100 firms, primarily at the expense of the business groups.

The lower panel of Table 9.5 shows the values of the explanatory variables in 1975 and 1995. Stock market capitalization grew in the three countries between 1975 and 1995, while state autonomy dropped in all three. The size of the state declined slightly in South Korea, and grew in both Spain and Argentina. The power distance index, the proxy used for sociological theories of business groups, does not change over such a short period of time as 20 years because the nature of social relationships and of culture is 'stabilized over long periods in history' and 'across many generations' (Hofstede 1980: 13, 26; 1991).

The data shown in the upper panel of Table 9.5 were treated using log-linear analysis for cross-classified categorical data (Fienberg 1980) to test if the differences across countries and over time are significant. Chi-square tests were calculated to evaluate the parameters predicting the counts in each of the 24 cells of the three-dimensional frequency table of country by organizational form and by year. Argentina, state-owned enterprises, and 1975 were used as the reference categories. All parameter estimates take these omitted categories as the reference benchmark. Country was modeled as a population variable because the number of firms in each country was fixed by design at 200:100 each in 1975 and 1995 (SAS Institute 1988).

Results

Only the saturated model (one degree of freedom) with all possible effects among the three variables was found to fit the data. Therefore, parameters accounting for the two main effects (excluding the population effect for country), three two-variable interaction effects, and the three-variable interaction effects are reported in Table 9.6. The parameters and χ^2 tests estimated for the interaction effect among country, control, and year reveal whether the dynamic differences across the three countries between 1975 and 1995 are significant or not.

Table 9.6   *Saturated log-linear model of the largest 100 non-financial firms in South Korea, Spain, and Argentina by form of control and year (N = 600)*

Country	Organizational form	Year
Spain	Business group firm	1975[a]
Korea	MNE subsidiary	1995
Argentina[a]	State-owned firm[a]	
	Other forms	

Effect	Parameter estimate	χ^2
Business group firm	0.33	12.24***
MNE subsidiary	−0.08	0.32
Other form	0.47	26.75***
Year 1995	−0.15	4.55*
Business group firm × year 1995	0.21	4.85*
MNE subsidiary × year 1995	−0.09	0.34
Other form × year 1995	0.12	1.74
Korea × business group firm	0.83	33.86***
Korea × MNE subsidiary	−1.41	25.34***
Korea × other form	0.96	47.72***
Spain × business group firm	−0.05	0.21
Spain × MNE subsidiary	0.41	8.28**
Spain × other form	−0.68	5.87*
Korea × year 1995	−0.18	1.61
Spain × year 1995	−0.72	31.81***
Korea × business group firm × year 1995	0.48	8.80**
Korea × MNE subsidiary × year 1995	−0.50	17.92***
Korea × other form × year 1995	0.09	1.27
Spain × business group firm × year 1995	−0.52	16.45***
Spain × MNE subsidiary × year 1995	0.37	5.14*
Spain × other form × year 1995	−0.15	1.62

Notes:
*** $p < 0.001$; ** $p < 0.01$; * $p < 0.05$.
[a] Category used as baseline.

Relative to the omitted categories (Argentina, state-owned firm, 1975), significantly *more* firms were controlled by a business group in Korea by 1995 ($\chi^2 = 8.80$, $p < 0.01$), and significantly *fewer* in Spain ($\chi^2 = 16.45$,

$p < 0.001$). These significant differences, while not representing a direct multivariate test of hypotheses 1–4 (as in the cross-sectional analysis reported above), are only comparatively consistent with hypothesis 4. The prediction that reduced market failure causes business groups to decline (hypothesis 1) is not consistent with the observed differences because all three countries experienced a sharp increase in stock market capitalization between 1975 and 1995. The vertical social relationships predicted in hypothesis 2 to increase the importance of business groups are stable over long periods of time, and thus cannot explain change within a mere two decades (Hofstede 1980: 13, 26). The prediction that state autonomy and size increase the importance of business groups (hypothesis 3) is inconsistent with the observed differences because between 1975 and 1995 state autonomy dropped in all three countries, and state size grew in Spain and Argentina while it declined slightly in South Korea. The observed differences are consistent only with hypothesis 4 predicting that the importance of business groups rises (declines) relative to other organizational forms as foreign trade and investment become more asymmetric (symmetric) over time because between 1975 and 1995 the asymmetry indexes grew in South Korea, fell in Spain, and zigzagged in Argentina.

TOWARD A RESOURCE-BASED UNDERSTANDING OF BUSINESS GROUPS

This chapter has approached the phenomenon of diversified business groups in emerging economies from a resource-based perspective. Theories emphasizing market imperfections, authority structures, or late development do not accurately explain the importance of business groups across emerging economies and over time. Firms and entrepreneurs create diversified business groups when they can accumulate an inimitable capability to combine domestic and foreign resources to enter industries quickly and cost effectively. This capability will only be inimitable if foreign trade and investment are asymmetric because such a conditions limits who can access resources. Diversification in the form of a business group follows a logic of repeated access to foreign and domestic resources under asymmetric foreign trade and investment rather than one of technological, marketing or financial strength. Thus, this chapter contributes an explanation of business groups that is firmly rooted in the managerial literature and speaks directly to the capabilities that sustain unrelated diversification in the long run.

Cross-sectional data on the importance of business groups in nine emerging economies confirmed that asymmetries in foreign trade and investment are associated with business groups, controlling for alternative explanations.

The cross-sectional analysis produced significant but unexpected signs for the predictions of market failure, sociological, and late-development theories of business groups. This puzzling finding may be due to the choice of proxies and/or to endogeneity. While stockmarket capitalization is a widely used proxy for market failure in the allocation of capital, large business groups are likely to list at least some of their companies, thus contributing to market capitalization. This problem, however, seems not to be at work in this sample because the lagged specifications of Table 9.4 should yield correctly signed estimates.

The consistently significant and negative estimates for power distance are also puzzling. Power distance is the only proxy available in the literature to measure the degree of vertical social relationships cross-nationally. The results of Tables 9.3 and 9.4 suggest that differences in vertical social relationships across East Asian countries explain the importance of business groups in those economies (Orrù et al. 1997), but not when the analysis is extended to include South Asian, Latin American, and southern European countries. Lastly, the choice of proxy used to test for the effect of state autonomy does not seem to account for the unexpected negative signs reported in Tables 9.3 and 9.4. An alternative ordinal measure of state autonomy (Gurr 1990) yielded results similar to those reported. Alternative measures of state size (number of state employees, value added of state-owned enterprises) are only available for a subset of the countries in the sample. It is possible to argue, however, that the consistently positive and significant estimates for corruption lend support to late development theories because corrupt governments allow business groups to grow by appropriating state resources, controlling for the amount of such resources with a proxy for state size (government consumption).

A comparative longitudinal analysis of the top 100 non-financial firms in South Korea, Spain, and Argentina at two points in time further showed that firms affiliated with business groups become more numerous over time in countries following an asymmetric development strategy (for example, Korea), and they decline in countries following a symmetric strategy (Spain).

It is important to note that the resource-based view advanced in this chapter regards diversified business groups not as substitutes for markets that fall but rather as an organizational form in competition against foreign MNEs and non-diversified firms lacking the capability to enter multiple industries. These two other types of firms are disadvantaged when foreign trade and investment are asymmetric. This argument represents a major departure from economic thinking. It is also important to highlight that a resource-based view can explain with the same causal mechanism – asymmetries – the rise of business groups in either export-oriented or import-substitution environments. This is a key improvement over late development theories that specified a different causal mechanism for each environment. Thus, the resource-based approach presented in this chapter offers a sound way to modify and enrich previous theories.

The theory and findings in this chapter have important implications for governments and managers alike. When governments privilege certain entrepreneurs or firms *and* restrict access by foreigners they should expect no less than the growth of powerful business groups. This situation, however, is not the only one under which business groups should be expected to rise. If the government encourages local and foreign firms to focus on the domestic market alone, without engaging in exports or outward investment, business groups will also thrive as they enter into coalitions with foreign MNEs to share the (limited) domestic market. In this second situation, business groups with a vested interest in import substitution are likely to oppose a shift to export-led growth. Being aware that the asymmetry is the root of the formation of business groups should inform government policies aiming at liberalizing imports and inward investment or at increasing exports and outward investment. For example, cutting off the connections between business groups and the state without allowing foreigners to do business as if they were locals, or vice versa, will not necessarily force business groups to concentrate on what they can do best. This is why recent economic reforms in several Latin American countries (Argentina, Brazil, Colombia) have not eroded the position of the business groups. Similarly, it is possible that the halfhearted economic reforms being pursued in Korea will not reduce the importance of the business groups as long as asymmetric access to resources is prolonged by keeping MNEs at bay.

Owners and managers of business groups are fully aware of what it means to lose asymmetric access to resources. This is why they oppose policies that diminish asymmetries in foreign trade and investment. When asymmetries fall, the scope and size of the group become a liability rather than a strength because competitive pressures from both foreign MNEs and non-diversified local firms intensify. Business groups have no option but to divest from certain industries and concentrate on those with the highest growth and returns. The framework presented in this chapter also has implications for MNEs planning to enter an emerging economy. Entering a country with asymmetric flows will be more likely to succeed if it takes place in collaboration with a local business group.

This chapter has developed a resource-based approach to the question of why the importance of diversified business groups differs across emerging economies and over time. More research is warranted to explore other important questions related to the phenomenon of business groups, namely: their emergence and growth, perhaps distinguishing between organic growth and mergers and acquisitions; their financial performance relative to non-diversified enterprises and foreign multinationals; and the ultimate origins of their re-sources and capabilities. More detailed data at the group level will be needed to extend the empirical tests offered in this chapter, which represent only a first effort to contrast the explanatory power of different theories.

The chapter is also limited in that it downplays the independent effect of cultural variables such as kinship structures, inheritance customs, or work ethics (Fields 1995: 38–44; Orrù et al. 1997). Future research should explore whether the same cultural institutions could have different effects depending on the nature of inward and outward flows. In general, more research is needed to assess the proxies used in this chapter to test for the effects of economic, sociological, and state-centered explanations. Another limitation that merits further research is the analysis of how specific development policies affect the rise of business groups. For example, governments frequently establish tariffs to encourage local production by foreign multinationals, which tend to estab-lish joint ventures with domestic business groups. Lastly, future research ought to explore whether the connection between development strategies and diversified business groups holds in the transition economies of Eastern Europe or the underdeveloped African countries.

The interaction between inward and outward trade and investment policies is a key feature affecting diversification and organizational dynamics inside emerging economies, and it provides a framework for understanding which organizational forms predominate, depending on the conditions of access to resources. A resource-based view of business groups in emerging economies helps surmount the theoretical and empirical limitations of economic, socio-logical, and late development theories precisely because it compares the advantages and disadvantages of focused firms, diversified groups, and for-eign multinationals under different political–economic circumstances. The resource-based view offers insights for policy makers and managers alike, and should provide the conceptual apparatus for further empirical research on the conditions under which entrepreneurs and firms in emerging economies find it strategically sustainable to diversify into new industries by leveraging their property and knowledge-based resources.

APPENDIX: DEVELOPMENT AND BUSINESS GROUPS IN ARGENTINA, KOREA, AND SPAIN

The ideal-typical development strategies described in Table 9.1 can be illus-trated with the cases of Argentina, South Korea, and Spain (see Guillén 2001 for more details). These are economies of similar size that barely relate to each other in terms of foreign trade or investment. During the 1960s and 1970s they entered manufacturing industries, transforming their economies into fully industrialized ones, with agriculture representing no more than 10 percent of output by the 1990s, down from around 50 percent in the 1940s. Spain's foreign trade and investment have increased symmetrically since the early 1980s, while Korea's outward flows have grown much faster than inward ones. Argentina has followed an erratic trajectory during this period (Gullén 2001).

South Korea

In the asymmetric South Korean political-economic context, firms and entrepreneurs diversified into unrelated industries since the 1960s creating large business groups known as *chaebol*. The state policy-making agencies created by General Park in the 1960s preferred to deal only with a handful of entrepreneurs, for obvious control reasons, and persuaded the favored ones to enter risky undertakings with expanded privileges in profitable industries, import protection, and subsidized loans. In addition, the Korean state protected the domestic market from imports and foreign MNEs (Fields 1995; Kim 1997: 125–32). The *chaebol* created group-level staff offices to manage the resources necessary for repeated industry entry (Kim 1997: 54–77; Fields 1995: 183–208; Ungson et al. 1997). When a *chaebol* targeted a new industry for entry – frequently in response to government incentives or guidance – the group-level office would conduct feasibility studies and facilitate access to resources and expertise from group companies, the state and foreign MNEs. Over time, repeated industry entry following the same blueprint allowed the *chaebol* to reduce the costs and time of setting up new ventures (Amsden and Hikino 1994). The *chaebol* continued to grow even after the state stopped subsidizing them. They opposed and circumvented attempts by President Chun in the 1980s to reduce asymmetries in trade and investment, knowing that their diversification and growth owed much to them. To the government's surprise, the biggest *chaebol* ended up benefiting from the reforms. They managed to access new sources of relatively cheap credit, acquire stakes in the privatized banks, set up financial management companies, and enter into new joint-venture agreements with MNEs (Fields 1995; Kim 1997: 181– 200).

Argentina

The growth of most Argentine *grupos económicos* began in the early 1950s, that is, towards the end of the populist presidency of General Perón, when the failure of nationalist–populist policies forced a 'retreat' from economic nationalism by stabilizing the economy and seeking foreign investment. The groups diversified into new industries with the cash flows generated in the profitable, and protected, domestic market. They obtained permits from the state and borrowed technology from foreign MNEs (Lewis 1992: 195–210, 349–59). The government privileged the groups when economic or financial crises afflicted the country. Trade and foreign investment policies oscillated between nationalism and pragmatism or vice versa in 1962, 1966, 1970, 1976, 1981, 1985, and 1990 (Lewis 1992). Previous research on Argentina supports the prediction that business groups expand more rapidly during periods of asymmetric pragmatic populism than during periods of symmetric nationalist populism (Bisang 1994: 20–24; Acevedo et al. 1990). For example, the groups expanded during the first military junta of 1976–81, whose neo-liberal policies increased imports and inward investment, while an overvalued currency made it difficult for firms to export (Acevedo et al. 1990: 147–8; Lewis 1992: 448–75). The groups also grew when the first democratic presidency attempted asymmetric policies of the pragmatic–populist kind in 1985–86. The groups, however, retrenched swiftly as more symmetric conditions set in during the late 1980s (Lewis 1992: 478–93). Under President Menem the groups expanded again because his asymmetric economic reforms produced a rapid expansion of imports and inward investment while exports and outward investment lagged (Toulan and Guillén 1997). The groups also benefited from privatization, taking over two-thirds of the state firms being sold, mostly in collaboration with MNEs. While the grupos are not as capable as the *chaebol*, they also developed the ability to set up new ventures quickly and cost effectively (Bisang 1994: 32).

Spain

A pragmatic–modernizing development strategy is not conducive to business groups, as the case of Spain illustrates. The country initially pursued an asymmetric nationalist–modernizing development strategy until the late 1970s. As a result, several diversified business groups formed around banks (Central, Bilbao, Vizcaya, Urquijo, Banesto), large chemical or steel companies (Unión Explosivos Río Tinto, Cros, Altos Homos de Vizcaya), as well as whenever entrepreneurs diversified out of traditional light industries like food and beverages (Rumasa). With the exception of Rumasa, the groups grew on the basis of connections to the state and foreign partners, as several meticulously researched case studies of these groups indicate (Muñoz et al. 1978). The process of market liberalization and integration with Europe during the 1980s and 1990s caused the definitive decline of many of the groups. Restrictions to foreign trade and investment were lifted during the 1980s, resulting in reduced asymmetries. Some of the business groups collapsed under international competitive pressure, while others succeeded in refocusing on one core activity or were acquired by foreign MNEs. By the mid-1990s only the industrial groups organized around such banks as BCH and BBV or large retailers (El Corte Inglés) had survived (Aguilera 1998), while virtually all others had disappeared.

NOTES

* A shorter version of this chapter first appeared as 'Business Groups in Emerging Econo-mies', *Academy of Management Journal*, 43(3), June 2000, 362–80. Funding from the Jones Center at the Wharton School is gratefully acknowledged. Helpful comments and/or data have been provided by N. Biggart, E. Bradlow, J. M. Campa, F. Duina, N. Fligstein, H. Haveman, W. Henisz, B. Kogut, D. Lessard, Y. Mylonadis, W. Ocasio, J. Pennings, S. Pérez, S. Suárez, K. Szafara, O. Toulan, A. Tschoegl, S. Wilk, and seminar participants at Carlos III, Valencia, Autònoma de Barcelona, California at Davis, Cornell, Massachusetts at Lowell, MIT, Harvard, and Princeton universities, as well as at the Sophienberg Institu-tional Analysis conference in Denmark. H.-K. Jun provided invaluable research assistance.
1. I have benefited from many conversations with Professor Omar Toulan, a former doctoral student of mine now at McGill University, who has conducted extensive research at Techint (see Toulan 1997).
2. Business groups in other Asian, Latin American or southern European emerging economies refuse to disclose sales figures aggregated at the group level. Other indicators of group size (for example, assets, employees) are even harder to obtain at the group level. The sources of data were: Argentina, Bisang (1994: 17), data for 1993; Brazil, *Exame* (www2.uol.com.br); Colombia, *Poder y Dinero*, March 1997 (www.dinero.com); India, Centre for Monitoring the Indian Economy, data are for 1993; Indonesia, www.indobiz.com; South Korea, Asia-Pacific Infoserv, *Korea Company Yearbook*, several years; Mexico, *Expansión*, as provided by McKinsey & Co., Mexico Office; Spain: Fomento (1996); Taiwan: China Credit Infor-mation Service, data for 1994.
3. Imports of raw materials and capital goods are usually very high in countries attempting to develop. Therefore, imports of consumer goods and passenger cars and not total imports were used so as to capture to what extent the country protects its domestic firms.

REFERENCES

Acevedo, M., E.M. Basualdo, and M. Khavisse (1990), *¿Quién es quién? Los dueños del poder económico*, Argentina 1973–1987, Buenos Aires: Editora/12.

Aguilera, R.V. (1998), 'Directorship Interlocks in Comparative Perspective: The Case of Spain', *European Sociological Review*, 14, 319–42.

Amsden, A.H. (1989), *Asia's Next Giant: South Korea and Late Industrialization*, New York: Oxford University Press.

Amsden, A.H. and T. Hikino (1994), 'Project Execution Capability, Organizational Know-how and Conglomerate Corporate Growth in Late Industrialization', *Indus-trial and Corporate Change*, 3, 111–47.

Barney, J. (1991), 'Firm Resources and Sustained Competitive Advantage', *Journal of Management*, 17, 99–120.

Bisang, R. (1994), 'Perfil tecno-productivo de los grupos económicos en la industria argentina', Working Paper No. 94-12-1671, Santiago, Chile: CEPAL.

Chandler, A. D. Jr (1990), *Scale and Scope*, Cambridge, MA: Harvard University Press.

Cohen, Jacob and Patricia Cohen (1983), *Applied Multiple Regression/Correlation for the Behavioral Sciences*, Hillsdale: NJ: Lawrence Erlbaum.

Evans, P. (1979), *Dependent Development*, Princeton, NJ: Princeton University Press.

Fields, K.J. (1995), *Enterprise and the State in Korea and Taiwan*, Ithaca, NY: Cornell University Press.

Fienberg, S. (1980), *Analysis of Cross-classified Categorical Data*, Cambridge, MA: MIT Press.

Fomento de la Producción (1996), *Las 2500 mayores empresas españolas*, Barcelona: Fomento de la Producción.

Granovetter, M. (1995), 'Coase Revisited: Business Groups in the Modern Economy', *Industrial and Corporate Change*, 4, 93–130.

Guillén, M.F. (2001), *The Limits of Convergence: Globalization and Organizational Change in Argentina, South Korea, and Spain*, Princeton, NJ: Princeton University Press.

Gurr, T.R. (1990), 'Polity III: Political Structures and Regime Change, 1800–1995' [computer file], Ann Arbor, MI: Inter-University Consortium for Political and Social Research.

Haggard, S. (1990), *Pathways from the Periphery: The Politics of Growth in the Newly Industrializing Countries*, Ithaca, NY: Cornell University Press.

Henisz, W. (2000), 'The Institutional Environment for Economic Growth', *Economics and Politics*, 12, 1–31.

Hill, C.W.L. and R.E. Hoskisson (1987), 'Strategy and Structure in the Multiproduct Firm', *Academy of Management Review*, 12, 331–41.

Hofstede, G. (1980), *Culture's Consequences*, Newbury Park, CA: Sage.

Hofstede, G. (1991), *Cultures and Organizations*, New York: McGraw-Hill.

Hoskisson, R.E. (1987), 'Multidivisional Structure and Performance: The Contingency of Diversification Strategy', *Academy of Management Journal*, 30, 625–44.

Hoskisson, R.E. and M.A. Hitt (1990), 'Antecedents and Performance Outcomes of Diversification', *Journal of Management*, 16, 461–509.

IFC (1998), *Emerging Stock Markets Factbook*, Washington DC: International Finance Corp.

Kaufman, R.R. and B. Stallings (1991), 'The Political Economy of Latin American Populism', in R. Dornbusch and S. Edwards (eds), *The Macroeconomics of Populism in Latin America*, Chicago: The University of Chicago Press, pp. 15–43.

Khanna, T. and K. Palepu (1997), 'Why Focused Strategies May be Wrong for Emerging Markets', *Harvard Business Review*, 75, 41–50.

Kim. E.M. (1997), *Big Business, Strong State*, Albany: State University of New York Press.

Kock, C. and M.F. Guillén (2001), 'Strategy and Structure in Developing Countries: Business Groups as an Evolutionary Response to Opportunities for Unrelated Diversification', *Industrial and Corporate Change*, 10(1), 1–37.

Leff, N. (1978), 'Industrial Organization and Entrepreneurship in Developing Countries: The Economic Groups', *Economic Development and Cultural Change*, 26, 661–75.

Lewis, P.H. (1992), *The Crisis of Argentine Capitalism*, Chapel Hill, NC: UNC Press.

Markides, C.C. and P.J. Williamson (1996), 'Corporate Diversification and Organizational Structure: A Resource-based View', *Academy of Management Journal*, 39, 340–67.

Miller, D. and P. Friesen (1980), 'Momentum and Revolution in Organizational Adaptation', *Academy of Management Journal*, 23, 591–614.

Miller, D. and J. Shamsie (1996), 'The Resource-based View of the Firm in Environments: The Hollywood Film Studios from 1936 to 1965', *Academy of Management Journal*, 39, 519–43.

Muñoz, J., S. Roldán, and A. Serrano (1978), *La internacionalización del capital en España, 1959–1977*, Madrid: Edicusa.

Murtha, T.P. and S.A. Lenway (1994), 'Country Capabilities and the Strategic State', *Strategic Management Journal*, 15, 113–29.

Orrù, M., N.W. Biggart, and G.G. Hamilton (1997), *The Economic Organization of East Asian Capitalism*, Thousand Oaks, CA: Sage.

Peteraf, M.A. (1993), 'The Cornerstones of Competitive Advantage: A Resource-based View', *Strategic Management Journal*, 14, 179–91.

PRS (1985–1996), *International Country Risk Guide: Political and Financial Risk Tables*, East Syracuse, NY: Political Risk Services.

Ramanujam, V. and P. Varadarajan (1989), 'Research on Corporate Diversification: A Synthesis', *Strategic Management Journal*, 10, 523–51.

SAS Institute (1988), *SAS/STAT User Guide*, Release 6, 03 edition, Cary, NC: SAS Institute.

Toulan. O. (1997), 'Internationalization Reconsidered: The Case of Siderar', Working Paper 3938, Cambridge, MA: MIT Sloan School of Management.

Toulan, O. and M.F. Guillén (1997), 'Beneath the Surface: The Impact of Radical Economic Reforms on the Outward Orientation of Argentine and Mendozan Firms, 1989–1995', *Journal of Latin American Studies*, 29, 395–418.

Ungson, G.R., R.M. Steers, and S.-H. Park (1997), *Korean Enterprise*, Boston: HBS Press.

Whyte, William Foote and Kathleen King Whyte (1991) [1988], *Making Mondragón: The Growth and Dynamics of the Worker Cooperative Complex*, Ithaca, NY: ILR Press.

PART III

Strategy and competition

10. Globalization of firms: strategies and outcomes

Saeed Samiee

The international business literature is replete with materials pertaining to the US, nature, prerequisites or drivers, imperatives, planning, and implementation of global strategy. Since 1980, the volume and the quality of the literature in Germany international strategic management have significantly increased. Much of the credit for developing this area goes to strategic management and, to some extent, marketing scholars who have, largely independently of one another, investigated and analyzed global strategy from different perspectives. Despite these advances, responding to research questions posed by technological advances and increasing internationalization and globalization drives remains a major challenge in strategic management (Bettis and Hitt 1995).

In relative terms, global strategy as a discipline is in its infancy. From its inception, strategic management has been concerned with business concepts and practices that affect performance. Presumably the development of relevant theories and concepts can capture dimensions that lead to superior performance and can be incorporated in the firm's strategic plan. However this objective may have been accomplished in a domestic sense, its international application is a debatable topic. In particular, performance consequences of globalization as a strategic thrust are not known. A range of strategies has been followed by firms in pursuit of internationalization, some of which fit the framework and strategies echoed in the literature and constitute globalization.

Three issues regarding globalization are noteworthy. First, there are clearly degrees of globalization. In general, globalization patterns tend to be unique to the firm (for example, international business knowledge and expertise, managerial orientation, motivation, and understanding of the globalization phenomenon), its resources, and the national and industry environments in which it operates. Second, globalization is a strategic thrust which occurs over long periods. Third, however different the globalization strategies deployed by firms, they share many similar drivers. In the case studies that follow, the importance of these variables is highlighted in the appliance industry.

The objective of this chapter is to explore the relevant antecedents and the processes that precede globalization in firms. In addition, the different

approaches to globalization used by three firms in the home appliance industry (Electrolux, Maytag, and Whirlpool) are analyzed and discussed. These
short case studies demonstrate the diversity of patterns used to achieve a
global status.

A secondary objective involves an attempt to incorporate perspectives
from both the international marketing and international management litera-
tures insofar as the relationship between the standardization of processes and
programs and the design and implementation of global strategies are concerned. The former is a central topic in the international marketing literature
whereas the latter, the main topic of this chapter, is a key consideration in the
international strategy literature. There is no assumption that the two fields are
necessarily mutually exclusive. A perusal of the two bodies of literature
makes it clear that scholars in both fields are increasingly leveraging off each
other's knowledge, approaches, and findings.

This chapter is divided into six sections. First, environmental factors favoring
transformation to a global paradigm will be discussed. Second, internationalization will be defined and compared with globalization from academic and
business perspectives. There is a great deal of confusion as to what constitutes globalization and whether firms that operate globally are necessarily
pursuing a global strategy. This section is intended to address the differences
in perspectives in light of key antecedents of global strategy (for example,
size, industry drivers, customer needs, product/technology). Third, the internationalization experiences of three firms in the home appliance industry are
explored and their transitions to adopting a global strategy are assessed.
Fourth, industry consolidation as a precursor to internationalization and globalization is discussed. Next, globalization is compared and contrasted with
standardization approaches. The final section consists of a discussion pertaining to the outcomes of the globalization experiences of these firms and ways
in which firms might become more successful in their globalization drives.

MACRO TRANSFORMATIONS FAVORING GLOBALIZATION

The importance of incorporating the institutional context in global strategy
has been highlighted in the literature (Bettis and Hitt 1995). The market
structures and governance mechanisms of host countries as well as the changes
infused by a variety of global institutions impact the feasibility of intensive
internationalization and the appropriateness of pursuing a global strategy. A
number of international developments have contributed to the rapid international expansion of firms and the transition of some into global enterprises.
Today, economic, regulatory, and political environments are favoring higher

levels of globalization. Furthermore, there is a strong move toward bilateral and multilateral cooperation to resolve a variety of problems and concerns, and international trade and economic considerations are central to many of these dialogues and treaties. In general, developed countries have been at the forefront of such initiatives, largely due to their greater dependency on international trade.

Examples of these initiatives are many. The successful implementation of the European Community (EC) 1992 Plan went a long way towards developing uniform market industry standards, logistics, government procurement, and consumer protection measures. The movement has led to an even greater level of cooperation in Europe (for example, the Maastricht Treaty). Parallel to this development was the formation of new multinational markets (for example, Mercosur) and the expansion, consolidation, and further integration of existing markets (for example, the North American Free Trade Agreement [NAFTA], and the Asia-Pacific Economic Cooperation [APEC] Forum). An unrelated event, namely the rapid political shift in the former Soviet Union beginning in the mid-1980s and the subsequent breakdown of barriers between the West and the East, has led to the further opening of markets that were previously difficult to access. For example, some former Soviet allies are now members of the Organization for Economic Cooperation and Development (OECD) and a few have been approved for membership in the European Union.

In particular, the successful conclusion of the Uruguay Round of the General Agreement on Tariffs and Trade (GATT) negotiations in 1993 and its transformation into the World Trade Organization (WTO) have had a profound impact on globalization trends. WTO serves as a central force in leveling the playing field and significantly reducing or removing visible and invisible barriers to world trade. Unilateral measures and counter-measures formerly exercised by various governments under GATT are virtually eliminated under the auspices of WTO.

Rapid technological developments in communications and travel as well as in the design and manufacturing of products (for example, CAD-CAM) contributed significantly to this globalization. These initiatives have, to a large extent, unified the business environment across national boundaries. However, despite these developments, environmental factors remain varied and complex, thus making theoretical developments in the area of global strategy difficult. Not surprisingly, researchers are embracing the complexity of international strategic issues by integrating multiple theoretical frameworks, as is evident from the more recent research (for example, Hitt et al. 1997).

INTERNATIONALIZATION VERSUS GLOBALIZATION

Despite their commonality, the terms 'internationalization', 'globalization', and 'global strategy' convey the presence of specific characteristics in the firm. The term globalization is often used interchangeably with internationalization, particularly in the business press (Kanter and Dretler 1998), to denote intense international expansion and business activities in markets abroad (for example, Freidheim 1999). Some sources use globalization in lieu of standardization. However active a firm may be in the international arena, the pursuit of a global strategy is an issue quite apart. That is, a firm may be very active internationally without being truly global. Clearly, these terms share many dimensions and components because the stages and the process of internationalization that a firm goes through shape its international portfolio of knowledge, resources, and capabilities. At the earliest stage of internationalization, these assets are in short supply within the firm and thus expose it to considerable risk of sub-optimization. Xerox, for example, possessed virtually no international business experience or knowledge initially and became dependent on other firms. However, they learned from this dependence and today they retain a similar international organization to that put in place some 40 years ago.[1] Yet, to be global demands a global mind set, a high level of coordination among divisions and functional areas, and an appropriate level of headquarters control across worldwide operations. The development of these capabilities within the firm typically occurs over long periods.

Globalization is a potentially desirable strategy because it permits the firm to leverage off capabilities that might otherwise be indigenous to a single division and/or country. Further, the prerequisite of a high level of intra-firm coordination permits the firm to globally consolidate many of its activities such as product development, manufacturing, warehousing, finance, marketing, and so on. As will be seen, in the extreme, a high level of globalization would embody a high level of standardization. For example, products are the same in all markets and are marketed in the same way under uniform brands.

Evidence regarding positive and significant performance consequences of the pursuit of global strategy is scarce. Also, the opportunities to become a truly global firm are constrained by several factors and the firm is not always in a position to pursue a global structure and strategy. For example, despite the many changes in the international business/trade environment that are supportive of globalization, local legal impediments alone can severely limit the firm's ability to become global.

Globalization is perhaps most likely in industries that to a large extent meet the antecedents to globalization. The actual number of industries that apparently meet the definitions used for global industries is relatively small (that is, fewer than three dozen at the 4-digit SIC level). The strategic management literature has identified dimensions of global industries and, using these dimensions, researchers have identified a number of industries. With some variation, the definitions used involve several facets. At the macro level, environmental forces play a pivotal role and create a *latent* potential for an industry to become global (Bartlett 1985). The industry in which the firm competes is a strong indicator for the suitability of globalization. First, the industry is becoming more global if some competitors are actively sourcing, manufacturing, and marketing in an increasing number of markets. As such, there should be at least one firm in the industry that competes globally (Hout et al. 1982; Hamel and Prahalad 1985; Porter 1986). Second, a high level of intra-industry trade (for example, 50 percent) is a further indication that the industry is increasingly global (Kobrin 1991; Porter 1980, 1986). Third, for globalization to occur, global customer needs should parallel global product information and awareness. Fourth, the convergence of various laws and regulations governing the conduct of business across national boundaries is essential. Such convergence may occur through international bodies such as those implemented for the benefit of the members of the European Union, or through periodic multilateral negotiations of the World Trade Organization. Fifth, the global purchasing practices of firms and customers turn increasingly global as a consequence of industry globalization. Thus, a firm like IBM would be expected to buy the necessary parts and components for its products and services on a global basis.

Two internal or micro aspects also serve as prerequisites to globalization. First, in order to implement a global strategy, the firm needs to meet the critical size criterion. In the strictest sense, smaller firms cannot pursue a global strategy, even though they may compete internationally. Serving customers in multiple markets and competing with a multitude of local and global competitors require an infrastructure that demands resources and capabilities that small firms lack. Second, even when firms are large and have a presence in many markets, they need to develop a global structure and corporate culture within the firm on a global basis (Maruca 1994).

Therefore, the pursuit of a global strategy implies a much higher level of knowledge, competency, and experience, and a network of operations in the international marketplace (compare Kobrin 1991). In particular, a network of operations implies a large size and, thus, to globalize a firm must necessarily possess an international network of operations.[2] Smaller firms do not have the resources and capabilities to develop and manage the large network of contacts, arrangements, and markets necessary for a global firm. In contrast, the pursuit of an international strategy encompasses the implementation of any strategy intended to expand the international scope of activities of the firm. This includes virtually any activity that involves another entity abroad and which is intended to enhance the revenue of the firm such as exporting, licensing, ventures and alliances, manufacturing and distribution agreements, and direct investment.

It would be tempting to discount the experience of a firm like Xerox as isolated and unique. However, similar patterns occur with some regularity for a variety of firms. Firms take different approaches to global expansion and implement vastly different strategies. Though the international strategies deployed by firms apparently vary based on the national origins of firms, there is no guarantee that a successful strategy duplicated by another firm will necessarily yield the same result.

THE EXPERIENCES OF THREE LEADING FIRMS

The globalization of the appliance industry and the experiences of three firms (Electrolux, Maytag, and Whirlpool) are explored in this study. This industry and its three leading competitors provide an excellent demonstration of the range of globalization activities while highlighting crucial success factors in the highly competitive global business environment. Firms may adopt a number of different approaches to internationalization. The pursuit of a global strategy is simply one approach. As will be seen later, transitions toward internationalization and attempts to globalize tend to be unique to the firm and, in some cases, the resources, the structure of the firm, and the stages followed in pursuit of globalization do not reflect those one would associate with a global firm.

The Home Appliance Industry

The appliance industry is fragmented and includes many competitors. The global appliance market is dominated by such firms as Bosch-Siemens, Electrolux, Matsushita, Merloni, Ocean, Whirlpool, and Thomson. Basic technologies for building 'functional' appliances are mature and fairly standard. As such, technological barriers to market entry are low and there are local competitors in virtually all countries. Aside from quality and ordinary functionality of the appliance, competitive advantage in such an industry is derived from incremental improvements in design and new features. Discrete product changes and introductions have been few and far between, the microwave oven representing the last discrete product introduced. The global market size is fairly large with over 235 million home appliances worth about $70 billion sold worldwide each year.

The globalization of appliance firms is further complicated by virtue of differences in consumer needs across national boundaries. The size of residences (apartments and homes) varies considerably around the world and manufacturers need to be particularly sensitive to this element. Preferences with regard to color, performance, wash temperature, water and power consumption, and price also vary considerably. For example, Germans like washing certain items in very high (boiling) temperatures. This demands that the washer have its own heating element to increase and retain high temperatures during the various cycles. In many parts of Europe, consumers like their laundry to be spun at extremely high speeds (for example, 1000 rpm) to prepare them for line drying. Japanese consumers, on the other hand, prefer cold water washing for the most part. In addition, space is a scarce resource in a Japanese home and the size of appliances needs to be as small as possible.

In such an international market environment, globalization may still be pursued at the organizational, technological, and sourcing levels. The core technology, for example, compressor, transmissions, and motors, can be shared. Furthermore, manufacturing processes can be similar, if not identical (Maruca 1994). Thus, similar technology, product platforms, and manufacturing processes can be used even when the product itself offers different features and sizes for each market. However, achieving any level of globalization at the firm level must be preceded by a series of globalization initiatives. Additionally, as noted earlier, the global economic, regulatory, and political environments are favoring higher levels of globalization.

Electrolux

Electrolux was formed by Axel Wenner-Gren in 1914 as a vacuum cleaner firm. It established itself as a premier manufacturer of vacuum cleaners in Europe in the mid-1960s by persuading the Vatican to use its products for a year free of charge (Tully 1986). In 1964, ASEA (now a part of ABB), an internationally-oriented electrical equipment company controlled by the Wallenberg family, acquired a large portion of Electrolux.

Although Electrolux had exported a great deal over the years, the firm's big push in the international arena resulted from the implementation of an international acquisition strategy in the early 1970s. Since 1978, it has acquired some 500 firms in 50 countries (Tully 1986; Jancsurak 1998a) and the firm amassed an invaluable knowledge base regarding the internationalization and management of its enterprise as a result of these acquisitions. However, organizational learning and the acquisition of internationalization knowledge are not always smooth and seamless. Electrolux developed a US presence as early as 1924. The company divested itself of its American division in 1968 by selling its interest, along with its right to the Electrolux brand in the US, to Consolidated Foods. This was a strategic error from a global strategy perspective since the US market is very large and affluent, is the source of many new technologies, and is where key players in the industry compete, making it an invaluable source of market intelligence. Sara Lee, Consolidated Food's successor, and three banks sold the North American business to Engles Urso Fullmer, Electrolux LLC, in 1998. In the meantime, AB Electrolux, the Swedish parent, re-entered the US market through its acquisition of Eureka in 1974. However, it could not use the Electrolux brand. The firm can begin using its original brand name in the US market within three years following its purchase from the American concern for $50 million (Beatty 2000).

In the US, Electrolux also purchased Tappan and in 1986 acquired White Consolidated Industries which marketed and manufactured such famous brands of appliances as Frigidaire, Westinghouse, Kelvinator, and Gibson. Likewise, in Europe they became the leading appliance manufacturer through their acquisition of Italy's Zanussi. Their more recent acquisitions have won them such internationally prized brands as AEG (German appliances) and WeedEater (US landscaping equipment). Additional brands sold by the firm include Allwyn (India), Arthur Martin, Bluebird, Corberó, Elektro Helios, Eureka, Faure, Flymo, Frigidaire Gallery, Husqvarna, Juno, Maxclean, McCulloch, Menalux, Partner, Poulan, Rex, Rosenlew, Samus, Tappan, Therma, Tornado, Volta, Voss, Zanker, Zanussi-Samus, and Zoppas.

The worldwide employment and sales figures of Electrolux were 93 000 and SEK120 billion, respectively, in 1999. It markets its products in over 150 countries where it sells more than 55 million consumer and industrial products and remains the most innovative firm in the industry. However, 93 percent of its sales come from North America and Europe.

Acquisitions at Electrolux have led to a very large portfolio of technologies, production plants, products, and brands that can be described as regional, if not multi-domestic. The nature of the industry, coupled with the sheer number of acquisitions in a broad range of countries (for example, India, Japan, and the US) has resulted in a multi-domestic structure by default. Throughout the better part of the twentieth century, however, the firm has amassed considerable knowledge in international business and as environmental forces have been working in favor of higher levels of globalization the firm is gradually moving towards global brands and designs (*Financial Times* 1999).

Electrolux is rationalizing its production facilities and warehouses on a global basis and is focusing on a smaller number of well-defined brand names, including a universal logo. Electrolux markets its products under 40 brands. As cooking, cleaning, and washing habits vary considerably on a country by country, products need to cater to the specific needs of each market. Thus, even when the firm has undertaken globalization initiatives, being global in this industry stops short of the full standardization of products and the corresponding marketing plans. For example, the common production platform strategy has led to the creation of the 'euro-oven' and 'euro-refrigerators' which will be produced at four plants (*Financial Times* 1999). However, in Italy the euro-oven will have a special pizza setting, while French customers will have special fish and shellfish compartments in their refrigerators.

Given the differences in tastes and diet, strict or forced standardization of appliances is inappropriate. Despite the necessity for localization, however, the number of products offered can be significantly reduced using a common platform (for example, Electrolux has reduced its refrigerator and freezer models by about 30 percent). However, trimming down the line is a decision independent of research and development. Despite the industry's mature status, the firm continues to innovate to retain its leadership position.[3]

With so many acquisitions, the firm has either inherited (as a part of a firm being acquired) or purchased firms operating in industries in which it has limited expertise. The firm has been proactive in divesting such lines (for example, sewing machine manufacturing, the kitchen cabinets market, and aluminum products) so that it might focus on globalizing its core appliance business.

Maytag Corporation

By most accounts, the Maytag Corporation manufactures and markets the premier brand of appliances for homes and businesses in the US. Based in Newton, Iowa, the firm was established in 1893 as a farm equipment manufacturer. To neutralize the cyclical effect associated with farm equipment, the firm began manufacturing a wooden-tub washing machine in 1907. For most of the twentieth century, Maytag remained a traditional domestically-oriented firm focused on improving its products and building its brand image. It was typically slow to respond to changes in the business and customer environments. For example, it did not eliminate wringer-type washers until 1983, at least a decade after other manufacturers had stopped manufacturing this type of washer. Over the years, the firm has acquired such well-known consumer brands as Jenn-Air (1982), Magic Chef (1986), and Admiral, as well as industrial food service brands such as Blodgett ovens, Dixie-Narco vending machines, Pitco Frialator, MagiKitch'n, Blodgett Combi, Norge, and Jade.

The domestic orientation and focus of Maytag is further surprising given that other leading appliance manufacturers with which it competed had expanded internationally decades earlier (for example, Frigidaire, Philco, and, in particular, General Electric). Until the mid-1980s, Maytag possessed no significant international expertise and relied on the domestic market for a significant portion of its revenues and profits. Maytag's expansion into international markets has been more reactive and by default. Over the years, the firm's main international activity was limited to exporting. However, the globalization theme was inescapable in the 1980s as virtually every firm was vying to become a global competitor. Amidst industry consolidation and a rapidly globalizing environment, Maytag awoke to the reality that to survive it too needed to globalize. As it lacked virtually any international business capability, it sought to acquire an existing complementary global firm.

Given the firm's excellent domestic image and the internationalization efforts of its major competitors into markets abroad, Maytag's late entry into the international arena is noteworthy. Virtually no one outside the US has ever heard of Maytag. It was not until the late 1980s that the firm would finally find a global white knight to use as its globalization platform. Maytag acquired Chicago Pacific Corporation (CPC) in 1989 and its prized possession, Hoover, along with it. CPC had purchased Hoover in 1986, two years after it emerged from Chapter 11 proceedings. To complete its line of home products, Maytag also acquired Rowenta, the top-selling German brand of irons and other small appliances.

Hoover was a perfect match for Maytag for several reasons. First, Hoover was an upscale and famous global brand. For example, in Britain the vacuum cleaner is commonly referred to as a Hoover. Second, the Hoover brand name has had a major following internationally since its inception in 1919, particularly in Europe and Australia. Third, the firm possessed considerable international business knowledge and experience. For example, Hoover began manufacturing in England in 1919 and was selling its products worldwide as early as 1921. Fourth, the Maytag and Hoover product lines were complementary. Hoover sold only vacuum cleaners in the US whereas internationally it offered a complete line of major appliances, including washers, dryers, dishwashers, refrigerators, and microwave ovens. Finally, as Maytag was very late in its attempt to globalize and possessed only limited international experience, it could not rapidly move up the 'globalization learning curve' without such an acquisition. The acquisition of the much smaller Rowenta was also a positive move for Maytag since the brand was widely known throughout Europe and it possessed considerable international marketing experience.

Maytag had hoped to use the Hoover organization as its springboard to become global. However, Maytag lacked the necessary organizational structure and knowledge either to integrate itself fully into its new, more international subsidiary or to leverage off their global business capability to establish the Maytag corporation and its brands internationally. As a late entrant and in the absence of substantial international business expertise and the lack of a full-fledged, long-term commitment to becoming global, Maytag was not positioned well for a smooth transition into the global arena.

From the start, Maytag almost totally lacked the capability to manage its European operations. The development of new products was slow and the firm faced significant manufacturing problems (Drown 1995). To complicate matters, the timing of the acquisition of Hoover was less than ideal as it was just in time for the onset of the recession in Europe which led to several years of losses at Hoover. As Europe was coming out of the recession, a marketing blunder in the UK led to substantial losses and placed the much coveted Hoover brand at risk.[4]

Maytag's globalization effort can be labeled as *ad hoc* at best. For example, in 1996 the firm entered into a joint venture agreement with Hefei Rongshida Group Corporation in China to produce washers and refrigerators for Chinese markets. However, this move was not a concerted effort to explore other China-like markets nor was it an integral part of a broader Asian strategy. About half of this venture was to upgrade washing machine production lines and the rest involved 'greenfield' development of refrigerator manufacturing (Holding 1999). More recently the firm acquired the Three Gorge Company, a Chinese domestic washing machine maker.

In the end, Maytag was unable to transform itself into a global competitor even though both Hoover and Rowenta possessed ideal attributes to enable Maytag to become global. Maytag eventually sold Hoover Australia to Southcorp Holdings Ltd in 1994 and Hoover Europe to Candy Sp.A. of Italy in 1995 at a substantial loss (Drown 1995). Maytag's attempt at becoming global demonstrates the complexity and the challenge of the task. The firm underestimated the levels of expertise, organizational knowledge and structure, and coordination and control of hundreds of activities that were necessary if it were to become a successful global competitor. Having remained domestic for most of its history, Maytag lacked the necessary infrastructure and knowledge for global operations. Given the mature market conditions, the competitive intensity in the industry, and the necessary critical size to become global, it is unlikely that Maytag can become a global player on its own.

This last ditch effort at Maytag to internationalize may have cost the firm its independence. In May 2000, Maytag changed certain corporate bylaws, making it an easier takeover target. At the time of this writing, the firm was holding merger or acquisition talks with a number of foreign firms, including Sweden's Electrolux and Korea's LG (Callahan and Scannell 2000).

Whirlpool Corporation

The Whirlpool Corporation began doing business in St Joseph, Michigan, in 1911, as the Upton Machine Company and produced motor-driven wringer washers. It merged with Nineteen Hundred Washer Company of Binghampton, New York, in 1929, and was renamed the Whirlpool Corporation in 1950. The firm expanded its washer line in 1955 with the addition of automatic dryers, refrigerators, ranges, and air conditioners to its product line. A relationship it cultivated with Sears Roebuck and Company in 1916 to supply the firm with home appliances under the Kenmore label has survived for over eight decades. Today, Whirlpool Corporation remains the principal supplier to Sears of many major home appliances under the Kenmore brand. This relation, in turn, became Whirlpool's first entry into the international arena. When Sears established an international division in 1936 (Sears International), it opened markets for Kenmore washers in England, Sweden, and the Canal Zone and, by extension, Whirlpool became an exporting firm. Concurrently, the Nineteen Hundred Corporation established a relationship with American Steel Export Company (NY) to handle the Whirlpool line through the firm's foreign distributors.

In 1999 Whirlpool had worldwide sales of $10.5 billion, employed 60 000, and sold its products in over 170 countries under major brand names such as Bauknecht (Europe), Laden (France), Estate and Ignis (Europe and Asia), Brastemp and Consul (Latin America), Cielo and Roper (US), Inglis (Canada), KitchenAid (US and Canada), Acros, Supermatic, and Crolls (Mexico), KIC (South Africa), Narcissus and SMC (Asia), and Whirlpool (global). It is the largest competitor in the US and Latin America and is in the third position in Europe. The company has manufacturing facilities in 13 countries on four continents.

Prior to the 1980s, the Whirlpool Corporation represented the traditional domestically-oriented American firm. However, the rapidly saturating domestic market coupled with the smaller margins associated with the highly competitive American market forced the firm to chart a new strategy for growth in the mid-1980s. The centerpiece of this strategy was developing a global presence, that is, entry into every market in which Whirlpool did not have a market presence (Maruca 1994). The goal was world leadership in a rapidly internationalizing major appliance industry. Given the mature nature of the industry, joint ventures and acquisition remained the main avenues for Whirlpool's globalization drive. The firm entered a joint venture agreement with a European firm which possessed a strong global brand and with companies in Mexico and India. It also increased its investments in Canada and Brazil.

Despite the early indirect exporting activities through Sears International, Whirlpool did not enter the globalization race until August 1988, when it entered into a $2 billion joint venture agreement and acquired a 53 percent interest in the home appliance division of N.V. Philips, with options to purchase the entire operation. The Philips venture was a good match for Whirlpool given their relative inexperience in managing a global enterprise. The Whirlpool brand was known largely in the US and Canada, but consumers worldwide were familiar with the Philips brand which appeared on a wide variety of consumer and industrial products. Whirlpool successfully leveraged off Philips' brand equity and its wide recognition to establish its own brand globally.

The Philips transaction was completed within five years and stipulated the rights to use the Philips name for an extended period in order to enable the firm gradually to introduce its own brands. The Philips acquisition also brought several Asian sales companies and distributors under the Whirlpool umbrella in Australia, Malaysia, Japan, Singapore, Thailand and Taiwan (Babyak 1995).

In contrast to Maytag which lacked virtually any international business experience, Whirlpool had fostered some international experience dating back to 1958 when the firm acquired an interest in a Brazilian appliance manufacturer and also because of its drive to export to Asia. However, this drive was neither persistent nor a central part of their overall strategy and the firm did not possess sufficient knowledge and structure for globalization. For example, Whirlpool's efforts in marketing a single 'world washer' failed because the firm did not consider the differences in washing habits across Europe.

Nonetheless the firm had gained some international marketing knowledge in the process of undertaking various international activities over the years. In the case of Whirlpool, the limited growth opportunity in the US market (where it held the leading position) was the motivation to become an international firm (Laabs 1991; Maruca 1994). Thus, the firm charted a new strategy to internationalize in the early 1980s. As a part of this strategic change, Whirlpool actively recruited individuals with training and interest in international business, thus enhancing the firm's international business competency. For example, the firm actively recruited from leading institutions of higher education in international business, for example, American Graduate School of International Management (Thunderbird) and the University of South Carolina.

The orientation and influences of top executives in rapidly transforming a multi-billion dollar firm from a market extension organization into a global competitor cannot be over-stressed. Although the initial entry phase as a joint venture partner rather than a fully independent foreign investor afforded the firm the opportunity to acquire critical international management expertise from its already global partner, Philips, much more was needed to change the orientation of its US management team and integrate its worldwide activities. The firm's CEO, David R. Whitman, who is largely responsible for making the transition from a domestic to an international firm did not immediately focus on performance. To become global, organizational and structural imperatives first had to be in place. Thus, Whitman sought to cultivate trust among the corporation's acquired international network and to create a common global vision. These were the focus of the firm for the first two years following the formation of the joint venture with Philips (Maruca 1994). However, much more organizational change needed to take place if the firm was to become global.

The first step on this road came in the form of a week-long international conference, titled 'Winning Through Quality Leadership: One Global Vision', held in 1990. Top executives from Whirlpool operations in 16 countries attended the conference in Montreux, Switzerland. This conference was critical to Whirlpool's globalization drive because, up to this point, Whirlpool's 140 managers from around the world had not had an opportunity to exchange information and views or seek synergies and ways in which they could fully collaborate across national boundaries. Despite its matrix organization structure, Philips's appliance division was largely a multi-domestic operation in which country managers were afforded significant latitude (Maruca 1994). As a testament to this operational mode, many managers present in Montreux had never met their counterparts from other countries.

Information acquisition activities, for example, external consultants, played a significant role in shaping the 'global' theme and objectives of the conference (Laabs 1991). In planning and organizing the conference, the assistance of nine key international business experts from such institutions as Wharton (Howard Perlmutter), INSEAD (Yves Doz), and Harvard (Stan Davis) was sought. Thus, every detail of the conference, including a seating chart that forced managers from different countries to sit next to each other, was worked out to achieve Whirlpool's 'global' objective for the meeting. The conference was exceptionally successful in achieving the stated objectives. As a result, it has now become an important annual event. Since the conference, the firm has gradually moved from a domestic firm and a multi-domestic enterprise, through acquisition to a corporation that is fairly global in perspective even if its product offerings in various markets are not standardized.

INDUSTRY CONSOLIDATION

Globalization is a likely alternative for larger firms and hence firm size is central in discussions pertaining to the formulation and implementation of a global strategy. We have been witnessing consolidation in a variety of industries and the emergence of mammoth corporations in the 1980s and the 1990s.[5] Global business forces and industry imperatives are commonly used as justifications for such consolidation.[6]

Industry consolidation through acquisitions and mergers offers the quickest way to expand in new markets and to secure resources for developing new technologies and products. Global strategy is meaningless if the firm's reach is limited to a few markets and if the profiles of its customers and supply chain and sources are not truly global. Concurrently, there is no indication that efficiencies, cost savings, and greater profitability have materialized in these larger firms (*The Economist* 2000; *Business Week* 1999). That is, empirical evidence pointing to the greater profitability of larger, global firms vis-à-vis multi-domestic or market extension firms is scant.

It is evident from the examination of the three firms in the appliance industry that consolidation has been an important tool in moving firms closer to becoming global entitles. In each case, firms acquired another firm to accommodate their internationalization effort. In the case of Electrolux, which already had a presence in the US, it acquired the third largest US appliance manufacturer (behind GE and Whirlpool), White Consolidated Industries, in 1986 (Tully 1986). White Consolidated itself was already an international firm by the international business base of the many brands it had acquired a few years earlier. Likewise, Maytag acquired Hoover and Rowenta, and Whirlpool acquired Philips's appliance business. Given the fragmented nature of the appliance industry, coupled with the relatively late globalization stage in the industry, mergers and acquisitions were and continue to be the major (if not the only) avenue to becoming a global competitor. Electrolux was the first firm aggressively to acquire firms around the world. Whirlpool was next in pursuing internationalization and in moving towards a global strategy. Maytag was the least prepared and the last to enter the international arena and its performance in this respect has been very poor.

The domestic and international sales between 1986–98 of the three firms are shown in Table 10.1. Not surprisingly, Electrolux was a major international force long before either Maytag or Whirlpool. In 1998, Electrolux derived 92 percent of its sales from global markets. Whirlpool's methodical implementation of its global strategy, on the other hand, increased its international sales from under 10 percent to almost half of its total sales. Finally, Maytag has been relatively erratic and has performed poorly in its globalization drive. Its international sales peaked to about 22 percent of its domestic sales and stood at about 10 percent in 1998. Maytag's results are dismal if the absolute value of international sales is considered. Maytag's international sales as a percentage of total sales of the three competitors is only 1.6 percent. In contrast, Whirlpool stands at 16 percent and the most international firm among the group, Electrolux, is at 46 percent.

GLOBALIZATION VERSUS STANDARDIZATION

The pursuit of a global strategy assumes the presence of two conditions. First, the industry the firm operates in must be either global or at least meet several of the prerequisites of globalization (that is, the presence of at least one global competitor; a high level of intra-industry trade; the global convergence of customer needs; the global availability of product information and awareness; the convergence of various laws and regulations governing the

Table 10.1   *International sales and growth patterns among leaders in the appliance industry, 1986–98*

	Electrolux		Maytag		Whirlpool	
	($)	(%)	($)	(%)	($)	(%)
1986						
Domestic	514	11	684	100	3 763	91
International	4 163	89	0		369	9
Total	4 677	100	684	100	4 131	100
1991						
Domestic	1 464	11	2 317	78	5 416	80
International	11 844	89	654	22	1 354	20
Total	13 308	100	2 971	100	6 770	100
1996						
Domestic	1 279	8	2 706	89	5 392	62
International	14 704	92	334	11	3 304	38
Total	15 983	100	3 040	100	8 696	100
1998						
Domestic	1 160	8	3 621	89	5 574	54
International	13 345	92	448	11	4 749	46
Total	14 505	100	4 069	100	10 323	100

Source: Companies' records.

conduct of business; and the emergence of global purchasing practices). In reality, relatively few industries meet these prerequisites and the great majority of industries identified as global industries are industrial firms. Samiee and Roth (1992), for example, identified 13 global industries, nearly all of which were industrial. However, other studies have identified as many as 36 global industries. In this sense, the firm cannot pursue a global strategy if environmental and industry conditions do not permit the implementation of such a strategy. The appliance industry is not a fully global one since it meets only some industry and market globalization prerequisites.

Second, the firm must have demonstrated the proclivity to globalize through a series of initiatives over a period of time. The fast-track globalization process at Whirlpool, for example, took approximately ten years. Furthermore, these initiatives need to be congruent with the external environment (that is, fit) because industries and markets abroad vary in degrees of devel-

Table 10.2   Relationship between industry environment and firm-level globalization initiatives

INDUSTRY ENVIRONMENT

		Few globalization drivers present	Most globalization drivers present
FIRM ENVIRONMENT	Few globalization initiatives	Market extenders Multi-domestic firms	*Ad hoc* or partial standardization
	Many globalization initiatives	Significant standardization (e.g. platforms, processes)	Full standardization

opment along the global industry dimensions. Thus, global strategy formulation ought to be conceived in stages and degrees.

Table 10.2 demonstrates the relationship between industry and market environment and firm-level globalization initiatives. When firms have undertaken few globalization initiatives (albeit international in perspective), regardless of the industry and market environments, they are not positioned well for globalization. In this light, Maytag's domestically-oriented profile should be a foregone conclusion. In situations where industry conditions are generally not supportive of globalization, firms like Maytag remain market-extenders or operate in a multi-domestic fashion. However, when industry and market conditions are generally supportive of globalization, the firm's limited globalization knowledge and capability prevent it from fully leveraging off industry globalization drivers. Over time such firms begin to gradually experiment with *ad hoc* or partial standardization (for example, on a regional basis or by standardizing certain processes and/or programs).

Firms that have moved along the globalization learning curve and have amassed considerable knowledge and organizational initiatives toward globalization are likely to possess a high level of intra-firm coordination and control. This capability in turn positions the organization for implementing systematic standardization. Where market and industry conditions are generally not supportive of globalization, such firms attempt systematically to standardize technologies, rationalize global manufacturing facilities, develop and implement uniform global processes, and standardize as many functions as industry conditions permit. That is, globalization may be limited to just a few processes or functions, for example, sourcing and distribution, but not programs (for example, the marketing plan). In the case of the appliance industry, for example, regulations, customer needs, and product differences have circumvented the standardization of marketing programs. As a result, firms operating in this industry have relied on local marketing programs. However, the most global of the three firms reviewed, Whirlpool, depends on standardized technologies, product platforms, and sourcing (*The Economist* 1995). Clearly, where both industry conditions and firm globalization initiatives permit, the most detailed process and program standardization is likely to occur.

In a relatively mature industry such as appliances, global competitive strength is based on, *inter alia*, the successful delineation and cultivation of global intermarket segments in which a firm chooses to compete. Intermarket segments embody some of the key environmental prerequisites (for example, global customer awareness, uniform uses for the product) to globalization. Within each intermarket segment, the homogeneity of consumers with respect to product and usage allows the firm to compete more effectively across national boundaries. Thus, globalization makes a high degree of standardization possible, but the appropriateness of pursuing a global strategy is contingent upon the identification and cultivation of intermarket segments (Kale and Sudharshan 1987; Jain 1989; Samiee and Roth 1992). Considerable conceptual and empirical research has been devoted to uncovering the nature of products and services that lend themselves to standardization. In general, standardization is thought to be possible if products and services meet certain conditions, including uniform benefit and use conditions across intermarket segments. This being the case and given the divergence of consumer preferences and tastes for consumer appliance products internationally (for example, washing habits and preferences), the validity of a high level of program standardization in the appliance industry comes into question.

CONCLUSIONS

It is clear from the foregoing discussion that globalization is a knowledge-based capability which is not possessed by all firms. This capability permits the firm to develop and implement a strategy that involves the rationalization of processes and functions which may include significant or full standardization of products, centralization of research and development efforts, and/or vertical or horizontal integration of manufacturing (Kobrin 1991). Globalization also implies the dependence of foreign subsidiaries and divisions on a multinational system for information, management orientation and method, resource allocation, and supply and product access.

In the sample of firms examined in this study, Maytag's experience represents a clear internationalization failure. Maytag has a long journey if it is to become a global firm. Electrolux is the one firm that clearly possesses the knowledge-based capability for globalization. It began its internationalization drive long before the others and has expanded throughout the world. However, by virtue of its acquisition style, international expansion and the industry imperatives, to date it has largely functioned as a multi-domestic firm. Currently the firm is undertaking a series of globalization initiatives that in time should make it as global a firm as industry and market conditions permit. Whirlpool, which is the relative newcomer to the international business scene, is the most global of the three leading firms in the industry. From its inception, the globalization of Whirlpool has taken about 10 years.

Financial performance should constitute the most important motivation for globalization. Firms often pursue globalization to reduce or eliminate redundancies and duplication of assets and functions, with the goal of lowering their overall costs. Although cost reduction should be an ongoing corporate thrust, it represents only one side of the equation. The more critical objective is profit maximization which is incongruent with a cost minimization focus. There is also no evidence in the literature pointing to the greater profitability of global firms. Consider, for example, that global rationalization of production or warehousing facilities may result in greater in-transit inventory cost, transportation, and tariffs, and a lower customer service level. The rationalization of production functions is an explicit goal of globalization and standardization strategies. However, global rationalization of manufacturing scale has been shown to be an insignificant factor leading to the global integration of industries (Kobrin 1991). This is an important consideration if the firm's intermarket segments are not stable because globally or regionally rationalized product/service packages would not offer optimal fits for these segments.

Ultimately, the firm's main goal centers on providing 'differentiated' products of appropriate quality level at the highest possible margins. At a conceptual level, the delineation of intermarket segments permits the firm to offer a differentiated product which is (substantially) standardized across markets. This approach affords the firm relative freedom in pricing and, hence, greater margins vis-à-vis its competitors. However, as the global market and industry environments are dynamic, global strategies need to be updated and modified regularly in response to changes in the marketplace.

NOTES

1. Haloid Corporation of America (the predecessor of Xerox) entered international markets through a 50–50 joint venture (Rank Xerox) with a major UK film producer and movie theater owner, J. Arthur Rank Production Ltd., in 1956. Haloid had initially approached IBM and others for assistance but was turned down. By the late 1960s, Xerox realized that the control of its operations was critical if it were to succeed internationally. Thus, it purchased a controlling interest (1 percent) in the venture for $22.6 million (*Wall Street Journal* 1969). Subsequently in 1995, Xerox increased its share in the joint venture from 51 percent to 71 percent plus 80 percent of the profits (up from 67 percent) at a cost of $968 (Hays 1995).

    In the Far East, it developed a venture with Fuji in 1962 to manufacture and market products in the region (Bostock and Jones 1994). Fuji-Xerox eventually became a critical asset to Xerox as its designs and manufacturing methods rescued its parent firm from the competitive threats posed by Japanese firms in various markets, notably in North America. For example, the Fuji-Xerox venture assisted its parent in cutting duplication, reducing its number of suppliers from 5000 in the early 1980s to about 400 in 1992 (*The Economist* 1995). Today Fuji-Xerox continues to operate as an autonomous unit. Its relative independence is partially reflected in the fact that Fuji-Xerox's financial statements are not consolidated into Xerox's operations. Despite Xerox's global presence (it derives 64 percent of its revenues from non-domestic sources), the firm's international activities are, at the very least, unusual.

2. Some authors advocate that environmental changes accommodate globalization for virtually any firm (for example, Rennie 1993). Indeed, the term 'born global' refers to firms that are basically global at their inception. This is a rare occurrence, if possible at all, even for such Internet-based firms as E-Trade which currently maintains operations in 33 nations. It is also noteworthy that the term 'born-global' is frequently used with imprecision. Arnold and Quelch (1998), for example, have used it in connection with Mary Kay Cosmetics' expansion into emerging markets. There is no empirical evidence that supports the presence of born-global firms or refutes the many internationalization models supported in the literature.

3. For example, Electrolux is introducing 'pay per wash' on a limited basis in its home market. In this scheme, Electrolux is distributing washing machines among 7000 households on the Swedish island of Gotland free of charge. Electrolux maintains the machines free of charge and households can replace or upgrade the machines after 1000 washes (representing a normal usage rate in 4–5 years). Households, in turn, reimburse Electrolux on a pay per wash basis. In this scheme, washing machines are connected to Electrolux's central database via the Internet and 'smart energy meters' in every home. Households receive a specified electric bill that includes their wash. Electrolux, in cooperation with the Swedish power utility Vattenfall, will be the first to take advantage of the smart home technology. In addition, Electrolux and Ericsson have formed a joint venture to link appliances to the Web and to one another via a central server. The first product of this venture will be the Electrolux 'Screenfridge', with a computer screen on its door that links users to the Internet and scans expiration dates to alert homeowners of spoiled food. These are the first of several products and services planned by Electrolux for the smart home (see *Appliance Manufacturer* 2000). Electrolux has also been a concerned and proactive 'green citizen'. The company now markets Creation ovens that consume 60 percent less energy and Recycle-40 washers that use 20 percent less water than their predecessors. Its own 150 manufacturing plants have also reduced water consumption by 50 percent and energy consumption and carbon dioxide emission by 25 percent from 1988 to 1996. Electrolux is serious about the environmental impact of its products and its manufacturing and publishes an Environmental Annual Report (Jancsurak 1998b). The firm is also introducing solar power lawn mowers and other outdoor products (see Jancsurak 1998c).

4. Hoover Europe offered free air travel within Europe and to the US to consumers buying $150 and $375 worth of appliances and floor-care products, respectively. Unfortunately for

Maytag, Hoover Europe set no limits and misjudged consumer response. In the end, the company ended up flying more than 220 000 people at no charge to the destination they qualified for at an estimated cost of $72 million. Three Hoover International executives were fired because of the blunder. See *HFD* (1993) and Hartley (1998) for details.

5. The consolidation in the pharmaceutical and telecommunications industries is representative of the trend. For example, the mergers of Upjohn and Pharmacia (1995), Ciba-Geigy and Sandoz to form Novartis (1996), and Bristol-Myers with Squibb, and the acquisitions of Wellcome by Glaxo, Smithkline by Beecham, Genentech by Roche, and Warner-Lambert by Pfizer are representative of the global consolidation in the pharmaceutical industry.

6. The research and development activities in the pharmaceutical industry are a case in point. The development of new drugs is time-consuming and expensive. For example, it takes an average of 15 years to develop a new drug at an estimated cost of $400–$500 million (Haseltine 1999; *Purchasing* 2000). This represents an eightfold increase as compared to the 1976 estimate of $54 million (Hansen 1979). The justification for mergers is frequently based on the firm's ability to develop, secure governmental approval for, and market new products to remain globally competitive. The argument is indeed a compelling one since the cost of researching and seeking approval for a drug is very high.

REFERENCES

Appliance Manufacturer (2000), 'Electrolux News', January, 48(1), 20.

Arnold, David J. and John A. Quelch (1998), 'New Strategies in Emerging Markets', *Sloan Management Review*, Fall, 40(1), 7–20.

Babyak, Richard J. (1995), 'Strategic Imperative', *Appliance Manufacturer*, February, 43(2), 19–22.

Bartlett, Christopher A. (1985), 'Global Competition and MNC Managers', ICCH Note No. 0-385-287, Harvard Business School.

Beatty, Gerry (2000), 'Electrolux Buying Electrolux Name from Electrolux', *HFN*, 15 May, 51.

Bettis, R.A. and M.A. Hitt (1995), 'The New Competitive Landscape', *Strategic Management Journal*, 16 (Special Issue), 7–19.

Bostock, Frances and Geoffrey Jones (1994), 'Foreign Multinationals in British Manufacturing, 1850–1962', *Business History*, January, 36(1), 89–126.

Business Week (1999), 'Addicted to Mergers', 6 December, 3658, 84.

Callahan, Patricia and Kara Scannell (2000), 'Maytag Discusses Acquisition with Three Firms', *The Wall Street Journal*, 25 August, B4.

Drown, Stuart (1995), 'Maytag Corp. Selling Hoover's European Unit at a Loss', *Akron Beacon Journal*, 30 May.

The Economist (1995), '… and Other Ways to Peel the Onion: Company Management', 7 January, 52–3.

The Economist (2000), 'The New Alchemy', 22 January, 354 (8154), 61.

Financial Times (1999), 'Electrolux Plans Global Platforms', 17 February, 23.

Freidheim, Cyrus F., Jr (1999), 'The Battle of the Alliances', *Management Review*, September, 46.

Hamel, Gary and C.K. Prahalad (1985), 'Do You Really Have a Global Strategy?', *Harvard Business Review*, 63 (July–August), 139–48.

Hansen, R. (1979), 'The Pharmaceutical Development Process: Estimates of Current Development Costs and Times and the Effects of Proposed Regulatory Changes', in R.I. Chien (ed.), *Issues in Pharmaceutical Economics*, Lexington, MA: Lexington Books.

Haseltine, William (1999), 'A Crisis Lurking Within', *Financial Times*, 28 Oct, 7.

Hartley, Robert F. (1998), 'Maytag: A Bungled Promotion in England', *Marketing Mistakes and Successes*, 7th edition, New York: John Wiley.

Hays, Laurie (1995), 'Xerox Agrees to Raise Stake in Overseas Unit', *The Wall Street Journal*, 13 January.

HFD-The Weekly Home Furnishings Newspaper (1993), 'Maytag Picks Up Pieces After Free-flyer Crash', 12 April, 67(15), 127(3), 127–9.

Hitt, Michael A., Robert E. Hoskisson, and Hicheon Kim (1997), 'International Diversification: Effects on Innovation and Firm Performance in Product-diversified Firms', *Academy of Management Journal*, August, 40(4), 767–98.

Holding, Robert L. (1999), 'Globalization: The Second Decade', *Appliance Manufacturer*, May, 47(5), 34.

Hout, Thomas, Michael E. Porter, and Eileen Rudden (1982), 'How Global Companies Win Out', *Harvard Business Review*, 60 (September–October), 98–105.

Jain, Subhash (1989), 'Standardization of International Marketing Strategy: Some Research Hypotheses', *Journal of Marketing*, January, 70–79.

Jancsurak, Joe (1998a), 'Right Reasons for Rightsizing Right Now', *Appliance Manufacturer*, January, 46(1), E5–E7.

Jancsurak, Joe (1998b), 'In Pursuit of a Greener Bottom Line', *Appliance Manufacturer*, January, 46(1), E23–E25.

Jancsurak, Joe (1998c), 'The Great Outdoors', *Appliance Manufacturer*, January, 46(1), E28–E29.

Kale, Sudhir H. and D. Sudharshan (1987), 'A Strategic Approach to International Segmentation', *International Marketing Review*, 4 (Summer), 60–71.

Kanter, Rosabeth Moss and Thomas D. Dretler (1998), '"Global Strategy" and its Impact on Local Operations: Lessons from Gillette Singapore', *The Academy of Management Executive*, November, 12(4), 60–68.

Kobrin, S. (1991), 'An Empirical Analysis of the Determinants of Global Strategy', *Strategic Management Journal*, 12, Special Issue, 17–31.

Laabs, Jennifer J. (1991), 'Whirlpool Managers become Global Architects', *Personnel Journal*, December, 70(12), 39–44.

Maruca, Regina Fazio (1994), 'The Right Way to Go Global: An Interview with Whirlpool CEO David Whitman', *Harvard Business Review*, March–April, 72(2), 134–45.

Porter, Michael E. (1980), *Competitive Strategy*, New York: The Free Press.

Porter, Michael E. (ed.) (1986), *Competition in Global Industries*, Boston, MA: Harvard Business School Press.

Purchasing (2000), 'Pharmaceutical Companies Face Tough Challenges', 13 January, 128(1), 40.

Rennie, M.A. (1993), 'Born Global', *McKinsey Quarterly*, 4, 45–52.

Samiee, S. and K. Roth (1992), 'The Influence of Global Marketing Standardization on Performance', *Journal of Marketing*, April, 1–17.

Tully, Shawn (1986), 'Electrolux Wants a Clean Sweep; the Swedish Company is on a Worldwide Buying Spree Designed to Make it the First Global Appliance Maker', *Fortune*, 18 August, 114, 60–62.

The Wall Street Journal (1969), 'Xerox to Pay Rank $22.6 Million to Control Joint Venture's Board, End Royalties to It', 6 December.

11. Entering foreign markets through strategic alliances and acquisitions

Michael A. Hitt and Klaus Uhlenbruck

INTRODUCTION

Over the last decade, we have witnessed a revolution in the business world. For example, there are now approximately 40 000 multinational enterprises that are responsible for about 25 percent of the world's GNP. In fact, this understates the actual amount of GNP accounted for by international businesses as there are a number of small and medium-sized firms that also have substantial amounts of international operations and sales. Additionally, an increasing percentage of the large number of mergers and acquisitions undertaken each year are between firms in different countries, in other words, cross-border acquisitions (Hitt et al. 2001a). Thus, globalization is creating a revolution in the business world.

Globalization creates a number of new opportunities as well as challenges for businesses (Hitt et al. 1997b). For example, new market opportunities have been created, but also new competitors. New markets have opened due to free trade agreements and the liberalization of markets (for example, Latin America). These changes have also led to new types of competition. For example, the potential for multipoint competition whereby two firms simultaneously compete against each other in two or more product markets has existed for many years. However, increasing globalization has enhanced the potential for multipoint competition based on geographic markets across country borders. Thus, one firm may have a strong presence in the North American market while another may have a strong presence in the European Union or Asian markets. If these firms compete against each other in each of these markets, they may forestall a competitive action in one of the geographic markets where they are particularly weak by responding to a competitor's action in that market in the geographic market(s) where they are strong. Therefore, multipoint competition is no longer based only on product markets but also on international geographic markets (Hitt et al. 1998b).

Globalization has been fueled by worldwide economic growth and emerging markets in various regions of the world. In the earlier 1990s, the economic growth in Asia served as a catalyst for increasing globalization. This was followed by economic growth in many countries throughout Latin America. While the economic growth has not been as dramatic in Eastern Europe as in Asia and Latin America, the opening of these markets helped increase globalization as well (Czinkota and Ronkainen 1997; Uhlenbruck and De Castro 2000). The effects of globalization are also evident from economic downturns. For example, the economic problems in Asia in the middle and latter part of the 1990s affected economic growth in the other parts of the world. Kotabe (1998) suggested that the economic crisis in Asia at its height reduced worldwide economic growth by approximately 25 percent. Of course, globalization has enhanced the free flow of goods across country borders exemplified by the flow of trade across the borders throughout the European Union and among the US, Canada and Mexico based on the North American Free Trade Agreement (Birkinshaw et al. 1995).

The factors fueling globalization and the outcomes that have resulted from it have changed the nature of firms' strategies, of competition in markets and industries, and the nature of competitive advantage (Sanders and Carpenter 1998). In short, globalization has been described as the third great revolution (Luo 1998). This revolution is increasing the integration of business across country borders and regions of the world. The increasing globalization and its effects have enhanced the importance of international strategy. Thus, we focus on firms' international strategy and, in particular, on the means by which firms enter international markets. Specifically, we address two increasingly popular entry modes, strategic alliances and acquisitions. We begin with a discussion of international strategy, followed by an exploration of strategic alliances, with particular emphasis on partner selection, and acquisitions as modes of entry. Finally, we contrast alliances and acquisitions as alternative entry mode choices.

INTERNATIONAL STRATEGY

International and product diversification play key roles in the strategic behavior of firms (Hitt et al. 1994). It has been proposed and empirically shown that international diversification produces a number of positive benefits for firms. For example, international diversification produces the opportunities to obtain economies of scale, of scope and of learning (Rugman 1979; Kogut 1985). As firms expand the markets in which they sell their current product lines, they can gain economies of scale in the manufacture, sale and distribution of those products. In addition, firms can gain economies of scope through exploiting relationships between business units across geographic areas (Porter 1990). The economies of scope also produce the opportunity to share distinctive firm capabilities across business units operating in different international markets (Hamel 1991; Kochhar and Hitt 1995). Expanding into international markets also produces the opportunity to exploit differences in factor markets that occur across countries as well as the opportunities to learn from different approaches to business. As an example, employees in particular countries may have a specific set of unique skills and capabilities that can be learned and therefore shared by others throughout the company's operations in other countries.

While empirical research has supported the derivation of these benefits from international diversification, the research is mixed in the effects of such international strategy on firm performance. For example, Geringer et al. (1989) hypothesized a positive relationship between international diversification and firm performance but found no relationship. In a *post hoc* analysis, they found that the relationship between international diversification and performance was, indeed, curvilinear, with the shape similar to an inverted 'u'. This finding suggests that international diversification can have a positive effect on firm performance, but the results by Geringer et al. (1989) also suggest that there are costs to such an international strategy and that increasing international diversification may reach a point where the costs exceed the benefits.

Geographic dispersion often increases transaction costs and managerial information processing demands (Jones and Hill 1988). As firms operate in more regionally dispersed global markets, generally they must conduct increasing numbers of transactions in local markets and across country borders. Additionally, the dispersed operations increase the coordination, distribution and other types of management costs. All of these operations must be coordinated and products, raw materials and employees must be distributed effectively between and across the units operating in different international markets. In addition, as firms move into multiple international markets, they must deal with different government regulations and trade laws, and are subject to greater risks of currency fluctuations. In addition, they must deal with differing trade barriers, increased logistical costs and cultural diversity. All of these challenges clearly increase managerial information processing demands.

Combining the two sets of arguments suggests that the relationship between international diversification and firm performance is likely curvilinear and similar to an inverted 'U'-shaped curve. The apex of that curve is likely to differ by firm depending upon the managerial skills and capabilities existing within the firm. Firms with a high degree of managerial knowledge and expertise operating in international markets are likely to gain greater benefits from international diversification and be able to diversify into more international markets before the costs exceed the positive returns from this international strategy.

The research also suggests that the relationship between international diversification and firm performance may be moderated by the firm's product diversification. For example, Hitt et al. (1997b) found that firms that were product diversified before they entered international markets were able to earn positive returns faster than those firms that were not product diversified before entering those markets. They suggested that these firms were better able to manage across multiple markets because they had developed internal structures that helped them to manage the diversity and complexity created by international diversification. Therefore, they found single business firms often performed more poorly in early international diversification efforts, but as they learned how to operate effectively in these markets, they began to earn positive returns. Furthermore, they found that firms that engaged in unrelated product diversification were able to obtain greater returns, partly because they did not have the internal transaction costs experienced by related product diversified firms. In other words, the internal coordination and other types of transaction costs are higher in related product diversified firms than in unrelated product diversified firms. Thus, we conclude that an international strategy can be valuable and produce positive returns but the effects of such a strategy are likely to be complex and specific to the firm's capabilities and skills as well as based on the configuration of international markets entered. The effectiveness of an international strategy can also be affected by its mode of entry into those markets. In recent times, two of the most popular modes of entry for international diversification have been strategic alliances and acquisitions. Next, we discuss strategic alliances.

INTERNATIONAL STRATEGIC ALLIANCES

Strategic alliances have become a popular strategy for entering international markets (Osborn and Hagedoorn 1997). The popularity of alliances is based on the desire to share risks and resources, increase one's knowledge and obtain access to markets (Hitt et al. 2000). However, while the general intent of partners in international strategic alliances is to establish and maintain a long-term cooperative relationship, many alliances are not successful (Madhok and Tallman 1998; Park and Russo 1996). One of the most important decisions in the success of these international strategic alliances is the selection of compatible partners that have complementary resources and strategic orientations (Hitt et al. 1995). Several have argued that strategic alliances provide good opportunities for organizational learning and for building firm capabilities (for example, Kogut and Zander 1992). In fact, Lane and Lubatkin (1998) suggested that alliances provide, perhaps, the best opportunity for learning tacit knowledge of another firm. Therefore, firms are likely to select partners for access to resources and knowledge (Hitt et al. 2000). Accordingly, the selection of partners who have the complementary resources and appropriate knowledge becomes critical to the success of those alliances. Additionally, the selection of partners who are willing to share their resources and knowledge is also critical to the success of these alliances. As such, firms must know their partners well before selecting them to participate in a strategic alliance.

All firms have some specific resource endowments (Barney 1991) but oftentimes need additional resources in order to be competitive in particular markets (Hitt et al. 1999). Even firms with larger resource endowments still may need special or particular types of resources in order to be competitive in particular markets. For example, if firms from developed markets move into emerging markets, they may not have the appropriate knowledge of these markets nor the contacts for distribution, government approvals, or direct linkages to customers necessary to be successful. As a result, they often want to select partners who have access to and knowledge of these markets. In addition, these developed market firms often seek to leverage their resources by selecting partners that have complementary and/or unique resources. In these ways, they can build a competitive advantage (Hitt et al. 2000). Alternatively, less resource-endowed firms may desire to gain access to new technologies, managerial skills and oftentimes to financial resources. In addition, they may desire alliances in order to have access to other intangible assets such as their partners' reputations. As a result, firms then seek to establish international strategic alliances to gain access to both tangible and intangible resources. Firms seek to learn from the experience of their partners, one of the most productive means of organizational learning (March and Levitt 1999). Learning from experience has a higher probability of producing a competitive advantage because of the higher probability of transferring tacit knowledge (Lane and Lubatkin 1998).

As suggested above and found in empirical research, firms from different types of markets and institutional infrastructures often require different types of resources. Thus, these firms search for particular partners that can help them meet their resource needs. If they select partners who do not have these particular resources or who will not allow access to them, the alliance is likely to fail. Alternatively, if firms select the right partners, they are more likely to learn new capabilities (even more resource-rich firms seek to learn from their partners in alliances). Therefore, the interactive learning opportunities and the sharing of critical resources become the primary basis for success in international strategic alliances.

The overall failure rates of strategic alliances have been reported to be high and they are even higher for alliances between firms with home bases in different countries (Hennart and Zeng 1997). One problem in international strategic alliances is the likelihood of different strategic orientations of the partners (Hitt et al. 1997a). Thus, because partners may enter alliances for different reasons and seek different types of resources and knowledge, there is the potential for conflict. Alternatively, when a firm selects the 'right' partners and is able to work cooperatively and effectively with those partners, the probability for success of these alliances is greater. Certainly, there are other factors that contribute to success in alliances, such as having substantial alliance experience. Such experience coupled with effective managerial capabilities can reduce the spatial transaction costs of international strategic alliances (Hitt et al. 2000). We believe, however, that one of the most critical factors in the success or failure of alliances is the selection of the right partner. Of course, some firms prefer even more control over the assets when they enter a new international market. As a result, a number of firms acquire existing firms in those markets.

CROSS-BORDER MERGERS AND ACQUISITIONS

Over 40 percent of the mergers and acquisitions in 1999 were across country borders. This number represents a significant increase over 1998 while the value of cross-border acquisitions also increased greatly in 1999. The increase in cross-border acquisitions has been clearly evident in Europe and the Pan Pacific (Hitt et al. 2001a). Much of the merger activity in Europe has been a result of the development and implementation of the European Union. In addition, these cross-border acquisitions prepare the firms not only for competition within the European Union, but also help them gain competitive parity or perhaps even an advantage over foreign competition from outside Europe (Angwin and Savill 1997).

While there has not been much research on cross-border mergers and acquisitions, the increasing number of such strategic moves suggests their importance and the need better to understand the reasons for these acquisitions and their outcomes. Clearly, to make cross-border acquisitions effective, top executives must develop not only an international but, indeed, a global mindset (Dutton 1999).

There are multiple reasons for cross-border acquisitions, some of which are similar to the reasons for domestic acquisitions. For example, a primary reason for many of the recent acquisitions has been the desire to increase market power and for consolidation in the industry (Hitt et al. 2001b; Ramaswamy 1997). This rationale is effective for both domestic and cross-border mergers and acquisitions. Additionally, acquisitions increase one's ability to move into a market (McCardle and Viswanathan 1994). Certainly, acquiring a firm that already operates in a market increases the speed with which a firm can enter that market and begin business operations. The acquired firm already has established distribution systems and customers as well as relationships with the various government entities important to operating in that market. By acquiring an existing business, a firm obtains access to these distribution systems and customers. Furthermore, it acquires the knowledge of customers in this market and access to social capital through relationships with government entities as well. Finally, acquisitions provide the opportunity for greater product diversification. This can occur in either domestic or cross-border acquisitions (Bergh 1997).

However, cross-border acquisitions may occur for other reasons as well. For example, they may offer the opportunity for greater learning by the acquiring firm (Barkema and Vermeulen 1998). While all acquisitions provide some opportunity for learning, acquiring a firm in another country provides greater opportunity for learning, because of the often substantial differences between the firms. Firms from different countries may have different sets of capabilities and knowledge bases (Morosini et al. 1998). Of course, different capabilities and knowledge bases may lead to another reason for acquisitions, that is, to enhance innovation (Hitt et al. 1997b). While any acquisition, whether domestic or international, may increase innovation (Hitt et al. 1996a), cross-border acquisitions offer greater opportunities to enhance innovation. Again, cross-border acquisitions offer the opportunity for access to different innovation systems and new product ideas as well as possibly different technologies. However, moving into international markets often increases the market for new products and therefore provides a larger market in which to sell the innovations and earn a return. Furthermore, by increasing the number of markets and thereby enhancing revenues, there are greater funds to invest in developing innovations. Lastly, cross-border acquisitions are more likely to overcome entry barriers to these markets (Hitt et al. 2001a).

Therefore, while there are multiple reasons for acquisitions, there are an even greater number of reasons for cross-border acquisitions. They provide additional opportunities for firms. At the same time, they also are much more complex and difficult to manage. Much has been written about the problems of integrating domestic firms that are acquired, and these difficulties are only multiplied in cross-border acquisitions (Haspeslagh and Jemison 1991). Therefore, while cross-border acquisitions offer an increasingly popular opportunity to enter new international markets, they also present multiple managerial challenges.

ALLIANCES VERSUS ACQUISITIONS AS ALTERNATIVE MODES FOR INTERNATIONAL EXPANSION

Entry mode optimization is a classic topic in international business research (Anderson and Gatignon 1986; Hill et al. 1990; Root 1980). Cross-border acquisitions and strategic alliances with foreign partners are increasingly popular options, but there is limited research in international business comparing these potential substitutes. The advantages and disadvantages of each option, however, are overlapping, and the choice is rather complex (compare Folta 1998). The choice depends on numerous firm external and internal conditions. Occasionally, firms choose first to engage a potential target in an alliance and later propose a full merger (Hitt et al. 1998a; Kogut 1991). In the following, we compare the two entry modes and then discuss the conditions that influence the choice between them. We close with a case study on the 1993 BMW–Rover cross-border acquisition that is considered a failure, resulting in divestiture, restructuring of Rover and significant losses for BMW. This case highlights the risks involved in foreign acquisitions.

Above, we introduced numerous benefits to alliances and acquisitions as modes for international expansion. Many of the benefits are common to both. Clearly, both cross-border acquisitions and alliances can support market access and reduce barriers to entry. Both also create the potential for learning. Firms entering an international market can learn about the foreign culture, customers, governments, or technologies in use from the foreign alliance partner or the acquired organization (Bresman et al. 1999; Lane and Lubatkin 1998). The combination of complementary resources with a partner or an acquired firm may result in innovation and create competitive advantage.

There are also common costs to international acquisitions and alliances. Both, for instance, involve spatial transaction costs. Also, both may be difficult to manage, although acquisition costs often are higher than costs of collaboration in an alliance. Nevertheless, when merging or cooperating firms are less compatible, costs associated with integration or collaboration are likely to be higher than if the two firms are more compatible (for example, similar firm cultures, compatible information systems).

Of course, there are numerous differences between foreign acquisition and alliances that may determine the choice between these two expansion routes. Most salient are risk differences involved with each of the expansion routes (Anderson and Gatignon 1986). Alliances involve the risk that the foreign partner is not willing to share resources and knowledge, thus limiting the potential for learning. At the same time, one partner may be able to absorb proprietary knowledge of the partner firm; thus alliances involve dissemination risk (Hamel 1991; Hill et al. 1990). Finally, the entering firms risk misjudging the strategic goals and behavior of the partner, which often leads to a rapid dissolution of the alliance (Berg and Friedman 1980). Acquisitions, however, allow for more control of the foreign firm, its assets, knowledge, and strategic orientation, thus reducing the above-noted risks of alliances.

On the other hand, acquisitions involve a higher investment risk because they are costlier, even compared to joint ventures, where investment risk is shared with one or more partners. In particular if the entering firm's intent is to access the capabilities and assets of a technological and/or market leader, an acquisition may be extremely costly. For example, the acquiring firm may be forced to pay a high premium for the leading firm. This risk may be particularly high in countries where capital markets are inefficient and over-payment or losses in case of divestiture can more easily occur. The risk involved with target valuation has been addressed by extant international business research (Balakrishnan and Koza 1993; Singh and Kogut 1989).

Resource commitments to an acquired foreign entity may also be higher than expected if costs of integration of the acquired firm exceed those antici-pated. High costs of integration are a critical concern in domestic acquisitions, particularly if there is little organizational fit between the acquirer and target (Jemison and Sitkin 1986). In conclusion, the choice between international alliances and acquisitions often represents a trade-off between risks involved in either of the expansion modes. Of course, the choice of international entry mode may be limited by the foreign government. For instance, full ownership of businesses by foreign firms was not permitted in the former Soviet Union. Foreign ownership was only allowed in the form of joint ventures with local firms. Thus, acquisition as a mode to enter Soviet markets was not a feasible alternative. There are several factors that may affect the risks of entry modes. These are explained in the next section.

MODERATORS OF ENTRY MODE RISK

The level of risk associated with foreign acquisitions or alliances varies depending on the conditions of the acquiring and target firms, or the partners, and their environment. Cultural differences between firms from different countries represent one such environmental condition (Kogut and Singh 1988; Uhlenbruck 2000; Very et al. 1997). Large cultural differences may reduce organizational fit between merging firms and thus increase the risk of high integration costs. Thus, in the case of significant cultural differences between the home countries of potential acquirer and target, an alliance between the firms may be preferable, because while the risks even for alliance success may be high, less investment is at risk.

Business strategy of the entering firm also can influence the choice of entry mode (Yip 1995). If a foreign market is of particular importance to the strategy of the firm, for instance because a potential host country is leading in relevant technology, the entering firm may select to acquire a local firm rather than partnering to avoid the risk that the local partner will not share its know-how. In markets critical to an entering firm, the higher level of control provided by ownership reduces the risk of goal incompatibility between partnering firms. Similarly, if the entering firm's new foreign operation requires a high level of alignment between existing operations, it may prefer an acquisition to avoid the risk that the strategic orientation between the partners diverges, which leads to a significant increase in coordination costs (Hitt et al. 1995, 1997a).

In addition to strategy, capabilities of the acquirer also affect risk associated with entry mode. Research on domestic acquisitions has identified that firms' capability successfully to integrate acquired firms varies (Haleblian and Finkelstein 1999; Jemison and Sitkin 1986). Finns that have developed such capabilities therefore have lower integration costs than firms that do not. Firms without these capabilities may also be less able correctly to estimate integration cost prior to the acquisition. One might make similar claims regarding the cost of target valuation and restructuring. The expedience and ability in managing acquisitions will likely reduce the risks involved. Similarly, firms engaged in alliances often develop barriers to undesired knowledge transfers to their partners (Hamel et al. 1989). Thus firms experienced in alliances may reduce the dissemination risk of its proprietary know-how.

Characteristics of the target firm can influence risk associated with acquisition. If the reason for an acquisition is specific assets of the firm only (for example, location-specific resources such as a local sales force), but not all of the firm's assets, the acquiring firm faces the task of divesting parts of the organization. This task contains uncertainty regarding the ability to divide the target's assets and selling portions of them. Hennart and Reddy (1997) consider the indivisibility of targets' assets and costs of disintegration a critical reason why firms may prefer cooperation (alliances) rather than an acquisition.

On the other hand, if entering firms are searching for assets they cannot find all in one firm, alliances provide an opportunity to access various resources distributed across multiple firms in the host country (that is, by creating a network of alliances). Acquisition and integration costs will likely prohibit acquisition of some firms in the host country. Possibly, under these conditions, entering firms might use both acquisition and alliance as entry modes.

In summary, the risk associated with acquisition is high, relative to alliance risk, if cultural distance between acquirer and target is high, if the acquirer has little or no international and acquisition experience and has not developed associated capabilities, if the target firm includes many undesired assets that may be difficult to divest, or if the resources desired by the acquirer are distributed across several firms. The risk associated with an alliance is high, compared to acquisition risk, if the alliance is of critical importance to the global strategy of the entering firm or the firm feels incapable of protecting proprietary knowledge from appropriation by the partner. Following is a case that portrays the risks involved in acquisitions.

THE BMW–ROVER CASE[1]

BMW, the German luxury carmaker, acquired Rover Group, Inc., for $1.26 billion from British Aerospace in 1994. The stock market reacted positively to this transaction, with BMW's share price rising 8.3 percent on the day the acquisition was announced. Numerous benefits were perceived as being derived from this acquisition. In a consolidating industry, both BMW and Rover were considered too small to survive independently. Also, this acquisition added important products to BMW's product line, namely sports utility vehicles, which were particularly popular in the US market. It also added smaller vehicles, which BMW lacked, but which can generate significant sales volume.

Although BMW had to take on substantial debt for this acquisition, a number of reasons favored acquisition over a less costly alliance. First, the automobile industry is considered a global oligopoly, where tight control over foreign units is necessary in order to implement firm strategy (Hill et al. 1990). Also, Rover at the time was already involved in an alliance with Honda, the Japanese car manufacturer, and aligning the strategy of all three firms may have been quite difficult. Second, cultural differences between the UK and Germany were considered limited and BMW has significant international experience, thus costs of integration were expected to be relatively low.

Yet, the expected benefits of the acquisition never emerged. Despite investing $5.4 billion in Rover over six years, BMW decided to divest most of the Rover Corporation in Spring of 2000, resulting in significant write-offs for the German firm. With no experience in large-scale acquisition, an incomplete understanding of Rover's problems, and little competitive pressure in its own market niche, BMW chose to allow Rover executives significant autonomy. In addition, Rover engineers and management rejected any German domination. But Rover's technological problems were significant. A large part of the technology in recently developed automobiles had been supplied by Rover's former partner Honda, but Honda had retained the associated know-how. Rover engineers did not have the necessary knowledge to continue using this technology without Honda's help. Also, quality problems in Rover vehicles were much worse than expected. In 1996, the US consumer information firm JD Power rated Rover's vehicles 37th and thus last in customer satisfaction among automobile brands. Also, efficiency at several Rover plants was well below industry standards. Output per employee was about one-third of comparable plants in England. Finally, as these problems led BMW to become more strongly involved in Rover operations, the focus was on technological issues. A clear marketing strategy, one of BMW's strengths, was never developed for Rover.

These substantial shortcomings likely caused Rover's decline. Rover's market share in the UK, its home market, declined from 13.4 percent in 1993 to only 5 percent at the beginning of the year 2000. The appreciation of the British pound in the late 1990s further reduced Rover's competitiveness abroad. When losses at Rover reached almost $1 billion in 1998, BMW's CEO, who had championed the acquisition, was forced to resign, followed by several of his top managers. External observers suggested that the management turnover and heavy financial losses have left BMW significantly weakened and even a potential takeover target.

While it is difficult to evaluate all the reasons for BMW's failure with Rover, some may be identified from our earlier, more theoretical discussion. One notable concern is the lack of experience with large-scale acquisitions. While BMW has a strong technological know-how and has developed a well-conceived market niche strategy for its automobiles, it apparently was ill-prepared to take the actions necessary to achieve synergies between the two businesses and turn around a failing brand. The late recognition of Rover's quality problems and technological deficiencies, as well as the willingness to exercise only limited control of this foreign operation in the first few years after acquisition, are likely the result of BMW's lack of experience in mergers and acquisitions.

Also, BMW seemed unable or unwilling to break up Rover and divest parts of the acquired assets, although one of Rover's product lines was in direct competition with BMW. However, BMW was forced to break up Rover as part of the divestiture. The Land Rover brand and physical assets were sold for $3 billion to Ford Motor Company. Under political pressure from unions and the British government, the Rover brand of luxury automobiles, a traditional competitor of BMW, was transferred to former Rover managers for a symbolic purchase price of £10. BMW retained the popular and profitable small car brand (Mini) together with new and efficient manufacturing facilities.

In hindsight, BMW may have been able to achieve the goal of extending its product line into new markets via an alliance with Rover. BMW now manufactures and markets a sport utility vehicle under its own brand. It likely adapted some of the technology for this new model from its Rover investment, but may instead have been able to access the know-how from Land Rover through an alliance instead of acquisition. Also, an alliance may have led to an eventual acquisition of the Mini brand, which extends the BMW product line to the small car market, but with a better understanding of the problems involved and at a much lower overall cost.

Finally, the differences between the German and British managers indicate the intricacies of foreign direct investment, even if cultural differences are limited. BMW underestimated the resistance of the British managers to German leadership, possibly for historical reasons. German and British automakers have been competitors for decades and the latter have suffered from a decline in market share worldwide for many years. Thus, German automobile manufacturers may claim superiority in quality and technology, which may be hard to accept in the UK (compare, Barkema and Vermeulen 1998). As a result, communication and learning between the two firms may have been severely restricted.

It is interesting to note that Rover was involved in a strategic alliance with the Japanese car manufacturer Honda before the BMW acquisition, where the partners owned cross-shareholdings of 20 percent. Honda successfully used the alliance to improve its market share and production capacity in Europe. The firm is widely credited with achieving a turnaround of the declining Rover brand before 1994. Despite the limited control Honda held in Rover, the collaboration between the two firms was deeper and richer than that achieved between BMW and Rover with an acquisition. Honda became a major supplier of technology and parts for Rover, while the British firm manufactured parts for Honda's UK plant and built two Honda models under license. However, Honda dissolved the alliance following BMW's acquisition of Rover.

CONCLUSION

We have examined the general effects of increasing globalization heightening the importance of firms' international strategies. Most of the research suggests that international diversification has a positive effect on firm performance. However, the positive effects depend on how the entry and operations in international markets are managed. Recent research found that the relationship between international diversification and performance is similar to an inverted 'u' shape. Moderate international diversification generally produces positive benefits. However, at some point with increasing international diversification, the costs (for example, transaction costs, coordination costs) exceed the benefits. A critical factor in the positive outcomes to international diversification is the mode of entry chosen and how entry is managed.

Two increasingly popular modes of entry into international markets are strategic alliances and acquisitions. Both have positive benefits but also carry specific risks. For example alliances provide the opportunity for sharing and combining resources to compete most effectively in a particular market. There are opportunities for learning new knowledge (for example, about technology and markets) as well as sharing the costs of competing in a market. The success of alliances begins with the selection of the best partner (that is, one with the most complementary resources and a willingness to share them with a partner) (Hitt et al. 2000) If a compatible partner with complementary resources is not chosen, the probability for success is low. Of course, there are risks involved in an alliance as well. One of the most critical is appropriation of a partner's specialized assets (for example, technology).

Acquisitions afford more control over the assets, but also are more costly and carry specific risks. Acquisitions may be critical if the market entered is highly important to the success of the firm's strategy. Alternatively, the potential for synergy in an acquisition and achieving it are not the same as many executives have discovered (Hitt et al. 2001a). The problems of integrating the acquired firm into the acquiring firm are often substantial (Haspeslagh and Jemison 1991). Managing the acquisition and assets in the most effective manner is as important as shown by the example of BMW and Rover. Because the investments required to complete cross-border acquisitions are substantial, the risks are even greater.

Therefore, while strategic alliances and acquisitions are growing increasingly popular as a means of entering international markets, many are unsuccessful. They must be carefully selected and effectively managed to maximize their potential returns. The rate of failure in these modes of entering international markets threatens the positive returns to international diversification. Obviously, we need more research on both modes of entering international markets to develop a better understanding of when to undertake these means of entering markets and how they should be managed to ensure success. A better understanding of international strategic alliances and cross-border acquisitions has implications for the theory and practice in international strategy.

NOTE

1. The information for this case builds on the following sources: *The Economist* (2000a, b, c, d); Hitt et al. (1996b); *Wall Street Journal* (1994, 2000); *Wirtschaftswoche* (1996).

REFERENCES

Anderson, E. and H. Gatignon (1986), 'Modes of Foreign Entry: A Transaction Cost Analysis and Propositions', *Journal of International Business Studies*, 17, 1–26.
Angwin, D. and B. Savill (1997), 'Strategic Perspectives on European Cross-border

Acquisitions: A View from the Top European Executives', *European Management Review*, 15, 423–35.

Balakrishnan, S. and M. Koza (1993), 'Information Asymmetry, Adverse Selection and Joint Ventures: Theory and Evidence', *Journal of Economic Behavior and Organization*, 20, 99–117.

Barkema, H.G. and F. Vermeulen (1998), 'International Expansion through Start-up or Acquisition: A Learning Perspective', *Academy of Management Journal*, 41, 7–26.

Barney, J.B. (1991), 'Firm Resources and Sustained Competitive Advantage', *Journal of Management*, 17, 99–120.

Berg, S.V. and P. Friedman (1980), 'Corporate Courtship and Successful Joint Ventures', *California Management Review*, 22(3), 85–91.

Bergh. B.D. (1997), 'Predicting Divestiture of Unrelated Acquisitions: An Integrated Model of *ex ante* Conditions', *Strategic Management Journal*, 18, 715–31.

Birkinshaw, J., N. Hood, and S. Jonsson (1998), 'Building Firm-specific Advantages in Multinational Corporations: The Role of Subsidiary, Initiative', *Strategic Management Journal*, 19, 221–41.

Birkinshaw, J., A. Morrison, and J. Hulland (1995), 'Structural and Competitive Determinants of a Global Integration Strategy', *Strategic Management Journal*, 16(8), 637–55.

Bresman, H., J. Birkinshaw, and R. Nobel (1999), 'Knowledge Transfer in International Acquisitions', *Journal of International Business Studies*, 30, 439–62.

Czinkota, M.R. and I.A. Ronkainen (1997), 'International Business and Trade in the Next Decade: Report from a Delphi Study', *Journal of International Business Studies*, 28, 827–44.

Dutton. G. (1999), 'Building a Global Brain', *Management Review*, May, 23–30.

The Economist (2000a), 'Walking Away from Longbridge', 18 March.

The Economist (2000b), 'BMW after Rover – Milberg's Mission', 1 April.

The Economist (2000c), 'The Pilloried Professor', 6 May.

The Economist (2000d), 'Rover – Faulty Towers', 13 May.

Folta, T.B. (1998), 'Governance and Uncertainty: The Trade-off between Administrative Control and Commitment', *Strategic Management Journal*, 19, 1007–28.

Geringer, J.M., P.W. Beamish, and R.C. DaCosta (1989), 'Diversification Strategy and Internationalization: Implications for MNE Performance', *Strategic Management Journal*, 10, 109–19.

Haleblian, J. and S. Finkelstein (1999), 'The Influence of Organizational Acquisition Experience on Acquisition Performance: A Behavioral Learning Perspective', *Administrative Science Quarterly*, 44, 29–56.

Hamel, G. (1991), 'Competition for Competence and Interpartner Learning within International Strategic Alliances', *Strategic Management Journal*, 12, 83–103.

Hamel, G., Y.L. Doz, and C.K. Prahalad (1989), 'Collaborate with your Competitors – and Win', *Harvard Business Review*, 67(1), 133–9.

Haspeslagh, P.C. and D.D. Jemison (1991), *Managing Acquisitions: Creating Value through Corporate Renewal*, New York: Free Press.

Hennart, J.-F. and S. Reddy (1997), 'The Choice between Mergers/Acquisitions and Joint Ventures: The Case of Japanese Investors in the United States', *Strategic Management Journal*, 18, 1–12.

Hennart, J.-F. and M. Zeng (1997), 'The Differences in the National Origin of Partners Affect the Longevity of Joint Ventures? A Comparative of Japanese–Japanese and Japanese–American Joint Ventures in the United States', unpublished working paper, University of Illinois at Urbana-Champaign.

Hill. C.W.L., P. Hwang, and W.C. Kim (1990), 'An Eclectic Theory of the Choice of International Entry Mode', *Strategic Management Journal*, 11, 117–28.

Hitt, M.A., M.T. Dacin, B.B. Tyler, and D. Park (1997a), 'Understanding the Differences in Korean and U.S. Executives' Strategic Orientations', *Strategic Management Journal*, 18, 159–67.

Hitt, M.A., M.T. Dacin, E. Levitas, J.-L. Arregle, and A. Borza (2000), 'Partner Selection in Emerging, and Developed Market Contexts: Resource-based and Organizational Learning Perspectives', *Academy of Management Journal*, 44, 449–67.

Hitt, M.A., J.S. Harrison, and R.D. Ireland (2001a), *Creating Value through Mergers and Acquisitions*, New York: Oxford University Press.

Hitt, M.A., J. Harrison, R.D. Ireland, and A. Best (1998a), 'Attributes of Successful and Unsuccessful Acquisitions of U.S. Firms', *British Journal of Management*, 9, 91–114.

Hitt, M.A., R.E. Hoskisson, and H. Kim (1997b), 'International Diversification: Effects on Innovation and Firm Performance in Product-diversified Firms', *Academy of Management Journal*, 40, 767–98.

Hitt, M.A., R.E. Hoskisson, R.A. Johnson, and D.D. Moesel (1996a), The Market for Corporate Control and Firm Innovation', *Academy of Management Journal*, 39, 1084–119.

Hitt, M.A., R.E. Hoskisson, and R.D. Ireland (1994), 'A Mid-range Theory of the Interactive Effects of International and Product Diversification on Innovation and Performance', *Journal of Management*, 20, 297–326.

Hitt, M.A., R.D. Ireland, and R.E. Hoskisson (1996b), *Strategic Management: Competitiveness and Globalization*, 1st edn, Cincinnati, OH: South-Western Publishing Company.

Hitt, M.A., R.D. Ireland, and R.E. Hoskisson (2001b), *Strategic Management: Competitiveness and Globalization*, 4th edn, Cincinnati, OH: South-Western Publishing Company.

Hitt, M.A., B.W. Keats, and S.M. DeMarie (1998b), 'Navigating in the New Competitive Landscape: Building Strategic Flexibility and Competitive Advantage in the 21st Century', *Academy of Management Executive*, 12(4), 22–42.

Hitt, M.A., R.D. Nixon, P.G. Clifford, and K.P. Coyne (1999), 'The Development and Use of Strategic Resources', in M.A. Hitt, P.G. Clifford, R.D. Nixon, and K.P. Coyne (eds), *Dynamic Strategic Resources: Development, Diffusion and Integration*, Chichester: John Wiley & Sons

Hitt, M.A., B.B. Tyler, C. Hardee and D. Park (1995), 'Understanding Strategic Intent in the Global Marketplace', *Academy of Management Executive*, 9(2), 12–19.

Jemison, D.B. and S.B. Sitkin (1986), 'Corporate Acquisitions: A Process Perspective', *Academy of Management Review*, 11, 145–63.

Jones, G.R. and C.W.L. Hill (1988), 'Transaction Cost Analyses of Strategy-structure Choice', *Strategic Management Journal*, 9, 159–72.

Kochhar, R. and M.A. Hitt (1995), 'Toward an Integrative Model of International Diversification', *Journal of International Management*, 1, 33–72.

Kogut. B. (1985), 'Designing Global Strategies: Comparative and Competitive Value-added Change', *Sloan Management Review*, 27, Summer, 15–28.

Kogut, B. (1991), 'Joint Ventures and the Option to Expand and Acquire', *Management Science*, 37, 19–33.

Kogut. B. and H. Singh (1988), 'The Effect of National Culture on the Choice of Entry Mode', *Journal of International Business Studies*, 19, 411–32.

Kogut, B. and U. Zander (1992), 'Knowledge of the Firm, Combinative Capabilities, and the Replication of Technology', *Organization Science*, 3, 383–97.

Kotabe, M. (1998), 'The Four Faces of the Asian Financial Crisis: How to Cope with the Southeast Asia Problem, the Japan Problem, the Korea Problem and the China Problem', *Journal of International Management*, 4(1), 1S–6S.

Lane, P.J. and M. Lubatkin (1998), 'Relative Absorptive Capacity and Interorganizational Learning', *Strategic Management Journal*, 19, 461–78.

Luo, Y. (1998), 'Timing of Investment and International Expansion Performance in China', *Journal of International Business Studies*, 29, 391–408.

Madhok, A. and S.D. Tallman (1998), 'Resources, Transactions and Risks: Managing Value through Interfirm Collaborative Relationships', *Organization Science*, 9, 326–39.

March. J.G. and B. Levitt (1999), 'Organizational Learning', in J.G. March (ed.), *The Pursuit of Organizational Intelligence*, Oxford: Blackwell Publishers Ltd.

McCardle. K.F. and S. Viswanathan (1994), 'The Direct Entry versus Takeover Decision and Stock Price Performance around Takeovers', *Journal of Business*, 67, 1–43.

Morosini, P., S. Shane, and H. Singh (1998), 'National Cultural Distance and Cross-border Acquisition Performance', *Journal of International Business Studies*, 29, 137–58.

Osborn, R.M. and J. Hagedoorn (1997), 'The Institutionalization and Evolutionary Dynamics of Interorganizational Alliances and Networks', *Academy of Management Journal*, 40, 261–78.

Park, S.H. and M.V. Russo (1996), 'When Competition Eclipses Cooperation: An Event History Analysis of Joint Venture Failure', *Management Science*, 42, 875–90.

Porter, M.E. (1990), *The Competitive Advantage of Nations*, New York: Free Press.

Ramaswamy, K. (1997), 'The Performance Impact of Strategic Similarity and Horizontal Mergers', *Academy of Management Journal*, 40, 697–715.

Root, F.R. (1980), *Entry Strategies for International Markets*, Lexington, MA: D.C. Heath.

Rugman. A.M. (1979), *International Diversification and the Multinational Enterprise*, Lexington, MA: Lexington Books.

Sanders, W.G. and M.A. Carpenter (1998), 'Internationalization and Firm Governance: The Roles of CEO Compensation, Top-team Composition, Work Structure', *Academy of Management Journal*, 41, 158–78.

Singh, H. and B. Kogut (1989), 'Industry and Competitive Effects on the Choice of Entry Mode', *Academy of Management Proceedings*, 116–20.

Uhlenbruck, K. (2000), 'Foreign Direct Investment in Transitional Economics: The Development of Acquired Subsidiaries', Academy of International Business National Meeting, Phoenix, AZ.

Uhlenbruck, K. and J.O. De Castro (2000), 'Foreign Acquisitions in Central and Eastern Europe: Outcomes of Privatization in Transitional Economies', *Academy of Management Journal*, 43, 381–402.

Very, P., M. Lubatkin, R. Calori, and J. Veiga (1997), 'Relative Standing and the Performance of Recently Acquired European Firms', *Strategic Management Journal*, 18, 593–614.

Wall Street Journal (1994), 'Honda Plans to Unwind Cross-holding with Rover, Dealing a Setback to BMW', 22 February, A3.

Wall Street Journal (2000), 'Ford Grabs Big Prize as Steep Losses Force BMW to Sell Rover', 17 March, A1.

Wirtschaftswoche (1996), 'Rover: Probleme ausmerzen', 29 August, 35.

Yip, G.S. (1995), *Total Global Strategy: Managing for Worldwide Competitive Advantage*, Englewood Cliffs, NJ: Prentice Hall.

12. Towards a research agenda on hybrid organizations: R&D, production and marketing interfaces

Xavier Martin

INTRODUCTION: THE SCOPE OF HYBRID ORGANIZATION

One of the most significant developments in international strategy formulation since the early 1980s has been the growth and maturation of research on hybrid organizational forms. By hybrids, I refer to intentionally and extensively coordinated arrangements whereby two or more firms pool resources in an explicit and durable manner to the intended benefit of each party. Hybrids lie between the business firm (the unified hierarchy) and the spot arm's length transaction among altogether independent parties (the atomistic market). Pure markets and pure hierarchies are the conventional solutions most readily studied by business scientists (Williamson 1991; Hennart 1993). Hybrids, however, are both empirically common and more challenging to research (for example, Contractor and Lorange 1988; Harrigan 1988).

Forms of hybrid arrangements include alliances, equity joint ventures, long-term collaborative procurement arrangements for components and technology, extended licensing, and assorted ties such that two or more firms remain legally autonomous but commit to durably and substantively coordinating their activities. Research has shown that participation in hybrid arrangements has implications for firms' performance, whether measured by financial indicators, innovation, or survival (for example, Singh and Mitchell 1996; Uzzi 1996; Ahuja 2000; Park and Martin 2001). An extensive literature has examined the motivations for entering into hybrid arrangements, and research shows that understanding the motivations helps understand the performance implications (Shaver 1995). Furthermore, understanding how firms set the functional boundaries of hybrid arrangements matters to managers and business scholars alike.

The upshot of hybrid organization is that it calls for coordination of business functions not only within a firm, but also between firms. Within a firm, management's role includes coordinating the business functions. For simplicity, I focus here on R&D, production and marketing – the three main functional areas that exist in one form or another in most companies. R&D is shorthand for the generation and absorption of new process technologies and new products or services, including but not limited to 'whitecoat' lab activities. Production is shorthand for the ongoing making of goods and services, including assembly manufacturing. Finally, marketing is shorthand for sales and distribution of finished goods and services, and related communication and support activities.

Management research has described in ample detail the workings, governance and implications of the interfaces between R&D, production and marketing within a firm. By contrast, research on interfirm arrangements has typically examined links between whole firms rather than between functions – even though not all functions of each partner firm may be involved. This chapter reviews what we know about interactions among the R&D, production and marketing functions as they occur *between* firms that participate in hybrid arrangements.

The chapter proceeds in four sections. The first section draws on the existing within-firm research to identify basic concepts and findings about functional coordination in business enterprises. The second section addresses functional interfaces between horizontally related firms, that is, between firms that operate in overlapping product markets and in the same stages of the industry chain. The third section addresses functional interfaces between vertically related firms, that is, between a buyer and supplier. While each context yields distinct questions and research challenges, some plausibly generalizable patterns emerge. The fourth section draws some conclusions and extends the chapter's ideas to broader community-level interfaces.

FUNCTIONAL INTERFACES WITHIN FIRMS

From its very inception, the field of business management has been concerned with how to shape the interfaces among business functions (Barnard 1938; Koontz 1955). More recent research on sources of competitive advantage further highlights the role of these functions. Evolutionary, transaction cost and resource-based approaches each in their own way view the firm as a bundle of resources whose boundaries and leveraging require managerial attention (Penrose 1959; Nelson and Winter 1982; Williamson 1985).

Much has been said of the tacit and ineffable nature of the most critical corporate resources. For that reason, it is not always easy to match strategic resources onto traditional organizational functions. Still, the traditional concept of the business function remains critical to the examination of sources of

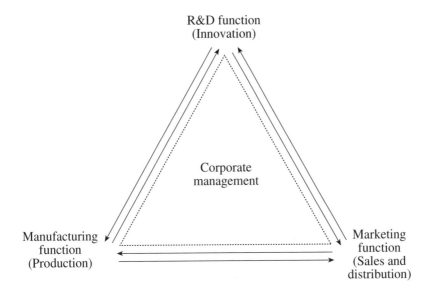

Figure 12.1   Functional interfaces within a firm

competitive advantage. Most valuable resources reside either in a firm's R&D, production or marketing function or in the managerial function that coordinates them (Figure 12.1). The potential for R&D and marketing to generate distinctive resources has long been acknowledged (for example, Morck and Yeung 1991; Ettlie 1998; Martin and Mitchell 1998). R&D creates new products and processes, in some cases protected by intellectual property rights. Thus, it can yield uniquely low costs, differentiated offerings, superior operations, and the ability to appropriate and regenerate these advantages in the face of competition. Marketing, meanwhile, serves to shape markets. It can allow firms to establish and maintain strong brands that translate into added consumer loyalty and price premiums, or to otherwise define offerings that best exploit demand conditions.

Traditionally, the role of the production function has received less attention in this line of research. This may be because most conventional models describe production as a function driven by explicit, replicable cost-lowering mechanisms such as economies of scale, scope and learning. In recent years, production has received more attention as a potential source of differentiated competitive advantage. This occurred as North American and European firms in various assembly-based industries were experiencing severe competition from Japanese rivals, especially during the 1980s. Some Japanese rivals, it turned out, organized production operations in a manner that generated magnitude improvement in efficiency. Furthermore, their production systems yielded products of superior quality. Therefore production, like R&D and marketing, could be a source of multifaceted and sustainable advantage (Womack et al. 1990).

Thus, each of the three business functions – together with the managerial skills involved in leading and coordinating them – can generate competitive advantage. This is not to say, however, that they all do in a given firm. On the contrary, most firms rely on a small number of activities in a single function – if that – as a source of competitive advantage. They leverage a small core of distinctive competence (Prahalad and Hamel 1990).

The notion of a limited corporate core, in fact, has antecedents in the academic literature. Thompson (1967) describes the core of a firm as a small number of functional activities that are most critical to its smooth functioning. The economist's concept of the core, too, reminds us of the power of thinking in terms of the smallest possible set of value-adding activities or participants (Telser 1978).

Why do many firms rely on a relatively small functional core for competitive advantage? Plausibly, because developing any source of sustainable advantage at all is very hard for firms competing in efficient input and output markets, and firms tend to focus on accumulating one advantageous resource rather than developing multiple competencies (Barney 1986). In such a context, the cost of developing a resource tends to match the benefits from using that resource, and firms find it easier to accumulate any one resource than to develop multiple competencies (Rumelt 1984; Dierickx and Cool 1989). This means that a firm that is strong in one function is likely to outperform many rivals lacking such strength, but will also find it difficult and typically fruitless to develop another unrelated source of advantage (for example, Porter 1980). Such a firm would be better off fostering and protecting its current functional strength instead. Focus may also alleviate any limitations on management's ability to cope with the tensions and trade-offs inherent in simultaneously pursuing multiple sources of competitive advantage.

All this suggests that a firm should foremost seek to develop and protect a narrowly defined functional strength. This is not to say, however, that management should ignore functions other than those in which it currently possesses a competitive advantage. Evidently, some minimum level of performance in each function is required. Furthermore, there may be complementarities both within and across business functions (Milgrom and Roberts 1990). Indeed, research suggests that firms need to achieve substantial coordination among business functions in order to exploit any latent complementarities. For example, to build on an innovation-based strategy requires ongoing communications and simultaneous efforts from the production and marketing functions (Nonaka 1990; Clark and Fujimoto 1991). Generally, multiple and simultaneous interactions increase the rate and accuracy of feedback to decision makers, promoting faster and more specific learning (Sterman 1989; Sengupta and Abdel-Hamid 1993).

In summary, research within firms suggests an important tension that is bound to affect hybrid interfirm relationships too. On one hand, a firm typically relies on a small set of distinctive resources such that it should protect a small functional core from external imitation and interference. On the other hand, the firm needs to coordinate among its various functions so as to leverage its core competency. Next, I turn to the challenges that this tension stands to generate in interfirm relationships, and discuss some evidence as to existing solutions.

FUNCTIONAL INTERFACES IN HORIZONTAL INTERFIRM RELATIONSHIPS

This section addresses functional interfaces among firms that are horizontally related. By horizontally related, I mean that the firms engage in similar activities and are therefore potential rivals, as opposed to vertical relationships among complementary buyers and suppliers. In the horizontal context, the dual-edged potential of hybrid relationships becomes all the more relevant. For simplicity, I deal in this section primarily with interfirm alliances. However, the main conclusions plausibly apply to other forms of horizontal hybrid arrangements, such as licensing (Martin and Salomon 2001).

The two faces of hybrid arrangements are as follows. On the one hand, a relationship such as an alliance can allow a firm to access precious new capabilities. Consistent with this premise, Park and Martin (2001) show that the more valuable, rare and inimitable the resources possessed by an airline are, the more positive will be the stock market reaction to a partner airline that announces an alliance with the first airline. On the other hand, alliances can cause firms to expose their core capabilities. In the resulting learning race, a firm may end up losing the distinctiveness of its capabilities without obtaining countervailing gains in know-how from its partner (Hamel 1991). This tension results in hybrids that mix competitive and cooperative motives (Kogut 1988; Brandenburger and Nalebuff 1996).

Previous research has discussed the implications of this dual concern for the management of existing joint ventures (for example, Hamel et al. 1989; Gulati 1998). Other research has described possible patterns of specialization among alliances' partners (for example, Porter and Fuller 1986; Buckley and Casson 1988; Hennart 1988; Garrette and Dussauge 1995). Here I focus on the implications for the scope of the alliances that firms are willing to form, since this decision determines subsequent organizational and managerial considerations. As illustrated in Figure 12.2, firms may engage either in

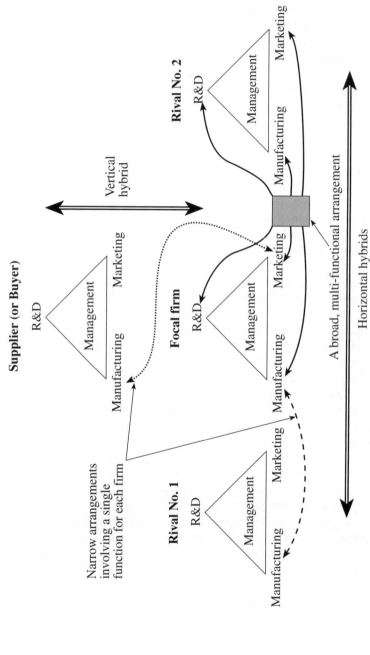

Figure 12.2   Functional interfaces between firms

single-function arrangements, which I refer to as narrow alliances; or in arrangements that involve several functions for each participating firm, and that I refer to as broad alliances. Firms that seek to access particular external capabilities while protecting their own operations will tend to form narrow alliances with a limited functional scope. We can examine this prediction and gain further insights into hybrid arrangements by observing the functional scope of the alliances that firms form in practice.

Martin and Park (2001) describe the scope of alliances in the international airline industry. The industry is a particularly proper context to look at alliance scope, because of its regulatory environment. International airlines' activities are governed by international agreements that prevent *de novo* foreign direct investment. They also make cross-border mergers and acquisitions effectively impossible in most cases. This has two interesting implications for our purposes. First, regulatory oversight is such that alliances are clearly announced, and their functional contents can be examined accordingly. Second, some alliances substitute for more direct modes of entry that would normally entail the full spectrum of business functions. Thus alliances in the international airline industry overstate the extent of multi-functional alliances elsewhere, if anything. Altogether, this represents a suitable and conservative setting in which to examine whether horizontal alliances will tend to be narrow in scope. Indeed, the data support this prediction.

Martin and Park (2001) describe the functional contents of alliances set up by 32 randomly selected international airlines between 1982 and 1994. During that 13-year period, the 32 airlines initiated a large number of horizontal alliances with rival airlines based in other countries – 389 of them to be exact. Figure 12.3 reports the functional contents of these alliances.

Because technical innovation plays a limited role in the industry, it is not surprising that only 18 alliances had R&D contents; all but three of these were single-function, that is, focused on R&D-type innovation only. Given the scarcity of R&D activities, I use a generous definition of broad alliances to include any alliance that encompasses two or more of the three main functions: production (transportation operations), marketing, or innovation. Among the other 371 alliances, 315 had a single function in scope: 218 dealt with production-type transportation activities only, while 97 dealt with marketing activities only. The remaining 56 alliances combined two or more functions. Overall, less than one alliance in six in this industry had multi-functional content. This is consistent with the proportions reported by Ghemawat et al. (1986) for various other industries during the period 1970–82. In summary, the data show that managers strongly prefer their firms' horizontal alliances to remain narrow in functional scope. It would be interesting to examine further the determinants of alliance scope itself, for we know little about this.

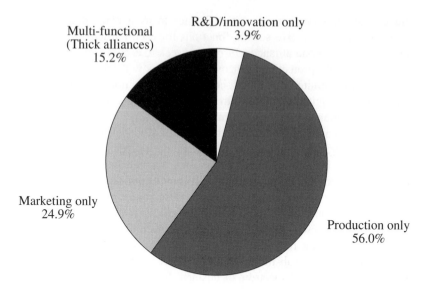

Multi-functional
(Thick alliances)
15.2%

R&D/innovation only
3.9%

Marketing only
24.9%

Production only
56.0%

Source: Martin and Park, 2001.

*Figure 12.3   Functional scope of 389 alliances among international
                  airlines, 1982–94*

Martin and Park (2001) provide further evidence worth considering for the purposes of academic research. Most of the best-known studies of interfirm alliances describe learning effects whereby firms learn about alliances through repeated action. That is, the number of alliances a firm has entered into in the past affects how likely the firm is to enter into future alliances, and what benefits it will obtain from alliances. Some of these studies also find industry effects whereby the alliances entered into among firms elsewhere in the industry make a difference, perhaps due to information spillovers. However, most of these studies also combine alliances regardless of their functional contents. They measure experience accumulation at the firm (and industry) level, ignoring whether a particular function was or was not involved in past alliances.

Martin and Park (2001) start by replicating these past results. They show that, when alliances are combined regardless of their functional contents, the propensity of a firm to engage into an alliance varies non-monotonically with both the number of alliances that the firm has entered into before, and the number of alliances that other firms in the industry have entered into. That is, alliances at the firm level are predicted both by past firm alliances and by past industry-wide alliances.

Martin and Park (2001) then show that a different picture emerges when a refined analysis takes into account the functional content of the alliances. They do so by generating separate counts of production, marketing, and other types of alliances. Past firm-level marketing alliances predict future firm-level marketing alliances, but have no substantial effect on production-type alliances. Conversely, past firm-level production alliances predict future production alliances, but not marketing alliances. Furthermore, there is no effect of past industry-level marketing alliances, and past industry-level production alliances only weakly predict future firm-level production alliances.

The results of Martin and Park (2001) show that the dynamics of interfirm alliances occur overwhelmingly at the functional level, and that function-specific experience accrues mostly from firm rather than industry effects. For researchers, the implications are as follows. First, when it comes to alliances among rival organizations, learning effects should be expected to occur within business functions. Second, the function, rather than the whole firm, is the more promising level of analysis. Third, the dynamics of hybrid arrangements among potential rivals generally keeps their scope narrow rather than broad.

This confirms the prediction advanced earlier: when rivals ally, they usually prefer narrow single-function alliances to broad multi-function arrangements. However, broader horizontal arrangements are common enough that they deserve explicit attention too. Furthermore, as I will discuss next, the dynamics are rather different in arrangements among vertically linked buyers and suppliers. Future research may examine what prompts broad rather than narrow hybrid arrangements among rivals as well as among vertically related firms. It should also examine what the consequences are for alliance and parent-firm performance – where attention to business functions would again be particularly worthwhile.

FUNCTIONAL INTERFACES IN VERTICAL INTERFIRM RELATIONSHIPS

Next, let us consider the case of vertical arrangements between buyers and suppliers. In this context, a tradition going back to Adam Smith has emphasized the virtues of a strict division of labor between successive stages of the industry chain. Thus, one might expect narrowly defined arrangements to predominate. However, there are also reasons to expect vertical arrangements often to involve complex combinations of business functions. This section examines this issue theoretically and then presents some evidence from the automotive industry.

By vertical hybrids, I refer to arrangements whereby a buyer and a supplier undertake extensive and durable collaboration on a substantive project that may involve the design, production, and/or marketing of a component. As with horizontal relationships, the logic for vertical hybrids is best understood by comparison both with a market solution of short-term arm's length contracting and with outright vertical integration (Eccles 1981; Hennart 1993; Hemmert 1999). Hybrid arrangements combine intermediate levels of market-like incentives with intermediate levels of firm-like control by authority (Williamson 1991).

Above I discussed the knowledge advantages and disadvantages of horizontal hybrids. These considerations also apply to some extent to vertical hybrids. Consider the negative consequences of know-how leakage first. At first blush, this issue would appear to be less salient in vertical relationships, where the buyer and the supplier have distinct specialization and do not normally compete head-on in the end product market. Nevertheless, some residual concerns arise due to two secondary mechanisms. One is the possibility that the other party will integrate vertically – that is, from the supplier's perspective, the possibility that the buyer with which the supplier shares knowledge will use that knowledge to start its own upstream activities (or reciprocally). The second is that knowledge could flow from the focal firm through the trading partner back to a rival of the focal firm – that is, the buyer takes the supplier's knowledge and shares it with another supplier (or reciprocally). In fact, the buyer may use the threat of either mechanism to discipline the buyer on an ongoing basis. Of course, the supplier could make the reverse threat too.

Notwithstanding these concerns, the potential benefits of high-involvement vertical relationships are substantial. Simple arm's length relationships, that minimize the functional interface between buyer and supplier, may be suitable for transactions with high transparency and limited information impactedness. However, in more complex situations, more extensive interfaces may be called for. This includes situations where specialized equipment and knowledge are involved in the transaction, and where the relationship builds on ongoing mutual adaptation between the buyer and the supplier (Martin 2001). Furthermore, multiple functions are likely to be involved where firms seek to leverage complementarities within and between their operations (Milgrom and Roberts 1990; Asanuma 1989; Helper 1991; Dyer and Singh 1998).

Previous research has examined the potential implications of buyer–supplier systems for firm expansion and scope, in domestic contexts (for example, Levinthal and Fichman 1988) and international contexts (Martin et al. 1994, 1995, 1998). Research also shows that intense and tightly integrated buyer–supplier relationships can substantially affect firms' performance domestically (Kotabe et al. 2000) and in international operations (Martin 2001). Here, I focus on the pattern of functional interfaces in vertical hybrids. Specifically, I examine the extent to which a supplier's influence over the buyer is related across business functions.

If the specialized division of labor and the protection of corporate boundaries and resources are the main concerns, then we should observe a supplier's influence to be very limited in scope – typically, to a narrowly defined production function. This would be the equivalent for vertical hybrids of the narrow relationships found prominently among horizontal hybrids. However, to the extent that firms seek to exploit complementarities among functional interfaces, then interactions around one business function will tend to be associated with interactions around the other business functions in a given buyer–supplier relationship.

To explore this issue I turn to data on the US and Japanese automotive industries that is discussed more extensively in Kotabe et al. (2000). The automotive industry has given rise to some of the most insightful comparisons between US and Japanese assemblers. The data were collected from suppliers, who contribute the bulk of a vehicle's value and play a critical role in shaping competitive advantage in the industry. Kotabe et al. (2000) surveyed 97 US and 105 Japanese suppliers regarding the management and consequences of their relationships with assemblers. The relationships in these data are mostly extensive first-tier partnerships. These relationships are better described as hybrid links than discretionary arm's length purchasing deals.

The data describe a variety of procurement practices covering the three business functions of interest, plus general management. Items were measured on a five-point Likert scale. Here I focus on items that measure a supplier's influence on the buyer. Automotive assemblers play a dominant economic and technological role in the industry. Therefore we would expect the automotive data, if anything, to understate the breadth of influence of suppliers relative to what it would be in other industries.

Principal components factor analysis with varimax rotation generates interesting results in this respect. Items pertaining to production and R&D load together. These include questions about product design, manufacturing process, materials and component procurement, and quality control. This indicates that extensive information exchange in production matters is associated with complementary knowledge flows in innovation-related matters. This result is consistent with previous descriptions of interfirm relationships in the Japanese automotive industry (for example, Asanuma 1989; Clark and Fujimoto 1991; Lamming 1993). What is even more interesting is that a similar pattern was found in the US data. This suggests that the connection between innovation and production functions is relevant in the automotive industry outside of Japan too (for further discussion see Kotabe et al. 2000).

The factor analysis also showed that items pertaining to the marketing and general management functions load together. These include questions on

sales force training, advertising, promotion, brand name selection, and pricing (where data were available) as well as human resources and management
recruitment. Again, the same pattern arose in the US and Japanese data. Thus,
in this industry, the technical functions of R&D and production tend to
overlap in hybrid relationships. Likewise, managerial and marketing functions tend to overlap.

For further insight, we can also examine the overlap between technical
(R&D/production) and managerial/marketing influence. Table 12.1 reports
the Pearson correlation coefficients between the two factors just discussed. It
also reports the correlations with a measure of how crucial the component's
technology is to the buyer's competitive advantage. This measures the strategic importance of the supplier's components. Three sets of correlations are
reported in Table 12.1. The top of the table (12.1a) reports results combining
the US and Japanese sample, while the next two segments (12.1b and 12.1c)
report correlations for the US and Japanese samples separately.

In all three specifications, one finding stands out: the influences of all the
main business functions are strongly associated. Where the supplier's influence in R&D and production matters is high, its influence in managerial and
marketing matters also tends to be high (and reciprocally). This finding is
stronger in the US sample ($r = +0.53$, $p < 0.001$) but is also evident in Japan
($r = +0.29$, $p < 0.01$). Thus, in these vertical hybrids, the functions of R&D,
production, marketing and management appear to complement each other
quite strongly. (By contrast, the data in Figure 12.3 imply a strongly negative
correlation between dummy indicators of production and marketing contents
in airline alliances; however, differences in measures prevent a direct statistical comparison between the vertical and horizontal results.)

Regardless of whether the US and Japanese data are combined, there is
no statistically significant evidence of correlation between management/
marketing influence and the component's technological crucialness. There
is a difference between the US and Japanese samples, however, regarding
the correlation between technical influence and crucialness. In the Japanese
data, the exercise of technical influence by the supplier is positively associated with the crucialness of the technology for the buyer ($r = +0.24$, $p <
0.10$). In the US sample, the association is negligible and tends to be
negative ($r = -0.16$, not statistically significant). A plausible interpretation
is that Japanese firms, having more experience on average working with
their current suppliers (Kotabe et al. 2000), open up interfirm interfaces
more selectively. This assumes that the most technologically crucial components are also those where supplier input is most required; alternatively,
this may also indicate that Japanese assemblers have become dangerously
dependent on suppliers in technologically critical areas. Further research in
this area would be interesting. Kotabe et al. (2000) provide more evidence

Table 12.1   Correlations among dimensions of supplier influence

(a)   Combined sample (N = 202)

	Technical influence (R&D, production)	Marketing and managerial influence
Marketing and managerial influence	+0.50***	
How crucial the component's technology is to the assembler's competitive advantage	+0.04	−0.04

(b)   US sample (N = 97)

	Technical influence (R&D, production)	Marketing and managerial influence
Marketing and managerial influence	+0.53***	
How crucial the component's technology is to the assembler's competitive advantage	−0.16	−0.05

(c)   Japanese sample (N = 105)

	Technical influence (R&D, production)	Marketing and managerial influence
Marketing and managerial influence	+0.29**	
How crucial the component's technology is to the assembler's competitive advantage	+0.24*	+0.04

Note: The *p*-values are indicated as follows: * for $p < 0.05$; ** for $p < 0.01$; *** for $p < 0.001$.

about the performance implications of functional interfaces between buyers and suppliers.

Overall, the evidence suggests that interfirm interfaces tend to be quite broad in vertical hybrids. The main purpose of some outsourcing may be the specialized division of labor, with relatively narrow interfirm interfaces. However the buyer–supplier relations I described mostly exhibit intense interactions across multiple functions. A possible interpretation is that these broad interfaces develop where procurement requirements are complex and where there is the potential to exploit multi-functional complementarities across (as well as within) firms. Opportunities exist for further research to examine what determines the functional make-up of a buyer–supplier relationship – and how the performance of firms and relationships varies with the breadth and functional diversity of the linkages in vertical hybrids.

It is also interesting to consider the contrast between horizontal and vertical hybrids. We observe comparatively narrow functional scope in horizontal hybrids (in the international airline industry), while the data on interfirm influence indicate broader relationships in vertical hybrids (in the automotive industry). Certainly, multi-functional complementarities may exist in horizontal hybrids too. It may be, however, that their exploitation through multi-functional interfaces is pre-empted in some cases by concerns about protecting core activities in the midst of rivalry. Likewise, concerns about potential rivalry exist in vertical hybrids too. However they may be low enough for richer, broader interfirm relationships commonly to develop.

Might differences in industry context exaggerate this contrast? Differences in measures may account for some of the contrast. Overall, however, I believe that the data I used may actually understate the magnitude of the difference. In the international airline industry, regulation reduces the threat of direct rivalry and would therefore encourage broader horizontal alliances. In the automotive industry, the bargaining power of assemblers makes very real the threat of upward integration and knowledge pass-through. This effect should be all the more salient when surveying suppliers, as in the data reported here. It would therefore encourage narrower buyer–supplier relations. Thus, on balance, I believe that research in other contexts would also find a contrast in multi-functional breadth between horizontal and vertical hybrids. One issue that requires further attention is what would encourage or discourage the exploitation of complementarities through broad multi-functional interfaces in horizontal hybrids.

IMPLICATIONS FOR FUTURE RESEARCH

Generally, this research confirms the importance of examining hybrid relationships at the level of business functions, rather than solely at the level of the firm as a whole. In some situations, firms benefit most from the careful selection and isolation of a single function (or even part thereof) in any hybrid arrangement. In other cases, advantage arises from the strategic combination of various functional activities both within and between firms. Choices about which functions to interface, and how to govern them, stand to have a substantial impact both on the hybrid arrangement and on its parents. The theory and data I presented show distinct patterns in horizontal and vertical hybrids. Each pattern is interesting for future research, as is the contrast between the two contexts. This means that the most insightful research programs will examine both horizontal hybrids among potential rivals, and vertical hybrids linking buyers and suppliers.

There are implications for research specification too. When a firm announces that it will enter into an alliance, complex procurement deal, or other form of hybrid arrangement, we typically get to observe the decision and its consequences at the parent firm level. Some hybrids exist as stand-alone legal entities that report information about themselves independent of their parent firms (for example, widely-held equity joint ventures). Even then, researchers seldom disaggregate the information at the level of the business function. Firms are the basic legal entity for most regulatory reporting and for understanding strategic competition and performance. Thus most of our theories of strategic and international management focus on whole firms rather than business functions. I believe, though, that examination of individual business functions can be fruitful in refining and complementing theories of competitive advantage. A firm's distinctive capabilities and resources reside in its business functions. For this reason alone, it is important to study functions as such. Just as importantly, the combination and interfacing of various functions across firms can critically affect a firm's competitive outlook; the definition and management of sound interfaces can be a source of competitive advantage by itself (Dyer and Singh 1998; Martin 2001). Thus, to paraphrase Penrose (1959), research in strategic and international management can be informed by conceptualizing firms and hybrid arrangements alike as combinations of business functions.

In practice, firms typically enter into multiple hybrid arrangements simultaneously (Martin et al. 1998; Martin and Park 2001). In so doing, they weave a web of relationships (Uzzi 1997; Gulati and Gargiulo 1999). The resulting networks and communities, in turn, stand to affect entire industries (Martin 2001). Conversely, this means that the building blocks of networks and communities may vary sharply in their functional contents. Networks, clusters, industry ecosystems, distributed activity systems, virtual organizations, and like phenomena each have distinctive functional dimensions. Research on these broader aggregations of businesses, too, should be informed by considerations of the interfaces between R&D, production, and marketing. Further research on these functional interfaces as they operate between firms stands to be fruitful for academics and practitioners alike.

ACKNOWLEDGMENTS

This research was supported by the Stern School of Business at New York University and the Graduate School of Business at Columbia University. I am grateful to Namgyoo Park for allowing me to draw on our joint research on international airline alliances, and likewise to Masaaki Kotabe and Hiroshi Domoto regarding research on buyer–supplier partnerships in the US and Japanese automotive industries. Thanks are due for helpful comments and suggestions from the organizers and participants of the conference on Emerging Issues in International Business at Temple University. I am particularly grateful to Masaaki Kotabe for his contribution and support of this research.

REFERENCES

Ahuja, Gautam (2000), 'Collaboration Networks, Structural Holes, and Innovation: A Longitudinal Study', *Administrative Science Quarterly*, 45(3), 425–55.

Asanuma, Banri (1989), 'Manufacturer–Supplier Relationships in Japan and the Concept of Relation-specific Skill', *Journal of the Japanese and International Economies*, 3(1), 1–30.

Barnard, Chester (1938), *The Functions of the Executive*, Cambridge, MA: Harvard University Press.

Barney, Jay B. (1986), 'Strategic Factor Markets: Expectations, Luck, and Business Strategy', *Management Science*, 32(10), 1231–41.

Brandenburger, Adam M. and Barry J. Nalebuff (1996), *Co-opetition*, New York: Currency-Doubleday.

Buckley, Peter J. and Mark C. Casson (1988), 'A Theory of Cooperation in International Business', in Farok J. Contractor and Peter Lorange (eds), *Cooperative Strategies in International Business: Joint Ventures and Technology Partnerships between Firms*, Lexington, MA: Lexington Books, pp. 31–53.

Clark, Kim B. and Takahiro Fujimoto (1991), *Product Development Performance*, Boston, MA: Harvard Business School Press.

Contractor, Farok J. and Peter Lorange (eds) (1988), *Cooperative Strategies in International Business: Joint Ventures and Technology Partnerships between Firms*, Lexington, MA: Lexington Books.

Dierickx, Ingemar and Karel Cool (1989), 'Asset Stock Accumulation and Sustainability of Competitive Advantage', *Management Science*, 35(12), 1504–11.

Dyer, Jeffrey H. and Harbir Singh (1998), 'The Relational View: Cooperative Strategy and Sources of Interorganizational Competitive Advantage', *Academy of Management Review*, 23(4), 660–79.

Eccles, Robert G. (1981), 'The Quasi-firm in the Construction Industry', *Journal of Economic Behavior and Organization*, 2, 335–57.

Ettlie, John E. (1998), 'R&D and Global Manufacturing Performance', *Management Science*, 44 (1), 1–11.

Garrette, Bernard and Pierre Dussauge (1995), 'Patterns of Strategic Alliances between Rival Firms', *Group Decision and Negotiation*, 4, 429–52.

Ghemawat, Pankaj, Michael E. Porter, and Richard A. Rawlinson (1986), 'Patterns of International Coalition Activity', in Michael E. Porter (ed.), *Competition in Global Industries*, Boston, MA: Harvard Business School Press, pp. 345–65.

Gulati, Ranjay (1998), 'Alliances and Networks', *Strategic Management Journal*, 19(4), special issue, 293–317.

Gulati, Ranjay and Martin Gargiulo (1999), 'Where do Interorganizational Networks Come From?', *American Journal of Sociology*, 104(5), 1439–93.

Hamel, Gary (1991), 'Competition for Competence and Organizational Learning within International Alliances', *Strategic Management Journal*, 12, special issue, 83–103.

Hamel, Gary, Yves Doz, and C.K. Prahalad (1989), 'Collaborate With Your Competitors – and Win', *Harvard Business Review*, 67(1), 133–9.

Harrigan, Kathryn R. (1988), 'Joint Ventures and Competitive Strategy', *Strategic Management Journal*, 9, 141–58.

Helper, Susan (1991), 'Strategy and Irreversibility in Supplier Relations: The Case of the U.S. Automobile Industry', *Business History Review*, 65(Winter), 781–824.

Hemmert, Martin (1999), '"Intermediate Organization" Revisited: A Framework for the Vertical Integration Division of Labor in Manufacturing and the Case of the Japanese Assembly Industries', *Industrial and Corporate Change*, 8(3), 487–517.

Hennart, Jean-Francois (1988), 'A Transaction Costs Theory of Equity Joint Ventures', *Strategic Management Journal*, 9, 361–74.

Hennart, Jean-Francois (1993), 'Explaining the "Swollen Middle": Why Most Transactions are a Mix of Market and Hierarchy', *Organization Science*, 4(4), 529–47.

Kogut, Bruce (1988), 'Joint Ventures: Theoretical and Empirical Perspectives', *Strategic Management Journal*, 9, 319–32.

Koontz, Harold (1955), *Principles of Management: An Analysis of Managerial Functions*, New York: McGraw-Hill.

Kotabe, Masaaki, Xavier Martin, and Hiroshi Domoto (2000), 'How Relation-specific Assets Matter: Knowledge Transfer and Supplier Performance Improvement in the U.S. and Japanese Automotive Industries', Working paper, New York University.

Lamming, Richard (1993), *Beyond Partnership: Strategies for Innovation and Lean Supply*, Englewood Cliffs, NJ: Prentice Hall.

Levinthal, Daniel A. and Mark Fichman (1988), 'Dynamics of Interorganizational Attachments: Auditor–Client Relationships', *Administrative Science Quarterly*, 33, 345–69.

Martin, Xavier (2001), 'Effects of Relation-specific and General Assets on International Corporate Expansion', Working paper, New York University.

Martin, Xavier and Will Mitchell (1998), 'The Influence of Local Search and Performance Heuristics on New Design Introduction in a New Product Market', *Research Policy*, 26(8), 753–71.

Martin, Xavier, Will Mitchell, and Anand Swaminathan (1994), 'Recreating and Extending Buyer–Supplier Links Following International Expansion', in Paul Shrivastava, Anne Huff, and Jane Dutton (eds), *Advances in Strategic Management*, volume 10B, Greenwich, CT: JAI Press, pp. 47–72.

Martin, Xavier, Will Mitchell, and Anand Swaminathan (1995), 'Recreating, and Extending Japanese Automobile Buyer–Supplier Links in North America', *Strategic Management Journal*, 16(8), 589–620.

Martin, Xavier and Namgyoo Park (2001), 'Why Firms Enter into Successive International Alliances: Bounded Momentum and Alliance Formation', Working paper, Stern School of Business, New York University.

Martin, Xavier and Robert Salomon (2001), 'Knowledge Transfer Capacity: Implications for the Theory of the Multinational Corporation', Working paper, Stern School of Business, New York University.

Martin, Xavier, Anand Swaminathan, and Will Mitchell (1998), 'Organizational Evolution in an Interorganizational Environment: Incentives and Constraints on International Expansion Strategy', *Administrative Science Quarterly*, 43(3), 566–601.

Milgrom, Paul and John Roberts (1990), 'The Economics of Modern Manufacturing: Technology, Strategy, and Organization', *American Economic Review*, 80(3), 511–28.

Morck, Randall and Bernard Yeung (1991), 'Why Investors Value Multi-nationality', *Journal of Business*, 64(2), 165–87.

Nelson, Richard R. and Sidney G. Winter (1982), *An Evolutionary Theory of Economic Change*, Cambridge, MA: Harvard University Press.

Nonaka, Ikujiro (1990), 'Redundant, Overlapping Organization: A Japanese Approach to Managing the Innovation Process', *California Management Review*, 32 (Spring), 27–38.

Park, Namgyoo and Xavier Martin (2001), 'Resource Access and Firm Value: A Test of Resource Effects in the International Airline Industry', Working paper, Stern School of Business, New York University.

Penrose, Edith (1959), *The Theory of the Growth of the Firm*, Oxford: Blackwell.

Porter, Michael E. (1980), *Competitive Strategy: Techniques for Analysing Industries and Competitors*, New York: Free Press.

Porter, Michael E. and Mark Fuller (1986), 'Coalitions and Global Strategy', in Michael Porter (ed.), *Competition in Global Industries*, Boston: Harvard Business School Press, pp. 315–43.

Prahalad, C.K. and Gary Hamel (1990), 'The Core Competence of the Corporation', *Harvard Business Review*, May–June, 79–91.

Rumelt, Richard P. (1984), 'Towards a Strategic Theory of the Firm', in B. Lamb (ed.), *Competitive Strategic Management*, Englewood Cliffs, NJ: Prentice Hall, pp. 556–70.

Sengupta, Kishore and Tarek Abdel-Hamid (1993), 'Alternative Conceptions of Feedback in Dynamic Decision Environments: An Experimental Investigation', *Management Science*, 39(4), 411–28.

Shaver, J. Myles (1995), 'Accounting for Endogeneity when Assessing Strategy Performance: Does Entry Mode Affect FDI Survival?', *Management Science*, 44(4), 571–85.

Singh, Kulwant and Will Mitchell (1996), 'Precarious Collaboration: Business Survival after Partners Shut Down or Form New Partnerships', *Strategic Management Journal*, 17 (Summer Special Issue), 99–115.

Sterman, John D. (1989), 'Modelling Managerial Behavior: Mis-perceptions of Feedback in a Dynamic Decision Making Experiment', *Management Science*, 35(3), 321–39.

Telser, Lester G. (1978), *Economic Theory and the Core*, Chicago: University of Chicago Press.

Thompson, James D. (1967), *Organizations in Action*, New York: McGraw-Hill.

Uzzi, Brian (1996), 'The Sources and Consequences of Embeddedness for the Economic Performance of Organizations: The Network Effect', *American Sociological Review*, 61(4), 674–98.

Uzzi, Brian (1997), 'Social Structure and Competition in Interfirm Networks: The Paradox of Embeddedness', *Administrative Science Quarterly*, 42(1), 35–67.

Williamson, Oliver E. (1985), *The Economic Institutions of Capitalism*, New York: Free Press.

Williamson, Oliver E. (1991), 'Comparative Economic Organization: The Analysis of Discrete Structural Alternatives', *Administrative Science Quarterly*, 36, 269–96.

Womack, James P., Daniel T. Jones, and Daniel Roos (1990), *The Machine that Changed the World*, New York: Rawson Associates.

13. The Internet and international business: a cross-regional study

Indrajit Sinha and Yaniv Gvili

Online retailing consists of transactions of products and services over the Internet to final consumers. The Internet has now become globally pervasive and widely accessible, and, by all estimates, the commercial potential of e-commerce belies usual estimates. Today 373 million people are connected to the Internet[1] and more than 2 million new users get connected each month in North America alone.[2] For them 20 million domain names (Web sites) have been established.[3] Despite the recently documented high-profile dot-com failures, the worldwide start-up rate of companies selling products and services on the Internet still remains impressive. Analysts predict that the online sales to consumers (B2C) will touch $45 billion in 2000 while total Web sales will reach $190 billion.[4] More generally, the Internet has evolved into an extremely powerful and versatile marketing medium for many traditional brick-and-mortar firms.

From an international business perspective, the issue that is of interest is to identify the commonalities and variations in the perceptions of global e-shoppers toward e-commerce. How are online shopping criteria differentially important to shoppers in different regions? Do non-American buyers perceive that their own country's e-retailers serve their needs better than American ones? It has been widely reported that the Internet, as a direct channel to global buyers, will help US suppliers extend their reach and target market and circumvent trade barriers imposed by foreign governments. But this theory presupposes that all things being equal international buyers will likely buy from US-based e-tailers over their own-country ones that may be better localized and customized to their preferences.

Additionally, several articles in the popular press have highlighted the relatively higher price consciousness and deal–prone behavior of American consumers on the Internet versus in traditional shopping contexts. An interesting research question is whether this phenomenon extends to other countries as well, particularly in those regions (like Western Europe and South Asia) where shoppers are not likely to expect lower prices due to either governmental regulations or the lack of competition among suppliers.

The above questions form the central focus of this exploratory study. Other specific issues that are also investigated are as follows:

1. *Decision making factors* What are the most important factors that shoppers consider during their online buying process vis-à-vis traditional buying? Do these factors vary across different geographic regions?
2. *Price sensitivity* How deep is the expected discount that consumers around the world expect to obtain from Internet retailers in comparison to traditional ones?
3. *Domestic versus US retailer sites* How do consumers in different geographic regions compare the attributes of their own-country e-tailers relative to the better-known and recognizable US brands like Amazon.com?
4. *Intention to buy* Considered by region, how willing are shoppers to buy from their domestic, own-country Internet retailers compared to international (especially, US) ones?

In this chapter we address such questions through a global survey of consumer perceptions of Internet retailing, and their online expectations and behavior. The objective is to identify and measure cross-regional differences on a number of buyer-based variables. The focus of the study is thus more exploratory than confirmatory, since we seek to gain new insights into issues pertinent to web retailing at a global level, and, particularly since we do not propose any preconceived hypotheses for subsequent confirmation or rejection. Indeed, owing to the evolving nature of online retailing and its global scope, aside from a few industry reports, very little academic research is available that has examined these issues.

Before we describe the data collection procedure and report our research findings, it may be useful to motivate the discussion by summarizing the innate attractiveness and challenges of online retailing from the perspective of *both* consumers and suppliers (that is, manufacturers and retailers).

ATTRACTIVENESS OF ONLINE RETAILING

From the standpoint of an individual buyer, the Internet offers a convenient, hassle-free medium for shopping, one that offers privacy and is not limited by stringent time schedules or the constraints of a store-level inventory. Additionally, the Web provides a number of buyer-empowering sites that permit an easy comparison of the prices and features of products that are available from different e-tailers. This latter feature contributes to more informed decision making and more comprehensive evaluation not possible before in the traditional shopping context. For instance, in the past, buyers often faced an array of choices and had to bear onerous search costs if they wished to evaluate their alternatives in greater depth. However, the ease and convenience of comparison shopping that is possible today on the Internet tends to cause many prospective buyers to become deal-prone as they are better able to sift through the value propositions of their offered choices. As we discuss below, this new-found facility represents a negative development for online suppliers because it stands to hasten a phenomenon known as *cost transparency*, which dilutes brand loyalty and makes consumers reluctant to pay any 'unreasonable' price premiums (Sinha 2000).

Viewed from the perspective of suppliers, the Internet represents a new and inexpensive distribution channel that provides direct and instant access to prospective buyers on a global level. Additionally, it facilitates the implementation of hitherto difficult marketing objectives of personalized (or relationship) marketing and securing consumer involvement at various stages of new product development. Several authors have recently discussed how the Net may allow suppliers to co-opt customer competencies and leverage *their* knowledge for such expensive and risky tasks as product design and testing in ways never possible before. An oft-cited instance is how the Microsoft Windows 2000 software was beta-tested by more than 200 000 unpaid consumer volunteers who pointed out bugs and made invaluable suggestions that significantly decreased the time to market the product.

THE CHALLENGE OF COST TRANSPARENCY

A key threat that the Internet poses to retailers is the seamless access to information of product attributes that consumers are able to secure at no or very little cost. Information has a way of making buyers more sensitive to prices and therefore more averse to paying any excessive premium. For the first time in the history of economic exchange, the buyer is presented with a wealth of information about competing offerings, their attributes and characteristics, as well as objective (third-party) evaluations of their quality. Moreover, the Internet equips the buyer with sophisticated software tools that process the complex information and determine the value that each represents on a host of buyer-specified yardsticks. Not surprisingly, marketers are therefore compelled to compete on price and ultimately end up engaging in a self-sacrificing price war.

Viewed more subtly, the new information that the Internet offers buyers tends to rewrite the rules of the products' price–cost equations that buyers held in their minds. Where previously consumers had thought the price of an established product was commensurate with the costs incurred by its manufacturer, now with the Net making him or her aware of cheaper alternatives of similar quality, this higher price seemed absurdly (and vexingly) out of line. In other words, the Internet usually succeeds in making the costs of the product category *transparent* to the buyer. Car dealerships are waking up to this new reality as customers now walk in armed with dealer invoice prices downloaded free of cost from sites like AutoByTel.com. Inevitably, these cost-aware buyers force dealers to charge only minimal margins, thereby squeezing their profits. Traditional newspapers are finding more and more of their readers balk at having to pay for renewals of their print subscriptions especially since they can read the electronic versions (and only the desired sections at that) free of cost on the Web. A similar plight afflicts travel agencies who are finding their business increasingly endangered by upstart internet sites like Priceline.com or Expedia.com that allow buyers to quote their own prices as well as by airlines offering cut-rate air tickets to customers directly by e-mail.

The interesting aspect of the Internet-led cost transparency phenomenon is that it is not just limited to the US. A similar plight currently afflicts traditional suppliers from their online rivals in other countries and geographic regions. Britain's lastminute.com site, which sells excess or unused inventory in the travel and hospitality industries, has dented the sales of many established brick-and-mortar travel agents. In Japan, online brokerages are as much a hit as in America, and have won over many Japanese investors who were used to paying the high commissions of the well-established brokerage firms.

Next we discuss the methodology and the salient findings of the cross-regional survey that is the focus of this chapter.

STUDY DATA

The data for this study were collected through an online survey of subjects located in US and in various Internet-ready countries across the globe. Respondents were contacted by e-mail once their addresses were obtained from a database that is freely available on the Web. They were subsequently screened to select those who had had some experience in online shopping. The selected subjects were then requested to visit the survey site and complete a brief questionnaire. Approximately, 500 responses were obtained, out of which some were missing data cases. The eventual sample consisted of 436 respondents from 23 nations, and was subsequently grouped into six regional categories: North America (US and Canada), Latin America, South East Asia (including Australia), Middle East, Western Europe, and Scandinavia. Response rates were in general satisfactory (mean = 14 percent) but varied somewhat across regions from a minimum of 13 percent in Western Europe to 20 percent in South East Asia.

ANALYSIS OF RESULTS

Broadly, the findings of the study can be categorized under the following headings.

Decision Factors in Online Shopping versus Traditional Shopping

In the aggregate, price was seen as the most important factor vis-à-vis shopping on the Internet. Subjects from all geographic regions perceived 'low price' to be significantly ($p < 0.05$) more important in online shopping than in traditional shopping. Results were consistent across regions although Asian and North American subjects accorded price a higher weight in general than European and Latin American subjects (Figure 13.1).

When it came to the reputation of the (online or brick-and-mortar) store, once again subjects of all regions rated its importance to be more in the Internet context than for a brick-and-mortar establishment. Interestingly, while these differences were significant for Western Europe, Scandinavia, and S.E. Asia, they were not so for North America and the rest. In other words, respondents in the latter regions viewed reputation to be equally important for online and traditional retailers (Figure 13.2).

Next, we looked at the relative role of convenience across Internet shopping and traditional shopping. We expected that subjects would perceive this

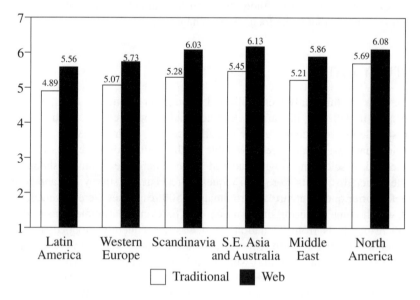

Figure 13.1   Online shopping: relative importance of low price

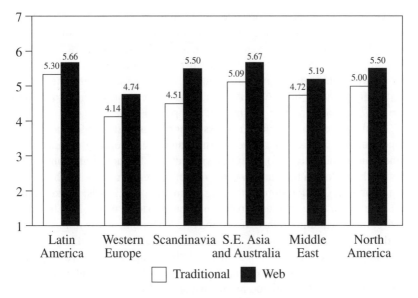

Figure 13.2   Online shopping: relative importance of reputation

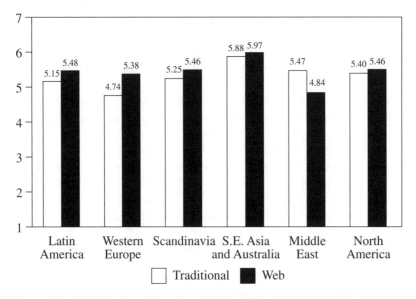

Figure 13.3   Online shopping: relative importance of convenience

aspect to be significantly more relevant to the former since the Web allows seamless browsing of product offerings unlike in a traditional store. While our results showed that convenience was generally valued more in Internet shopping, it was not necessarily so in all regions, and the differences were not always significant (significantly higher only for Europe and the Middle East). Importantly, North American subjects viewed convenience to be only *marginally* more important for Internet shopping (Figure 13.3).

The most interesting variation across regions was observed for the relative importance of service in online versus traditional shopping. While North American (principally, US) shoppers viewed it to be more important on the Web, although not significantly so, the rest of the regions rated it as being less important than in a traditional shopping setting. In other words, unlike Americans, the rest of the world seem to perceive the Web to be more of a self-service environment. The importance of service of a Web retailer was in fact significantly lower than traditional shopping for Scandinavia (Figure 13.4).

Finally, subjects of every region rated 'branding' to be more important online than in the brick-and-mortar world. This belies the popular belief that brands are destined to oblivion in the virtual era (Figure 13.5).

Price Expectations of Online Shoppers

The next set of questions addressed subjects' beliefs about the price they expect to pay when they are shopping on the Internet. A majority of respondents in all regions agreed that, as a rule, they would expect lower prices on the Internet (inclusive of all tax and shipping charges) versus traditional shopping for the identical item. However, the majorities varied from a low of 70 percent for S.E. Asia to a high of 87 percent for Scandinavia (Figure 13.6).

When asked about the exact percentage reduction in price when shopping online, the mean responses tended to vary across regions. Surprisingly, subjects in more developed countries (like the US and Western Europe) tended to be more conservative in their expectations (15 percent lower on average), shoppers in the rest of the world seemed more optimistic, with Latin American consumers expecting in excess of 20 percent lower prices (Figure 13.7).

Comparison between Domestic versus US E-tailing Sites

To the question 'how difficult it is to purchase items from Internet sites not from your own country (1: not very difficult–7: very difficult)', responses indicated that subjects did not perceive this exercise to be particularly difficult. However, Scandinavian and Western European subjects viewed it as being the least onerous as compared to the rest (Figure 13.8).

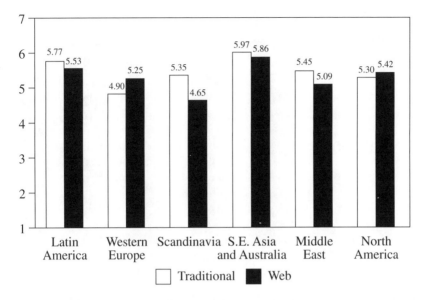

Figure 13.4   Online shopping: relative importance of service

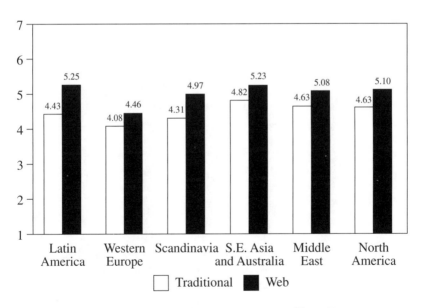

Figure 13.5   Online shopping: relative importance of branding

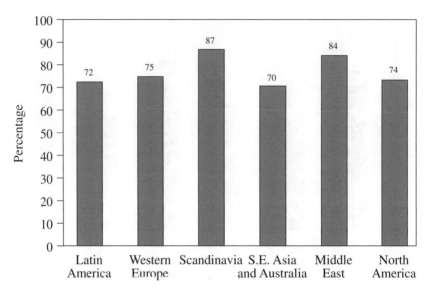

Figure 13.6   Percentage agreeing that prices are lower on the Internet

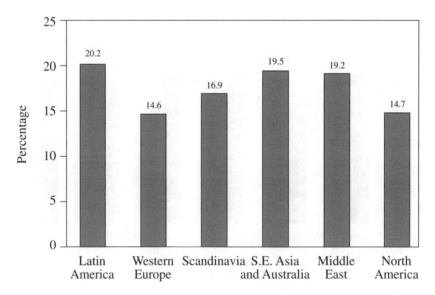

Figure 13.7   Percentage expected discount on the Internet

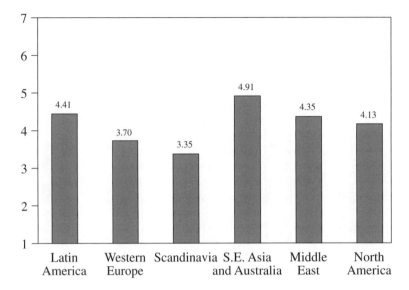

Figure 13.8   Difficulty in buying from another country's sites

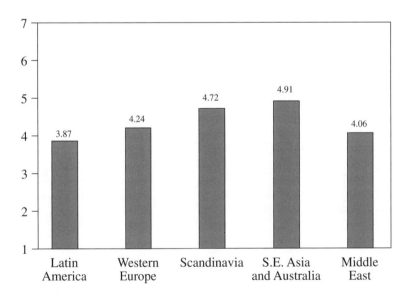

Figure 13.9   Need fulfillment by domestic e-tailers relative to US sites

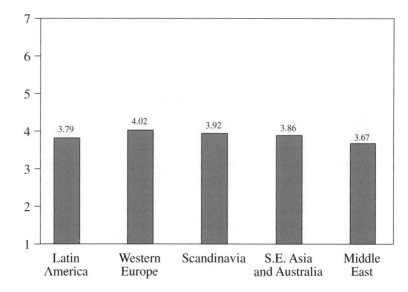

Figure 13.10   Product selection of domestic e-tailers relative to US sites

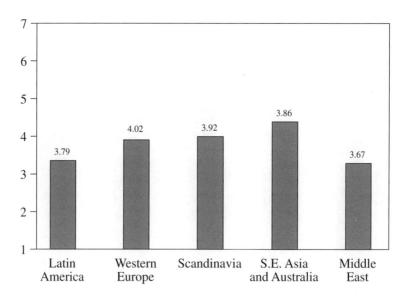

Figure 13.11   Quality of 'deals' offered by domestic e-tailers relative to US

Next, subjects in every region except North America were asked to compare their own-country e-tailers with established US sites. First, they responded to the question as to whether their domestic e-tailers understood their needs better than US sites. Responses indicated a high level of dissatisfaction with their own-country Internet retailers. Shoppers in Latin American and the Middle East were the most critical, while the rest were not significantly more satisfied with their domestic equivalents (Figure 13.9).

Finally, shoppers worldwide expressed a high level of dissatisfaction with their domestic e-tailers in terms of both product selection (Figure 13.10) and offered deals (Figure 13.11). It is understandable that US e-tailers scored higher on such characteristics perhaps due to the significant advantages that they enjoy from being first movers in various categories of e-commerce.

Likelihood of Shopping on the Internet

The final issue in the survey sought to elicit the respondent's likelihood of purchasing an item on the Internet in the very near future. Responses to this question varied in an expected manner consistent perhaps with the spread and penetration of e-commerce, with North American shoppers expressing the strongest inclination and the Latin American ones the least (Figure 13.12).

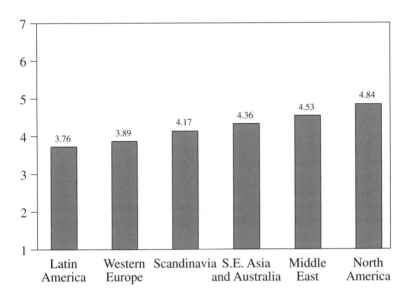

Figure 13.12   Likelihood of shopping online

GENERAL DISCUSSION AND CONCLUSION

The above results show that price, convenience, brand, and reputation are the most important factors for online shoppers, regardless of region. Interestingly, in North America consumers perceive service to be more important in an Internet context than in traditional buying. In other regions, people regard the Internet more as a 'self-service' medium. In regions where e-commerce is not as well developed, buyers are *more* focused on securing price reductions. Consumers generally expect to pay less for the same products when they buy them online than from brick-and-mortar stores. However, the expected discounts appeared to vary according to region. Consumers from relatively less-developed regions expect to gain higher reductions than those in more affluent ones. It is a testament perhaps to their experience with online shopping that consumers in North America and Western Europe are more conservative in their expected price discounts on the Web.

On the whole, the findings should be heartening to the managers of US Internet shopping sites. Shoppers in other geographic regions viewed US e-tailers as superior to their domestic alternatives on such important dimensions as need fulfillment, selection, and quality of offered deals.

A key finding of this study is the remarkable convergence in online buyer perceptions that exists around the world. On most criteria, there were few significant differences among subjects in different regions. Considering the increased globalization and rapid diffusion of ideas and knowledge that the Internet has facilitated, this conclusion may not be entirely surprising.

NOTES

1. http://www.glreach.com/globstats/evol.html
2. http://www.clicksites.com/internet.html
3. http://www.dotcom.com/facts/quickstats.html
4. http://www.epaynews.com/statistics/transactions.html#1

REFERENCE

Sinha, Indrajit (2000), 'Cost Transparency: The Net's Real Threat to Prices and Brands', *Harvard Business Review*, March–April, 43–54.

Index

Abdel-Hamid, T. 245
Acevedo, M. 175, 176, 195
acquisitions
  BMW-Rover case 9, 233–5, 236
  cross-border 228–9
    versus strategic alliances 230–31
  Electrolux case 207–9
  entry mode risk 230–33, 235–6
  failure rate 236
  global strategy 8–9, 214–15
agglomeration 23, 24
Aguilera, R.V. 196
Ahmed, A. 103
Ahuja, G. 241
airline industry 245, 247–8, 254
Alden, D.L. 89
Aliber, R.A. 71
Alster, N. 45
Amsden, A.H. 163, 164, 165, 167, 168,
    172, 173, 180, 194
Anderson, E. 230
Angwin, D. 228
APEC *see* Asia-Pacific Economic
  Cooperation
Appadurai, A. 83
Appiah, K.A. 82
Argentina
  business groups 186–90
  development strategy 175–6, 194–5
Arnold, D.J. 220
Asanuma, B. 250, 251
Asia-Pacific Economic Cooperation
  (APEC) 203
Asian financial crisis
  FDI liberalization following 112–13
  structural uncertainty 144
  worldwide economic growth,
    reduction in 224
asset seeking, FDI motivation 20, 21,
  22
Aulakh, P.S. 1–10, x, xvii, xviii, xx–xxi

automotive industry
  US and Japan 251–4

Babai, D. 109
Babyak, R.J. 213
Bachman, D. 69
Balakrishnan, S. 231
Balassa, B. 15
Baldwin, R. 32
Balkanization *see* cultural Balkanization
Barber, B. 84
Barkema, H.G. 229, 235
Barney, J. 168, 169, 179, 227
Bartlett, C.A. 205
Barton, T.D. 83, 84
Bayard, T.O. 109
Beatty, G. 208
Belisle, D.J. 132
Belk, R.W. 84, 87, 89
Benko, R. 58
Bennet, W. 83
Berenbeim, R. 57, 61
Berg, S.V. 231
Bergh, B.D. 229
Berman, P. 49
Bernard, A.B. 132
Berne convention 55
Bettis, R.A. 201, 202
Bhagwati, J. 15, 19–20, 32, 111
Bilateral Investment Treaties (BITs)
    102, 109, 110–11, 118
Bilkey, W.J. 128
biotechnology 58
Birkenshaw, J. 224
Bisang, R. 195
BITs *see* Bilateral Investment Treaties
Blank, S. 27, 28
Blass, A. 52
Blecker, R.A. 127
Blonigen, B.C. 77
Bodnar, G.M. 73

Boli, J. 82
Bonham, Y. 40
Borsuk, R. 47
Bostock, F. 220
Bowersox, D.J. 126
Brady plan 112
Brandenburger, A.M. 245
Brennan, A. xxi
Bresman, H. 230
Brewer, T. 2
Brosius, P. 92
Buckley, P.J. 66, 106, 245
Bush, R. 45
business groups
  defining 164–7
  development strategies
    FDI flows and resource access
      169–70, 171
    impact of 170–72
    modernizing 169, 170, 171
    nationalist 170, 171
    nationalist-modernizing 170, 172–4
    nationalist-populist 175, 176–7
    populist 169, 170, 171
    populist-modernizing 173
    pragmatic 170, 171
    pragmatic-modernizing 177–9
    pragmatic-populist 174–6
  diversification 163, 167
  economic sociology theory 166, 167,
    181, 182, 190, 191
  emerging economies, study of 7–8
    data and methods 181–2
    OLS regressions 182, 184, 185,
      186
    results 182–6
    statistics and correlation coeffi-
      cients 182, 183
  importance, study of 179–80, 181
    data and methods 186–8
    largest 100 firms 187–8, 188–9
    results 188–90
  inimitability 179–80
  late development theory 167, 181,
    182, 190
  market failure view 165–6, 167, 181,
    182, 190
  resource-based view 164, 168–9, 186
    asymmetry 191–2
    competition 169

cultural variables 193
implications 192
inputs 168
knowledge 168
markets 168
research avenues 192–3
towards an understanding of
  190–93
state, role of 167

Callahan, P. 211
Canada-US Free Trade Agreement
  (CAFTA)
  expansion into NAFTA 29, 31
  FDI and trade 27, 28–30
  hub-and-spoke relationship 26
  MNC response to 26
  US-Mexico trade 29, 30
Casson, M. 66, 245
Cava, A. 91
Caves, R.E. 1, 65, 66, 142, 143
Cavusgil, T.S. 128
Cervantes, M. 40
Chandler, A.D. Jr 163, 165, 168
Chandran, R. xx–xxi
China
  copying in 50
  FDI policy 118
Chinese Economic and Technological
  Development Zones (ETDZs) 150
Chirico, J. 84
Choi, J.J. 5, 65–77, 70, 71, 73, 74, 77, x
Christophe, S.E. 69
Clark, K.B. 244, 251
clusters 18, 23–4
  horizontal and vertical 24
  impact of regional integration 24–5
  MNC trade and FDI patterns 26–30
  types 23
Cohen, D. 40
Cohen, J. 181, 182
Cohen, P. 181, 182
common currencies 17, 31
common markets 17
competition
  business groups 169
  export performance 132–3
  industry concentration level 151–2
  international expansion 142
  multipoint 223

strategy 8–10
structural forces 145–6
computer chip protection 40, 58
Conner, K.R. 39, 60
Contractor, F.J. 142
Cool, K. 244
copyright 37
  databases 57
  versus patent 48
  software 58, 61
core competency, corporate concept of
  244–5
corporate citizenship 91–2
counterfeiting 43
Cox, E.P. 41
Craig, C.S. 1
cultural Balkanization 83–5
  brokers, cultural 90
  business ethics 90–92
  cross-vergence framework 86, 88
  culture, meaning of 87
  fundamentalism 84
  globalization 82–3, 87
  glocalization 85
  homogenization 4, 5–6
  hybridization 83, 84, 85, 86, 87–8, 89,
    92
  management 88
  marketing 89–90
  meaning of 83–4
  processs leading to 85
  work values 86–7
currency premium theory 71
customs unions 17, 19
Cutts, S. 130
Czinkota, M.R. 6–7, 123–37, 124, 126,
    128, 131, 132, 135, 224, x–xi

Davis, W. 81
Dawson, L.L. 84
D'Cruz, J.R. 22, 27
De Castro, J.O. 224
De Melo, J. 32
decline stage, industry life cycle 155
Delmar, J. 43
Den Hartog, N. 88
Dienickx, I. 244
DiMaggio, P.J. 82
diversification 224–5 *see also* business
  groups

firm performance 225–6, 235
  product diversification 226, 229
Donaldson, T. 91
Double Taxation Treaties 102
Douglas, S. 1
Dretler, T.D. 204
Drown, S. 210, 211
Dumas, B. 73
Dunfee, W.D. 91
Dunning, J.H. 1, 15, 18, 20, 23, 30, 32,
    65, 66, 67, 99, 142
Dussauge, P 245
Dutton, G. 228
Duvall, D.K. 49
Dyer, J.H. 255, 360

e-commerce 9–10
  attractiveness of 261–2
  cost transparency 262–3
  decision making factors
    branding 266, 272, 277
    convenience 264–6, 272
    low price 264, 272
    reputation 264, 265, 272
    service 266, 272, 277
  domestic *versus* US retailer sites 261,
    266, 269–71
  explosive growth of 9–10
  exports 135–6
  intention to buy 261
  likelihood of shopping 271
  price expectations 266, 268
  price sensitivity 261
Eaton, C. 23, 32
EC *see* European Community
Eccles, R.G. 250
economic growth, worldwide 223–4
Eden, L. 4, 15–32, 18, 20, 22, 24, 27,
    29–30, 32, xi
EEC *see* European Economic Commu-
    nity
El-Agraa, A.M. 32
Electrolux 207–9, 215, 219
Elliot, K.A. 109
embryonic stage, industry life cycle 154,
    155
Engle, T.T. 69
Enright, M.J. 23, 32
entry mode risk 230–31
  alliance *versus* acquisition 232–3

business strategy 231–2
firms' capability 232, 236
environmental movement 92
EPO *see* European Patent Office
Errunza, V. 69, 74
ETDZs *see* Chinese Economic and
Technological Development Zones
Ethier, W.J. 18
Ettlie, J.E. 243
EU *see* European Union
Eun, C.S. 74
European Community (EC) 1992 Plan
203
European Economic Community (EEC)
15, 18
European Patent Convention (1973) 55
European Patent Office (EPO) 45, 55–6
European Union (EU) 31
merger activity 228
Evans, P. 167, 168, 174
executives, influence of 213–14
export promotion
environment, changes in
bureaucratizaton 130
expenditure returns 130–31
firms' satisfaction 131
OECD restrictions 130
trade imbalances 129
WTO influence 129–30
export performance, determinants of
budgeting 133
captive trade 134
competitiveness 132–3
demand-oriented focus 134
new technologies 135–6
resource-sharing 136–7
unplanned exports 135
exports as special 123–4
government, changing role of 6–7
reasons for
market gaps, bridging 125–7
obstacles abroad, overcoming 125
trade deficit, alleviating 127
traditional approaches
knowledge transfer 127–8
red tape, reducing 128
subsidization 128, 137
value of 131–2

Fagre, N. 100, 101, 103, 118

FAO *see* Food and Agriculture Organization
Fatemi, A. 69
Fayerweather, J. 3
FDI *see* foreign direct investment
Feinberg, R.M. 39, 49
Fichman, M. 250
Fields, K.J. 166, 169, 193, 194
Fienberg, S. 188
financial markets, global
corporate decisions 67–8
exchange rates and finance, effects of
75
FDI 71–2
financial-market-decision variables
67–8
firms
and markets, profile of 75–6
risk and cost capital of 72–4
valuation 66–70
ownership-location-internalization
67–8
potential *versus* realized gains 76–7
research issues 65–6, 77
Finkelstein, S. 232
Folta, T.B. 230
Food and Agriculture Organization
(FAO) 52
foreign direct investment (FDI) 4, 6
bargaining 103–4, 107–10
bilateral negotiations 110–12
business groups 169–70, 171
CAFTA 27, 28–30
China 118
clusters 26–30
competition for 114, 117
duration control 150
efficiency 20, 21, 22
entry mode control 149
equity control 149
financial markets 65, 71–2
firm valuation 66–8
government policies 149–50
horizontal *versus* vertical 159
industrial structure 141
liberalization 6, 99–100, 101–3
backlash 117
and emergency finance 112–13
Latin America 105
reasons for 105–7

location control 149–50
market seeking 20, 21, 22
NAFTA 30, 109
partner control 150
project orientation control 150
regional integration 15–16, 18, 20–30
resource seeking 20, 22
size control 150
strategic asset seeking 20, 21, 22
tariff jumping 20, 22, 23
timing control 150
unilateral sanctions 111–12
Fox School of Business and Manage-
    ment xvii, xviii–xix, xx–xxi
Free Trade Area of the Americas
    (FTAA) 31
free trade areas (FTAs) 17
Freeman, J. 88
Freidheim, C.F. Jr 204
Friedman, J. 83
Friedman, P. 231
Friesen, P. 182
Froot, K.A. 71
Fuji-Xerox 220
Fujimoto, T. 244, 251
Fuller, M. 245
fundamentalism 84

Ganesan, A.V. 116
Gargiulo, M. 255
Garrette, B. 245
Gatignon, H. 230
GATS *see* General Agreement on Trade
    in Services
GATT *see* General Agreement on Tariffs
    and Trade
General Agreement on Tariffs and Trade
    (GATT) 109, 115
  intellectual property rights 56
  norm of national treatment 17
  predecessor of WTO 4, 203
  Uruguay Round talks 57, 61, 114–15,
    203
General Agreement on Trade in Services
    (GATS) 114, 116
Generalized System of Preferences (US)
    111–12
Gentry, W.M. 73
Geography and Trade 23
Ger, G. 84, 87, 89

Geringer, J.M. 142, 225
Gestrin, M. 20, 29, 32
Ghemawat, P. 247
Givon, M. 40
Gleason, E.S. 119
globalization
  born-global firms 220
  cultural Balkanization 5–6, 82–3, 87
  as divisive 84
  executives, influence of 213–14
  financial performance 219
  global strategy 201–2
  home appliance industry 206–7, 216
    218
    Electrolux 207–9, 215, 219
    Maytag Corporation 209–11, 217,
      219
    Whirlpool Corporation 211–14,
      216, 219
  hybridization 85
  industry
    consolidation 214–15
    suitability 204–5
  institutional context 6–8, 202–3
  intermarket segments 218, 219
  versus internationalization 8, 204–6
  knowledge-based capability 218–19
  local, increased appreciation of 89
  multipoint competition 223
  versus nation-states xviii
  prerequisites for 204–6, 215–16
  revolution in business 223–4
  size criticality 205–6
  versus standardization 204, 215–18
  technological development 203
Globerman, S. 32, 40
glocalization 83, 84, 85
Goldman, N.D. 38
Gomes-Casseres, B. 101, 103, 104, 106,
    118
Gopal, R.D. 38, 39
Granger, C.W.J. 69
Granovetter, M. 163, 164, 165, 180
Grönroos, C. 135
growth stage, industry life cycle 154,
    155, 160
Guillén, M.F. 7–8, 163–96, 168, 178,
    193, 194, 195, xi–xii
Guisinger, S.E. 119
Gulati, R. 245, 255

Gurr, T.R. 181, 191
Gvili, Y. 9–10, 260–72, xii

Haar, J. 28
Hagedoorn, J. 226
Haggard, S. 169, 170, 174, 177
Haleblian, J. 232
Hamel, G. 205, 225, 230, 232, 244, 245
Hannan, M.T. 88
Hannerz, U. 83, 89
Hansen, R. 221
Hanson, G.H. 29, 32
Hartley, R.F. 221
Harvey, M. 40
Haseltine, W. 221
Haspeslagh, P.C. 229, 236
Hays, L. 220
Head, K. 24
Helfgott, S. 39
Helper, S. 250
Hemmert, M. 250
Henisz, W. 124, 181
Hennart, J.-F. 20, 227–8, 232, 241, 245
Higgins, R.S. 39, 49
Hikino, T 163, 165, 168, 172, 180, 194
Hill, C.W.L. 168, 225, 230, 233
Hilts, P. 42
Hitt, M.A. 8–9, 163, 164, 168, 180, 201, 202, 203, 223–36, 224, 225, 226, 227, 228, 229, 236, xii–xiii
Hodder, J.E. 70
Hofstede, G. 87, 88, 181, 188, 190, 197
Holding, R.L. 211
Hoover, and Maytag 210–11
Hoskinsson, R.E. 163, 164, 168, 180
host government-MNC relations 6
  bargaining models 100–101, 107–10
  traditional 100, 103–5, 106
  two-tier multi-party 100–101, 107–10, 118–20
  developing countries, defined 101
  FDI liberalization 99–100, 101–3
  reasons for 105–7, 120
  research avenues 119–20
  tier-1 bargaining, determinants 110–16, 120
  bilateral negotiations 110–12
  multilateral financial institutions 112–14

  multilateral trade agreements 114–16
  tier-2 bargaining 117
Hout, T. 205
hub-and-spoke relationship 23, 24
  CAFTA 26
Hufbauer, G. 32
Huntington, S.P. 84
Husted, B.W. 5–6, 81–92, 87, 91, xiii
hybrid organizations 241–56
  business functions
    coordination of 241–2
    as research focus 255–6
  defining 241
  forms of 241
  functional interfaces 9
    within firms 242–5
    interfirm 245–9, 245–54
  hybridization 83, 84, 85, 86, 88, 89, 92
  Hymer, S. 65, 66, 142
  Hyundai group 172–3

ICSID *see* International Center for the Settlement of Disputes
IGMS *see* Institute of Global Management Studies
IIPA *see* International Intellectual Property Alliance
IMF *see* International Monetary Fund
In the Hurricane's Eye 99
industry
  endowment 140–41
    and MNC performance 7
  life cycle 153–5
innovation
  intellectual property protection 57–8
  investment return 53
  patent protection 51–2
insider firms
  inward FDI 30
  regional integration 21, 24–5
Institute of Global Management Studies (IGMS) xviii–xix, xx–xxi
integrative social contracts theory 91
intellectual property protection 4–5
  agreement administration 55–6
  competitiveness 48–9
  confusion over 37–8
  copyright 42, 46, 55
  economic growth, hindrance to 49–51

economic rationale of 59
enforcement issues 38, 40, 45, 47–8,
    56–7, 59–60
free access *versus* protection 52–3
industrial property 37, 54–5
industrialized *versus* developing
    countries 48–53, 57
information 57–8
innovation 51–3, 53
international rules 39–40, 45–6, 54–6,
    61
job losses 43
literature on 38–40
marketing strategies 60–61
mask work 40, 42, 46, 58
new technologies, problems of 57–8,
    61
patents 41, 45, 46
philosophical issues 57
piracy 40, 43–5
sales losses 38–9, 43, 44, 46
trade secrets 42–3, 46
trademarks 42, 46
TRIPS agreement 114, 115
WIPO role 56
internalization theory 20
International Business (IB) research
    current state of 1–2
    functional boundary to issue-oriented
        approach 1, 2–3, 2
    new directions in 30–31
International Center for the Settlement
    of Disputes (ICSID) 103
International Intellectual Property
    Alliance (IIPA) 43, 48
International Monetary Fund (IMF) 100,
    107, 108, 109, 110, 112–13
International Trade Commission (ITC)
    28, 39–40, 43, 44
internationalization, *versus* globalization
    8, 204–6
Internet *see also* e-commerce
    marketing tool 9–10
    and smart homes 220
ITC *see* International Trade Commis-
    sion

Jain, S. 4–5, 37–62, 218, xiii
Janakiramanan, S. 74
Jancsurak, J. 207, 220

Jemison, D.B. 231, 232
Jemison, G.D. 229, 236
Jensen, J.B. 132
Jensen, M.C. 69
Johnson, F. 28
joint ventures 21
Jones, G. 220, 225
Jorion, P. 73, 74

Kale, S.H. 218
Kallab, V. 15
Kanter, R.M. 204
Kaufman, R.R. 170, 177
Keck, M.E. 91
Kennedy, C. 107
Keohone, R.O. 82
Khanna, T. 163, 165, 166
Kim, E.M. 173, 194
Kim, W.C. 142
Kim, Y.C. 75
Kindleberger, C. 65, 66
Kobrin, S. 18, 101, 103, 205, 219
Kochhar, R. 225
Kock, C. 168
Kogut, B. 224, 226, 230, 231, 245
Koontz, H. 242
Kotabe, M. 1–10, 39, 41, 131, 224, 250,
    251, 252, xiv, xvii, xviii, xx–xxi
Koza, M. 231
Kraidy, M.M. 83, 85
Krajewski, S. 26
Krugman, P. 23, 32
Kung, H. 90, 91
Kuttner, R. 59
Kwok, C.C.Y. 73

Laabs, J.J. 213, 214
labor pooling 24
Laird, S. 129
Lamming, R. 251
Landes, W.M. 59
Lane, P.J. 227, 230
Lechner, F. 84
Lecraw, D.J. 101, 102, 103, 104
Leff, N. 165
Lenartowicz, T. 87–8
Lenway, S.A. 164
Lesch, W.C. 127
Lessard, D. 77
Levinson, B.A. 90

Levinthal, D.A. 250
Levitt, B. 227
Levitt, T. 3
Lewis, P.A. 176, 195
Li, J. 142
Lin, J. 84, 89
Lins, K. 77
Lipsey, R. 15, 19
Lipsey, R.G. 32
Little, J.S. 28
location 18
    centralization *versus* decentralization
        23, 25
    clustering 23–4
    control, FDI policy 149–50
    firm type 24–5
    preferential trading agreements 24
Lorange, P. 142
Losq, E. 74
Lubatkin, M. 227
Luo, Y. 7, 140–61, 224, xiv

Ma, H.K. 91
Maastricht Treaty 203
MacLeod, M. 136
macro-environment 3, 4–6
Madhok, A. 226
MAI *see* Multinational Agreement on
    Investment
Majluf, N.S. 75
Makihara, M. 136
managerial function
    within firms 243, 244
    interfirm relationships
        horizontal 246
        vertical 251–4
Mann, C.L. 127
Mansfield, E. 51, 52, 53
March, J.G. 227
market seeking, FDI motivation 20, 21,
    22
marketing function
    within firms 242–5
    interfirm relationships
        horizontal 246, 247, 248, 249
        vertical 251–4
marketing tool, Internet as 9–10
Markides, C.C. 164, 168, 172
Markusen, A. 18, 23, 32
Marshallian new industrial district 23

Martin, X. 9, 241–56, 243, 245, 247–9,
    250, 255, xiv–xv
Maruca, R.F. 205, 207, 212, 213, 214
Maslow, A. 129
mature stage, industry life cycle 155
Mayer, D. 91
Maytag Corporation 209–11, 217, 219
McAuley, A. 135
McCardle, K.F. 228
Meckling, W.H. 69
Mehra, K. 142
Menell, P.S. 58
Mercosur agreement 109, 203
mergers
    cross-border 228–9
    global strategy 8–9
Mexico
    extension of CAFTA to 26
    impact of NAFTA 28, 29, 30
    peso crisis 32
MFN (Most Favored Nations) treatment
    111, 116
Michel, A. 77
micro market structure 76
MIGA *see* Multilateral Investment
    Guaranty Agency
Milgrom, P. 244, 250
Miller, D. 165, 168, 182
Miller, K.D. 75
Milner, H. 32
mimetic isomorphism 82
Mitchell, W. 241, 243
Mittelstaedt, J.D. 49
Mittelstaedt, R.A. 49
MNCs (multinational corporations) *see
    also* host government-MNC
    relations
    and business groups 188, 191
    development strategies 170
        nationalist-modernizing 172, 173
        pragmatic-modernizing 177
        pragmatic-populist 174–5
    factor endowments 141
    industry selection 142–3, 157
        capability 158–9
        competitive behavior 159–60
        entry, timing of 160–61
        local partner collaboration 161
        longitudinal and comparative
            pattern for 157–8, 160

strategic goals 159, 160
international expansion 140–41
location 18, 25
NAFTA 27–8, 29–30
oligopolistic advantages of 66, 69, 71,
  142, 143
as proportion of world GNP 223
PTAs, impact of 30–31
pull and push factors 140
risk management 74
structural dynamics 143–61
technological change 141, 147
MNEs (multinational enterprises) *see*
  MNCs
Molot, M.A. 22, 32
Mondragón group 178–9
monopoly power 49, 52, 151
Monteils, A. 24, 29–30, 32
moral absolutism *versus* relativism
  90–91
Morck, R. 69, 243
Morosini, P. 229
Mudambi, R. 137
Multilateral Investment Guaranty
  Agency (MIGA) 102–3
Multinational Agreement on Investment
  (MAI) 115–16, 117
multinational corporations *see* MNCs
multinational enterprises *see* MNCs
Muñoz, J. 177, 195
Murtha, T.P. 164
Myers, S.C. 75

NAFTA *see* North American Free Trade
  Area
Nalebuff, B.J. 245
Nash, L. 89
Nath, R. 87
nation states, and regions 18
Nelson, R.R. 242
Nigh, D. 1
Nonaka, I. 244
nontariff barriers (NTBs), lowering of 4,
  16, 17, 18
North American Free Trade Area
  (NAFTA) 18, 20, 32, 111, 129, 203
challenges for Canadian firms 27
expansion from CAFTA 29, 31
impact on FDI patterns 30, 109
regional integration 25–30

Nye, S.J. 82

OECD, ses Organization for Economic
  Cooperation and Development
Ohmae, K. 18
oligopoly 66, 69, 71, 143, 151, 233
online shopping *see* e-commerce
Organization for Economic Cooperation
  and Development (OECD) 59, 203
export credits 130
MAI 115–16, 117
Orrù, M. 164, 166, 191, 193
Osborn, R.M. 226
Ostergard, R.L. Jr 59

Palepu, K. 163, 166
Panagariya, A. 15, 32
Paris Convention (1883) 47, 54
Park, General 194
Park, N. 25, 241, 245, 247–9
Park, S.H. 226
Parliament of the World's Religions
  (1993) 90, 91
patents
computer chips 58
cost of 45
electronic 40
enforcement 48
'first-to-invent' *versus* 'first-to-file'
  principle (US) 41
need for reform 48
patent protection and innovation 51–2
piracy of 43–4
varying laws on 38–9
Patrick, H.T. 111
Peace, A. 90
Penrose, E. 242, 255
Pérez Companc 175, 177
Peteraf, M.A. 164
pharmaceutical industry, consolidation
  in 221
Phatak, A. xxi
Philips, and Whirlpool Corporation
  212–13, 214
Piertersc, J.N. 85
Pillai, R. 88
piracy
computer chips 58
ease of 44–5
international trade, distortions in 43–4

pluralism 84–5
Porat, M.M. xvii, xviii, xx–xxi
Porter, M.E. 141, 142, 145–6, 151, 205, 224, 244, 245
Porter, M.F. 23, 32
portfolio theory 68–9, 76
Posner, R.A. 59
poverty, alleviation of 7
Powell, W.W. 82
power distance index 181, 182, 183, 184, 185, 188, 191
Prahalad, C.K. 205, 244
Prasad, A.M. 73, 74
preferential trading agreements (PTAs) *see also* regional integration
    advantages 20
    firm types 20–22, 31
    hub-and-spoke relationship 22
    impact of 30–31
    'new regionalism' 4, 18, 26
    rebirth of 15
privatization of SOEs, and FDI liberalization 113–14
production function
    within firms 242–5
    interfirm relationships
        horizontal 246, 247, 248, 249
        vertical 251–4
project orientation control, FDI policy 150
PTAS *see* preferential trading agreements
Puga, D. 24, 32
Putzger 139, 135

Quelch, J.A. 220

Rajan, M. 77
Rajan, R. 70
Ralston, D.A. 86, 87, 88
Ramamurti, R. 6, 99–120, 114, 120, xv
Ramanujam, V. 163
Ramaswamy, K. 228
R&D function 9
    within firms 242–5
    intellectual property protection 39
    interfirm relationships
        horizontal 246–8
        vertical 251–4
Reddy, S. 232

Reeb, D.M. 73
regional integration *see also* preferential trading agreements
    domestic firms 21–2, 25
    economic effects 16
    entry mode 31
    FDI, impact on 15–16, 18, 20–30
    intellectual property protection 17
    macro-regions 20–22, 26–8
    micro-regions 23–5, 28–30, 31
    MNC strategic responses to 15–16
    NAFTA, lessons from 25–30
    outsider firms 21, 22, 25
    research 15–16, 30–31, 32
    theory of 16–20
regional integration schemes *see* preferential trading agreements
religion, and globalization 84
Rennie, M.A. 220
research and development *see* R&D function
resource seeking
    clustering 24
    FDI motivation 20, 22
Reuer, J.J. 75
Ricardo, D. 123
Richardson, J.D. 124
Ricks, D. 1, 86, 131
Rindal, K. 124
risk 72–4
    acquisitions *versus* alliances 230–33, 235–6
Roberts, J. 244
Robertson, R. 82, 84, 85
Rocca, A. 176
Rokeach, M. 87
Ronkainen, I. 40, 224
Root, F.R. 103, 230
Ross, D. 152
Roth, K. 87–8, 216
Rousslang, D.J. 39
Rover, acquisition by BMW 9, 233–5, 236
Rozek, R.P. 51
Rubin, P.H. 39
Rugman, A. 2, 20, 22, 26, 27, 29, 32, 69, 224
Rumelt, R.P. 39, 142, 244
Russo, M.V. 226

Sader, F. 114
Salacuse, J.W. 111
Saloman, R. 245
Samie, S. 8, 216, 218, xv–xvi
Samsung 173–4
Sanders, G.L. 38, 39
Sassen, S. 82
satellite industrial platform 23
Savill, B. 228
Scannell, K. 211
Scherer, F.M. 152
Schott, J. 32, 130
Schwanen, D. 27
Semiconductor Chip Protection Act
    (1984) (US) 40, 42
Senbet, L. 69
Sengupta, K. 245
Serra, J. 15
Servaes, H. 77
Severn, A.K. 77
Shaked, I. 77
shakeout stage, industry life cycle
    154–5
Shamsie, J. 165
Shaver, J.M. 241
Sherwood, R.M. 41, 56
Sikkink, K. 91
Singer, T.O. 128
Singh, H. 231, 255, 360
Singh, K. 241
Sinha, I. 9–10, 260–72, 262, xvi
Sitkin, S.B. 231
size control, FDI policy 150
Sklair, L. 82
Smith, A. 123
software piracy 38, 39, 42, 43
Solnik 72
Solnik, B. 73
South Korea
    business groups 172–4, 186–90
    development strategy 172–4, 194
Spain
    business groups 186–90
    development strategy 177–9, 195–6
Spero, D.M. 37
Spradley, J.P. 88
Stallings, B. 170, 177
standardization 8, 204, 215–18
state-centered district 23
Stein, J. 71, 77

Sterman, J.D. 245
strategic alliances
    versus acquisitions 230–31
    entry mode risk 230–33, 235–6
    failure rate 227–8, 236
    functional interfaces 245–6
        alliance scope 247–9, 254
    partner selection 8–9, 226–8, 236
    resource endowment 227
    Rover-Honda 235
strategic behavior, international 224–6,
    235
structural dynamics 143–4, 160–61
    attributes 150–53, 156, 157–8
        asset intensity 152
        capital requirements 152–3
        concentration level 151–2
        industrial profitability 150–51
        sales growth 151
        technological intensity 153
    complexity 144–5, 156
    deterrence 145, 156, 157–8
    dimensions 144, 156, 157–8
    evolution 153–5, 156, 157
    forces 145–6, 156–7
        buyers, MNC bargaining power
            over 147
        distributors 148
        government policies 148–50
        new entrants, threat of 146
        rivals 148
        substitutes 147
        suppliers, bargaining power of
            146–7
    integrating with other factors 156–8
    uncertainty 144
Stulz, R.M. 71, 74
Subramanian, A. 49
Sudharshan, D. 218
Sun, M. 52
supplier influence, vertical interfirm
    relationships 251–4

Tallman, S. 142, 226
tariffs
    barriers, lowering of 4, 16, 17, 18
    control programs 57
    jumping 20, 22, 23, 24
Taylor, C. 124
Techint, development strategy 175–6

technological change 4
  economic growth 51
  export performance 135–6
  industry structure 141, 142, 147
  intellectual property rights 5, 37,
    48–9, 57–8
Teece, D.J. 141, 142, 143
Telser, L.G. 244
Thomas, G.M. 82
Thomas, R.J. 40
Thompson, J.D. 244
Tichey, N.M. 92
timing control, FDI policy 150
Tomlinson, J. 83
Toulan, O. 176, 195, 196
Toyne, B. 1, 2
Trade-Related Aspects of Intellectual
    Property Rights (TRIPS) 56, 114,
    115, 116
Trade-Related Investment Measures
    (TRIMS) 114, 115–16
trade secrets 48
trademarks
  law 48
  piracy 44
Treaty of Rome (1957) 15
Trigeorgis, L. 77, 80
TRIMS *see* Trade-Related Investment
    Measures
TRIPS *see* Trade-Related Aspects of
    Intellectual Property Rights
Tully, S. 207, 215
Turner, R. 47

Uhlenbruck, K. 8–9, 223–36, 224, 231,
    xvi
UNESCO *see* United Nations Educa-
    tional, Scientific, and Cultural
    Organization
Ungson, G.R. 194
Unión Explosivos Rió Tinto (UERT)
    177–8
United Nations Educational, Scientific,
    and Cultural Organization
    (UNESCO) 56
United States 28
  FDI liberalization 108, 112–13, 117
  NAFTA impacts 28
  political union 17
  trade deficit 28, 127, 129

trademark law 40
Universal Copyright Convention (1952)
    55
Uruguay Round talks (GATT) 57, 61,
    114–15, 203
Uzzi, B. 241, 255

Vandevelde, K.J. 109, 111
Varadarajan, P. 163
Venables, A. 24, 32
Vermeulen, F. 229, 235
Vernon, R. 9, 32, 105
Very, P. 231
Viner, J. 16
Viswanathan, S. 228

Walker, M. 32
Wapner, P. 91
web retailing *see* e-commerce
Weigel, D.R. 99, 102
Weintraub, S. 32
welfare effects
  foreign counterfeiting 39
  regional integration 16, 19, 20
Wells, L.T. 100, 101, 103, 105, 112,
    118, 119
Wenner-Gren, A. 207
West, J. 130
Whirlpool Corporation 211–14, 216,
    219
Whiting, R. 58
Whitman, D.R. 213
Whyte, K.K. 178, 179
Whyte, W.F. 178, 179
Wieczorek, M. xxi
Wilk, R.R. 85, 89, 90
Wilkinson, I.F. 136
Williamson, O.E. 241, 242, 250
Williamson, P.J. 164
Willmore, L. 141
Wint, A.G. 101
Winter, S.G. 242
WIPO *see* World Intellectual Property
    Organization
Womack, J. 244
Woo, J. 47
World Bank 3, 100, 107, 108, 109, 110
  emergency finance and FDI liberaliza-
    tion 112–13
  policy-making influence 112

World Intellectual Property Organiza-
    tion (WIPO) 55–6, 59
World Investment Report 99
world polity theory 82–3
World Trade Organization (WTO) 3, 4,
    18, 100, 107, 108, 109
  Council for Trade in Goods 115–16
  export promotion activities 129–30
  intellectual property rights 56–7, 59
  protesters at 1999 meeting 92
  transformation from GATT 203

WTO *see* World Trade Organization

Xerox 204, 206

Yatsko, P. 50
Yeung, B. 69, 243
Yip, G.S. 141, 231

Zander, U. 226
Zeng, M. 227–8
Ziele, W.J. 134